# Generalist Social Work Practice with Groups

**Stephen J. Yanca**

*Saginaw Valley State University*

**Louise C. Johnson**

*University of South Dakota*

Boston    New York    San Francisco
Mexico City    Montreal    Toronto    London    Madrid    Munich    Paris
Hong Kong    Singapore    Tokyo    Cape Town    Sydney

**Senior Acquisitions Editor:** *Patricia Quinlin*
**Editorial Assistant:** *Carly Czech*
**Marketing Manager:** *Wendy Albert*
**Production Editor:** *Pat Torelli*
**Editorial Production Service:** *Progressive Information Technologies*
**Manufacturing Buyer:** *Debbie Rossi*
**Electronic Composition:** *Progressive Information Technologies*
**Cover Designer:** *Joel Gendron*

For related titles and support materials, visit our online catalog at www.pearsonhighered.com.

Portions of this text have been adapted from Louise C. Johnson and Stephen J. Yanca, *Social Work Practice: A Generalist Approach,* Ninth Edition, published by Allyn and Bacon, Boston, MA. Copyright © 2007 by Pearson Education.

Portions have also been adapted from Stephen J. Yanca and Louise C. Johnson, *Generalist Social Work Practice with Families,* published by Allyn and Bacon, Boston, MA. Copyright © 2008 by Pearson Education. Adapted by permission of the publisher.

To obtain permission(s) to use material from this work, please submit a written request to Pearson Higher Education, Rights and Contracts Department, 501 Boylston Street, Suite 900, Boston, MA 02116 or fax your request to 617-671-3447.

Between the time website information is gathered and then published, it is not unusual for some sites to have closed. Also, the transcription of URLs can result in typographical errors. The publisher would appreciate notification where these errors occur so that they may be corrected in subsequent editions.

ISBN-13:  978-0-205-47009-9   ISBN-10:  0-205-47009-2

**Library of Congress Cataloging-in-Publication Data**

Yanca, Stephen J.
    Generalist social work practice with groups / Stephen J. Yanca, Louise C. Johnson. —
1st ed.
        p.  cm.
    Includes bibliographical references and index.
    ISBN-13: 978-0-205-47009-9
    ISBN-10: 0-205-47009-2
  1.  Social group work. 2.  Social service.  I. Johnson, Louise C.  II. Title.
    HV45.Y36 2009
    361.4—dc22

                                                                    2008033511

Printed in the United States of America

10 9 8 7 6 5 4 3 2 1    HAM    12 11 10 09 08

# CONTENTS

## 5   Interaction and Engagement with Groups      112

# PREFACE

We are pleased to present the first edition of *Generalist Social Work Practice with Groups*. This text represents the completion of a trilogy of texts that covers the entire generalist social work practice curriculum using one model of generalist practice, the Johnson/Yanca model. To our knowledge this has not been done before. Other texts on generalist practice are written with singular texts on generalist social work practice, on generalist practice with families, and one on generalist practice with organizations and communities. Generalist social work programs that wish to concentrate on studying generalist practice with multiclient systems have to be prepared to teach and have students learn new models of generalist social work practice every time they use a different text. Our three texts will take students from an introductory course on generalist practice to more advanced courses on working with families and with groups, organizations, and communities. At the same time, each text can also be used as a stand-alone text for a course on any of these areas.

In many ways this is a group work version of our text *Social Work Practice: A Generalist Approach*, ninth edition. Using our Johnson/Yanca model for generalist social work practice, we have converted portions of the practice text and our text *Generalist Social Work Practice with Families* into material that is specific to working with groups. We have included generalist practice with organizations and communities as well. The conversion was quite easy, as we found that our model can readily be applied to working with groups and with organizations and communities as well as with families and family subsystems. At the same time, we are cognizant of the need to emphasize that in generalist social work practice the social worker must be prepared to work with any size system as a client system, as a target for change, or as part of the support system. This text has been written to fill a gap in terms of providing an approach to working with groups from a generalist perspective. We provide a means for determining which size client system is appropriate. The text assumes that once it has been determined that group work is appropriate, the generalist social worker will need to have an effective approach to forming and facilitating groups.

The text is intended for use by BSW students and practitioners, first-year MSW students, MSW programs that offer a generalist degree, and practitioners looking for a text about working with groups using a generalist approach. Most other group work texts seem to be oriented toward providing group therapy with a heavy emphasis on a theoretical approach to group work. Our research and practice indicate that generalist social workers do not typically do group therapy, but they work with groups quite often. We have categorized these types of groups into change oriented, support and self help, growth and development, and prevention groups. In addition, we found that generalist social workers typically work in organizations and that they need to learn how organizations are structured, how they function, and how to work with organizational task groups as either facilitators or group members. Similarly, we found that generalist social workers need to understand the community and need to know how to work with community task groups.

While it is helpful to have used our generalist practice text before or along with this text, it is not necessary. For those who have read the practice text and/or our family text, some of the material will sound familiar and will serve as a refresher with a concentration on applying concepts to working with groups. We hope that instructors, students, and practitioners find it useful to have three texts that use the same model. Typically texts by different authors use different approaches, leaving it to the reader to bridge the gaps between approaches or make the translation for one to the other.

For those who have not read an edition of our practice or family texts but have been exposed to other versions of generalist practice, this text will add to that understanding by presenting an approach to group work from a generalist perspective. Foundation material provided in Part One provides a base for understanding our perspective on generalist social work practice with groups. It is assumed that students and practitioners will have had some exposure to or understanding of generalist social work practice and are using this text to gain a more thorough understanding of how to work with groups using a generalist approach.

As with our practice and family texts, generalist social work as developed in this text begins with the need of a client system. This might be an individual, a family, a family subsystem, or a social system. The social worker explores or assesses the situation in which the need exists with the client system and significant others. Based on the findings of this exploration, a plan for work to alleviate the situation is developed and an agreement between the worker and the client system is drawn up. The focus of the plan can be an individual, a small group, a family, an organization, or a community. Once the plan is developed, the worker and client system, and perhaps other persons, work to carry out the plan. At some point, the worker and client system decide whether to terminate their relationship or continue to work together on further plans.

Students should have certain prerequisites before using the material covered in this book. These include:

1. At least one introductory course covering the history and development of social welfare and an introduction to the profession.
2. A broad liberal arts base providing a wide variety of knowledge pertaining to the human situation, an appreciation of history, and some understanding about the nature of knowledge.
3. Courses providing an understanding of human behavior and the social environment such as those in psychology, sociology, anthropology, political science, and economics. Courses that include understandings of human development and human diversity, including racial and ethnic differences, are particularly important.
4. Some exposure to generalist social work practice either through academic experiences or practice that uses a generalist approach.

The text presents our model for generalist practice with groups, but no attempt is made to consider practice with any particular population or social problem area. Rather, the assumption is made that the generalist approach with groups can be used in a wide variety of situations. These can range from children to adults to people who are older. Groups can serve those who have medical and mental health problems and can include those who are discriminated against because of diversity or those who have a social situation that does not provide for their basic needs. We have included groups that serve those in need of support, those who wish to promote their own growth and develop new skills, and those who may need alternatives that prevention groups provide. We also provide an approach that is readily applied to social work practice in any setting from rural to urban.

One more important note. We have chosen to alternate the use of male and female pronouns when referring to the worker and to clients throughout the text, with perhaps some bias toward female pronouns. We have done this because the majority of readers are likely to be females. We believe that social work texts should be more inclusive with regard to using female pronouns. We think that the overuse of male pronouns in almost every other area of our society including most texts sends a different kind of message than a more balanced use of male and female pronouns.

## Plan for the Text

Part One provides an overview of foundation material that will assist the reader in understanding our approach to generalist social work practice with groups. A more thorough presentation of our approach to generalist social work practice can be found in our companion text *Social Work Practice: A Generalist Approach*. Chapter 1 introduces the reader to group work and introduces the types of groups that we examine in greater detail in Part Two. It also considers group work across the life span, ethical considerations, and a model for good practices with groups. Chapter 2 provides background material on generalist social work practice along with an overview of the Johnson/Yanca model. It includes a basic understanding of diversity and the concept of diversity competent practice. Of course no single chapter, or text for that matter, can make someone diversity competent. Diversity competence is a lifelong learning process that is never really fully achieved. This chapter provides a means of organizing that process and presents some foundation material on understanding diversity competence. Chapter 3 is adapted from our practice text and provides a vital understanding of the application of our model to individual group members. Chapter 4 is also adapted from our practice text and describes our approach to generalist practice with groups. This includes presenting the version of group development first developed by Louise Johnson in the original edition of the practice text now in its ninth edition. Group development is conceptualized as consisting of orientation, authority, negotiation, functional, and disintegration stages. Chapter 5 is adapted from our practice and family texts and examines relationship, interaction, and engagement in groups. It includes a description of typical group sessions, group facilitation skills, group process, and records.

Part Two comprises four chapters that represent the application of the Johnson/Yanca model for generalist group work practice to the types of groups that generalist social workers are most likely to encounter. We have chosen to write this portion of the text as a practical guide to working with each type of group. We have included assessment and planning before the group begins. The chapters cover assessment, planning, practice actions, and evaluation and termination with each type of group during each stage of our group development process from Chapter 4. Chapter 6 includes a schema for planning groups that can also serve as a proposal. Chapter 8 has a schema for developing and using program materials in groups.

Part Three applies our model to working with organizations and communities. This type of work invariably involves working with various types of task groups. Again we have chosen to write these from more of a practice perspective rather than presenting a myriad of organizational and community organization theories. Chapter 10 provides a schema from our practice text that outlines an organizational study. It presents our concept of organizational structure and good practice as a manager in organizations from the worker's perspective. Chapter 11 examines various types of task groups in organizations and how the worker can facilitate and participate in each. Chapter 12 considers understanding the community, and Chapter 13 presents working with various community task groups.

The authors have based the organization for this text on years of experience in generalist practice and in teaching generalist social work practice. As the concepts are developed, attention is given to building on material presented in earlier sections of the book. Repetition is used to reinforce learning. The authors assume that the present cannot be understood apart from the past; thus, historical as well as contemporary aspects of the material covered are noted.

An attempt has been made to minimize the use of jargon yet to introduce the reader to professional language. Charts and schemas are provided to help the reader organize considerable amounts of information into a coherent whole to maximize understanding.

The text contains several case examples. An attempt has also been made to use case examples from practice in a variety of settings. Each chapter contains a statement of learning expectations for that chapter, a summary, study questions, and suggested readings for use by students, teachers, and practitioners. An appendix with chapter notes, a glossary of key terms, and an index are included at the end of the text.

For this first edition of *Generalist Social Work Practice with Groups*, special recognition is given to Kim Sawatzki and Tony Moore, students at Saginaw Valley State University who worked on the research project on generalist practice with families, groups, organizations, and communities. Their contribution was invaluable in confirming our practice experience with generalist practice with these systems. Thanks also go to the reviewers of the manuscript for their helpful comments: Ray Feroz, Clarion University; Diane Mirabito, New York University; and Matthew T. Theriot, University of Tennessee, Knoxville.

We would like to dedicate this text to our instructors, especially our group work instructors and our field instructors in the social work programs at the University of Connecticut in Hartford, Connecticut, and at Wayne State University in Detroit, Michigan. Their dedication and commitment to advancing the practice of social work with groups inspired us in our own practice with groups and in our teaching and writing about groups. Their shadow is cast over what we have written here and what we became as social workers, as social work educators, and as authors of social work texts.

S. J. Y.
L. C. J.

# PART ONE

# Foundations of Generalist Practice with Groups

Generalist social work practice involves working with individuals, families, groups, organizations, and communities using a structured approach that includes assessment, planning, action, evaluation, and termination. As generalist social workers practice in agencies, they inevitably find themselves in groups. In addition to serving clients in groups, social workers participate in groups in their agencies. Task groups within organizations are used to maintain the organization, carry out its functions, and plan and implement change. Working with communities involves working with various types of task groups that may include organizations, governmental systems, or community members as either members of the group or as units of attention for the change effort.

Generalist practice with groups as presented in this text assumes that the reader has an understanding of the nature of generalist social work practice. This text is based on understandings of the Johnson/Yanca model of generalist social work practice. A summary of the model is presented in Chapter 2. This model of practice is based on the understanding that an assessment of the individual(s) and situation(s) leads to a decision that the group is the desired method of providing service and the group is the unit of attention. This text is based on material presented in our basic text for generalist social work practice, *Social Work Practice: A Generalist Approach*.

Most group work texts are highly theoretical. Many tend to assume that the practitioner will be engaged in group therapy. This text is not about therapy. It is about practicing and participating and facilitating the myriad of groups that generalist social workers are likely to encounter in their work. It is heavily oriented toward real practice with groups.

Chapter 1 begins with an overview of generalist social work practice with groups. It begins with an examination of the assumptions we have made in writing this text. Next it presents different types of groups that are explored in greater detail in Part Two. The chapter goes on to examine the history and development of group work. Finally, there is a discussion of age considerations, ethics, and good practices with groups.

Chapter 2 is a summary of the Johnson/Yanca model of generalist social work practice. It begins with a brief history of generalist practice. After summarizing the model, there is a discussion of the environment as an ecosystem. It ends with a description of diversity competent practice.

Chapter 3 is an overview of the change process with individual group members. This includes assessment, planning, direct and indirect practice actions, and evaluation and termination.

Chapter 4 is an overview of the change process with groups. It includes a description of our approach to group development.

Chapter 5 describes interaction and engagement with groups. It includes a discussion of relationships and communication, a description of group sessions, and an examination of skills used by the worker in groups.

# 1 Generalist Social Work Practice with Groups

## LEARNING EXPECTATIONS

1. Beginning understanding of reasons for using groups in generalist social work practice.
2. Knowledge about some assumptions relative to social work with groups.
3. Identification of major types of groups with which social workers are involved.
4. Knowledge about the historical beginning and development of social work with groups.
5. Understanding age considerations, ethics, and good practices with groups.

Working with and within groups is a fact of life for most generalist social workers. There are several different types of groups that are used and each has some aspects that are shared and some that are different. To understand the process of working with and within groups and developing skills in doing so, the worker needs to have a foundation on which to work. An understanding of the history of group work and an understanding of the variety of groups both make up this foundation. It is also important to understand the use of groups with different ages across the life span. However, before we begin we need to share some assumptions we have made in writing this text.

## Assumptions about the Use of Groups in Generalist Social Work

In our individualistic society, the power of the group is often overlooked. Humans are inherently social beings. We assume there is a deep longing to relate to others, to be cared for, and to be accepted. Small groups can fill that need. Groups can provide members with opportunities to socialize with other people. They can reassure members that they are not alone in their need; others have similar needs. Groups can provide individuals with opportunities for belonging and satisfaction in engaging in collective endeavors. Providing mutual aid gives members the experience of pleasure in giving as well as receiving help from their peers. Through group discussion more ideas for problem solving are generated.

We have made several other assumptions. First is a definition of the small group as we consider it. A small group is comprised of three to twelve or fifteen individuals who have sufficient commonality and goals so that they are able to work together on a common or similar goal. If the group is focused on a task outside of the group, as is often found in organizations and community-focused groups, the number involved can be larger. However, it is important that there be face-to-face interaction among all members of the group. Consideration needs to be given to social functioning of individuals. If they have well-developed interactional skills, then the group's size can be about fifteen. If these are less well developed, it is better to have a smaller number of individuals involved.

It should also be noted that group therapy is not covered in this text. It is our belief that group therapy is a specialty that should be practiced only by advanced master's level social workers, psychologists, and psychiatrists who are trained in group therapy. We see group therapy as usually more focused on the individual group member than is true in social work with groups as presented here. It is our observation that the majority of texts on working with groups are focused on therapy, thus the need for another focus. It is a focus that is concerned about the use of group process for responding to the concerns and needs of individuals. It is a focus that grows out of an assessment in the Johnson/Yanca model of generalist practice. It is a focus for practice by BSWs and by MSWs who are generalists.

This leads to another very important assumption that we make. The primary focus is on the group as a system: its structure, functioning, and stage of development. This interactional system is more than the sum of its parts. The group is usually used to enable individuals to meet concerns and needs; the focus is on helping individuals to function within the group to meet concerns and needs. These concerns and needs may be of an individual nature or they may relate to the group as a whole. The interactional process within a group is group discussion with all group members participating. The worker role is dependent on the nature and development of the group. This is discussed in Chapter 4.

Certainly, from time to time the worker with the group focuses on individuals. This is especially true during the assessment of concern and need and the consideration of a plan of action that then chooses the group as the unit of attention. It is often a necessary part of the group formation process. From time to time a worker may need to focus on an individual to enable him to make use of the group and its process. There may be a need to refer individuals to other resources. (See Chapter 3.) We are also aware that at times a social worker may be called on to serve an already formed group. These may be natural groups or those formed by another worker. An example of a natural group would be a neighborhood friendship group or a gang. Then assessment and planning processes must be adapted.

Another assumption is that a generalist approach to a situation is used in deciding that the group is the desirable manner in which to meet the concern and need. The Johnson/Yanca generalist approach calls for an assessment to be made of the situation which any size system, individual, family, group, agency, or community brings to the table. Thus, an individual or family assessment may be called for as a starting point. This assessment leads to a plan of action that includes goals, objectives, tasks, units of attention, and strategy. Groups can be useful when individuals face similar situations and can benefit from interchange with others. Groups are also important, when the group influence on individuals is great (teens), development of socialization skills is indicated, use of activity is desirable, the focus is on environmental change, and usable natural groups exist. The group should not be used when individuals might be overwhelmed by a group, individuals might be destructive in the group, a common purpose or goal does not exist, the environment will not allow the group to function, or the environment will not allow the group to meet its goals, at least to some extent. (See Table 1.1.) As a general rule groups should not be seen as saving time by serving multiple clients. This is a false assumption. Often, group work takes as much or more time than working with the same

**TABLE 1.1    Indications and Counterindications with Client Systems and Units of Attention**

|  | Indications | Counterindications |
|---|---|---|
| **Individuals** | ■ Information giving<br>■ Information gathering<br>■ Concrete service<br>■ Referral service<br>■ Need relates primarily to an individual without significant family<br>■ No other involvement feasible<br>■ Intrapsychic difficulties<br>■ Individual who with help can involve significant systems in the change process<br>■ Individual choice | ■ Cannot function in a one-to-one helping relationship<br>■ Action-oriented service needed<br>■ Focus on interactional aspects of family or peer group needed<br>■ Need fulfillment best reached by change in larger system |
| **Family** | ■ Major difficulties seem to exist in family interaction<br>■ One family member undercuts change efforts of other members<br>■ Family needs to respond to individual need<br>■ Need for understanding family interaction to understand individual functioning<br>■ Family needs to examine role functioning or communication<br>■ Chaotic families where there is a need to restore order<br>■ Family choice | ■ Irreversible trend toward family breakup<br>■ Significant impairment of individual family member prevents participation<br>■ Need for individual help precludes work with family<br>■ No common concern or goal<br>■ Worker cannot deal with destructive interactions |
| **Small Group** | ■ Individuals face similar situations and can benefit from interchange<br>■ Group influence on the individual is great<br>■ Development of socialization skills is indicated<br>■ Use of activity is desirable<br>■ Focus on environmental change<br>■ Usable natural groups | ■ Individual overwhelmed by the group<br>■ Individual destructive to group<br>■ A common purpose or goal does not exist<br>■ Sufficient cohesive factors do not exist<br>■ Environment will not allow the group to function<br>■ Environment will not allow the group to reach its goal to at least some extent |
| **Organization** | ■ Difficulty related to organizational functioning<br>■ Number of individuals are affected and needs not being met because of organizational factors<br>■ Workers are overconstrained from providing service to clients | ■ Dangers of further negative results to clients are great<br>■ Client service will be neglected or negated |
| **Community** | ■ Lack of needed resources and services<br>■ Lack of coordination of services<br>■ Community influence on organization or family prevents meeting of need<br>■ Community functioning affects a large number of individuals and families negatively | ■ Same as organization |

individuals singly. This is especially true in the planning and start-up phases. There is also preparation time for each session and time for debriefing after each session.

When working with groups, the environment is an important consideration. Group work is often more visible than work with individuals. Even though confidentiality norms are in place, what is happening can become known and misinterpreted. Activities and behaviors are sometimes questioned by outside observers. Knowledge of what the environment will accept is important and needs to be considered in any planning. This, of course, means that agency policy should always be adhered to. Individual group members may feel conflict between expectations from the environment and those of the group situation. Diversity considerations play a strong role in this issue. We deal with diversity issues in Chapter 2.

Consideration must be given to the values of the members and their immediate environment, especially family and diversity values. Social work values and community and agency values must also be considered. In the Johnson/Yanca model of generalist practice, and thus practice with groups in a generalist framework, it is important to focus on group member strengths, not weaknesses. Members must be involved in decision making to the maximum extent possible.

Two intertwined processes are continually taking place when the generalist social worker is working with a group: the social work process and an interactional process. We separate discussion of these processes for learning purposes but point out that they are not separate when working with or being in a group. We use the Johnson/Yanca model in this text: identifying concern or need, assessing, developing a plan of action, acting, and evaluating. The interactional process with groups is a group discussion process. These processes are further developed in Chapters 4 and 5.

Work with groups can be a challenging but exciting means for meeting client concerns and needs. It calls for social workers who understand how individuals function in groups, how groups function, and how to influence groups to meet their goals. It is hoped this text will provide social workers, particularly at the BSW and beginning MSW levels, with the knowledge with which to explore this challenge. One means for further developing skill in using groups is observation using the material provided on group structure, functioning, and development (see Chapter 4) with groups of which they are a part in their everyday lives. Supervision by a knowledgeable social worker can be very useful in developing skills. Workshop attendance is also helpful.

## Types of Groups Used in Generalist Social Work Practice with Groups

In Parts Two and Three of this text, we discuss five types of groups that are a part of the interventive repertoire used by generalist social workers. In this section, we briefly identify and discuss these types as an introduction to our model of social work with groups. A more detailed examination of each type of group takes place in Parts Two and Three.

### Change-Oriented Groups

Groups organized to facilitate problem solving and decision making or counseling groups are **change-oriented groups**. Our differentiation of counseling and therapy groups is mainly in terms of the types of needs and concerns dealt with. We view therapy groups as concerned with situations in which people are experiencing significant barriers to healthy functioning. These groups also call for a worker with considerable expertise who is usually more focused on the individual than the group process. Advanced MSWs, psychologists, and psychiatrists generally lead these groups. Sometimes BSW workers in structured environments such as residential and day treatment, with advanced training and close supervision, may work with therapy groups. However, therapy groups are beyond the purview of this text. They are discussed here only to differentiate them from problem-solving and decision-making groups, often called counseling groups.

We view **counseling groups** as made up of members who are capable of making decisions and carrying them out. Group members generally work on similar problems of social functioning. Workers are BSWs and generalist MSWs. It is most desirable that supervision by someone who is skilled in social work with groups be available. These groups may be found in domestic violence agencies, substance abuse programs, and residential and day programs.

## Support and Self-Help Groups

The number of so-called self-help and support groups has seen tremendous growth in recent decades. An early version of the self-help group is Alcoholics Anonymous (AA). Modeled after it have been Narcotics Anonymous, Gamblers Anonymous, Overeaters Anonymous, and Sex Addicts Anonymous, among others. These groups do not typically use professional leadership; rather, group members assume the needed roles. Professionals may assist them by providing a place to meet and advertising for the group. Professionals may encourage a self-help group as a resource for clients and others who have addiction problems.

Conversely, **support groups** usually involve professionals. The purpose of these groups is to provide support for their stipulated purpose. It is the members of the group who provide the support for one another during and between sessions, not the social worker. These groups can focus on any difficult situation, including illnesses or health problems such as cancer, Alzheimer's, dementia, and so forth. Some groups are limited to those who are directly affected by the difficulty. Other groups may be for family members and other concerned individuals. Some contain both the person affected and other supportive individuals. Workers usually provide technical information to aid the discussion. One of the strengths of these groups is that other members or sponsors are usually more available to members. In fact, in many cases the availability is around the clock.

Social workers need understanding about self-help groups and support groups because they are important resources for many individuals. Workers also need to assess the functioning of these groups to make referrals that match the needs and characteristics of people with the group to which the referral is being made.

## Growth and Development Groups

**Growth and development groups** are the most common type found in society. Many are focused on recreational and educational activities, but are not led by social work professionals. However, they remain an important resource for our clients. The purpose of these groups is to promote healthy social, physical, emotional, and spiritual growth of their members. Many of these types of groups are intended to teach or increase a variety of skills.

Social workers are involved with this type of group when the members have special challenges that make it difficult to participate in existing groups. Social workers may provide supervision or consultation to the nonprofessional who is working with this type of group. They also need to be able to determine if a particular group can meet the needs of clients. Social workers are found working with groups in youth organizations such as the YMCA, and the YWCA, Boy's and Girl's Clubs, community centers, and present-day descendants of settlement houses. They also can be useful in working with adults who are very active. Skill development groups include education groups, parenting groups, life skills training, social skills training, and assertiveness training.

### Prevention Groups

**Prevention groups** tend to use the same or similar activities as growth and counseling groups, but prevention groups generally limit their membership to an identified "at risk" population. Funding sources often specify eligibility criteria for membership in these groups. In other situations, there may be an assumption that certain groups or individuals are "at risk." Examples might be those at risk of using drugs or alcohol, being delinquent, or exhibiting destructive gang behavior.

### Task Groups

**Task groups** are formed to accomplish a task or achieve a goal. Usually they are related to an organization or a community. There are differences between the task group and other groups. The purpose for the group lies outside the group and is not focused on meeting individual needs, although often individuals derive considerable personal benefit in the form of opportunities for socialization and a sense of achievement for being part of a project. The focus is on a needed change in the ecosystem or the environment. The social worker is often a member of a task group focused on planning for service to individuals or for a needed service. Interdisciplinary teams are another example of task groups of which social workers may be a part. In this text, task groups are discussed as we consider generalist practice with organizations and communities in Part Three. Much of generalist practice with organizations and communities is carried out through task groups.

## History and Development of Social Work with Groups

It is the opinion of the authors that in using the group as the unit of attention, it is desirable that the social worker have some understanding of the historical use of group methods in social work practice. With this understanding the worker can then choose from a variety of approaches for working with groups the one most appropriate for the given situation. In this text we use the term *social work with groups*, not *social group work*. Social work with groups is a more inclusive term and better reflects the thinking used in generalist social work. As we develop the historical material, this stance should become more clear.

The origins of the use of groups in social work have a very important source in the social group work tradition. (Other sources will be considered subsequently.) The beginnings of social group work are found in the late 1800s in the work of the settlement house and a variety of group serving agencies including the YMCA; the YWCA; the Boy and Girl Scout movements; and other youth-serving, recreation, and informal education agencies.

The settlement movement began in England with the establishment of Toynbee Hall in London in 1886. The movement quickly spread to the United States with New York's Hudson Guild (1876) and Neighborhood Guild (1877). Subsequently, other settlement houses developed in the larger cities of the United States. Hull House (1889) under the leadership of Jane Addams, has become particularly famous.[1] She had a strong relationship with John Dewey and his developing work on informal education. She was involved in many civic activities including the developing labor movement. Hull House focused on the democratic way of functioning.

A major component of the settlements was that workers, often university women, lived in the neighborhood, usually in a large house, with those with whom they were working. Some of the work, which focused on helping people to help themselves, took the form of clubs and recreation activities. There was a strong focus on the surrounding community and how it could better meet the neighborhood's needs (a form of social action). Many settlements had a strong tie to a specific group of recent immigrants. An important part of their focus was on helping these immigrants find ways to function comfortably in their new environment.

A movement, then, was taking place: Each agency developed its own way of work. The settlement houses tended to have three foci: the individual, the group, and the social environment. They focused on helping people help themselves rather than on problems or establishing who was deserving as did the Community Organization Societies (COS). This was a time of great migrations from Europe and from rural areas to large cities. The industrial revolution was having an important impact on the social situation, and many people had to adjust to new situations, and to new ways of functioning.[2]

Gradually, by the early 1930s those working in the various group-centered agencies began to come together in small discussion groups. Training opportunities formerly carried out only in a specific agency began to become more generally available. Participants shared their understandings about work with small groups. These participants could have recreation or informal education foci as well as what gradually began to be identified as social work. Some of the participants came from developing disciplines of sociology, social psychology, or group dynamics. They were concerned with not only sharing their understandings about work with groups but also how to incorporate the research knowledge learned from the developing disciplines about the nature of groups. Another concern developed as refugees from fascist Europe pointed out how small groups could be used for negative as well as positive purposes.

In 1910, Jane Addams became president of the National Conference of Charities and Corrections and in 1917, showed her support for social work by supporting the National Conference's name change to the National Conference of Social Work. Clara Kaiser offered the first course in group work at Western Reserve University in the early 1930s. After 1935 this course was continued by Grace Coyle. In 1936, the American Association for the Study of Groups was founded. In 1939, this organization established the publication *The Group*. Gisela Konopka has stated: "Identification of group work with social work can be dated and credited to a person; 1946, Grace Longwell Coyle,"[3] at the National Conference on Social Work of the American Association for the Study of Group Work (AASGW). The AASGW decided to become a professional organization, the American Association of Group Workers (AAGW). Some individuals more identified with recreation, group dynamics, and the like chose not to affiliate with AAGW. In 1939, there were

21 institutions offering group-work training, most in schools of social work. A method of social work was developing with an emphasis on assisting individuals with *normal* growth and development, promoting citizen and social responsibility, focusing on the importance of group process, and focusing on activities and programming as essential.[4] By 1949 the method of social group work had developed to the point that four important texts had been published: Gertrude Wilson and Gladys Ryland's *Social Group Work Practice* (1949), Harleigh B. Trecker's *Social Group Work* (1949), Grace Coyle's *Group Work with American Youth* (1948), and Gisela Konopka's *Therapeutic Group with Children* (1949). The method was finding a place in the services of broadened areas of practice, particularly in therapeutic settings.

In 1955, the National Association of Social Workers (NASW) was formed by uniting seven professional organizations including AAGW. With this development, social group work became not only a method of social work but a field of practice as well. Group work became one of the sections of the new organization. *The Group* ceased to publish with an assumption that articles on group work would be included in a new publication, *Social Work*. However, this generally did not prove to be the case. Membership in the new organization was limited to graduates (master's level) of accredited schools of social work. (Those who were members of ASSW were grandfathered into NASW.) Group workers maintained a sense of identity for a time through the group work section but NASW abandoned sections in 1962. Some group workers began to feel that they had lost their identity. They had always been a smaller cadre of social workers. They felt the stronger emphasis on talk therapy tended to place them in a lesser role because they used activity tools or were seen as just recreation workers. They felt there was a loss of the emphasis on the use of group process as an important element in bringing about change. They felt there was a movement away from social concerns with an emphasis on individuals and their problems. In other words they felt they had become second-class citizens in the social work profession.[5] It should be noted that in 1979 some social group workers formed the American Association of Social Work with Groups (AASWWG). Also in 1979, the journal *Social Work with Groups: A Journal of Community and Clinical Practice* began publication. These two mechanisms as well as a dedicated group of practitioners and educators work to keep the traditions of social group work alive today.

Another influence on social work with groups has come from the casework stream of social work. Early on, Mary Richmond of the COS and considered to be the mother of casework late in her career acknowledged that work with groups was a part of social work.[6] This thinking was soon lost as casework became engrossed with psychoanalytical thinking and its emphasis on the individual and therapy. However, as psychiatry began to develop methods for working with groups about 1950, social caseworkers began to use some of this way of working with groups. In addition, the move of social group work into therapeutic settings, which were often related to psychiatric settings, found some social workers influenced by this trend.[7] One concern, then as now, is that some of this work is in reality working with people in collectivity and has little concern for the group's process. In our thinking, group process is essential to social work with groups. As psychoanalytic thinking had a lessened influence on thinking in psychiatry, psychology, and social casework, many new approaches to working with groups developed. These too found a place in the practice of many social workers.[8]

In social work with groups there was a growing realization that there was not just one approach for social workers when working with groups. In 1966, Catherine Papell and Buelah Rothman identified three models: social goals, remedial, and reciprocal. The social goals model aims to develop a citizenry knowledgeable and skilled in discussing social issues and moving to social action. The remedial model aims at treatment and adjustment in personal and social relations. The reciprocal model suggests a dual approach with both the individual and the social environment and aims to assist in finding common grounds for work together.[9]

In 1974, a meeting was held at the University of Southern California in which social workers presented papers describing nine theories used by social workers in working with groups. These theories included: Organizational (the Remedial model of Papell and Rothman); Psychosocial; Functional; Mediating (the Reciprocal model of Papell and Rothman); Developmental; Task-Centered; Socialization; Crisis Intervention; and Problem-Solving. These nine theories represent a variety of sources including some that were developing within social casework. Most were focused on individual change.[10]

Two other developments in the mid 1960s significantly affected the practice of social work with groups. First was the input from social systems theory. This allowed for a new view of group process. The nature of group process as presented in this text was strongly influenced by this new understanding. (See Chapter 4 for a presentation of this material.) Social systems theory also provided an understanding about the similarities of various systems with which social workers are engaged, individuals, families, small groups, organizations, and communities. The second development was the beginning conceptualization of integrated social work practice, the forerunner of today's generalist practice on which this text is based.

Today, focus on the group is used in a wide variety of settings with a wide variety of approaches. There is a small group of practitioners who strive to preserve the social group work tradition (AASWG). A few schools of social work still have a graduate focus on social group work. Many social workers who are employed in traditional casework agencies and in therapeutic settings are using a wide variety of approaches for working with groups. Generalist social workers (the focus of this text) have in their repertoire many possibilities for ways of working with a group when it has been determined that the group is the approach of choice. We believe that when a group modality is used, the process of the group is of great importance and should receive considerable attention. We believe that activity as well as group discussion are powerful tools for the social worker. We believe that the social environment has a considerable influence on the functioning of the group and that groups are very important in bringing about change in that environment and its agencies and communities. This is the heritage of traditional social group work. But we also believe in the generalist approach because the social worker then has a wide variety of other approaches to used as they work with groups. Thus we have chosen to use the term *social work with groups* rather than *social group work*. In this text we do not deal with therapy as a goal, so group therapy approaches are not discussed. However, many of the groups are therapeutic for their members because group is used to bring about individual change or to provide support.

## Group Work Across the Life Span

Generalist social workers work with a wide variety of groups across the life span. Groups can be formed with almost any age group. Human beings are very social. Wherever we go, we form groups. When the social worker considers working with clients in groups, she needs to take into consideration age as an important factor in terms of group composition, the content of group discussion and activities, and the purpose of the group. There are no absolute rules, but there are some basic guidelines to consider.

Children tend to be very active and are usually more interested in doing rather than talking. Thus, children's groups should be planned around activities. Even if there is a discussion component, it is best to plan for relatively brief discussion and to include more activity. The activity itself should be age appropriate and preferably fun for the children. The worker should consult a developmental guide to determine whether an activity is a good fit with the physical and mental abilities of the members of the group. Children with mental or physical disabilities will need activities that are suitable for their condition. For children under 10, boys and girls can usually combine to form a mixed group.

Young adolescents still tend to be action oriented, but are capable of handling more discussion than are children. Males especially tend to prefer competitive activities or teams. Most groups should be separated by gender at this age group. Females are typically more interested in males than males are in females, but both sexes tend to be very self-conscious around the opposite sex. Older adolescents (15 and older) are capable of participating in groups that are exclusively group discussion, and by this age they can be included in groups of both males and females for most subjects. However, victims of sexual abuse or sexual assault should be separated by gender.

Age span is important when considering groups for children and adolescents. A general rule to follow with children is to have members be within two or three years of one another, especially if most of the group is in the middle of a three-year span. Older adolescents can have a slightly larger age span, but younger adolescents are probably best served in a two-to three-year age span as well. Social and emotional development needs to be taken into consideration so that children and adolescents are relatively close to each other in these areas.

Adult groups can have a much wider age range, sometimes a decade or more. A good general rule to follow is to have members be within a generation of each other. This ensures some common experiences that will make group cohesion easier to attain. For some adult groups it may be more important that members share the same needs or concerns regardless of their age differences.

Groups are particularly important in serving people who are older in senior citizen centers and agencies, retirement communities, assisted living facilities, and nursing homes. Some groups focus on a particular activity such as cards or knitting but much socialization and discussion usually occurs in the groups, which can be used to help members become aware of resources or deal with feelings. Discussion groups are also popular with this age group. Groups fill an important role for older persons in helping them deal with loneliness.

Some groups can be intergenerational, with members being parents and children or grandparents and grandchildren. The former may have activities designed for children and activities designed for parents or activities that parents and children can enjoy together as a family with other families. Intergenerational activities for older adults and young children do not necessarily involve members who are actual grandparents and grandchildren. Many people who are older enjoy having contact with young children, and given the joy expressed by many of the children involved in these types of activities, the feeling is mutual. Some nursing homes and adult day activity programs have set up intergenerational activities.

In fact, some adult day activity programs may be combined with child-care programs. This can be especially beneficial for employees who have both children and a parent in need of care.

When we consider the different types of groups outlined earlier, adults and older adolescents tend to be in change-oriented groups. These groups primarily use group discussion as the group methodology. Most prevention groups are made up of children and adolescents, because the nature of prevention is oriented to the future. Growth and development groups tend to be offered across the life span in a wide variety of settings with a wide variety of purposes and group modalities. Support and self-help groups are mainly composed of adults, but can include adolescents, usually those who are older.

## Ethical Considerations

As professionals, social workers have an obligation to act in an ethical manner and to avoid engaging in unethical conduct. This obligation is both moral and legal. In exchange for the sanction to practice as a professional social worker, society expects that social workers will conduct themselves in a manner that helps rather than harms or exploits clients. The ethical guide for social workers is the *NASW Code of Ethics*. Although not all social workers belong to the National Association of Social Workers (NASW), most state licensing boards have adopted the code as a guide for ethical behavior for licensed social workers. It is clearly the standard for ethical practice in the profession. Social workers who work with groups can practice ethically as long as they are familiar with and abide by this code of ethics. A copy of the code, can be found at the NASW website, www.socialworkers.org/pubs/code/default.asp. In many respects, ethical practice reflects the primary values of social work, including valuing each individual, respecting self-determination, maintaining confidentiality, competence, and promoting social justice. An additional aspect is the admonition to refrain from any form of exploitation.

There are several other organizations that have standards and ethical guidelines for working with groups, including the Association for the Advancement of Social Work with Groups (AASWG). Their *Standards for Social Work Practice with Groups* can be found at www.aaswg.org/Standards/standards1.pdf. The American Group Psychotherapy Association has *Guidelines for Ethics* that can be obtained at www.agpa.org/group/ethicalguide.html. While generalist social workers do not typically offer group psychotherapy, their ethical guidelines are compatible with expectations for social workers and for working with other types of groups. The Association for Specialists in Group Work has *Ethical Guidelines for Group Counselors* that are compatible as well. These last two groups include professionals from disciplines other than social work. However, their ethical guides are generally consistent with the code for the NASW. For professional social workers, the *NASW Code of Ethics* takes precedence over any other code or standards. The reader is encouraged to obtain copies of these codes and guidelines, become familiar with them, and keep a copy of them close at hand. Ethical practice involves more than reading about it or engaging in an academic study. Ethical practice means incorporating ethical considerations into everything that the professional social worker does.

A full examination and comparison among these codes and guidelines is beyond the scope of this text, but it is essential that social workers who work with groups become familiar with them. There are a few areas that are basic for all of these guidelines. For the most part, they are similar in the expectation that group workers practice within their area of competence and engage in continuing education and training to advance their skills. Workers need to treat group members with dignity and respect and ensure that members do the same with one another. Group workers must avoid dual relationships with group members. This includes engaging in any type of personal relationship, financial transactions outside of those related to group participation, and avoiding any situation that might lead to or be interpreted as exploiting group members.

For groups that involve self-disclosure, typically change-oriented, support, and self-help groups, members need to receive informed consent that includes the potential risks and benefits of participation. Of special concern is the issue of confidentiality. Maintaining privacy is vital to establishing trust, and members and the worker must agree to do so. However, members need to be informed that the worker cannot guarantee that other members of the group will maintain confidentiality. In addition, there are some circumstances in which the worker is obligated to reveal information. These include suspected child abuse or neglect, or if the worker believes that a member is a danger to himself or others. There may also be legal circumstances in which a court might require the worker or members to give testimony. Most of the laws regulating this last circumstance vary from state to state and the reader is encouraged to become familiar with the legal aspects of privileged communication for social workers in his or her state. This should be identified in the statutes and administrative rules for social work licensing.

There are several proposed models for the application of the *Code of Ethics*. The issue is what is ethical when more than one ethical principle is relevant in a given situation—an *ethical dilemma*. Often social workers find themselves in situations in which acting in one way may adhere to one ethical principle but would actually violate another. For example, if a client threatens to harm himself or others, the worker would be violating confidentiality if she informed the police about the threat. However, protecting the well-being of the client and others is her first obligation. So, in cases of life or death, preserving life clearly takes precedence over confidentiality. However, there are many situations in which the decision about what is ethical is not clear cut.

Philosophically, there are two primary concepts that have been proposed to guide ethical decision making. One involves applying the principle of the greatest good for the greatest number. In this approach, the worker considers both harms and benefits and makes the decision based on maximizing benefit while minimizing harm. The other approach is based on the idea that certain actions are inherently right or wrong and these can be codified into ethical principles. The NASW *Code of Ethics* describes the purpose of the code as providing a guide to ethical decisions.[11] It recognizes that dilemmas will occur, but does not prescribe a specific approach in reaching a decision that is ethical. Thus, the approach that we propose is based on a blend of these two approaches in adhering to the *Code of Ethics*.

In applying the *Code of Ethics* to working with clients, it seems clear that the worker's first obligation is to her client. We surmise this by examining the code itself. Not only does the ethical responsibility to clients come first in the Ethical Standards, but it is by far the longest of the standards and the very first standard states that the "Social worker's primary responsibility is to promote the well-being of clients."[12] There are some limits to this, such as instances of child abuse, but it is consistent with the idea that society expects professionals to act in the best interests of those they serve provided that other people are not harmed. If we assume that the first obligation is to the client, then identifying who is the client takes on greater significance. For the generalist, the client may be any size client system. In groups, the client is the group, but each member is also a client. Thus the situation is ripe for many ethical dilemmas to arise.

An assumption that we make is that ethical dilemmas are best resolved through open discussion. It seems that what cannot be discussed is most often that which is unethical. Bringing the dilemma out in the open by discussing it with one's supervisor or colleagues at the very least protects clients from exploitation. It is very important that this be done in a manner that preserves the client's right to confidentiality. Therefore, the worker does not need to identify the client system except on a need-to-know basis. Revealing the identity of the client to one's supervisor is appropriate, because he or she has an obligation to be familiar with the work of those who are supervised. Revealing the identity to one's colleagues may not be necessary, except in more formal situations such as case conferencing or when colleagues are called on to cover for each other. In many instances, it might also be appropriate to involve the client in the discussion when it involves the rights of the client. In groups, it may be possible or even essential to discuss the ethical dilemma within the group.

It is proposed that in applying the NASW *Code of Ethics,* the worker should take the following steps:

1. Analyze the situation and identify the client system
2. Identify the relevant values, ethics, and legal issues
3. Identify potential positive and negative outcomes
4. Discuss with supervisor and/or colleagues and with client when appropriate
5. Decide on the most ethical process and outcome based on ethical principles using a mutual decision making process

At each step in this process, the worker should take great care to document what took place.

## Good Practices and Empirically-Based Practice

Over the recent past, professional social work and other human services professions have increasingly emphasized the need to incorporate empirical data into the decision process about interventions including those that are used in group work. These are generally referred to as "best practices," "empirically-based practice," or "evidence-based practice." These approaches advocate the use of research-based outcomes to determine the interventions that are used with clients. The impetus for these seems to come from the desire to become more scientific or clinical in working with clients and from managed care systems, which use similar approaches in medical settings. While the expressed intent of these practices is to develop protocols for effective intervention, we are concerned about the potential misuse of this approach by social workers. We have several concerns regarding this. The first is that these approaches may be used by some social workers as "expert systems" in which the worker rather than the client is viewed as the expert concerning the client's life and circumstances. This is diametrically opposed to our approach, especially in terms of the use of naturalistic inquiry and facilitating change through group process in partnership with group members. Respecting the client includes respecting the fact that the client is the expert on his or her life. We support the need to acquire sound knowledge and skills on which professional social work practice should be based. However, we are not in favor of the use of research in promoting social workers as experts. Instead, we prefer to emphasize the worker's expertise in assisting group members in meeting their needs.

The second concern has to do with social work values, in particular the value of self-determination. If not properly used, these systems could undermine clients' right to make their own decisions, as would be the case if the social worker uses one of these systems to decide what is best for the client or the group or exercises undue influence in doing so. This type of approach is basically the medical model, which is essentially diagnosis and prescription. The expert diagnoses the disease and prescribes treatment to remedy it. This approach does not include the important role that the client plays in determining her own life.

A third concern is that these approaches tend to be reductionist—they seem to attempt to reduce the complexity of human beings and their environments to a more simplistic understanding and intervention. In particular, the term *best practices* implies that there are only certain ways or a set of ways to provide services to clients who experience certain needs. While it may be possible to identify protocols for fighting certain diseases and medical conditions, it does not appear this lends itself as well to the variety that is found in the human condition. There is a real danger that in the process of seeking reimbursement from insurance, social workers may preclude the use of more effective approaches because they will not be listed under accepted protocols. We do not think that it is wise to limit potential interventions. Instead, we think that it is best to expand possible solutions before deciding on what course of action to take. Good social work practice involves the creative blending of knowledge, values, and skills. Expert-based approaches would seem to miss the inclusion of the creativity of the worker and the client or group in developing effective change strategies. A related concern here is that best practices can be used in a way that is actually the opposite of what social work has championed. It can be used to categorize clients and their situations rather than to individualize them and recognize each person's uniqueness as an individual. With the development of diversity-competent approaches to practice, there is an added imperative to serve clients in a manner with which they are comfortable or that is expected within their diversity group. This requires that best practices in diversity-competent practice be client centered, which may not always fit with approved or researched approaches.

Finally, there is a concern that there has not been sufficient research to begin to cover the wide array of challenges that people face in meeting their needs. Research that has not been replicated or confirmed may not be reliable. The subjects may be too different from the client to ensure success. Environments are also quite different. In addition, research is often driven by a variety of agendas. Clients with unusual or unpopular characteristics and circumstances may not have studies done that will accurately portray their circumstances. There may be insufficient evidenced-based practice to support group work with certain clients or certain situations. An additional related concern is that many approaches that have been studied are primarily oriented toward individual change. Much less has been studied with regard to environmental change. This might preclude focusing on the environment or on interactions between client and environment in the change effort.

These concerns do not preclude the use of research in social work practice. We heartily endorse the need for social workers to use research findings in their practice. The question is how that information is used. We are opposed to its use in a way that puts the worker in the position of expert. Instead, we support incorporating research into the approach that is presented in this text.

## A Model for Good Practices in Generalist Social Work Practice

There is a need to incorporate knowledge gained from research and from practice into working with clients. The approach presented here is one that we developed in the ninth edition of our text *Social Work Practice: A Generalist Approach*. It recognizes both of these needs. We call it *good practices* in professional generalist social work practice. Good practice is broadly defined as accepted practice in the field or setting or with a population that is based on empirically-based research and practice, practice experience, and the empowerment of clients. In addition to acquiring knowledge and skills through empirical means, the social worker uses her practice wisdom. Good practices also incorporate social work values into each intervention, in terms of both process and content. Good practices use the knowledge and skills of the worker in service to the client. The term *good practices* implies that there are many ways to meet the needs of clients. Our model for good practices in generalist social work practice is as follows:

1. Through research, practice experience, and life-long learning, the professional social worker develops the knowledge, values, and skills needed to serve her diverse client systems, including individuals, families, groups, organizations, and communities.
2. The social worker shares her knowledge and skills from research and practice experience with her client systems as they proceed through the change process.
3. The social worker and the client system mutually decide on a plan that is most likely to be effective in bringing about the desired change and work together in taking actions to implement the plan.
4. The social worker and the client system evaluate the outcome to determine if the desired change has occurred.

These steps are applied throughout the change process with groups as the worker and the group or its members develop assessments and plans, then take actions to carry out those plans.

David E. Pollio suggested an approach that is similar to what we have proposed but with less emphasis on client involvement. He included the following:

1. Critically appraising evidence gathered from a variety of sources
2. Acquiring knowledge from professional sources and conferences as well as the group worker's own experiences
3. Evaluating the outcomes
4. Implementing existing models and those developed by the worker
5. Considering individual differences in making decisions
6. Incorporating evidence-based knowledge of group process, leadership, and development into practice

He also identified behaviors of evidence-based group workers:

1. The worker communicates evidence that supports treatment decisions and techniques.
2. The worker takes time to learn about evidence-based approaches.

3. The worker uses his own evaluations and other sources in building his knowledge and skills.
4. The worker adapts evidence-based models and techniques to each group.

We suggest adding a more inclusive decision-making process so that group members become partners in making decisions about what may work best for them.[13]

Mark J. McGowan has published a text that outlines how to develop skills as an evidence-based group worker using a four-stage process. The first stage is the development of a practice question that is answerable. The second involves searching for the best evidence that is available. The third stage is critically analyzing the evidence by evaluating the rigor, assessing its impact, and identifying its application to various groups and situations. The final stage is to use the technique or approach in the group and evaluate the results. McGowan provides some excellent resources and suggestions for conducting searches and also presents guides to evaluating various studies. He mentions consideration of client preferences, but does not highlight this in the application of his approach. He also includes what social workers refer to as practice wisdom, but again his emphasis seems to be primarily on evidence from outside sources.[14]

The knowledge and skills necessary for professional generalist social work practice with groups will be identified throughout the text. These include knowledge and skills necessary to build relationships and engage groups and group members in the change process and for completing assessments, such as knowledge about groups and group process, human need, human development, diversity, person in environment, and ecosystems. Social workers use their knowledge and skills to explore with groups and their members the nature of needs and potential strengths and resources in their ecosystems. In the process, the worker and the group listen to group members' stories about their lives and their situations. Workers use their knowledge and skills to develop understandings of persons in environments or ecosystems and they facilitate the development of these understandings within the group experience. They clarify their own and the group's perceptions of the ecosystem with group members who validate or correct this understanding. In the process the group and its members gain a better understanding of their own lives and the situation with which they are faced.

An important aspect of knowledge and skills for practice is understanding the models of practice with groups that social workers use. The models serve to help the worker to formulate ideas or theories about how groups develop and function. In turn, this provides workers with a framework for understanding the group. In presenting the types of groups we identified earlier, we see elements of the three models presented by Papell and Rothman[15] as relevant for understanding the functioning of these groups as well as the roles that group workers have in various types of groups. The reciprocal model that Papell and Rothman described is most closely associated with our overall approach to social work with groups.[16] We favor the development of group process and mutual aid whenever it is feasible. We see the worker as primarily a facilitator. We favor using this model with most change-oriented groups. The exception might be when members have limited social skills and may need more direction and encouragement, such as groups of children or of adults who are mentally limited or have a major mental illness. With these groups, the model typically used will look more like the remedial model, in which the worker uses her expertise and knowledge to lead the group more directly. It may also be necessary for the worker with groups for delinquents or criminals to be more active and directive at times to prevent the group from being used as a support for inappropriate behavior, such as that of a gang. However, even in these circumstances we do not favor having the worker take the role of expert, as in the case of the remedial model.

We advocate the use of the reciprocal model with support and self-help groups and as much as possible with growth and development and prevention groups. However, these latter two often involve teaching and imparting information to group members. As such, there are elements of the remedial model in working with these types of groups.[17] It is incumbent on the worker to gain knowledge and expertise in the areas that the group will cover. At the same time, how group members learn and use the information and incorporate it into their life outside of the group should be more closely associated with the reciprocal model in that members should have opportunities to interact with one another and receive support.

The model that we present for working with community task groups in Part Three is essentially the social goals model.[18] The worker facilitates group development and change through collective action that is inclusive. Her role is that of enabler, and goals are identified by the group.

Group workers develop knowledge and skills necessary for planning with groups and their members. They use their knowledge and skills to assist groups and their members in developing goals, objectives, strategies, and tasks to bring about the changes necessary to meet needs. Plans are developed that are consistent with the development and diversity of group members and the purpose of the group. While developing plans, group members learn how to plan. Workers use their knowledge of models of practice, which helps them to formulate ideas or theories about how people change and how groups are used to facilitate and support change. This lays the foundation for working with groups and their members to identify change strategies that are likely to be effective. Good practices give guidance to workers regarding procedures and practices that are necessary to fulfill the expectations of their groups and the members, their agencies, their community, and their profession in a given area of practice.

Social workers acquire knowledge and skills in facilitating the change process through direct and indirect practice actions or interventions with groups and their members. These are used to assist groups and their members in carrying out plans or removing barriers to success. This is the essence or substance of good practices presented in this text. When the worker is able to identify the theory or model or method on which her actions are based, she receives some sanction for those actions. In many respects, models and good practices, along with professional roles needed to carry them out, exemplify what it means to say, "This is what social workers do." This also gives the group and group members some reassurance that the worker is not merely guessing or experimenting with what might work, but she actually has a theoretical basis or practice background that supports why it should work.

Social work values and ethics are used throughout this process. Social workers use their values to guide both the content and the process of change. Values guide the work and provide a purpose for it. As a result of working with a social worker, clients should feel valuable and worthwhile as human beings. This is achieved by treating clients with dignity and respect and by valuing them as human beings and respecting their position as experts on their own lives. Self-determination goes hand-in-hand with this. Respecting clients means respecting their right to make their own decisions. Social workers should inform clients about what is likely to work or not work given their knowledge and practice wisdom, but clients need to be included in the decisions regarding what is done to meet their needs. A third cardinal value is that clients have a right to get socially accepted needs met in socially accepted ways. Workers should support choices that clients make that are congruent with this value. When working with groups, the professional social worker facilitates the use of these values by the group throughout the life of the group.

Throughout the change process, the worker and the group and its members evaluate the process and the outcome. Group members need to be able to give feedback about what feels right and what does not and about what is working and what is not. How change occurs is as important as what change occurs. We are confident that when groups and their members are included in determining the process and the outcome of the change process, the probability of success is increased along with the likelihood that the change will endure over time.

The chapters that follow present our model of generalist social work practice and its application to various groups that are typically facilitated by generalist social workers. It represents our view of what comprises good practices with groups in various settings. We call it an *ecosystems strengths approach to change.* While we are reluctant to classify our model in terms of a particular theory other than generalist practice utilizing an ecosystems strengths approach, we see it as most closely associated with person in environment, client-centered, and solution-focused approaches. Actually, any social work intervention can be used during the action phase to facilitate implementation of the plan.

## Summary

This chapter provides an overview of social work with groups from a generalist perspective. It introduces several assumptions when considering social work with groups. Two of the most important are that the material presented in this text is built on the authors' generalist text, *Social Work with Groups: A Generalist Approach.* Second, the worker focuses on the group as a system and on its process as the major means for meeting concerns and needs. The discussion provides an overview for the remainder of Part One.

Also identified and briefly discussed are five types of groups that the generalist social worker may find appropriate for service to clients. Four of these types are further discussed in Part Two. The fifth, task groups, is found in Part Three, where work with agencies and communities is the focus.

The chapter presents a brief historical summary of how social work has used groups. This then prepares the reader to consider social work with groups from a generalist perspective in considerably more depth than can be presented in a generalist text. It also contains information on groups for various ages across the life span, ethical considerations, and good practices with groups.

## QUESTIONS

1. Describe some of your experiences as a member of a group.

2. Discuss how group work has evolved as a part of the history of the social work profession.

3. Discuss whether group work is becoming a lost art in social work.

4. Describe some of the groups that people might experience during the course of their life span.

## SUGGESTED READINGS

Breton, Margot. (2005). Learning from Social Group Work Traditions, *Social Work with Groups* 28 (3/4): 107–119.

Drumm, Kris. (2006). The Essential Power of Group Work, *Social Work with Groups,* 29 (2/3): 17–31.

Edwards, Richard L., Ed. (1995). *Encyclopedia of Social Work,* 19th ed. Washington, DC: NASW Press, 1995 ("Group Practice Overview").

Gitterman, Alex, and Shulman, Lawrence. *Mutual Aid Groups, Vulnerable and Resilient Populations, and the Life Cycle,* 3rd ed. New York: Columbia University Press, 2005.

Johnson, David W., and Johnson, Frank P. *Joining Together: Group Theory and Group Skills*, 9th ed. Boston: Allyn & Bacon, 2006.

Kurland, Roselle, and Salmon, Robert. "Making Joyful Noise: Presenting, Promoting, and Portraying Group Work to and for the Profession," *Social Work with Groups*, 29, 2/3 (2006): 1–15.

Kurland, Roselle, and Salmon, Robert. "Education for the Group Worker's Reality: The Special Qualities and World View of Those Drawn to Work with Groups," *Social Work with Groups*, 29, 2/3 (2006): 73–89.

Kurland, Roselle, and Salmon, Robert. "Purpose: A Misunderstood and Misused Keystone of Group Work Practice," *Social Work with Groups*, 29, 2/3 (2006): 105–120.

McGowan, Mark J. *A Guide to Evidence-Based Group Work*. New York: Oxford University Press, 2008.

Northern, Helen. "Ethical Dilemmas in Social Work with Groups," *Social Work with Groups*, 21, 1/2 (1998): 5–17.

Northern, Helen, and Kurland, Roselle. *Social Work with Groups,* 3rd ed. New York: Columbia University Press, 2001.

Pollio, David E. "The Evidence-Based Group Worker," *Social Work with Groups*, 25, 4 (2002): 57–70.

Schwartz, William. "The Group Work Tradition and Social Work Practice," *Social Work with Groups*, 28, 3/4 (2005): 69–89.

Shulman, Lawrence: *The Skills of Helping: Individuals, Families, Groups, and Communities,* 6th ed. Belmont, CA: Thomson-Brooks/Cole, 2009.

Steinberg, Dominique Moyse. "The Art, Science, Heart, and Ethics of Social Group Work: Lessons from a Great Teacher," *Social Work with Groups*, 29, 2/3 (2006): 33–45.

Toseland, Ronald W., and Rivas, Robert F. *An Introduction to Group Work Practice,* 6th ed. Boston: Allyn & Bacon, 2009.

Zastrow, Charles. *Social Work with Groups,* 6th ed. Belmont, CA: Thomson-Brooks/Cole, 2009.

# 2  Foundations of Generalist Social Work Practice

## LEARNING EXPECTATIONS

1. Understanding the foundations of generalist social work practice.
2. Understanding the history of generalist social work practice.
3. Understanding the Johnson/Yanca model for generalist social work practice.
4. Understanding the environment as an ecosystem.
5. Understanding the development of diversity competence.

This chapter presents some of the fundamentals of social work practice from the generalist perspective. As indicated in the introduction to Part One, a more thorough presentation of generalist social work practice can be found in our companion text *Social Work Practice: A Generalist Approach*. Some material from that text has been adapted and will appear throughout this text. It is important for the reader to have an understanding of what it means to be a generalist social worker and how generalist practice has evolved over time. This background information gives some direction to the work that is done with various client systems in the wide variety of settings in which generalist social workers practice. The foundation material in this chapter provides a base for understanding our perspective on generalist social work practice in preparation for understanding our approach to generalist practice with groups. It is assumed that the reader has had some exposure to generalist social work practice and that this text is being used to gain a more thorough understanding of how to work with groups using a generalist approach.

As we indicated in the introduction to Part One and in Chapter 1, in a generalist approach the social worker assesses the situation with the client system and together they decide which systems are the appropriate *units of attention,* or focus of the work, for the change effort. Choices also need to be made regarding the best method of delivering services. Group work is one of those methods. The client system or the unit of attention may be an individual, a family, a small group, an agency or organization, or a community. The units of attention may also be any of the transactions among these systems. Working with organizations and communities generally involves working with task groups. Thus, the generalist social worker needs to have knowledge that can be applied to a variety of systems.

The first part of this chapter will consider important aspects of generalist social work practice that form a foundation for professional practice as a social worker. This is intended to provide a common base for anyone using this text. This is followed by a brief history of generalist practice. The next part of the chapter will consider generalist practice from our perspective. It is important to understand our blending of an ecosystems approach and a strengths approach to change and the ecosystem. This is followed by a presentation of understanding the environment as an ecosystem. Finally, we present our approach to working with diverse clients, which we call diversity competent practice.

# A Brief History of Generalist Practice in Social Work

The more formal development of generalist practice as an approach to social work practice took place in the 1960s and 1970s. This is the same time that BSW (Bachelor of Social Work) programs began to become accredited. Generalist practice was adopted as the required curriculum for accredited BSW programs. During this time, most MSW (Master of Social Work) programs were organized by sequences such as casework, group work, and community organization. More recently, the Council on Social Work Education (CSWE), which accredits both BSW and MSW programs, has required that the BSW and the first year of the MSW curricula be generalist practice. Although the formal development of generalist practice is more recent, the basic practices associated with generalist practice have been used since the very beginnings of social work. It is a blending of the two major approaches that evolved in early social work practice. Charity organization societies and settlement houses were developed during the late 1800s and early 1900s.

The early practice of social work can generally be characterized as pretheoretical. Workers saw needs and responded. They were caught up in the pragmatic philosophy of the times. They had preconceived views of the causes of poverty from individual defects such as laziness, mismanagement, or alcoholism. Workers used a "friendly visitor" approach to help people overcome their difficulties. The first major statement of social work practice theory was Mary Richmond's *Social Diagnosis,*[1] in which she developed the original framework for assessment. However, rather than the term **assessment,** she used the term **diagnosis,** borrowing medical terminology from the **medical model.**

It was assumed that a cause-effect relationship existed; in other words, the social worker was looking for the cause of the problem. The cause was generally assumed to be either moral inadequacy or lack of appropriate use of social resources. The process of careful, thorough, systematic investigation of the evidence surrounding those in need of service and then the putting together of that evidence so that the worker gained an accurate picture of the situation were the heart of the social work process. This was **scientific philanthropy,** the study of the social situation. The information to be gathered was comprehensive and specific. The sources to be used included not only the client but also the family, other relatives, schools, medical sources, employers, neighbors, and pertinent documents.[2]

There seems to have been an assumption that the painstaking gathering of information would lead to an understanding of the cause of the problem. Further, it was assumed that if the cause were known, then the remedy would be simple to apply. This idea, which grew out of the Charity Organization Society, assumed that the problem lay primarily within the individual. For example, poverty was considered a result of immorality, misuse of money, and excessive drinking. The Charity Organization Societies tended to focus on individuals and families and later developed the casework approach.

Settlement houses, the originators of the group work and community organization methods, responded to the same social conditions differently. The source of problems was in the environment and in a lack of understanding about how to cope with one's surroundings. Workers used educational and enriching group activities and worked within the political system to bring about change.

The Charity Organization Society saw the cause of poverty as lying with the person, representing the conservative perspective. Settlement houses saw people who were poor as caught in situations that were not of their own doing. Economic and political conditions, including discrimination, oppression, and exploitation, left many people powerless to change their circumstances. Settlement workers sought to empower people through collective action to bring about change in the system. The radical version of this view was that a complete change in the system was needed. The liberal view held that radical change was unlikely but that amelioration of some social problems was possible by making the system more humane and responsive to people's needs.

The beginning of professional social work was a response to the social milieu of the early twentieth century, a time when new immigrants, with their different cultures and lifestyles, were of concern to the larger society. Progressives were working for reforms they believed would eliminate poverty. The developing social sciences were rooted in the belief that application of a scientific method could identify the causes of poverty and deviance. It was felt that if these causes could be identified, solutions would be apparent and social ills eliminated.

The early theory about the practice of social work reflected efforts to work with the new immigrants in ways that would enable them to live "moral lives" and thus avoid poverty. This theory was strongly based on the new sociological understandings and called for meticulously searching for facts that would illuminate the causes of deviance. This reflected the conservative perspective of the Charity Organization Society, which also sought to make helping more scientific. Science was seen as based on facts; facts led to answers. Thus, the answers as to how to help lay in the collection of facts. A strong emphasis on diagnosis (assessment) developed and remains an important legacy in contemporary social work practice.

In the late 1950s, a new statement of casework was presented by Helen Harris Perlman in *Social Casework: A Problem-Solving Process.*[3] She saw the casework endeavor as "a person with a problem comes to a place where a professional representative helps him by a given process."[4] Perlman continued using the term *diagnosis,* but her meaning seems closer to that of the term *assessment,* as used in contemporary social work literature. She saw diagnosis as dynamic, as "a cross-sectional view of the forces interacting in the client's problem situation."[5] Diagnosis was seen as an ongoing process that gives "boundary, relevance, and direction"[6] to the work. It was considered to be the thinking in problem solving.

Perlman saw casework as a process—a problem-solving process—and she developed the process or movement idea throughout her book. She held that the caseworker–client relationship was essential to the movement or work of problem solving. The professional relationship was perceived as being purposeful, accepting, supportive, and nurturing. Underlying Perlman's work is the assumption of human competence, with a goal of developing this competence. Problems are seen not as pathological but as part of life. The social-functioning focus of social work began to emerge.

Another trend of that era was the emergence of literature that began to identify and specify the theory base underlying practice. This base included not only the casework method but also group work and community organization, which drew heavily from a sociological theory base. Knowledge of small-group process was a major interest, and the assessment of group interaction was a major concern. The focus of these two methods was in part on growth as a process. Relationship with nonclients began to be considered. The groundwork was being laid to identify the common base of social work practice—those concepts that applied to practice regardless of the system being worked with.

The era was rich in theory development, just as it was rich in the development of new service possibilities, concern for new problem areas and new client groups, and the use of old methods in new ways. Theory development in that era focused on (1) the continuing development of traditional methods, (2) the development of generic or integrated approaches to practice, and (3) the development of new approaches to practice using new underlying assumptions for use in service to specific groups of clients.

During the 1960s, both the **diagnostic approach** (now called the **psychosocial approach**) and the **functional approach** were expanded and updated.[7] Both were approaching the stage of well-developed theory. These new formulations took the five concepts (assessment, person in situation, process, relationship, and intervention) and incorporated developments from the social sciences. Use of social systems theory and communications theory began to appear.[8]

During this period, important formulations of group work and community organization became available. These not only continued to develop the practice theory of these methods but also made it possible to identify the concepts that were universal to casework, group work, and community organization. Thus, the theoretical commonalities of all types of social work practice could be distilled.

Of particular interest is the movement from the use of the medical terms *diagnosis* and *treatment* to the more general terms *assessment* and *intervention*. As community organization theory developed, the use of the terms *assessment* and *intervention* was given additional support as commonalities were found.

Examination of the concept of **problem-solving process** during the early part of the era indicates that it was being used in all three traditional methods of social work: casework, group work, and community organization. The casework use of the problem-solving process is reflected in the continued importance of Perlman's approach during that era. Process came to imply movement through time.

The concepts of person in situation and client–worker relationship were expanded in the period by the application of new social science theory. The 1970s saw a rapid rise in the use of social systems theory as important supportive knowledge for all social work. The concept of relationship enlarged. Relationship was seen as important for work with the client. The importance of many other relationships was noted in group work and community organization literature. There began to be discussion of **interactional skill**.

In 1970, two early attempts to conceptualize social work from an integrative point of view were published. Carol Meyer's *Social Work Practice: A Response to the Urban Crisis* stressed the need for a new conceptual framework because of limitations of current theory in relating to urban turmoil in the 1960s.[9] Harriett Bartlett's *The Common Base of Social Work Practice* was written out of the need of the social work profession for specification about the nature of practice.[10] Both books reflected the development of five concepts: assessment, intervention, person in environment, relationship, and process. Although the books focused on the problems of integration rather than on the development of theory, they did introduce several useful concepts. Bartlett identified *social functioning, professional judgment in assessment,* and *interventive action.* Meyer noted *process of individualization, interventive points,* and *plan of action.* She saw the diagnostic process as a tool of assessment and intervention as having a variety of possibilities known as the **interventive repertoire**. These two books marked a turning point in theory development. No longer was theory to be developed for the traditional methods of casework, group work, and community organization. It was to be developed for the unified social work profession and to respond to particular problems and needs.

During the early 1970s, several textbooks appeared that presented conceptualizations that were integrative in approach.[11] A text by Allen Pincus and Anne Minahan received the widest acceptance. In their approach, social work was seen as a planned change, with the intervention plan being based on problem assessment. The assessment "identified problems, analyzed dynamics of the social situation, established goals and targets, determined tasks and strategies, and stabilized the change effort."[12] One major aspect of the approach was the use of influence—"effecting the condition of development of a person or system."[13] The use of relationship was seen as part of this process. In the Pincus and Minahan approach, the five concepts are used, but they are put together in new ways and new concepts are added. The developing profession was moving toward new ways of thinking about practice, toward new practice conceptualizations.

Given the growing commonality of social work practice, it is not surprising that an important contribution of this era was the effort to develop what came to be known as *integrated methods* or **generalist practice**. New services were evolving and new groups of clients were being served. It was discovered that these clients did not fit nicely into traditional casework, group work, or community organization categories. Instead, a combination of methods was needed to respond to the complex problems and situations these clients presented. The efforts of the National Association of Social Workers and others toward the unification of the profession provided a milieu in which efforts toward identifying the commonality of theory could go forward. The federal legislation of the Great Society and the War on Poverty provided training funds that increased the capacity for knowledge building. The rediscovery of rural social work called for a generalist approach. The time was right, both in a societal and a professional sense, for this forward movement in the development of the theory base of social work.

A third trend of this era was the development of new approaches to practice that focused on specific needs. This trend began in the 1960s as the family became a unit of attention and as approaches for work with the family developed. Interest in short-term casework, particularly crisis intervention, also contributed to this trend. As social workers began to work with new problems and new client groups, approaches with a more specific focus were needed for action with and for clients after a generalist approach had been used in the early stages of service. Concurrently, examination of current group work and community organization practice yielded the understanding that more than one approach had developed in each of these traditional methods.[14] The 1969 Charlotte Towle Memorial Symposium was a presentation of major theoretical approaches to casework practice.[15]

In this era, there was not as much agreement about practice approaches as there once had been. For example, social workers no longer agreed that the conceptual framework of person in situation underlay professional practice. Some of the important new practice approaches that evolved were crisis intervention, task-centered casework, and social-behavioral social work.

A social work practice was emerging in which a general theory base was used for the original response to need and for the assessment of client in situation. Then, using a relationship developed in the process, an intervention based on one of the more specific approaches was chosen from the intervention repertoire. The essence of generalist practice began to appear. Since that time several texts have been published on generalist social work practice. The first such text devoted to practice at the BSW level was the first edition of our companion text, *Social Work Practice: A Generalist Approach* by Louise C. Johnson, published in 1982. Since then, the text has been adapted for use in the first year of an MSW program, now that generalist practice is the required curriculum.

The philosophy underlying generalist practice is best exemplified by practices that arose in the settlement houses. While practice in the Charity Organization Societies saw the need for change as lying with the individual, the settlement houses saw the need for environmental change. This broadened the arena for social work practice considerably. While collective action was preferred, workers in settlement houses worked at whatever level was most appropriate. They would work with individuals, families, groups, organizations, or the community to bring about change. This is the basic approach used by the modern generalist social worker.

## The Johnson/Yanca Model of Generalist Practice

In this chapter, we present a summary of the Johnson/Yanca model of generalist practice.[16] It is important for the reader to be familiar with this generalist model of social work practice for two reasons. First, generalist practice with groups assumes that a generalist approach to the situation has chosen to use group work as a method for delivering services. It is recommended that the reader have an understanding of and use this model to determine if group work is appropriate. Second, group work practice as presented in this text uses the Johnson/Yanca model for working with client systems and the model is the fundamental approach used throughout the text. In this chapter, the Johnson/Yanca model is presented in summary form.

This model of generalist practice is one that is continually evolving. It first began to develop in the 1970s when Louise Johnson began to specify the nature of integrated practice, which was a developing conceptualization of social work practice at that time. It looked at practice with individuals, small groups, and communities for concepts that were used in practice with all of these systems. In doing this, five concepts were identified in a historical context: assessment, relationship, person in the environment, process, and intervention. As the integrative model became the generalist model of social work practice, two other systems were included, families and organizations or institutions. This work resulted in the publication of *Social Work Practice: A Generalist Approach* in 1982. The model continued to evolve with each subsequent edition of the book based on teaching, practice experience, and developing trends within the profession. With the seventh edition published in 2001, Stephen Yanca joined Louise Johnson as coauthor. He has contributed to the work by providing material on newer understandings used in generalist practice: an **ecosystems** approach to practice, a strengths consideration, and most recently diversity competence.[17] Another assumption made in developing the model was that it would focus on the learning needs of the undergraduate (BSW) student. As the Council on Social Work Education required a generalist approach for the first year curriculum for graduate programs the text can also be used at the foundation level of master's practice.

Discussion of the major concepts concern to need, creative blending of knowledge values and skills, a change process focused on intervention into human **transactions** contained in the model follow. Also discussed are the two interwoven **processes** of the model, the interactional process and the social work process.

## Concern or Need

In the model, a concern or need is brought to a worker or an agency. **Concern** is defined as: a feeling that something is not right. It is interest in, regard for, and care about the well-being of oneself or other individuals. **Need** is that which is necessary for a person or a social system to function within reasonable expectations in a given situation. " They need" is need identified by others. "**Felt need**" is need identified by the client. The worker starts with need identification.

The identification of the need is considered by using several points of view representing the complexity of the human situation. These points of view are human development, human diversity, an ecological perspective, and a strengths approach. The **human development perspective** includes social, emotional, cognitive, physical, and moral or spiritual development. The **human diversity approach** brings together understandings about the nature of culture, disability, gender, age, and sexual orientation and their effect on the development and functioning of human beings and other systems. An **ecosystem perspective** considers how environmental factors (including the physical environment) exchange matter, energy, and information over time past, present, and possible future. In the early consideration of conceptualizations that helped to explain concern and need, we used social systems theory. Now we believe that the ecosystems approach encompasses social systems theory. Important is the focus on change as change in one part of the environment affects change in other systems in the environment (family, small groups, organizations, and communities) and impacts on individual functioning. Social systems theory also brings to ecosystems theory the knowledge that all systems have structural, functional, and developmental aspects. A strengths approach calls for an assessment with emphasis on abilities and assets rather than on deficits, and uses an ecosystems approach. This recognizes the importance of empowerment, resilience, healing, and wholeness in working with people. It reduces the emphasis on deficits and pathology and sees a focus on strengths and resources that can be used to facilitate growth and change. It places less emphasis on **problems** and problem solving than was true in earlier conceptualizations of the model.

Finally a concern/needs approach to social work practice considers social functioning which is seen as people coping and environmental demands.[18] Thus, a focus of the social work endeavor as it considers concern and need, is on helping individuals and systems to cope and to deal with environmental factors impinging on social functioning.

## Creative Blending of Knowledge, Values, and Skills

Social work has thinking, feeling, and doing aspects. In some ways, these three elements relate to knowledge (thinking), values (feeling), and (doing) skills. This model identifies **knowledge** as a picture of the world and humans in it, and the ideas and beliefs about this world that are based on reality, which is confirmable or probable. The knowledge base used by social workers is a broad one. It is obtained from liberal arts with emphasis on the social sciences and human biology. It contains knowledge about persons, their interactions, and social situations and about practice theory that involves the nature of helping interactions; the process of helping and a variety of intervention strategies; specialized knowledge needed to work with specific groups of clients; and the capacity to be reflective, imaginative, and creative in the use of the knowledge base.

To have a sufficiently broad knowledge base, a social worker needs the following:

1. *A broad liberal arts base*—This includes a knowledge of the social sciences (sociology, psychology, anthropology, history, political science, and economics) to provide explanations about the nature of human society and the human condition. Study of the natural sciences provides tools for scientific thinking and an understanding of the physical aspects of the human condition. Study of the humanities aids in the development of the creative and critical thought processes; it provides an understanding of the nature of the human condition through the examination of creative endeavors and of the cultures of human society. The latter is especially important for diversity competence. A social worker is a person with a developed and expanded personal capacity gained by exposure to a broad, liberal educational experience.

2. *A sound foundation knowledge about persons, their interactions, and the social situations within which they function*—This includes knowledge about persons from emotional, cognitive, behavioral, spiritual, and developmental points of view. Such knowledge must consider the diversity of the human condition and the effect of diversity on functioning and development. Understanding of human interaction in depth is also essential. This knowledge includes one-to-one relationships, family relationships, and small-group relationships and the variety of these relationships in diverse populations. It also includes understanding of the societal organizations and institutions that are a part of contemporary society and of the social problems that affect human functioning, especially those that are exacerbated by prejudice and discrimination.

3. *Practice theory, with concern for the nature of helping interactions, of the process of helping, and of a variety of intervention strategies appropriate for a variety of situations and systems*—This includes knowledge of professional and societal structures and institutions for delivery of service to individuals in need of help and methods of adapting and developing the service structure for more adequate need fulfillment.[19] It also includes knowledge about effective ways of providing service to diverse individuals and families.

4. *Specialized knowledge needed to work with particular groups of clients and in particular situations*—The choice of knowledge each worker includes in this area is dependent on the practice situations and on career aspirations. In diversity competent practice, the worker needs to be knowledgeable about the values and beliefs of the population, its experience with the dominant society, the manner in which help is given and received, and good practices that need to be used with each group.

5. *The capacity to be reflective, imaginative, and creative in the use of knowledge obtained from a variety of sources*—It is especially important to be able to see the strengths in people and in their environment, and to be able to use those strengths to

build a vision for the future. To become diversity competent, the worker must be able to reflect on her knowledge about herself and knowledge about each diverse group. She must be willing to critically examine her knowledge and be open to considering distortions that might be present as a result of prejudices and stereotypes. She must be able to acquire and use new knowledge about diversity from her clients and from professional sources such as articles, books, professional training, colleagues, and other sources.

6. ***The ability to learn new and different ways of acquiring and using knowledge***—In diversity competent practice, the worker needs to become more familiar with different ways of knowing that each diverse group may use in acquiring knowledge. In white male, Eurocentric society, great value is placed on knowledge that is gained by the scientific method. Other groups value knowledge that is more experiential and passed on from earlier generations. Women may value knowledge that is acquired through relationships.

**Values** are not provable. They are what is desirable. They identify what is preferred. They act as guides for behavior. The social work endeavor considers several sets of values, the client's, those of the community and agency, the worker's and those of the social work profession. The latter have been clearly spelled out in the National Association of Social Workers *Code of Ethics*. (The *Code of Ethics* is available online at www.socialworkers .org/pubs/code/code.asp.) These values have often been expressed as principles of worth and dignity of the individual, the right to self-determination, and the right to confidentiality. Another way of looking at the professional values is to recognize the dual worth of individuals and social responsibility.

The social work endeavor is based on the dual values of the worth and dignity of individuals and of social responsibility. These values can be expressed in these principles for action:

1. People should be free to make choices.
2. Individuals are important; individual needs and concerns cannot be totally subjected to community needs.
3. Workers should use a nonjudgmental approach to persons and their concerns, needs, and problems.
4. The social work role is helping or enabling, not controlling.
5. Feelings and personal relationships are important.
6. People have responsibility for others, for their needs and concerns.

Diversity competent practice requires the recognition and valuing of diversity. It does not see differences as one being superior and one being inferior, resulting in value judgments of good and bad instead of just different. Good and bad judgments lead to prejudice, discrimination, and oppression. This in turn negates the worth and dignity of individuals and cultural groups and is counter to the social work value system.

**Skill** brings knowledge and values together and converts them to action that is a response to concern or need. Skill may be defined as a complex organization of behavior directed toward a particular goal or activity. Social workers need both cognitive and interactive skill. Betty Baer and Ronald Federico have organized the skill component into four areas:

(1) information gathering and assessment; (2) the development and use of the professional self; (3) practice activities with individuals, groups, and communities; and (4) evaluation.[20]

The *Educational Policy and Accreditation Standards* of the Council on Social Work Education[21] provide the official statement of the skill level expected of baccalaureate- and master's-level social work graduates. Two types of skills are called for (although it is impossible to completely separate them): cognitive skills and interactive or relationship skills. *Cognitive skills* are those used in thinking about persons in situations, in developing understanding about person and environment, in identifying the knowledge to be used, in planning for intervention, and in performing evaluation. *Interactive skills* are those used in working jointly with individuals, groups, families, organizations, and communities; in communicating and developing understanding; in joint planning; and in carrying out the plans of action. A social worker must be proficient in both types of skills.

This model sees the three elements—knowledge, values, and skill—as a creative choosing of what is applicable to a particular situation and creatively blending them for use in responding to client and others' concerns and needs. The ability to combine appropriately and creatively the element of knowledge, values, and skill calls not only for choosing and applying appropriate knowledge, values, and skills but for blending the three elements in such a manner that they fit together and become a helping endeavor that is a consistent whole. It involves identifying and choosing appropriate, often unrelated, bits of knowledge and using not only social work values but also those of the client and the agency as a screen for tentatively chosen knowledge. It calls for skillful application of the knowledge and values. Because each person and situation is different, the knowledge, values, and skills are different in any situation. There are no "cookbooks" or standardized procedures; rather, there are generalized ways of approaching persons in situations.

## The Change Process

The blending of an **ecosystems** and a **strengths approach** with problem solving forms a **change process** that allows the social worker to be creative and allows for organization of a complex array of knowledge into a cohesive whole. It calls for moving from understanding need to identifying assets, abilities, and capacities of all systems involved in the situation. This process is seen as facilitating growth. It also sees the primary interventions as intervention into human transactions rather than change focused on interior systematic change. Originally, we conceptualized the change process as a problem-solving process. Newer thinking, which focuses on strengths, resources, and growth, has seen problem solving as focusing on deficits. Thus, we now talk about the change process. We conceptualize the change process (social work process) as having four phases: assessment, planning, action, and evaluation and termination. The assessment process is further seen as identification of concern and need, identification of the nature of concern or need, identification of potential strengths or resources in the ecosystem, selection and collection of information, and analysis of available information. The change process then involves two types of activity: (1) working within a relational/interactional framework with clients and others, and (2) carrying out the helping process. Both are essential concerns of the model and each is described as we envision them in subsequent sections of this chapter.

A strengths approach has contributed to practice theory by reducing the emphasis on deficits and pathology and focusing on strengths that can be used to facilitate growth and change.[22] An **ecosystems perspective** offers a way to organize and understand the environment and the transactional nature of person in environment. In this model, a strengths approach and an ecosystems perspective are blended with the traditional problem-solving process to form an ecosystems strengths approach to change. This approach views problem solving as meeting needs in a way that facilitates natural growth and change in the person, the environment, and the transactions between person and environment. It sees the social work endeavor as aimed at identifying and utilizing the assets that are available in the person, the environment, and transactions between person and environment to bring about change that fits with what the client desires and the reality of his situation.

Ecological and strengths approaches have a health-based orientation. Both see growth and change as a natural part of human development over time and consider healthy functioning as a goal and as a reality for most areas of the client's life. It is not necessary to change everything about the person or the situation, only the area in which need is not being met. In general, people are able to meet the majority of their needs in socially accepted ways.

An ecosystems approach sees need as arising out of an imbalance or incongruity in the transactions among systems. Person in environment is viewed as a system of systems in which the client and his natural environment are all a part of one ecosystem. The social worker and the client work together to identify the transactions that are out of balance. Using a strengths approach, they seek to rebalance the transactions based on the abilities, capacities, and resources available within both the client and the environment. The knowledge, values, and skills of social work, along with the strengths and resources within the client and the client's environment, are used in understanding the situation and in identifying possible goals.

Contributions from a strengths approach can become an integral part of the change process used in social work practice when: (1) the focus of the helping process is on the unique individual or client system involved and on the possibilities for positive growth and change; (2) the strengths and competencies of the client system are respected and valued by the social worker and utilized as a major resource in the helping process; and (3) the client is involved in all phases of the helping process and is given maximum opportunity for self-determination. Social workers who incorporate these principles in their work with client systems will discover that the change process is a useful tool to help the client reach his goals and objectives.

Blending these two approaches into assessment, planning, action, and evaluation allows the worker and the client to build on environmental and personal strengths in discovering ways to meet unmet needs.

## Diversity Competence

A recent addition to the model, although this way of thinking has been implicit for some time, is the concept of diversity competence. We use the term *diversity competence* rather than *ethnic* or *cultural competence* because there is great diversity in American society; there is diversity beyond that related to culture or to ethnic groups. That diversity relates to socioeconomic class, gender, sexual orientation, political beliefs, religious beliefs, age, education, and culture of origin, to name a few of the differences that exist in modern society. Diversity competence calls for the use of **naturalistic inquiry**. That is, the worker assumes that she does not know what she does not know. It is a form of **inductive learning** and calls for the worker to learn from the client or others, not making assumptions based on preconceived notions. This makes clients and others equal partners in the change process. The client or others are expected to provide the understandings of their way of functioning, their cultural history, their view of what is important in the change process. Diversity competence calls for the worker to seek from the diverse group understandings about culture, values, expectations, and other things that affect the use of help. It calls for the worker to develop a level of self-knowledge so that they do not bring expectations and beliefs to the helping situation that preclude gaining the necessary understandings for diversity competent practice. Later in this chapter we develop this aspect of the model to a greater extent.

In terms of the phases of the change process, a diversity competent approach is used throughout the process. The diversity competent worker incorporates her learning from the diverse people into each phase of the process. She is careful to consider diversity as she conducts her assessment. She works with the group member and the group to develop plans that are consistent with the diversity of group members. She uses direct and indirect practice actions that are comfortable for the group and its members. She considers diversity in evaluation and is knowledgeable about the termination process for diverse groups.

## Two Intertwined Processes

The separation of the interactional and the social work processes is artificial at best. Both are taking place at the same time. Each is dependent on the other. However, for purposes of understanding, we have chosen to discuss each process separately.

*The interactional process.* In its simplest form, the **interactional process** is a worker and a client together working on a concern/need in an environment. However, there are other interactional forms as well. Several clients may make up a family or small group. The "worker" may be a team of several helpers, all social workers, an interdisciplinary team, or worker and other interested people. For a social worker to be most able to use the interactional process, she must have begun the life-long task of self-understanding from several viewpoints: lifestyle and philosophy of life, her moral code and value system, her family and cultural roots, and personal needs, to name a few viewpoints. (See Table 2.1 .) She also must have a sense of the use of self in professional activities, being able to use responsibility and authority appropriately. She needs to have developed skill as a diversity competent social worker. Furthermore, it is important to have skills for working with multiperson helping teams. This includes skill in collaboration, referral, and consultation.

The social worker understands what it means to become a client and how to develop a workable social history. (See Table 3.1 A Guide for Developing a Social History.) She recognizes the place of motivation, capacity, and opportunity in the helping endeavor and how to assess stress levels and crisis situations. Clients are always seen as individuals who are unique and have strengths. When the client or focus of service is a larger system, a systemic assessment is used to understand and work with that system.

All interaction takes place within an environment or ecosystem. This environment includes the client's personal life system, the agency providing the service, and the community of client and agency. (See Table 13.1 Schema for Study of a Geographic Community.) Social workers need to develop skills in assessing and understanding the structure, functioning, and development of agencies, institutions, and various kinds of communities.

**TABLE 2.1   A Guide for Thinking about Personal Need**

■ **My Common Human Needs**

1. What are my needs for food, shelter, and clothing? How do I meet these needs?
2. What are my needs for safety so as to avoid pain and physical damage to self? How do I meet these needs?
3. What are my health care needs? How do I meet these needs?
4. What are my needs for love and belongingness? How do I meet these needs?
5. What are my needs for acceptance and status? How do I meet these needs?
6. What are my needs for developing my capacity and potentiality? How do I meet these needs?
7. What are my needs for understanding myself and the world in which I live? How do I meet these needs?
8. What other biological needs do I have?
9. How do I describe my spiritual development? What are major sources for this development? What are my present needs in this area?

■ **My Developmental Needs**

1. What are my needs because of my experience in developing physically? How do I meet these needs?
2. What are my needs in relation to my cognitive development? How do I meet these needs?
3. What is my present stage of psychosocial development?
4. What are my needs because of the development tasks of my current stage of development?
5. How well have I accomplished the tasks of earlier developmental stages?
6. What present needs do I have because of challenges related to not accomplishing these tasks?

■ **My Needs Arising from Human Diversity**

1. What in my lifestyle is "diverse" from the dominant lifestyle of my community?
2. What is the basis of the diversity? Race, cultural group, gender, religion, disabling conditions, other?
3. What is the meaning of this diversity to me? How do I feel about myself in relation to this diversity?
4. What is the meaning of this diversity to my immediate environment? How does the environment deal with me as a diverse person?
5. How do I deal with the stresses and strains that exist because of diversity?
6. What strengths or special needs do I have because of my diversity?

■ **My Needs Arising from Social Systems of Which I Am a Part**

1. What expectations do the various social systems of which I am a part have of me? (These include family, peer group, school or work, organizations of which I am a member, neighborhood or cultural group, etc.).
2. What do I see as my responsibility toward the social systems of which I am a part?
3. What needs do I have in relation to these social systems, including the expectations and responsibilities related to them?

(See Table 12.1 Schema for Study of a Social Agency.) They need understanding of how to work in bureaucratic settings.

Of prime importance for use of the interaction process with worker and client in an ecosystem are communication skills. These are necessary for the development of helping relationships. Communication skills are the heart of the interview and for work with small groups, prime tools of the social worker.

Thus, we see the interactional process are client (one or multiple persons), worker (one or multiple persons) in an environment using communication as a primary tool. This is one of two major processes within the social work endeavor as seen in the Johnson/Yanca model.

***The social work process.***   The second process, which as noted is intertwined with the interactional process, is what we call the **social work process**. This is the process that encompasses the work that the worker(s) and client(s) do together. In the Johnson/Yanca model, it has four phases: assessment, planning, action, and evaluation and termination. Although it is recognized that usually it is important to return to an earlier phase, and sometimes the phases seem to be overlapping, for developing understanding, here each part is considered separately.

The assessment phase is carried out with the client(s). They are prime sources of information and verify conclusions that are drawn based on that information. This is the stance of the culturally competent social worker. There is a progression within the assessment process: (1) identification of the concern/need; (2) identification of the nature of the concern/need; (3) identification of the potential strengths and resources in the ecosystem; (4) selection and collection of information; and (5) analysis of the available information.

The work then begins to move into the planning phase of the process. Of prime importance again is the involvement of the client in this process. As assessment and planning progress, the worker and client identify the most appropriate target for developing change possibilities. It is here that individual, family, small group, organization, or community systems become the focus and the work returns to the assessment process applied to the chosen focus for attention. (See Table 1.1 Indications and Counterindications with Client Systems and Units of Attention.)

The planning phase not only involves identification of the most appropriate unit of attention based on client desires, worker competence, and the usual way of work of the agency, planning also involves identification of a strategy to be used. Strategy is an overall approach with specified roles for worker and client, tasks to be carried out, and methods and techniques to be used. Of great importance in developing a **plan of action** is the specification of goals, the overall, long-range expected outcome of the process. As with assessment, the client is involved in the planning process and the plans developed are within the diversity context of the situation. Thus, we conceptualize a plan as having a unit of attention, goals and objectives (intermediate steps in reaching a goal), and a specified strategy for the work to be done. If the assessment yields desirability for a plan beyond the competence of the worker or the scope of the agency, then referral to another source for help should be considered. If such a resource is unavailable, then worker and client return to the assessment planning process and seek a workable plan.

The action phase can be direct or indirect. Direct action is action with clients. It focuses on transactions of individuals with their environment or actions with families or small groups.

**Direct practice** action strategies that fall within the purview of the generalist practitioner include action to enable the development of relationships, action taken to enable development of understanding of person in the environment, action taken in the planning process, action taken to enable the client to know and use available resources, action taken to empower or enable clients, action taken in crisis situations, action taken to support the social functioning of clients, action taken that uses activity with clients as the base for help, and action taken to mediate between clients and a system in their environment. Generally, generalist social workers, particularly at the BSW level of practice, do not use a clinical model of practice.

**Indirect practice** strategies are actions taken with persons or systems other than clients in order to help clients. The actions include those that use influence in service of clients, actions designed to change **social systems** or the environment, and actions that coordinate services. Case management is one of the approaches to coordination of services.

The fourth phase of the social work process is evaluation and **termination.** While it is assumed that evaluation will be a part of the termination phase, it is also recognized that evaluation is an ongoing part of the process. Termination, it is hoped, will come as a result of meeting the goals of the plan of action, of resolving the concern/need that initiated the work together. This kind of termination is planned for from the beginning of the social work process. However, it is recognized that termination can take place in an unplanned manner with clients deciding to discontinue the endeavor. It can also take place when a worker leaves agency employment. Three components of termination work are disengagement, stabilization of change, and evaluation. As in all parts of the social work process, clients are heavily involved.

The social work process usually begins with a **feeling** of concern about something. This concern arises because a need is not being met. After **thinking** about the situation in a particular way—a process called assessment—some **action** is taken. This response—feeling, thinking, acting—is cyclical in nature. As the worker and client think and act together, new feelings of concern arise and new needs become apparent. As they act, they think about what is happening and gain new insights into the situation. The worker's knowledge about human development, human diversity, social systems theory, ecosystems, and a strengths approach is used in thinking about the situation. (See Figure 2.1.)

In working with groups, the phases of the change process are used in different ways at different times during the life of a group. For instance, assessment and planning for a group needs to take place before a group begins, or for some groups, before new members join. In many respects, the group itself may represent the action phase with evaluation taking place throughout the process and termination occurring when the group ends or a member leaves. Similarly, each group session requires assessment and planning beforehand, with the group session being the action phase. Evaluation occurs throughout this process and termination comes at the end of the session. For change-oriented groups, the change process is used by the group during group sessions. The worker assists the group to learn and use the change process as it works to develop and achieve either group or individual goals. This is developed further throughout this text.

What has been presented in this chapter is the current formulation of the Johnson/Yanca model for generalist social work practice. It is assumed that this model will continue to develop as new understanding of social work practice emerges. It is a model developed for use by BSW workers and useful to the MSW worker, especially since it comprises the first year of the MSW curriculum. It is a model that can be adapted for use in a variety of social work practice settings and for use when the individual, family, small group, organization, or community become the unit of attention. It is used with clients to determine the appropriate unit of attention. It stresses a naturalistic approach, involving the

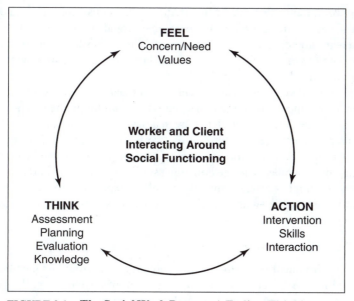

**FIGURE 2.1    The Social Work Process: A Feeling, Thinking, Acting Endeavor.**

client heavily in assessment, planning, action, and termination/evaluation. It is the model on which work with a group and its members is used in this text. Reader understanding of the model is essential for the group work discussed in the text.

## The Environment as an Ecosystem

Environmental aspects of the ecosystem have not been as well developed as theories and understandings about client systems. We know a lot more about the person or client side of the concept of person in environment. The environment as an ecosystem is introduced here to lay a foundation for understanding the environment as we discuss generalist practice with groups.

In using an ecosystems approach that encompasses person in environment, the *in* can serve as the focal point for social work services. The *in* can represent the *in*terface between the person and the environment. **Interface** is the point of contact between two systems. At the *in*terface there are *in*teractions that occur. To the extent that both the person and the environment exchange resources, energy, or *in*formation via these *in*teractions, transactions take place. When these *in*teractions or transactions are balanced, both the person and the environment benefit. *In*terrelationships are formed, and a certain level of *in*terdependence exists. Change in one part of the ecosystem will *in*fluence other parts of the ecosystem. When the *in*teractions or transactions are out of balance, an *in*congruity exists between the needs of the person and/or the environment and resources available to meet those needs. This imbalance or *in*congruity gains the attention of the social worker and is the reason for and focal point of social work *in*tervention.

In group work, there are several ecosystems that are considered. First, the group has an ecosystem made up of the group, its environment, and the interactions between the group and its environment. In addition, each group member has his or her own ecosystem, which includes the group. Finally, the worker has her ecosystem that is made up of both personal and professional aspects of her life.

A combination of ecosystems and strengths approaches gives the worker a powerful means to assist group members to meet their needs beyond the immediate situation. This approach also brings the environment into play in a positive way and dramatically expands potential resources for change well beyond the worker or the group. Instead of limiting the possibilities to whatever the worker or group members bring to the helping situation, the worker and group members can seek other possibilities by tapping into resources in the environment. In addition, as group members are able to experience this expanded range of resources with the worker, they are empowered to use this approach in working to meet other needs, now and in the future.

## The Immediate Environment

The immediate environment refers to the environment of the group, its members, and the social worker. It includes the environment that is present when and where the group meets and the environment with which members and the worker interact on a daily basis. Three segments of the immediate environment that are important in group work are families, the agency, and the community.

Included in the immediate environment of most group members are their families. Past and present experiences with their families have a profound influence on how people function in groups outside of the family. Some group workers consider the family as a special type of group. Others see group work as essentially working with members who seek to replicate their experiences in their families. Because the family is our first experience with relationships and with groups, it has a significant effect on how we relate to others in general, including when we are in groups. This is true for the social worker as well as for group members. Thus, family background is an important consideration in working with groups and the social worker needs to be aware of it as a factor in her own work with groups as well as that of each group member as he or she participates in the group.

The agency is part of the immediate environment of the worker and most groups. Most of the time the agency provides a space for the group to meet, a group leader or leaders, and materials that are needed for activities. For the worker, the agency is a very important part of her environment, generally providing employment, supervision, collegial relationships, and a sanction to function in the role of social worker including facilitating the group.

For group members, the agency may also provide ancillary services to the members, their families, and their neighbors in the community. The agency sanctions the group and provides qualified staff to facilitate it. The fact that the agency is typically chartered by the state or a part of federal, state, or local government means that group members can have some confidence that the social worker is properly trained and has the credentials that are appropriate for the work to be done. To the extent possible, the agency provides comfortable space that will meet the needs of the group. The agency and its functioning are covered in Part Three, when we consider organizational practice.

The community is a part of the environment of the group and the social worker. Group members live in the community and represent a segment of it. There are numerous resources in the community that are part of meeting most of the needs that people have. Each group member will have different experiences with various segments of the community. Some will have generally positive experiences, while others may not. The worker herself will likely have two types of relationships with the community at large. One will be as a member of the professional or human services community. Other relationships will depend on the personal circumstances of the worker. Most of the time, the worker either lives in the community or in the surrounding area. The worker uses both her professional and her personal knowledge and experiences in assisting the group and its members to meet needs. The community and community practice are studied in greater detail in Part Three of the text.

## Diversity Competent Practice

**Diversity competence** is an important aspect of social work practice. The great majority of clients are members of populations whose diversity places them at risk of experiencing prejudice, discrimination, and oppression. At one time, diversity was seen as a barrier to be overcome. More recently, theories evolved that called for ethnic-sensitive practice in which the worker respected and valued the ethnicity and culture of the client. However, being sensitive does not necessarily mean that the worker makes fundamental changes to the manner in which services are delivered. Thus, the next step in this evolution has been to develop **culturally competent practice**, which calls for the worker to be able to practice in ways that are consistent with expectations in the client's culture. In recent editions of our text, *Social Work Practice: A Generalist Approach*, we extended this a step further by considering diversity competent practice skills. This extends the concept of cultural competence to all forms of diversity. The Council on Social Work Education identifies diversity as differences related to age, class, gender, color, culture, disability, ethnicity, marital status, family structure, race, national origin, religion, sex, and sexual orientation.[23] The NASW includes most of these populations in its standards for cultural competence.[24] However, we believe that diversity competent practice is a more descriptive term. The lists of populations for both organizations extend well beyond culture and recognize that people can be different from each other in many ways, and in multiple ways, as well.

The diversity competent social worker explores ways to serve diverse clients in a manner that is expected within their diverse group. For instance, a white worker might need to be able to use an Afrocentric approach in working with some of her African American clients or a feminist approach in working with some of her female clients. The professional worker realizes that it is her responsibility to adapt her skills to meet the needs of her client. She meets that responsibility by engaging in life-long learning activities throughout her career. She reads materials and attends relevant training programs. She seeks to learn from knowledgeable colleagues and members of the community. She realizes the value of learning from her clients about how they would like to be served and incorporates this into her repertoire of skills. She uses diversity-appropriate skills in engagement and relationship building, assessment, planning, action, evaluation, and termination with every client she serves. She realizes that diversity competence is a life-long process that is never really achieved, but she seeks to add to her competence with every client she serves.

The importance of diversity competence can be seen in the demographic changes occurring in the United States. During the first half of the twenty-first century, sweeping demographic changes will alter the face of America. Population projections indicate that the number of elderly people will increase in the United States and in other industrialized countries. The United States will also experience dramatic changes in its ethnic and racial composition. It appears that sometime in the middle of this century, people of color will surpass whites in population, and we will become a nation of minority groups. By that time, over half of our high school graduates will be children of color, as will half of our working-age adults. Martha Ozawa studied these trends and raised concerns about the high rate of poverty among children, especially African American and Hispanic children. She pointed out that federal spending has been eleven times greater for people who are elderly than for children. She concluded that child poverty, especially among children of color, will lead to a decline in our economic and social well-being unless we dramatically increase our investment in children.[25]

## Knowledge, Values, and Skills Needed for Diversity Competent Practice

In order for the social worker to develop diversity competence, she must take a comprehensive approach to understanding the effects of diversity on herself, her clients, the environment, and the interactions among these. Table 2.2 is an outline for developing a diversity competent approach to practice. There are two important aspects to this work. The first is the need for the social worker to develop her ability to acquire and use knowledge, values, and skills in a way that makes diversity competent practice possible. This requires developing a view of the world and an attitude toward professional social work practice that is inclusive rather than exclusive, that seeks to include everyone rather than excluding anyone; that genuinely values differences and variation; that taps one's natural curiosity about difference; and that truly values every human being. This means developing a system of thinking, feeling, and acting that opens the door to actively seeking new knowledge, to developing values that are consistent with this approach, and to trying new skills that may be uncomfortable for a while. It means becoming a true professional by giving up the safety of what we know and risking to reach out and learn about what we do not know. This task also involves learning how to acquire knowledge in a variety of ways. It involves learning about values that are different from our own and respecting those values. It involves learning how to use new skills while coping with discomfort that may be associated with doing something different.

The second aspect is to actually acquire and use appropriate knowledge, values, and skills in practice with diverse groups. It means learning how to learn about others. It includes learning where to look, whom to ask, what it means, and how to use new knowledge about others. It requires the social worker to learn about her own values and those of others without preconceived notions or judgments that prevent including the client's value system in the work to be done. It means becoming adept at altering one's approach or even abandoning it in favor of one with which the client is comfortable.

Often students have difficulty in identifying their own diversity. Marty Dewees cited an unpublished paper by W. Nichols that found that "many students from White, dominant, middle-class status, particularly in geographical areas with limited racial diversity, regard

**TABLE 2.2   Outline for Developing Diversity Competence**

**I.** Understanding self
  **A.** Understand the social worker's own attitudes and beliefs about diverse groups
  **B.** Understand the influence of attitudes and beliefs of the worker's family on the social worker's own attitudes and beliefs about diverse groups
  **C.** Understand the influence of attitudes and beliefs of the worker's ecosystem on the social worker's own attitudes and beliefs about diverse groups
  **D.** Understand the influences of societal attitudes and beliefs on the social worker's own attitudes and beliefs about diverse groups

**II.** Understanding societal influences
  **A.** Understand the history of each diverse group in America
  **B.** Understand historical and current stereotypes, prejudice, discrimination and oppression
  **C.** Understand formal and informal mechanisms in American society that cause or reinforce discrimination and/or oppression (past and present)
  **D.** Understand privileges and advantages that dominant groups have over the population (male privilege, white privilege, heterosexual privilege, wealth or class privilege, etc.)

**III.** Understanding a diverse group
  **A.** Understand the particular culture and circumstances that make each group diverse
  **B.** Understand the values, beliefs, and customs of each diverse group
  **C.** Understand strengths of diverse groups and resources available in their ecosystems
  **D.** Understand the social, psychological, economic, and political effects of historical and current stereotypes, prejudice, discrimination and oppression on diverse groups

**IV.** Developing diversity competent practice skills
  **A.** Development of knowledge regarding relationship building, assessment, planning, action, evaluation and termination that are necessary to provide services in a manner that is expected within each diverse group
  **B.** Development of a personal and professional value system that values diversity
  **C.** Development of skills in providing direct and indirect services in a manner that is expected within each diverse group

themselves as having *no* culture or ethnicity."[26] This observation is consistent with the authors' experiences in teaching BSW students. Some of this lack of cultural identity may be attributed to the mixing of cultures and ethnic groups in American society. However, the inability to identify one's own culture or ethnicity does not mean that one does not have any cultural or ethnic influences. What it means is that one is not aware of these influences. In addition, the authors have consistently observed that many female students have difficulty in recognizing discrimination they have experienced as women. Often, this begins to slowly change when there are discussions about who did what around the house when they were growing up or in their current living arrangement. Unfortunately, this type of discrimination is only the tip of the iceberg.

The danger here is that the worker will not recognize or be open to the effects of diversity on the helping relationship and will not be prepared to deal with issues her client experiences that arise out of diversity. To become competent as a social worker, the student must become "diversity competent," or competent in working with diverse clients, especially those who are different from oneself. Competence in working with diversity begins with an awareness of one's own diversity and the effect that diversity has in one's personal life.

The preponderance of work that is being done on developing models for cultural competence in social work practice points out the need for the student or worker to develop cultural awareness of herself. We have extended this requirement beyond culture to all forms of diversity in society. To become diversity competent, the student or worker must begin with an examination of her own diversity, along with an examination of how her experiences have shaped her attitudes toward her own diversity and the diversity of others. Cultural influences play a major role in both of these endeavors. It is not enough to be "color blind" or "culture blind" or "diversity blind." Assertions of tolerance will not ensure the development of trust in clients who are different from oneself. In fact, it is more likely to lead to mistrust, since clients get the message that diversity does not matter when indeed they know that it does. Professing tolerance for diversity can easily come across as insensitivity toward diversity. Diversity competence calls for an active listening approach to diversity that seeks to know more. It uses diversity to create a dialogue with the client that will lead to a better understanding of the client and his environment.

Lu, Lum, and Chen suggested that the worker "engage in inductive learning that promotes investigation and inquiry."[27] Doman Lum also included this idea in his work on culturally competent practice.[28] The inductive approach is different from the deductive process that is used in the scientific method. The deductive process involves moving from theory to hypothesis to testing the hypothesis to see whether the theory is supported. The inductive process involves moving from making observations of phenomena to searching for patterns that may lead to theory development. Applying the inductive learning approach to becoming competent in working with diversity means adopting an open-minded inquisitive approach, laying aside preconceived notions, and listening to the experiences of the client. Self-knowledge must come first so that the worker can move away from experiencing the client's story out of her own experience and instead hear the client's story out of his experience.

Becoming diversity competent may seem like an insurmountable challenge, especially for a student or a new social worker. But this work is not completed over a semester or over a year. It is an ongoing process, over a lifetime. In fact, it is never really finished. However, the social worker can become more diversity competent if she is open to learning from each and every client she meets and if she accepts the responsibility to engage in the life-long learning that is expected of a professional.

As a professional, the social worker has a responsibility to engage in a process of life-long learning. An important area of life-long learning is learning about diversity. The student begins this process through course work, research, assignments, reading, class discussions, and examining herself as a person and as a developing professional. She learns to use inductive learning and natural inquiry in her approach to diversity. In field placement, the student is frequently put in a position of working with people who are diverse, often for the first time. Many of these people have experienced considerable prejudice and discrimination related to their diversity. The student learns how to work with diverse clients by applying what she has learned from her academic experiences along with her new field experiences. She learns from her field instructor and from others with expertise who may be available in her agency, the community, or her university. Most important, she learns to learn from her clients. They are the experts on their own experiences with diversity. As a professional social worker, she learns to continue this learning, and she seeks out additional training through in-service training, conferences, and other continuing education activities.

## Application of Diversity Competent Practice to Groups

When the social worker works with groups, it is important to know how diversity affects the group as a whole as well as individual members of the group. In general, diversity is healthy for groups. It provides the group with a variety of ways to experience life. Diversity also provides an opportunity for group members to become more familiar with people who are different from themselves. However, even when group members share the same diversity, each person will have experienced that diversity in her own unique way and will have her own story to tell.

Some groups will have a great deal of heterogeneity and others will be relatively homogeneous. There are advantages and disadvantages to each. One advantage with homogeneity is that group members will tend to have a lot in common with one another. This can help to create cohesion relatively quickly. A disadvantage can be that ideas may be somewhat limited because there is not as much variety in the group members' backgrounds. Thus, heterogeneity can bring more variety, but it can also lead to conflict. It is helpful if more than one member of the group shares the same diversity. Otherwise, members can feel isolated.

As the social worker works with groups, she promotes respect for and valuing of diversity. This is in keeping with the cardinal social value of a belief in the inherent value and worth of every human being. The worker can promote the treatment of each group member with dignity and respect by modeling this for the group in her interactions. She can encourage the group to adopt norms that reflect mutual respect. She can raise awareness when the group or group members say and do things that do not reflect these values. She can suggest ways to incorporate diversity and diverse experiences into the functioning of the group. As we focus on working with various types of groups, we will highlight some ways in which diversity can be used to strengthen a group and help it to achieve its goals.

Following through with the spirit of naturalistic inquiry, the worker continues to employ the basic aspects of this approach throughout the action phase. If the worker has been successful in employing naturalistic inquiry, she should have an assessment that incorporates diversity as it applies to group members. She should also have a plan that reflects group members' perspective on their diversity, including goals, objectives, and tasks that are appropriate for their diversity. Using naturalistic inquiry during the action phase means that the worker consistently engages in dialogues with the group about the actions that are taken. Before she or the group takes action, she discusses who, what, where, when, how, and why. Who is going to take what action? Where and when will it take place? How will it be carried out? Why are we doing this? In addition, the worker confirms that the action is something that the group approves so that it is consistent with the diversity of group members or other factors. When the action takes place over time, the worker carries on a dialogue about the action with the group. She checks to ensure that group members are in agreement and that it fits for them and the situation at hand. When the action is completed, she discusses group members' level of comfort with the results and with the means by which the results were achieved.

Diversity competent practice actions with diverse group members requires the worker to learn practice actions that will facilitate successful completion of the plan in a manner that is expected within the culture or diverse group of group members. Knowledge that is needed to understand diverse group members is itself quite diverse. Similarly, ways of seeking and receiving help also varies. The foundation of diversity competent practice is the use of naturalistic inquiry, which has been described earlier. The application of this approach to direct practice actions means a continuation of the process in which group members are the source of what fits best for them. Thus, much of what makes up diversity competent practice actions with diverse group members is really a process or a "how" rather than a "what." It is more of a how to work with the group member rather than a what to do with him in terms of a specific approach. Just because the group member is diverse, does not mean that the worker should automatically assume that a certain approach is pre-scribed. For example, while an Afrocentric approach may be used with many African Americans, some may not be comfortable with it.

In diversity competent practice, the worker explores with group members actions that are consistent with their diversity as well as their own individual preferences as a unique person. She does not impose her own or society's view of what group members should do but seeks to find what fits for them as individuals. Most of the direct practice actions described in the text can be used with any group members, including those who are diverse. However, how they are used may be different based on either diversity or the unique individual with whom the action is occurring.

## Summary

This chapter provides a foundation for understanding generalist social work practice. It includes a description of the Johnson/Yanca model of generalist practice upon which this text is based. In generalist practice, the social worker and the client system together decide on the appropriate client system and the target for change. Either of these may be an individual, a family, a group, an organization, or a community.

The Johnson/Yanca model of generalist practice starts with an understanding of the concern or need. The model is based on a creative blending of knowledge, values, and skills for social work practice. The change process is characterized as moving through phases that include assessment, planning, action, and evaluation and termination. Included in the model is an approach identified as diversity competent practice.

This chapter also introduces the environment of the helping endeavor, the community and the agency. Both can be understood from a social systems perspective. The transactional nature of human functioning makes it essential that social workers understand the strengths and resources of the community and the agency and the influence of these two systems on the functioning of the worker, group members, and the group.

If the worker is to be a generalist, this understanding is essential in making decisions as to the target for change and the mode of intervention. If the target is to be the community or agency system, the worker needs in-depth understanding of that target. Communities and agencies are complex systems that must be understood in some depth before they become a target for change.

## QUESTIONS

1. Describe generalist social work practice and give an example.

2. Describe the Johnson/Yanca model of generalist social work practice.

3. Using Table 2.1, develop a survey of your own needs.

4. Describe the concept of the environment as an ecosystem.

5. Describe what it means to be diversity competent.

6. Select a diverse population and discuss how you might become more competent in working with members of that population using Table 2.2.

## SUGGESTED READINGS

Johnson, Louise C., and Yanca, Stephen J. *Social Work Practice: A Generalist Approach*, 9th ed. Boston: Allyn & Bacon, 2007 (Chapters 5–13).

Edwards, Richard L., Ed. *Encyclopedia of Social Work,* 19th ed. Washington, DC: NASW Press, 1995 ("Community"; "Community Needs Assessment"; "Community Organization"; "Community Practice Models"; and "Ecological Perspective").

Homan, Mark S. *Promoting Community Change: Making It Happen in the Real World,* 4th ed. Pacific Grove, CA: Brooks/Cole, 2008.

Kettner, Peter M. *Achieving Excellence in the Management of Human Service Organizations.* Boston: Allyn & Bacon, 2002 (Chapter 3).

Meyer, Carol. "The Ecosystems Perspective: Implications for Social Work Practice," in *The Foundations of Social Work Practice*, Carol Meyer and Mark Mattaini, Eds. Washington, DC: NASW Press, 1995 (pp. 16–27).

Netting, Ellen F., Kettner, Peter M., and McMurtry, Steven L. *Social Work Macro Practice,* 4th ed. Boston: Allyn & Bacon, 2008.

Netting, Ellen F., and O'Connor, Mary K. *Organization Practice: A Social Worker's Guide to Understanding Human Services.* Boston: Allyn & Bacon, 2003.

Rubin, Herbert J., and Rubin, Irene S. *Community Organizing and Development,* 4th ed. Boston: Allyn & Bacon, 2008.

Sheaford, Bradford W., and Horejsi, Charles R. *Techniques and Guidelines for Social Work Practice,* 8th ed. Boston: Allyn & Bacon, 2008.

Tropman, John, E., Erlich, John L., and Rothman, Jack. *Tactics and Techniques of Community Intervention,* 4th ed. Itasca, IL: F. E. Peacock, 2001.

# 3 The Change Process with Individuals in Groups

## LEARNING EXPECTATIONS

1. Understanding individuals as members of a small group in generalist social work practice.
2. Understanding assessment of individual group members.
3. Understanding planning with individual group members.
4. Understanding direct and indirect practice actions with individual group members.
5. Understanding evaluation and termination with individual group members.

Groups are made up of individuals. Ultimately, the purpose of most groups is to provide some sort of benefit to their members. In order to understand the functioning of the group, it is important to understand the functioning of and interactions between individuals within the group. This chapter presents a synopsis of the use of the Johnson/Yanca generalist practice model as it is applied to individuals. The emphasis is on working with individuals in groups, including assessing the appropriateness of using group work in serving a client. This material is presented here in order for the reader to have an understanding of individual group members. A more detailed version of the change process with individuals is presented in our text *Social Work Practice: A Generalist Approach*. The material presented here is intended to be foundational material for understanding our approach to generalist practice with groups and to provide the reader with an understanding of how this approach is used with individual group members either within the group or in addition to working with clients in groups. It is not intended to substitute for relying on the group for the work that needs to be done within the group. What is most important in a group occurs among its members, rather than between the worker and individual members. The interaction among members of a group is part of what is called group process. It has many layers and different meanings depending on the situation. Group process is discussed further in the next two chapters.

This chapter presents the change process as it applies to individual group members. The change process is conceptualized as follows:

### Assessment Phase
- Identify the initial concern or need.
- Identify the nature of the concern or need.

- Identify potential strengths and resources in the ecosystem.
- Select and collect information.
- Analyze the available information.

### Planning Phase
- Develop a plan based on analysis of available information.

### Action Phase
- Take action to implement the plan.

### Evaluation and Termination
- Evaluate results during each stage and after plan is implemented.
- Consolidate change at termination of service.

This process is used by the generalist social worker with any of her client systems. In group work, the change process may be used with individual clients and the means by which change is carried out is in a group. This might be the primary means, as is the case with counseling groups. It could be a secondary means, as would be typical of most of the other types of groups. In this respect, group work becomes part of the action phase of the change process.

The worker also facilitates the use of this change process within decision-making, problem-solving, or counseling groups and whenever other groups are faced with problem solving or decision making. It is used by individual members of the group as they work through resolution of their situations. The change process is also used by the group as a whole as it assists members in achieving their goals and meeting their needs. The change process also serves as a basic structure for task groups, which is discussed in Part Three of the text.

The change process with individuals begins with assessment, including a schema for an individual social history. The steps in the assessment phase of the change process with individuals is presented. The next phase of the change process is planning. This chapter considers planning with individuals. It considers the use of group work as a means of achieving individual goals and the process of incorporating individual goals into working with groups. Direct and indirect practice actions with individuals are discussed to give the reader a basic understanding of actions taken to facilitate the plan. At times, the group worker may need to work directly with an individual group member, either within the group itself or outside of the group. She may also need to act on behalf of a group member to ensure that certain needs are met. The basic concepts of evaluation and termination are presented here. A more detailed consideration of evaluation and termination with groups is presented in the next chapter.

## Assessment with Individuals in Groups

Assessment with groups can be a complex process, associated with the need to assess both the group as a system and individuals within the group. This is further complicated by factors such as diversity. In some groups, the main purpose and function of the group causes the assessment to be limited to the group itself. These are generally groups in which participation is the primary benefit, and the group is open to anyone interested in it. This is usually the case for growth and development groups and most self-help and support groups as well. In change-oriented groups, each individual needs to benefit from the group because the group is the mechanism for meeting some very important needs. Members of these groups may already have assessments or social histories that were developed by their original or primary workers. Others will need to have an individual assessment for the worker to ensure that they are appropriate for the group and will fully benefit from the group experience. In this chapter, we have included a schema for assessing individuals. Assessment of the small group as a social system is covered in the next chapter. The assessment presented here is one that is typical for an individual group member in a change-oriented group, to understand the more complex assessment associated with this type of assessment. Assessment with other types of groups is discussed in Part Two.

The purpose of assessment is twofold. It should give the worker an understanding of the person and the situation at hand. It should also lay the groundwork for change. Assessment is both content or product and process. Assessment as a product is represented by a document such as a social history. Assessment as a process refers to the means by which the worker develops the social history, along with gaining an understanding of person in environment and laying the foundation for change. As the worker gains this understanding he looks for strengths and resources that might be used to develop a plan that will meet the needs of his client. Table 3.1 is a typical social history for an individual. Generally in Part I of the assessment, basic demographic information is gathered and presented. Most social histories consider the person's family and her relationships within the family. The family has a profound influence on people and may also be a vital source of strength and resources. Education and work history give the worker a picture of how the person functions in society. Diversity considers how the person and the situation are influenced by these factors. Finally, factors in the environment are examined in terms of demands and expectations as well as strengths and resources.

Part II of the social history typically examines the concern or need that is the focus of the work. It is important that this need along with other needs be identified and thoroughly understood. A solid statement of need means a smooth transition to goals that will meet those needs. The worker should include some examination of the history of the need(s) and the effect it has on carrying out vital roles, including those of spouse, parent, child, student, employee, and the like. Needs related to development, diversity, and environmental expectations are typically present and effect the person's ability to meet his own needs. Parts I and II of the social history should give the worker a thorough understanding of person in environment.

Part III makes the transition from understanding to laying the groundwork for change. It examines strengths and resources in the person and her ecosystem along with challenges that might create barriers to change. It essentially represents the last step in the assessment phase in which the worker analyzes the information that is available.

Assessment as a process is made up of the steps identified above. The worker and the client identify the need or concern and formulate a need statement. The statement should incorporate the blocks that are preventing the need from being met as well as a sense of how the need will be met by removing blockages. For example, a client who has experienced difficulty in fulfilling the role of parent might have the following need statement:

Joyce needs to develop positive parenting skills that she can use to be an effective parent.

**TABLE 3.1  Schema for Development of a Social History: Individual**

**I.** Person

    **A.** Identifying information (as needed by agency): name, address, date and place of birth, marital status, religion, race, referred by whom and why

    **B.** Family

        **1.** Parents: names, dates of birth, dates of death, place or places of residence, relationship

        **2.** Siblings: names, dates of birth, places of residence, relationships

        **3.** Spouse: names, ages, dates of marriages and divorces, relationships

        **4.** Children: names, ages, dates of birth, places of residence, relationships

        **5.** Resources in the family for client—expectations for client

    **C.** Education and work experience

        **1.** Last grade of school completed, degrees if any, special knowledge or training; attitudes toward educational experiences; resources and expectations of educational system for client

        **2.** Work history—jobs held, dates, reasons for leaving; attitudes toward work experiences; resources and expectations of work system for client

    **D.** Diversity

        **1.** Disabling factors—physical, mental health history, current functioning

        **2.** Cultural and ethnic identification, importance to client

        **3.** Other diversity factors (include religious affiliation or spiritual factors, if any)

        **4.** Resources and expectations related to diversity characteristics of client

    **E.** Environmental factors

        **1.** Significant relationships outside family; resources and expectations for client

        **2.** Significant neighborhood and community factors; resources and expectations for client

**II.** Concern or need

    **A.** Reason for request for service

    **B.** History of concern or need; onset of concern or need; nature and results of coping attempts; factors that seem to be contributing to concern or need

    **C.** Capacity to carry out "vital roles"

    **D.** Needs of client (general)

        **1.** Needs based on common human need/development

            **a.** Stage of physical, cognitive, and psychosocial development

            **b.** Adequacy of need fulfillment in previous stages

            **c.** Present needs (needs for developmental stage and compensation for previous stage deficiency)

        **2.** Needs based on diversity factors

            **a.** What dominant societal factors and attitudes affect the way people of this diversity meet common human/developmental needs?

            **b.** What cultural group factors affect the way people of this diversity meet common human/developmental needs?

            **c.** Individualize client within the diverse group. What are this client's attitudes toward diversity, means of coping with diversity, adaptation or lifestyle within diverse group, coping or adaptation relative to dominant societal expectations?

            **d.** What incongruities exist between this client's way of functioning and the societal expectations due to diversity?

            **e.** What needs does this person have because of dominant societal attitudes and expectations, because of cultural factors related to common human need/human development, because of individual factors of attitudes toward the diversity and dominant societal expectations and impingements, or because of incongruities between the client's way of functioning and societal expectations due to diversity?

*(continued)*

**TABLE 3.1   (Continued)**

3. Needs based on environmental expectations
   a. Client's responsibilities toward family, peer group, work, organizations, community
   b. Other environmental expectations of client; client's attitudes toward these expectations
   c. Are responsibilities and expectations of the client realistic?
   d. Client needs because of the responsibilities and expectations
4. Needs of client in relation to the request for service
   a. What general needs of the client have bearing on the request for service?
   b. What is the specific need of the client in relation to the request?
   c. What factors seem to be blocking the fulfillment of that need?

III. Strengths and challenges for helping
   A. What does the client expect to happen during and as a result of the service to be provided?
   B. What are the client's ideas, interests, and plans that are relevant to the service?
   C. What is the client's motivation for using the service and for change?
   D. What is the client's capacity for coping and for change? What might impinge? What are the individual's internal resources for change?
   E. What are the client's strengths?
   F. What are the environmental resources and the environmental responsibilities and impingements that could support or mitigate against coping or change?
   G. Are there any other factors that affect the client's motivation, capacity, or opportunity for change?
   H. What is the nature of the stress factor?
   I. Are the client's expectations realistic?
   J. Summary of strengths and the challenges of client in situation as they relate to meeting need

Instead of using a problem-oriented approach that might identify Joyce as a bad or a poor parent, an ecosystems strengths approach to change identifies needs and formulates need statements that focus on meeting those needs.

The next two steps of the assessment phase focus on understanding the nature of the need and examining potential strengths and resources that will meet it. Identifying the nature of the need for Joyce might be as follows:

Joyce did not experience positive parenting as a child.

Joyce lacks knowledge about how to function in the role of parent in a positive way.

For the next step in identifying potential strengths and resources the following assumptions might be made about Joyce:

Joyce is motivated and has a strong desire to be a good parent.

Joyce is capable of learning positive parenting skills.

If Joyce learns positive parenting skills, she will be able to become an effective parent.

The next step is to select and collect information. The selection of information to be collected is driven by the assumptions that were made in the previous two steps. The worker examines Joyce's experiences growing up to see if there is evidence of positive or negative parenting. She tries to find out what Joyce knows or does not know about parenting. The worker assesses Joyce's motivation and desire for change and her capacity to learn new skills. As Joyce learns new skills, the worker watches for evidence that Joyce has the capacity to use those skills in parenting her children.

The final step in the assessment phase is to analyze the information that is available. The social worker collects evidence that supports or refutes her assumptions. She may find that Joyce was raised in a family situation that might be described as chaotic because her mother experienced difficulties with substance abuse. Joyce may have experienced neglect and abuse and so she would not have knowledge or experiences that would lead to positive parenting. The worker also might find that Joyce is highly motivated to have her children returned to her care and is willing to attend a parenting group. Joyce could have at least average intelligence and may have actually been doing a better job at parenting than was the case with her mother. Thus, it would appear that Joyce had learned some parenting skills that were more positive than the ones she had experienced. It is possible that she could implement new parenting skills if given the opportunity.

## Planning with Individuals in Groups

As with assessment, planning is both a product and a process. In working with individuals who may be candidates for group work, the plan might incorporate group work as a method of delivering services. In addition, plans may be developed with individual members of the group. The plan may be facilitated by other members of the group or by the worker or by both.

As a product, a plan encompasses goals, objectives, and tasks. The **goal** is the overall, long-range expected outcome of the endeavor that is intended to meet a need. Because of the complexity of the overall plan, a goal is usually reached only after intermediate goals or **objectives** have been attained. **Tasks** are steps that the worker and the client need to take to reach the objective and achieve the goal. Goals and objectives may relate to the client, the family, various family members, several different persons, or social systems involved in the situation. Goals and objectives develop out of assessment related to the needs of the client and various systems involved and the identification of the blocks to need fulfillment. They are generally related to the removal of a block or to developing new means of need fulfillment.

It is challenging to write appropriate goals and objectives using an acceptable format. Social workers are prone to qualify or hedge their statements to allow for flexibility or individuality. Much of this comes from a desire to respect client self-determination and to allow for unforeseen difficulties. However, planning calls for direct and definitive statements so that expectations and outcomes are clear and progress can be accurately measured. Otherwise, confusion will occur about who is responsible for what, and measuring progress and outcomes will be impossible. Although goal statements must be definitive, there is room for flexibility in that plans can be changed. When it is obvious that something is not working, the plan needs to be changed. However, the need for flexibility in planning should not obscure the need for clearly defined goals, objectives, and tasks.

Many social workers will see a variety of things that might be improved or changed as they assess the person in environment and will want to fix everything. It is best to keep things less complicated and focus on the main areas the client wishes to change and where change will likely make the biggest difference. A general guideline for individual group members is to limit the number of goals to no more than two or three at any given time during the process. For group members facing multiple barriers or difficulties, more goals may be necessary. However, it is not very likely that an individual will remember to work on more than two or three goals at a given time. For children and those who are under stress or have limitations, one or two goals may be the most they are able to handle at one time.

In developing a plan with individual group members in a change-oriented group, the challenge is to balance the needs and goals of each individual with each other and with those of the group. The first task is to identify individual or personal goals for each member. Although the worker may have discussed these beforehand, it is important for members to state their goals to other members of the group. The next step is for the worker to assist the group in articulating a common goal that includes everyone in the group. This inclusion process helps to establish and reinforce a sense of belonging and teamwork and increases a sense of cohesion. It is sometimes difficult to develop an all-encompassing goal; thus, the worker should keep the goal simple and straightforward. For example, for a parenting group, a common goal might be to learn to use positive parenting skills. Sensitivity to diversity and to at risk populations is essential when planning, as is building on the strengths of individuals and their environment. Once the group has established a common goal, the task is to assist them in finding ways to help one another achieve individual goals as well as to identify roles in helping the group to achieve its overall goal and to function as a group. The worker will need to use mediation and negotiation in helping the group in this process.

Goals should build on the strengths of individuals, the group as a whole, and the strengths and resources available in the larger ecosystem. In addition to personal or individual goals and a common goal for the group, there are two other types of goals that are important: mutual or shared goals and reciprocal goals. **Mutual goals** require two or more members to participate or act in certain ways regardless of the actions of others, for example, a goal in which everyone agrees to engage in positive parenting techniques, even if their partner did not do so. **Reciprocal goals** require different actions on the part of two or more members, for example, a goal in which a parent agrees to cook the family's favorite meal and the family members agree to make a commitment to sit together as a family for that meal. Reciprocal goals may also be contingent. This is usually stated as "if-then." For example, parents can agree to give each child an allowance based on completion of certain chores. This might be stated as, "If John cuts the grass when requested, then Mr. A will pay him $20.00."

If the worker and client have been able to formulate a good need statement, there is a simple process for developing a goal statement that may involve changing only one or two words. For the need statement for Joyce, a good goal statement would be:

> Joyce will develop positive parenting skills that she can use to be an effective parent.

Changing "needs to" to "will" makes this a strong goal that is designed to meet the identified need.

Care must be taken to express the objectives in terms of the behavioral outcomes desired rather than how the goal will be reached. In other words, receiving a service is not a goal but rather a task designed to meet a need or achieve the goal or objective. Also, each goal and objective should have a specified date for its accomplishment. Objectives should be specific, concrete, and measurable. Goal statements are usually broader and more general than objectives. If objectives have specific statements about frequency, duration, and time frame, then the goal statement can be more broad. For example, the goal statement for Joy is broad in that it does not specify how these skills will be learned or measured or the time frame for completion. In developing more specific, measurable statements for objectives, it is helpful to think in terms of a sequence of questions: who, what, how, where, and when. The "who" refers to the person or persons taking action and the targets of change. The person(s) taking action should appear first in both the goal statement and the objectives. The next word should be *will,* which conveys a positive, unequivocal statement about the desired state of affairs. Next comes a description of "what" and/or "how" the situation will appear if the goal or objective were accomplished or the need were to be met. Identifying "who" is the target of change may come next, if appropriate. "When" describes the time, frequency, and/or duration in which the action is to take place and the time frame for completion. An example of an objective written using these guidelines follows:

> Objective: Joyce will demonstrate at least three positive parenting techniques in interactions with her children during three visits by April 15.

Joyce and her children are the "who." "Positive parenting techniques" represents the "what." "During three visits" refers to both "where" and "when" along with the frequency. "By April 15" is the time frame. It is clear from this statement who will do what and where and when she will do it. There should be no confusion about expectations; both progress and outcomes can be measured with an identification of what makes up "positive parenting techniques."

Goals should be reasonably feasible; that is, there should be a good chance of reaching them. In thinking about feasibility, consideration is given to time and energy factors. It is wise to state goals and objectives in terms of a positive outcome rather than in negative terms. That is, goals should be stated as "the client will" rather than "the client will not." When goals and objectives are positive, they help to focus on the desired outcome instead of being problem focused. This reinforces behavior that is needed to bring about change. In addition, a positive focus gives the client more hope that the situation can be resolved. Finally, it creates a "self-fulfilling prophecy" that is more likely to result in success than failure. People tend to engage in behavior that is based on a prediction or "prophecy" of what they expect to have happen, not necessarily what they want to have happen. "Self-fulfilling prophecy" means that one's own behavior contributes a great deal to the outcome. When people are focused on behavior that is likely to bring about the desired change, they are more likely to succeed and are also more likely to receive positive reinforcement from one another and from their environment.

Group members can often be most helpful in evaluating the feasibility of a goal; thus, they should be involved in setting goals. This can motivate them for the work needed to reach that goal. As they reach objectives, the members gain hope for reaching other goals.

Different situations call for different kinds of change and different kinds of goals. The kinds of change that should be considered are:

1. *A sustaining relationship*—used when it appears that there is no chance to change the person in environment and when the person lacks a significant other who can give needed support or when a relationship with a significant other is threatened or has broken down

2. *Specific behavioral change*—used when people are troubled by specific symptoms or behavior patterns and are generally otherwise satisfied with their situation
3. *Relationship change*—used when the issue is a troublesome relationship
4. *Environmental change*—used when it is recognized that a part of the need is a change in some segment of the environment or in the transactions between person and environment
5. *Directional change*—used when values are conflicting or unclear, when a client is unclear about goals or direction of effort, or when aspirations are blocked in a manner that makes unblocking very difficult or impossible

In summary, goals and objectives for individual group members should relate to meeting a need. They should be stated in terms of an outcome, be specific, and be measurable. They should be feasible and positive in direction and developed with the group member to reflect the member's desires.

The **unit of attention,** or **focal system,** is the system being focused on for the change effort. This is generally in relation to the overall goals, but there may be different units of attention in relation to specific objectives. A unit of attention is either a person, a social system such as the family or an organization, or the transactions between them. It may be the client system or a person or system that has a significant influence on the situation. In other words, units of attention are systems that are the focus of the change activity.

Units of attention may be individuals, families, small groups of unrelated persons, organizations, or communities. Table 1.1 gives some indications and counterindications for the choice of each kind of system. It is important to specify appropriate units of attention for every goal and objective. Units of attention may be clients or other persons and social systems involved in the situation.

**Tasks** are steps that are necessary to achieve the objectives and ultimately the goal. Tasks may be used to describe events that occur only once or are ongoing. They should cover the "who, what, how, where, and when" for the actions that are planned. This is generally the first place the worker might appear in the plan. The exception would be cases in which the worker might be part of an objective by monitoring, prompting, or rewarding the group or a member to assist in accomplishing objectives.

The tasks should be sequenced and a time for the completion of each established. This results in an overall time frame or time line for the service. It is important to specify the resources needed to carry out the plan and to indicate how those resources are to be obtained. This would include the time investment of the worker and the client. Any monetary investment, such as fees or agency funds, should be specified. Other needed resources could be the use of an agency or community facility or service or the inclusion of other persons in the action system.

# Direct and Indirect Practice Actions with Individuals in Groups

Following planning, the next step in the generalist social work change process is action. One of the marks of a generalist practitioner is the capacity to choose from a wide variety of possibilities the action most appropriate for the specific situation. Social work action falls into two primary classifications: **direct practice** (action with clients) and **indirect practice** (action with people and systems other than clients). Direct practice primarily involves action with individuals, families, and small groups. Direct practice is focused on change in the thoughts, feelings, or actions of individuals, the transactions between individuals and their environment, the transactions within a family or a small-group system, or in the manner in which individuals, families, and small groups function in relation to persons and societal institutions in their environment.

Indirect practice involves those actions taken with persons other than clients in order to help clients. These actions may be taken with individuals, small groups, organizations, or communities as the unit of attention.

Direct practice falls within the following categories:

1. Diversity competent practice actions
2. Actions taken to enable development of relationships
3. Actions taken to enable clients to learn and use the change process
4. Actions taken to enable clients to know and use available resources
5. Actions taken to empower or enable clients
6. Actions taken in crisis situations
7. Actions taken to support the social functioning of clients
8. Actions taken that uses activity with clients as the base of help
9. Actions taken in using a clinical model of social work

In this section, actions related to developing relationships, to the use of resources, to empowerment and enabling of people, to crisis intervention, to support, and to the use of activity are discussed. Diversity competent practice is discussed in Chapter 2. Although assessment and planning have been discussed, these actions are also briefly reviewed here as these relate to facilitating clients learning the change process. Action taken in using clinical models of social work is beyond the scope of this book.

In the generalist approach to social work practice, the worker is not only involved in direct work with clients but is also involved in work with individuals, small groups, agencies, and communities on behalf of the group and its members. This work has often been characterized as indirect practice. It is very often work with the agency and community systems. This is sometimes described as *macropractice* when the work that is done with these larger systems involves them as a client system or when the target of change is a larger system in the environment. This type of practice is covered in greater detail in Part Three.

One of the identifying characteristics of the generalist social worker is the worker's ability to respond to many issues at several levels. In addition to macropractice, the generalist social worker is also prepared to work at the micro and mezzo levels. The *micro level* is working with individuals. *Mezzo* refers to working with families and small groups. The generalist social worker identifies both relevant factors at these various levels inherent in any practice situation and then decides on the appropriate focus of the action for change. This focus may be on micro (individual), mezzo (family or group), or macro (agency and community) concerns. Often the focus may call for work with both private parties and the public. Thus, the generalist practitioner must possess knowledge and skills for indirect as well as direct practice and be able to combine the two when appropriate. As we will see, it is possible to change the interactions between members of these systems and the client or group members without the necessity of bringing about change in these larger systems.

Indirect actions are aimed at bringing about change in the environment. Indirect actions can be learned by clients so that they can act on their own behalf in the future.

This chapter discusses four approaches that may be used in indirect practice:

1. Action that involves the use of mediation between the client and the environment
2. Action that involves the use of influence
3. Action designed to change the environment
4. Action relative to coordination of services

The generalist practitioner's repertoire includes actions for working with individuals, groups, families, organizations, and communities. Often, several types of action are needed to reach identified goals. In understanding generalist practice with groups, it is important that the worker understand how group work may be blended with other actions with clients to form a comprehensive, effective, and efficient delivery of services. There is overlap among possible actions or strategies, and often the worker creatively combines strategies or makes alterations to better respond to specific situations. The art of social work comes into play when action becomes the focus of service.

## Actions to Develop Relationships

Actions taken to develop relationships are essential to any form of social work. Relationship is the key element in working with groups. To function in group discussions and activities, members must have the level of relationship skills required for meaningful participation. Well-functioning individuals have healthy, well-functioning relationships that are commensurate with their age and developmental level. Often, direct practice actions involve developing, repairing, restoring, or strengthening relationships between clients and their environments as either the primary need or concern or the means by which the primary need or concern will be met.

A good relationship requires the ability to do three things: (1) communicate effectively, (2) make decisions and solve problems, and (3) resolve conflict constructively. Effective communication begins with the use of "I" statements (statements that begin with the word "I"). A successful process for decision making and problem solving needs to be one that the parties agree on and results in everyone's needs being met. The ability to resolve conflict in a constructive manner is using a win-win approach, as opposed to win-lose.

In constructive conflict resolution, a willingness to negotiate and compromise is a must. The parties should stick to the issue and stay in the present, not the past. Using "I" statements will tend to encourage expression of thoughts and feelings. "You" statements tend to create defensiveness and can easily lead to name-calling and attacking the other person. These situations are related to win-lose. Changing the subject, talking about the past, attacking the other person, using or threatening violence are ways that people use to win at the other person's expense. It is crucial to avoid violence and threats of violence. The problem with win-lose in significant on going relationships is that someone has to be a loser, which does not lead to a successful relationship.

The social worker uses her knowledge and skills in developing relationships to build a relationship with individual clients or group members and to assist them in strengthening relationships within the group and with others outside of the group. She models effective communication and teaches and guides clients or group members in communicating effectively. When inappropriate or harmful interactions occur, the worker helps those involved to restructure the interaction. For instance, making a derogatory remark generally occurs because the person is angry. The worker asks the person what he was thinking and feeling before he made the remark. As the reasons emerge, the worker asks for a direct statement about the person's real feelings using "I" statements. The person might say, "I feel hurt and angry because . . . ." Behind negative interaction is an unmet need. People need positive relationships to grow and develop and succeed. Good communication skills, an effective decision-making/problem-solving process, and constructive conflict resolution are necessary for maintaining positive relationships.

## Actions to Enable Group Members to Learn and Use the Change Process

Social work is a profession that has no trade secrets as such. Everything we learn can be given to our clients to assist them in improving their lives. This is fairly unique. Most professions maintain control over their knowledge and skills and do not allow others to use these. In addition, as social workers, a major goal with nearly all of our clients is to work ourselves out of a job. That is to say, our goal is to reach a point at which clients are able to meet their needs on their own without our assistance. In many respects, we believe in the old adage "Give a person a fish and you feed him for a day. Teach him to fish and you feed him for a lifetime." An important aspect of this is teaching clients the change process as we work with them.

Actions to enable clients to use the change process include helping them to use assessment, planning, action, and evaluation whenever they have needs or concerns. Helping them to learn to use the change process is important for their long-term success in meeting needs. When a client develops a better understanding of himself and his environment, he has learned the first step in the change process—assessment. This understanding allows him to change the interactions between himself and the environment. In an ecosystems strengths approach, need represents an imbalance in the transactions in the ecosystem. Changing the transactions is necessary to meet the need. Understanding the ecosystem is critical to restoring balance and meeting need. It helps the client to identify strengths and resources within himself and in the environment.

Understanding person in environment is the foundation for successful planning. Clients can learn planning skills as they work on resolving the current situation. Teaching planning skills is an important direct practice action with all client systems. The actions that follow can be learned in order to facilitate implementation of plans that the client formulates and to remove barriers.

## Actions to Enable Use of Available Resources

For some clients, the major block to meeting need is a lack of resources. Sometimes these resources are available, but the client is not aware of or does not know how to use them. Sometimes the resource is not responsive to some clients. In a complex and diverse society, all resources are not amenable to all clients. One part of the generalist social worker's understanding of a community is knowing which resources can meet the needs of which clients. An important part of the social worker's interventive repertoire is the ability to match clients with resources and to enable them to use the available resources.

Enabling clients to know and use resources is especially important when working with diverse clients. Experiences with prejudice and discrimination often result in becoming marginalized and isolated. Members of diverse groups may not be aware of resources or may not feel welcome in using them. The way in which resources are made available or services are delivered may not fit with their culture or diversity. In diversity competent practice, the social worker uses naturalistic inquiry to find out what clients know about resources that are available. She explores experiences that they have had or have heard from others regarding the use of those resources. She incorporates this into the actions she takes in enabling clients to use resources.

To help clients use the available resources, workers should have knowledge and skill in four areas: (1) knowledge of the service delivery systems of the community in which they practice and the community in which the client lives and functions; (2) knowledge of and skill in the use of the referral process; (3) knowledge of the appropriate use of the broker and advocate roles and skill in filling these roles; and (4) knowledge of how to empower clients to take charge of their life situation. The social worker takes action to enable clients to use available resources, with the purpose of enabling clients to meet their needs and thus enhance their social functioning and coping capacity.

When identifying components of the service delivery system, workers usually begin by identifying social service agencies and services provided by other professionals. A broader view needs to be considered. Within many neighborhoods, communities, and ethnic groups, a helping network outside the formal system exists. This **natural helping system** becomes known to social workers as they come into contact with diverse clients and groups in the community.

The natural helping system is made up of a client's family, friends, neighbors, coworkers, and others in her environment. These are the people to whom a person in need goes for help first. When clients come to a social worker, they have probably already tried to get help from these **natural helpers**. The use of the natural helping system has particular importance in working with diverse cultural groups. Past experiences with discrimination and oppression have led many people of color to rely on systems in their immediate environment for assistance. Often the relationship between the client and this system may need to be strengthened or restored or the systems themselves may need to be strengthened and supported in providing help. Social workers can sometimes strengthen or support the natural helping attempts rather than take over the helping function completely. The extended family has always been an important part of the helping system for many ethnic groups and in small towns and rural areas.

The first step in enabling clients to use resources is a thorough knowledge of the resources available. The second step is choosing the appropriate resource. This choice is based on matching client's needs and lifestyle with a resource that can meet the needs in a manner congruent with that lifestyle and culture. Client involvement in the choice is essential for matching and linking her to the resource. In addition, workers may use indirect practice strategies to work for change in the relational patterns characterizing segments of the service delivery system so that client need can be better met.

**Referral** is the process by which a social worker enables clients to know and use another resource. In addition, the referral process involves supplying the referral agency with information that may be helpful in providing service and then following up on the usefulness of the service to the client. The worker must obtain written permission from the client, usually called a release of information, before sharing any identifying information about the client system with an outside service.

Referral is used when the client's needs cannot be met by services provided by the agency that employs the worker or when a more appropriate service is provided by another agency. The worker uses knowledge of the potential resources and knowledge of the way service is delivered to match potential clients and potential services so that the service is acceptable to and usable by clients. The referral service may be used in conjunction with the service a worker is providing or as the primary service.

Referrals are made only with permission of the client. The worker and client discuss the potential service, and the worker helps the client make the initial contact with the new agency, if necessary. This can be done by giving a phone number or directions for reaching the agency or by making suggestions about how to approach the agency. Sometimes it is helpful for a worker to call the agency for the client or go to the agency with the client for the first contact. The worker must make sure the client has the resources needed to access and utilize the service, including transportation, access to a telephone, financial resources, and day care.

The worker and client also discuss the information that would be helpful to the agency. After receiving the client's permission and obtaining a written release of information, a worker provides this information to the worker at the new agency. It is often helpful if the two workers know each other and can discuss the client's needs.

An often overlooked final step in referral is follow-up. In determining whether the client is receiving the services sought, the worker gains information about the appropriateness of the service. This also enables the worker to make appropriate referrals in the future. If the client has not been able to use the service, the worker must advocate for the client or assist him in receiving the needed service elsewhere or determine why he was unable to use the service.

In enabling clients to use available resources, two primary roles are used: the broker role and the advocate role. It is important for the social worker to understand the difference between these two roles and to choose the one most appropriate to the situation. The **broker** helps a person get needed services. This includes assessing the situation, knowing the alternative resources, preparing and counseling the person, contacting the appropriate service, and ensuring that the client gets to the resource and uses it.[1] The goal is to expedite the linkage of clients to the needed resource. This involves giving information and support, teaching clients how to use resources, and also negotiating with the agency.

The role of **advocate** consists of "pleading and fighting for services for clients whom the service system would otherwise reject."[2] For example, a lesbian couple may be denied housing because of their relationship, or a group member with HIV or AIDS may be denied medical treatment. The worker as advocate seeks different interpretations or exceptions to rules and regulations, points out clients' rights to services, and removes blocks to receiving or using an agency's services.

In the advocacy role, the worker speaks on behalf of the client. Before engaging in advocacy, a worker must first be sure that the client desires the worker to intervene in this manner. Then the worker must carefully assess the risks involved for the client if advocacy is used. This includes consideration that any action taken might cause problems for the client or block access to the resources. The client should clearly understand the risks involved and be motivated to use the service if it is obtained. **Case advocacy,** advocacy for a single client, is most effective when used to obtain concrete resources for which the client is eligible. It is also useful when people and systems impinge on a client's functioning. To be a case advocate, social workers must be comfortable with conflict situations and knowledgeable about the means for conflict management. They must be willing to negotiate and be aware of the value of withdrawing application for service if the best interests of the client are not being served. Clients must have considerable trust in the worker before they will be willing for the worker to take an advocate role.

The worker uses the advocate role only when the broker role is not effective. Whenever possible, it is better for clients to act on their own behalf in order to strengthen their belief in themselves as well as gain a sense of empowerment. There are times, however, when an advocate stance must be taken in order to enable clients to obtain needed services. **Cause advocacy** is used to serve groups with similar difficulties. Both case and cause advocacy are important actions on behalf of clients who are members of populations that are at risk of prejudice, discrimination, and oppression. Case advocacy is used when barriers to resources and services exist for individual clients. Cause advocacy addresses issues on a larger scale. Mediation with the client and the environment as an alternative to advocacy is discussed later in this chapter.

## Actions to Empower and Enable Group Members

Empowerment and enabling involve validation of feelings, positive reinforcement, feedback, assertiveness, and cognitive and behavioral change. Clients can learn to use these actions to improve their self-esteem and to build strong relationships. The most powerful validation, reinforcement, and feedback come from significant others such as one's parents, spouse, family members, and friends. The fundamental basis for good self-esteem is love and acceptance from one's parents. Unconditional love for being, not doing, allows the child to internalize unconditional acceptance of himself as a human being who has worth. This is not unconditional acceptance of the child's behavior. It is the parent's responsibility to socialize the child so that he learns what is acceptable and not acceptable behavior. The message is "I love you as a person no matter what you or I feel, think, or do. However, your behavior is a separate matter. I do not have to love or even like your behavior and neither does anyone else." Group work allows clients to revisit issues that might be left over from their childhood regarding love and acceptance. Groups are excellent forums for people to experience a sense of acceptance and belonging that can help to overcome earlier negative experiences. The worker uses validation, reinforcement, and feedback to build healthy self-esteem in the client while also helping her to use these for herself and with others, and helping group members use these in the group. He also helps the client to appropriately use cognitive and behavioral change strategies in meeting her needs.

Most clients can benefit from taking an active role in changing the situations impinging on their functioning. **Empowerment** is "a process of increasing personal, interpersonal, or political power so that individuals can take action to improve their life situation."[3] Empowerment has been suggested as a strategy of choice when working with members of minority groups, populations at risk, and women.[4] Empowerment is particularly useful in the contemporary world in which power is an all-pervasive issue and in which the gap between haves and have-nots is growing dramatically. Empowerment means providing clients with the supports, skills, and understanding needed to allow them to take charge of their own lives and use their power in situations in which they have felt powerless.

Those caught in feelings or situations of powerlessness often lack knowledge of how to negotiate systems, feel hopeless that any change is possible, and may lack the self-esteem necessary for engaging in change activity. Empowerment involves assisting clients in negotiating systems. It involves motivating, teaching, and raising self-esteem so that clients believe they are competent individuals with the skills needed for negotiating community systems and they deserve the resources necessary for healthy social functioning. Empowerment enables clients to receive the benefits of society and increases their capacity to work toward resolving the conditions preventing them from providing for their needs.

According to Ruth J. Parsons, a literature search confirms that the important ingredients of an empowerment strategy are support, mutual aid, and validation of the client's perceptions and experiences. When these ingredients are present, there is a heightened degree of self-esteem, more self-confidence, and a greater capacity to make changes or take action. An empowerment strategy calls for building collectives; working with others in similar situations; educating for critical thinking through support, mutual aid, and collective action; and competency assessment, or identification of strengths and coping skills.[5]

Thus, the use of groups, particularly mutual aid groups, enhances this action strategy. Silvia Staub-Bernasconi pointed this out and called for a focus on consciousness development, social and coping skills training, networking, and mediation. Also, empowerment calls for work with power sources and power structures.[6] This strategy is congruent with the generalist social work model presented in this text. The strong emphasis on maximal client involvement in assessing, planning, and acting to meet goals is an important ingredient of empowerment. Teaching clients about meeting needs and about the nature of the systems in their environment is a part of empowerment.

A technique useful in an empowerment strategy is consciousness-raising, which involves giving clients information about the nature of the situation, particularly the various environmental forces affecting their functioning. This work can heighten client understanding of self in relationship to others. Workers must feel comfortable with the anger that can result from using this technique and be able to help clients use anger in ways that further the work at hand. When the time is appropriate, it is also important for the worker to help clients move beyond anger into other responses. It is hoped that clients can gain a more realistic view of the situation and then take advantage of change possibilities.

Groups are a powerful adjunct to consciousness-raising. It is helpful to group members to see others struggle with new understandings and to see the work of a group be of benefit. The group can be involved in collective action and thus enhance a sense of individual power. The group can also be a support system for mutual aid. Participation in a group can lead to enhanced self-esteem and can help members learn new skills. As members tell their stories and share their perceptions, new understandings can emerge.

The nature of the relationship between worker and client and relationships within the group are important considerations when using this strategy. Using an empowerment approach requires establishing mutual respect, building on strengths, sharing information and knowledge of resources in a sense of partnership, and considering clients or group members as "experts" on their own situation. Because the worker may be viewed as yet another person with power over the client, the social worker needs to act as a colleague or a member of the group rather than as a detached professional. This requires the worker to shift her frame of reference from that of an expert to that of a collaborator.[7] As the worker demonstrates belief in the client and points out competencies, the client will gain a sense of value and worth and a belief that he has the ability to bring about change.

Another valuable technique that can be an adjunct to an empowerment strategy is work focused on reducing self-blame. Clients need to see that the difficulties they are facing often have their source in the functioning of systems in the environment. The worker can help clients take responsibility for changing the environment by teaching specific skills for environmental change. Although the worker may also work for environmental change through advocacy and mobilization of resources, it is important that clients participate; otherwise, the feelings of inadequacy may be further reinforced.[8]

Empowerment is not a strategy that is used in isolation from other strategies. Instead, it aims to reduce helplessness so that clients can take charge of their lives.

Enabling or helping clients reach their goals may seem similar to empowerment, but there are subtle differences. **Enabling,** the broader term, refers to helping the client carry out an activity otherwise not possible. This term recently has taken on negative connotations when used with regard to alcohol and other addictions. For example, a spouse whose actions support the addictive behaviors of the partner is often called an enabler. As used in this text, enabling has a positive connotation in that the action being supported is desirable.

Sometimes in the process of empowering or enabling clients or group members, the worker may need to work directly with individuals to enhance positive thinking and actions, or she might need to encourage or support group members in doing this with one another. Often, clients have had experiences that reinforce a negative view of themselves or their situation. They may be frustrated or may have learned that it is safer to predict failure than to hope for success. Clients may blame themselves or others for the situation or be blamed by others. They may engage in self-defeating thoughts or actions. When the worker senses that this is happening, she can assist the client in changing thoughts or actions so that he can successfully meet goals and carry out the plan. The thinking part of this strategy is called a cognitive approach or intervention. The action part refers to behavior. Some theorists have combined these two approaches into what is called a cognitive-behavioral approach.[9]

The basic idea behind this approach is that thoughts lead to feelings and behavior. Negative thoughts lead to negative feelings and negative reactions, and positive thoughts lead to positive feelings and positive behavior. The BSW-level social worker is not generally trained to use this approach in a clinical model of practice. However, it is important to be able to work with clients and group members to develop positive thinking and actions as they carry out plans. Plans contain behaviors that clients or group members have agreed to do. These behaviors are stated in objectives and tasks. If the client does not think she can accomplish something, she is unlikely to do so. The worker asks the client what she is thinking about the situation and about the proposed goals, objectives, and tasks. The worker listens for thoughts that might be barriers to success. The worker helps the client to see how her thinking can have either a positive or a negative influence on carrying out the plan. A good set of questions to ask are: (1) What do you think will happen if you do this? or What were you thinking when that happened? (2) What do you want to have happen? (3) What could you do to make that happen today? This week? This month? (or next time?) (4) What could you tell yourself that would make you feel more confident in doing that? (5) What kind of payoff or reward could you identify that would help you to remember to do that?

An important technique in empowering or enabling clients that uses a cognitive- behavioral approach is assertiveness training. In this technique, the worker assists clients or group members to become more assertive about meeting their needs. The worker will generally engage in or facilitate practicing and role-playing assertive behaviors in situations in which the client or group member needs to advocate for herself. It is important that the worker help the client differentiate between assertiveness and aggressiveness. Assertiveness is the positive expression of oneself and is marked by the use of statements that begin with "I." Aggressiveness is imposing one's thoughts or feelings on others and is generally marked by statements that begin with "You." Assertiveness training is especially effective when used in groups.

Sometimes clients need to be able to use a behavioral approach for themselves or in their relationships with others. This is especially valuable for parents who need to influence their children's behavior. Social workers are generally uncomfortable with using punishment to modify behavior, because doing so usually violates social work values and ethics. In addition, clients may have experienced a great deal of punishment in their lives. The use of extinction and positive reinforcement tends not to be a violation of social work values and ethics. Basically, **extinction** involves ignoring undesirable behavior to eliminate it. The parent should be warned that the initial response of the child will be to increase the behavior in order to receive the customary attention. However, persistently using this technique generally results in the desired goal.

Positive reinforcement is giving a reward for or recognizing the desired behavior. Positive reinforcement can be given whenever the desired behavior occurs, or there can be an agreement beforehand that certain behavior will be rewarded. The strongest reinforcements are those that are identified by the person receiving them. If a reinforcement is given too frequently, it is more likely to change the behavior more quickly, but the strength of the reinforcement tends not to last very long. Conversely, if the reinforcement is infrequent or seen as unattainable, it will have little impact on changing behavior. Sometimes a smaller reward or a symbol can be used on a more frequent basis and a larger reward given less often. An example is a star chart, on which the child puts a star for each day of the week he has exhibited a positive behavior. When he earns enough stars, he is rewarded with a toy. In this way, the stars serve as positive reinforcement on a day-to-day basis, and the toy serves as a longer-term reward.

Positive feedback is a form of positive reinforcement that is extremely important in developing and maintaining positive relationships. Many clients may not have received much positive support in their lives. Thus, they may not be able to give or receive much positive support. Whenever the worker sees dissatisfaction with a relationship, he should look for the absence of positive feedback. The worker can suggest ways to give positive feedback and ways to receive it. Generally, giving positive feedback results in getting positive feedback in return, although this may take some time if the other person has become accustomed to negative feedback or no feedback at all. Feedback is an important part of parenting. Parents need to give consistent messages about the behavior they expect from their children and then follow up with positive or negative feedback. Positive feedback tends to be the strongest form of reinforcement a parent can give a child. Positive feedback is also an important aspect of change-oriented groups. The group worker facilitates exchanges of positive feedback among members of the group to reinforce changes in behavior.

Actions that assist clients to engage in positive thinking and positive behavior are important to empowering and enabling them. The ability to be assertive may be needed for clients to advocate or speak up for themselves. Positive reinforcement and feedback are essential to good parenting and to developing and maintaining successful relationships. The worker incorporates these tools into his work in empowering and enabling clients to carry out their plans.

## Actions in Response to Crisis

Frequently, the client is in a crisis when the service is initiated. During the course of participating in a group, members may experience a crisis either within the group itself or in their lives outside of the group. Unmet need can create a crisis situation. Situations in which clients may experience a crisis include financial woes, health problems, relationship difficulties, trouble with the law, and the like. During a crisis, the client's normal coping mechanisms are overwhelmed. The worker helps the client to restore coping abilities by developing and working on a plan that will meet needs and resolve the crisis.

Clients use many coping mechanisms as well as the resources of the natural helping systems and community institutions before coming to a social worker. They often are under considerable stress and may be in a state of crisis. If the client is in a state of crisis, it is important that the social worker be able to recognize this situation and respond appropriately. Crisis intervention is a model of social work practice that provides a knowledge base and guidelines for crisis response. All generalist social workers should develop knowledge of and skill in working with people in crisis. The major goal of action in response to crisis (*crisis intervention*) is resolution of the crisis and restored social functioning. If, after this goal is reached, the worker and the client then decide there is some other goal they want to work on together, another kind of action is taken.

A **crisis** exists when a stressful situation and/or a precipitating event causes an individual to develop a state of disequilibrium, or to lose her steady state. Coping mechanisms that have worked in past situations no longer work, despite a considerable struggle to cope. A person who is continually in a state of disorganization is not in crisis; working with such a situation requires a different kind of action.

Crisis is usually a part of the life experience of all people. Workers seeing clients in crisis should assume that these people were functioning adequately before the crisis event and should view the helping role as restorative rather than remedial. It is important not to base an assessment of clients' normal ability to function on the behaviors and coping mechanisms displayed during the crisis.

A crisis situation can develop because of situational and developmental factors. Situational factors include illness of the individual or close family members, death of a close family member, separation or divorce, change of living situation or lifestyle, and loss of a job. These situational factors call either for assuming new roles and responsibilities, or for changing the established way of functioning with others. Sometimes these factors cause considerable stress only temporarily; after a period of instability and trying new coping methods, the result is a new and comfortable way of functioning. At other times, an additional stressful situation precipitates the crisis situation. Developmental stress arises from the unsettled or stressful feelings that may occur as clients move from one developmental stage to another. This movement requires new ways of functioning.

When working with clients or group members in crisis, the worker needs to be aware of the time element of crisis. The true crisis situation generally lasts from four to eight weeks. After that time people find new ways of coping. Without appropriate help during the crisis stage, the result may be a reduced capacity for effective social functioning. Thus, help for people in crisis must be immediate and sometimes fairly intensive.

The worker has two crucial tasks: (1) to develop an understanding about the person in crisis and what precipitated the crisis and (2) to develop the helping relationship. In developing an understanding, the worker searches for the precipitating event—the event that pushed the person into crisis—as well as the nature of the underlying stressful situation. The worker also determines what the person has tried to do to resolve the stress (the coping mechanisms used) and encourages her to share how she feels about the situation.

The worker forms a helping relationship by actively responding to the client's concern and need. Together they explore the situation and determine the reality of the client's perceptions. The worker supports the client's strengths by acknowledging the coping attempts and makes specific suggestions for other means of coping. The worker shares with the client his understanding of the situation. The worker communicates realistic hope that the crisis can be resolved and that he will help her through this difficult time. The client is encouraged to express feelings about the situation. The worker is sensitive to the client's anxiety and to the possibility of depression. If excessive anxiety or depression develops, the worker helps the client seek the services of a competent mental health professional. The worker also links the client to other needed resources.

Through the work together in the four- to eight-week period of crisis, the client usually discovers new coping mechanisms, and the crisis is resolved. In the latter part of this period, the worker can often enhance the client's problem-solving and coping skills and thus prevent future crises. Working with clients in an intensive, fairly directive manner during the crisis helps prevent future social-functioning difficulties and restores the client to a state in which she can manage in an effective manner.

Sometimes it is possible to work with persons in crisis in small groups. When the worker has several clients in crisis situations, it can be helpful for these people to share perceptions and experiences as a part of the crisis response. Some crisis groups are open-ended, with people in the later stages of crisis gaining help by helping those in the early stages of crisis.[10]

## Actions That Are Supportive

**Support** has been a universal part of helping. Supportive means are a part of every generalist social worker's repertoire. Florence Hollis identified sustainment as one of the procedures of social work practice.[11] Her usage of the term *sustainment* seems very close to the notion of support and is primarily expressed by nonverbal means. Hollis identified some of the components or techniques of sustainment as expression of the client's abilities and competencies, expression of interest, desire to help, understanding of a client's situation and feelings about that situation, and use of encouragement and reassurance. Reassurance should be realistic. Emphasis should be on the feeling component and support for the acceptability of having feelings about the situation of concern.

Judith Nelson defined supportive procedures as "those intended to help clients feel better, stronger, or more comfortable in some immediate way."[12] She has identified four kinds of support: (1) *protection,* which includes giving directions and advice, setting limits, and giving structure to complex or overwhelming situations; (2) *acceptance,* which includes making clients aware that the worker is with them in their struggles, confirming the worth of the person, and communicating understanding of clients' feelings and situations; (3) *validation,* which includes showing clients ways they are effective and competent persons, giving feedback, providing hope, communicating praise and approval, and encouraging clients in their coping efforts and role performance; and (4) *education,* which includes teaching clients how to cope and function effectively, providing needed information, socializing clients to new roles, and helping clients develop self-knowledge. One of the ways of teaching is modeling effective methods of coping.

Not only is Nelson's classification useful for identifying what support will best meet a client's needs, it also is important in identifying which aspects of a client's functioning the worker desires to support. Two other useful ways to identify the specific area of social functioning that needs support might be in terms of coping tasks or life roles. Using the coping-task approach, the worker identifies the task or tasks a client confronts when coping with a life situation (e.g., acceptance of the limitations of chronic illness). Using the life-role approach, the worker identifies the client's limitations, difficulties, and strengths in carrying out a life role. For example, if the client has difficulty following through with disciplinary procedures as a parent, the worker might first note areas in which the client does follow through, such as meal preparation. The worker then helps the client determine what skills she uses to complete that task and teaches her how to use the same motivations and skills when disciplining her child. This approach builds on the client's strengths rather than weaknesses and reinforces the idea that the client has problem-solving skills useful in various situations.

When using support as an interventive strategy, the worker identifies the client's need (as in all social work practice). This assessment emphasizes the client's perception of the situation and the client's realistic experiences in attempting to fulfill the need. Feelings of threat or deprivation are particularly important to note. The assessment should also consider the client's capacity for hope, the client's strengths, and the support the environment can provide.

The worker then decides what behaviors and attitudes can be supported to enable the client to meet the need. A decision is made about the specific kind of support to provide. Sometimes it is useful to provide the client with concrete resources or tangible services as a means of demonstrating the worker's care and concern. Using a supportive approach, the worker tries to develop a climate for helping that is accepting, understanding, comfortable, and validating and in which the client feels free to discuss concerns and feelings openly. The worker expresses interest and concern, encourages and praises the client for appropriate efforts, expresses realistic confidence in the client's ability to cope and to carry out life tasks, guides the client, and provides needed structure for the client's work.

Problems can arise from the inappropriate use of support. For one thing, there is always a danger that the client will become overly dependent on the worker. Thus, the worker must guard against unrealistic expectations on the part of the client and avoid helping when clients can do things themselves or when the environment can provide the support. Workers need to be aware of their tendencies to be overly protective or to make up for the wrongs that clients have suffered. The worker also needs to be aware that an evaluative tone can create resistance in the client and thus be counterproductive.

Although worker support is an important component of the social work endeavor, the worker also should focus on helping the client build an adequate support system within the client's natural environment. Support from others is one of the most powerful tools in coping and change efforts. Support from relatives, friends, family, clergy, place of worship, and so on is essential to healthy functioning. If these systems have not been adequate or have broken down, the worker should assist the client in rebuilding or strengthening these relationships as a means of resolving the current situation as well as meeting future needs. Building a support system is especially important for diverse clients at risk of prejudice, discrimination, and oppression.

In the past, many social workers have become accustomed to spending extra time in a supportive role with clients. However, managed care and limitations on services have reduced the time available for such extra support services. Social workers need to be certain from the beginning that adequate support systems are in place for the client, especially in a situation in which time limits are placed on the service. If support is needed from more formal support systems, then developing a relationship with those systems must be a priority.

Small groups have been found to be effective for providing support. These support groups are of particular value for use with caregivers,[13] those who have family members suffering from chronic or life-threatening conditions,[14] and those who have had a common debilitating experience.[15] The worker should be aware of support groups and self-help groups that are available in the client's area. If a group is needed, the worker may initiate setting up a group through her own agency if appropriate or may approach another agency whose services might potentially include such a group. Generalist practice with support groups is examined in greater depth in Part Two. In the era of managed care and limited services, agencies need to sponsor these groups as a means of providing support beyond the time limits of service. If agencies collaborate and share this task, then the burden of committing staff and resources will not be overwhelming. For instance, a health care agency might agree to sponsor a group for cancer patients and their families; the local senior agency may sponsor a support group for caregivers; and the local substance abuse program may sponsor AA, Alateen, and Al-Anon groups.

Properly used, support can produce growth, not just maintain the status quo. It provides positive reinforcement and can give clients strength to live and to grow in difficult situations. Support should be a part of the generalist social worker's interventive repertoire.

## Use of Activity as an Interventive Strategy

**Activity** is doing something or performing tasks as opposed to talking about what to do or about feelings and ideas. Activity can take the form of helping clients or group members carry out normal life tasks. It can also take the form of activity constructed by the worker to enhance the helping process, such as role-playing a difficult situation, or in a group session, using an activity that requires cooperation. The use of activities in groups is covered in later chapters; however, the basic concepts regarding the development of activities are presented here.

"Homework assignments" help to carry over the work that is done in individual or group sessions to everyday life. Once clients begin to use the work from sessions, they can build on their success. The worker asks clients to describe in detail what happened and how they felt about it. If they feel good about the change, the worker discusses what it would take to make this happen more frequently.

Activity is a means for influencing change in the ways people function. Through action, clients or group members learn many of the skills needed for adequate social functioning. Socialization of people to the ways of their society and culture (that is, life experience) relies heavily on the use of action. Activity is a means for developing social-functioning skills and also for enhancing self-awareness. Activity leads to accomplishment, which in turn enhances self-esteem and a positive sense of self. Activity also has usefulness in developing an assessment. As the worker observes the client in action either in individual or group sessions, the client's interactional and communication patterns become evident. The worker can also assess the client's competence in functioning and the quality of the functioning by observing the client in action.

Traditionally, activity has been used in certain segments of social work, notably in the use of games and crafts in social group work. The use of play therapy with children has been another use of activity. Milieu therapy (use of the setting) in institutions also uses activity (as discussed later in this chapter). Some family therapists help families plan family activities. Literature on the ways people learn emphasizes experiential learning involving activity. Activity has been a major technique in working with children and is considered valuable in working with "action-oriented" persons.

Activity is also useful in a variety of other helping situations and can be used as a technique for meeting many needs of clients. It enhances physical development and neuro-muscular control and stimulates intellectual growth. Activity can be an acceptable release for feelings and emotions, teach patterns of behavior and provide self-discipline, enable acceptance by peers, and increase status. It can provide opportunity for making and carrying out decisions, for forming relationships, and for resolving conflict. Activity can also encourage the development of new interests, skills, and competencies. It can enhance social functioning by enabling movement along the normal growth processes and can be useful with persons who may be at risk of not developing. This risk is often related to lack of opportunity, and activity can provide needed developmental opportunities. In this sense, it can be a preventive approach.

Activity can be broadly defined as anything that involves action by the client or group. This includes structured activities that are a part of individual or group meetings. It includes activities that the worker may participate in as a leader or facilitator. It also includes actions that the client needs to take to accomplish various tasks associated with the plan. Some practitioners refer to these latter activities as "homework" in that the client or group member agrees to carry out certain tasks between sessions. There may be practice or role-playing that takes place within the session to prepare the client or group member for the work to be done outside the session. For example, in improving communication, the worker might ask the group to try to use "I" statements when they are speaking with one another. The worker has them use "I" statements throughout the session and allows group members to catch each other when they forget to use "I" statements. However, they have to use an "I" statement when doing so. When there has been enough practice and a sufficient level of proficiency achieved, the client is asked to try this at home. The client then reports back at the next meeting. It is essential to build activity into the work with clients so that they can "own" the work to be done. The more active clients are in accomplishing the goals in their plan, the more competent they will feel. Activity is especially helpful to clients who are depressed. Movement toward a goal brings hope and a sense of accomplishment.

Care should be taken in how activity is incorporated into work with clients from populations that have been oppressed or experienced discrimination or excessive control from others. If activities are imposed on these clients, it adds to their feeling of being controlled. The type of activity should enhance opportunities for choice, decision making, and empowerment. The way in which the activity is presented and carried out should also include these elements. Of course, clients or group members should be allowed to decline to participate at any time with any activity without fear of negative consequences.

Social workers must plan activity carefully. This calls for an expanded knowledge of the nature of action and skill in its use. Robert Vinter has identified three aspects of activity: (1) the physical space and social objects involved in the activity; (2) the behaviors essential to carry out the activity; and (3) the expected respondent behavior because of the activity. Before deciding to use any activity, a worker should assess these three aspects as they relate to the specific activity. Some dimensions discussed by Vinter that influence the action include: (1) its prescriptiveness about what the actors are expected to do; (2) the kinds of rules and other controls that govern the activity; (3) the provision the activity makes for physical activity; (4) the competence required for persons to engage in the activity; (5) the nature of participation and interaction required; and (6) the nature of rewards that are inherent in the activity.[16]

It is also important to assess clients' capacity and use of activity. Areas particularly important to consider include:

1. *The client's particular need and interests*—Need should be identified before deciding to use activity. Interest can be identified by considering the client's stated desires, skills, and interests.
2. *The capacity of the particular client to perform the tasks required in the activity*—An understanding of age-group characteristics is important, as is understanding of the usual activities of a client's cultural or other diversity subgroup.
3. *The client's motivation and readiness to use the particular activity*—Some clients cannot use certain activities because of cultural taboos. Others, who are work oriented, may not be able to use activity that appears to be play. Clients need to have an opportunity to make choices among possible alternatives. Activity that is relevant to the client's lifestyle is usually the activity most useful to him or her.
4. *The ability of the client's support systems and community to accept and support the activity being used*—Consideration should also be given to these factors.

A third kind of analysis that workers using activity should carry out is related to its use in a specific situation and includes:

1. The materials, equipment, and resources needed to carry out the activity
2. The time and capacity required of the worker to help the client or group carry out the activity

3. The climate and environment in which the activity will be carried out (the environment's ability to allow the activity and its support for carrying out the activity)
4. Directions for carrying out the activity
5. Precautions and safety measures that need to be taken in carrying out the activity
6. Adaptations of the activity that may be needed

Based on the four kinds of assessments discussed above, a decision is made to use a particular activity. In preparing to implement the activity, the following tasks may need to be carried out:

1. *An activity may need to be tested or carried out to determine if all aspects are understood*—It is usually best not to use an activity that the worker has not pretested. Adaptations should be made as necessary.
2. *All supplies and equipment must be obtained*—Rooms or other areas must be obtained. Responsibility is allocated for specific tasks to the worker, other staff, or family members.

As the activity takes place, the worker should be supportive and positive, show rather than tell, and set appropriate limits. It is also important to discuss the process and outcome of the activity with the client or group after its conclusion.

In using activity as an interventive strategy, the criteria for "good activity" should be kept in mind:

1. Good activity grows out of the needs and interests of the client.
2. Good activity takes into consideration age, cultural background, and other diversity factors.
3. Good activity provides experiences that enable or enhance the physical and psychosocial development of clients.
4. Good activity is flexible and offers a maximum opportunity for participation.

Because the possibilities for the use of activity are vast and varied, it is beyond the scope of this book to provide information about the use of specific activity. Social workers can make use of literature from the field of recreation; structured group or family experiences; and various forms of individual, family, or group work to gain knowledge about the use of specific activity.[17]

In using activity, the worker employs a creative approach and adapts the activity to the particular client's need. The creative use of activity can be a powerful influence for helping clients. Its use calls for skill and understanding on the part of social workers.

## Actions as Mediation with Group Members and the Environment

Sometimes, as the worker and client explore the client's needs, concerns, and situation, it becomes apparent that the way in which the client or group member and a system in the environment interact is not functional. Often the situation is of a conflictual nature. For example, a mother seems unable to communicate with a probation officer so that they can work together in setting limits for her son. The mother is afraid of the authority represented by the probation officer and does not respond to his suggestions. The probation officer is frustrated and believes the mother is indifferent to her son's need for limits. The worker knows this is not the case. In such a situation a **mediation strategy** can be useful.

William Schwartz described this strategy as "to mediate the process through which the individual and his society reach out for each other through a mutual need for self-fulfillment"[18] and as "helping people negotiate difficult environments."[19] The worker's concern—and the focus of the mediation action—is the social functioning of both the client and the system. The transaction between the two is the concern, the target for change.

Mediation is basic to an ecosystems approach to social work practice. This approach views need as arising out of incongruity between the client and systems in her environment. Restoring or developing a balance between the needs of the client and the needs of systems in her environment is necessary for the situation to be resolved. A mediating role allows the worker to work with the client and individuals or groups in her environment without taking sides. Mediation bridges the gap between direct practice actions, or work done directly with clients, and indirect practice actions, or work on behalf of clients with systems in the environment.

William Schwartz, Serapio Zalba, and Lawrence Shulman have written extensively about this type of action and strategy.[20] Shulman has identified three blocks in the interactions of clients with environmental systems:

1. *The complexity of systems*—The development of institutions and the bureaucratizing of their functioning have made it less possible for people to understand how to approach these systems or to use the resources they provide. These complex systems seem strange, impersonal, and often overwhelming to many clients.
2. *Self-interest*—The self-interest of systems often is in conflict with the interests of others or of the larger system of which they are a part. When such self-interest is predominant, it is necessary to make that system aware of the interdependence, and thus of the mutual interest, necessary for the functioning of the larger system.
3. *Communication problems*—Often, the inability of systems to work together is a result of a lack of communication or of inaccurate communication and thus of misconceptions about the other.[21]

In overcoming these blocks, the worker and client both have tasks. The purpose of mediation is not for the worker to be an advocate and challenge one or the other system but to help the client and the larger system reach out to each other so that together they can achieve a common goal. The worker helps or enables each of the two systems to accomplish the tasks necessary but does not do the work leading to the goal. That work belongs to the client and the environmental system.

The worker has three major tasks to accomplish: (1) to help the client reach out to the environmental system, (2) to help the environmental system respond to the client, and (3) to encourage both the client and the environmental system to do the work needed to reach the common goal.

In helping the client to reach out to the environmental system, the worker first points out to the client the interests and goals she has in common with the environmental system. The worker also identifies the blocks that seem to be preventing the client from reaching these goals. The worker challenges these blocks by pointing out ways they can be overcome and the advantages to the client of overcoming them. The worker tries to give the client a vision of what can happen if the client and the environmental system find a means of working together. In doing this, the worker reveals his own commitment and hopes for a society in which people and institutions work together for the common good. Through this, the worker gives hope to the client. The worker helps the client define what needs to be done in the reaching out, and together they decide how the client is to do it. The worker is careful to define the limits of what may be expected so that the client does not develop unrealistic expectations.

When helping the environmental system to respond to the client's reaching out, the worker points out their common interest and concerns and the obstacles that seem to prevent cooperative functioning. The worker tries to help the environmental system mobilize its concern and its resources for helping. Where appropriate, the worker can provide the environmental system with information that will enhance its understanding of the situation. In a sense, both the client and the environmental system are clients. In some situations (e.g., divorce) a social worker may be engaged as a mediator on initial contact. Both parties immediately are seen as clients under these circumstances.

In using this strategy, the worker negotiates a contract or agreement with the client and, when possible, with the environmental system as to the work (tasks) each will do in attempting to overcome problems. The worker helps both carry out their tasks by helping them adhere to the contract, clarifying what is expected in the situation, and requiring that they do their tasks.

When working in a mediation mode, the units of attention are both the client and the environmental systems involved. Each is helped to acknowledge the common interests and to become aware of the feelings, needs, and demands of all. This requires that the worker be aware of the rules and roles within the situation. The worker provides focus and structure for the work to be done. Based on his knowledge and understanding, the worker also supplies ideas and suggestions as to how the systems might better work together. Clarification and problem solving are important tools of the endeavor.

Although the mediation strategy was developed to use with small groups, it has proven equally effective in working with individuals and families and is particularly useful with institutionalized individuals.[22] It is often useful in situations in which empowerment is a goal.

## Actions Involving the Use of Influence

The social worker does not have complete control and cannot guarantee a specific outcome when working from an interventive-transactional stance. Clients and others involved in the situation maintain the ability to decide what their behavior will be in the situation. This ability makes control by the social worker impossible except in those areas in which she has been given the authority to control certain aspects of the client's behavior, such as in some institutional situations, some work with children, protective service work, and probation and parole work.

**Influence** has been defined as "the general acts of producing an effect on another person, group, or organization through exercise of a personal or organizational capacity."[23] Influence is powerful. It can produce change, persuade or convince, overcome obstacles, motivate, and bring about attitudinal changes. The social worker's input is to create a climate favorable for the needed work, heighten the motivation of those needing to do the work, "provide a vision"[24] for the work to be done together, and reduce the resistance involved.

Influence is an important aspect of working with clients and on behalf of clients. It is also an important aspect of working with groups. As the social worker works with indivdiuals or groups, the influence for change is heavily based on the worker–client or worker–group interaction, particularly on the relationship between worker and the client or the group members. In indirect practice, the worker works on behalf of the client or group to meet their needs. In doing so, the worker will be working with other inidviduals and systems. For the work to be successful on a long-term basis, the results also must meet the needs of these other individuals, small systems (the family or group or their members), or collectives (organizations, community, or community segments). Relationship remains an important aspect of influence, although other factors (such as the knowledge and expertise of the worker and the material resources and services the worker might have available) are also important. The worker's status and reputation are sources of influence. All these influences are used when the work together is collaborative and cooperative in nature. Sometimes persuasive techniques must be used for the other system or systems involved to become convinced that a collaborative or cooperative approach is of value to all concerned. Sometimes cooperation and collaboration are not possible, and confrontation, bargaining, and even coercion are necessary to reach the desired goals.

Sometimes the social worker initiates and participates in the action on behalf of the client. Sometimes mediation between systems is called for. At other times the social worker stimulates others to carry out the action. Regardless of who takes the action, some means of legitimizing any action taken must be sought. The social worker does not act in isolation but as a representative of an agency. Sometimes the social worker can act with or through an organization to which she belongs. Without the support of legitimization, the worker lacks the influence needed to support the change effort. Without legitimization, ethical issues can come into play. Influence is used as an indirect practice action with individuals and environmental systems on behalf of the client, as is environmental change and coordination of services. Generally, indirect practice actions are intended to be used to bring about changes in the actions of systems. Changes in feeling and thinking may be used as tactics in accomplishing this, but changing actions is the basic strategy. Generally, the worker uses influence on behalf of the client and refrains from using it with the client except in a crisis situation or as a last resort, when they are truly stuck.

Quite often, when people or staff in other agencies know that there is a worker involved with a client, this changes the way they act. People may give more credibility to the client's need because the worker has done so. They may be willing to defer to the worker because of her position or authority. Workers in other agencies may do this as a matter of policy or as a professional courtesy. Workers are more conscious of their work when a fellow professional is also involved. The majority of workers are conscientious and hardworking, regardless of the circumstances. However, the worker will naturally want to make a good impression on fellow professionals, and this fact alone can influence change on behalf of the client. For example, if the worker calls for services on behalf of the client whose situation requires immediate action, it increases the likelihood that the client will receive services more quickly. Similarly, accompanying a client or group member to an agency sends a strong message about the importance of the service.

The use of influence has potential ethical problems. The worker should use influence with the client or group only when absolutely necessary. This also applies to influencing other systems. The worker should not routinely use her influence as a shortcut or to gain favor for her client over other clients. This undermines client empowerment and self-determination. It can lead the other agency to see the worker in a negative light over time, limiting her ability to obtain services when she has a client who really needs immediate attention. Other agencies will expect reciprocity when they have clients who need immediate or special attention. A worker who abuses her influence may build up expectations with other agencies that she or her agency cannot meet.

An important base for influence is the skill and knowledge of the social worker in developing and using relationships with a variety of persons in a variety of situations. Influence can be exerted by those who know about and can use a planned change process. Influence derives from understandings about human development, human diversity, the variety of social problems, and the availability of services and resources.

Social workers use not only their own base of influence but that of other people with whom they are working. When working for change in situations, in organizations, and in communities, people with influence are very useful. This is covered in greater detail in Part Three. Influential people may be elected or appointed to positions of authority, are respected and looked up to, have control over resources and information, and are involved in important decision making. They often are people who control from behind the scenes. Values are another important factor to consider in relationship to influence. People are more apt to be influenced for change when the change is within their value system and provides something that is important to them.

Workers need to be aware of the nature of the power and influence they wield in relationships with clients or as the leader or facilitator of a group. Influence can be an inherent outgrowth of the power differential in the worker–client or worker–group relationship. Every effort needs to be made to guard against the potential for abuse of power with clients. In addition to professional expertise, which workers possess by virtue of their skill, values, and knowledge base, certain personal characteristics may also contribute to a worker's influence with a client.

Clients and group members do have some choice of whether they will be influenced or not. To be influenced, people must have at least some motivation for change. Some factors that affect willingness to be influenced include discomfort with the situation and a belief that it can be changed, a desire to gain position or resources, and a desire to change the situation for someone else.

Resistance is the opposite of motivation and is sometimes a sign that other influences on a person are stronger than the need for change. Barriers to change—to accepting influence—can be cultural in nature. Ideologies, traditions, and values are all part of cultural influences on situations. Barriers also may be social in nature. The influence of a person's family or peer group, the norms of the situation, or the reputation of the change agent can be social barriers to change. Or the barrier may be organizational in nature: a competitive climate or an organizational climate that considers procedure rather than people. Communication patterns can be a barrier to change. Personal barriers such as fear, selective perception, or lack of energy and skill also affect an individual's capacity to accept influence and to change. All of these barriers may be part of the transactive nature of relationships in a helping situation.

The influence process is carried out in a relationship with one or more of the systems involved in the transaction. This relationship is transactional in nature, in that it is affected by other relationships. The relationship between the social worker and the system being influenced is a major source of a social worker's influence. A major task in the social work endeavor is to foster the kind of relationships that allow the worker to bring other sources of influence to bear on the situation. As the worker applies these various sources of influence to the situation, change takes place in the relationships among the subsystems involved. The worker's knowledge and skillfulness as well as social work values guide the decisions about what sources of influence to use and how to use them.

There are also ethical considerations regarding the use of influence. Of particular importance is concern about the difference between influence and manipulation, control, or abuse of power. Clients and others typically do not understand the limits of the social worker's span of control and ascribe more authority to the worker than is legally allowed. Clients may believe that the worker can withhold an income maintenance check if they do not do what they think the worker wants them to do. Such situations can become complex when the client acts according to what she believes the worker wants rather than what the worker has said. Workers can use their ascribed authority to control clients. However, this negates the value of self-determination and also raises concerns about who has the right to do what and on what grounds.[25] In the contemporary situation, social work values, such as the right to self-determination and confidentiality, are often limited by agency mandates, statutory reporting laws, or other constraints of practice.

All three of the following questions can be used to determine if influence is being used within social work values:

1. Whose needs are being met by the use of the influence? If it is the client's needs, it is within the social work value system. If it is the worker's needs, it is not.
2. Have the goals been established by the worker and client or group together as part of a collaborative process?
3. Has freedom of choice for all concerned been considered and maintained to the maximum extent possible?

Influence is a major consideration for the social worker to take into account in planning and implementing interventions in transactions among people and their systems. Because a power differential often exists between social workers and their clients, attention must be given to prevent misuse of influence. Influence, or use of self, when used within the social work value system serves as an enabling function.

## Actions to Change the Environment

**Environmental manipulation** is the strategy that brings about alteration in the environment of a client as a means of enhancing the client's social functioning. Specifically, three factors in the environment are considered as appropriate targets for change: space, time, and relationships.

In using an ecosystems strengths approach, action takes place to change the transactions between the client and formal and informal systems in the immediate environment. In identifying the immediate environment, both proximity and relationships are important. For an individual, the family is often a primary system in the immediate environment. School or places of employment are important systems for individuals and families, as are the neighborhood, extended family, friends, and other significant individuals or systems. The first choice in working with clients is for the client himself to be able to mobilize these systems to assist him in meeting his needs. However, often relationships between clients and significant individuals and systems in their environment need to be developed, enhanced, or restored. This may be the reason needs are not being met and the client requires assistance from the social worker. In working on behalf of the client, the worker may need to have contact with these significant individuals or systems and take actions that will develop, enhance, or restore important relationships.

As we pointed out earlier, mediation is an important action with systems in the environment. Mediation can be used with both formal and informal systems. Other important skills are improving communication, bargaining, negotiation, problem solving, and conflict resolution. Either the worker may work jointly with the client and systems in the environment, or she may work separately with each. When working separately, the goal is usually to move toward some kind of joint effort to resolve the situation.

The social worker uses her communication skills to facilitate good communication. These skills are covered in Chapter 5. She models good communication and asks people to change their communication patterns to reflect good communication.

Decision-making and problem-solving skills involve the ability to work together to develop a plan that will resolve the situation. Since the social worker is familiar with various models of problem solving, she can assist clients and members of their ecosystem in doing this. In addition, the worker can assist them to develop an ongoing process of reaching decisions or solving problems.

Bargaining, negotiation, compromise, and conflict resolution are used when unresolved differences persist. These approaches involve identifying the needs and concerns of the parties involved and finding ways to meet those needs. As needs are identified, the worker elicits responses to need from others. She may ask those involved in the situation to give and take in order to have their needs met. She may suggest ways of reciprocally meeting needs between parties. Throughout the process, the worker attempts to reach a mutually beneficial arrangement that can be sustained over time. Some questions that might be used are: (1) What would you like to see happen in this situation? What would meet your needs? What would it take to satisfy you? (2) What would you be willing to do to resolve this? (3) Would you be willing to . . . ? (4) If . . . , then would you be willing to . . . ? (5) What do you want to do with this? These questions are designed to move people toward having their needs met by meeting the needs of others in their ecosystem. When needs are balanced, then the ecosystem is balanced.

When planning for change in the environment, a worker can use the variables of relationship, space, and time as a framework. Relationships should be influenced to enhance the competence of clients or group members. This can be illustrated by considering a person with physical disabilities. If those in this person's environment provide care so that the person makes few decisions and little use of the physical capacity she possesses, she will feel less competent. If caregivers encourage appropriate self-reliance, however, her competence will be enhanced.[26]

In an ecosystems strengths approach, client needs may involve incongruity in the transactions between the client and the environment. Changing the transaction to meet the need returns balance to the individual and his ecosystem.

Changes can be made in the spatial aspects of a client's environment. Space should be appropriate for the people who occupy it. According to Irene Gutheil, some of the factors important when considering physical space are the features of a space and whether they are fixed or can be changed through modifying the design of the building and placement of furniture. Also important are issues of territory, personal space, crowding, and privacy.[27] These concerns are particularly important in residential situations but should also be considered in evaluating offices and other areas in which services are provided.

For people with physical disabilities, physical barriers can be a block to relative self-sufficiency. A sense of competence is enhanced when barriers are removed. The physical environment should provide for the privacy a person needs. The effects of color and light in influencing feelings and behavior should be considered.

The activity that takes place in the space and the manner in which people interact during the activity are important considerations. There must be provision for proper spacing around people; being too close or too far apart can lead to discomfort and cause people to withdraw.

Spatial arrangement that allows for eye contact is important in working with groups. A circle arrangement encourages people to talk to one another, as each can see everyone else. Room arrangements in which all individuals face a speaker discourage group interaction and encourage attention on the speaker only. Social workers can use their understandings of groups and their needs and of spatial arrangements to determine how space can be changed to enable people to function more adequately.[28]

When a social worker working with a group arranges chairs at the meeting space to bring about interpersonal interaction or certain seating configurations among group members, he has manipulated space and created environmental change. The way the physical environment of a social agency is arranged can make people feel comfortable or uncomfortable and can cause undesirable behavior or enable constructive activity. Physical arrangement can sometimes make the difference in whether group members use the services offered or fail to get needs met.[29]

Changes in space can range from accommodating the client for an office visit to assisting in major moves, such as changing the place of residence for a client or a family or for one of its members. When the client decides to make a move from his current residence, the worker may need to assist in locating other living options, especially in instances of limited finances or that involve government funding. The client may need access to resources to assist with security deposits and other costs. Clients may experience discrimination and need to have their rights protected.

Placement of a child in a residential treatment facility is a form of environmental change. The facility uses the milieu (the arrangement of the space, program, and staff relationships) to help the child. Milieu therapy involves attitudes and relationships of the persons who occupy the space as a therapeutic tool. Hospitals, nursing homes, and other institutions can make use of milieu therapy.[30]

The social worker may become involved in accessing day programs or in arranging for residential, institutional, or alternative placement for one of the members of the family.

This is common in child welfare, mental health, disability services, health care, aging services, delinquency services, corrections, and similar settings. Social work services can include making referrals and securing placement, providing services to the family while the member is in care, or providing aftercare services. Social workers sometimes also provide services within a program.

Any environmental change should be preceded by a thorough study and assessment of the situation, with particular emphasis on relationship, space, and time factors that may be impeding the person's social functioning. Attention should be given to how culture and lifestyle prescribe the use of the physical environment and time so that the plan does not conflict with the client's culture and lifestyle.

Time factors can be changed in service of clients and groups by changing the schedule for activity. There is a time for physical or mental activity and a time for quiet in people's lives. By considering the client's needs at various times, the social worker uses the time allotted in ways that are congruent with the client's needs. For example, after children have been in school all day, they are usually ready for physical activity rather than for sitting quietly. When working with a mother, the worker should realize that times when family demand is high are not times the mother can reflect on her own needs. The timing of group sessions should take into consideration the time rhythms of the client's or group members' lives. Institutions often develop schedules to meet staff desires rather than considering the daily rhythms of those being served. Social workers can be alert to these time elements and work for changes in schedules so that service to clients can be facilitated.[31]

Changes in time with group work generally mean flexibility in scheduling, which is much more difficult with groups than it is with an individual. Environmental demands, such as work or school, affect the time that members have available to meet and to carry out various tasks. Not only must the group sessions be coordinated, but scheduling services and activities can be complicated. Working with groups generally requires more involved scheduling and arrangements.

When using the strategy of environmental manipulation, the worker assesses the situation and plans to bring about change in relationships, space, and the use of time. In planning for change, it is essential that the worker use her understandings about relationships, space, and time. The social worker also should be creative in structuring environments to support the client's efforts in social functioning.

## Actions to Coordinate Services

**Coordination** is the working together of two or more service providers. Coordination of activity can be focused on a client, such as an individual or family (microlevel coordination), or it can be focused on persons in a particular category, such as persons with AIDS or developmental disabilities (macro level coordination).

Coordination of services can be used on behalf of an indivdiual client, a family, or on behalf of a group or its members. When a client is in crisis or faces severe or multiple needs, she may require assistance in coordinating needed services. This is a common situation for social workers who work in the settings mentioned above. Case management is usually the model that is used (discussed below). Child welfare cases involve families who are having difficulty in meeting children's needs or are abusive. In the majority of cases, there are multiple needs experienced by the family and by individual members. The worker may assume initial responsibility for coordinating services, with the expectation that the family will eventually assume responsibility or will experience a reduction in the need for services. Given the tremendous rise in costs, various alternative models to residential and institutional care have evolved for the mentally ill, developmentally disabled, or mentally retarded. The juvenile and adult corrections systems have seen similar efforts. Services for aging individuals are becoming more community based and will inevitably require more alternative services as the costs of residential and institutional care mount. All of these services require the social worker to provide coordination or to participate in situations in which another worker is the primary coordinator of service.

When coordination of services is needed, the worker involves the client with the process as much as possible. Over time, some clients will be able to do this for themselves. Others will no longer need the array of services. Still others will require some assistance over an extended period of time. When working with an individual client, the worker attempts to involve the family in the process, if this is possible and the client is agreeable. The assumption is that the family will be an important and more consistent source of ongoing assistance in securing services. For some clients, this may not be so, but in most cases, the family remains an important resource. Sometimes all that is needed is for the worker to mobilize the family or give information to key members. Other times, the worker may supplement what the family provides, or she may find resources for the family that will ease some of the burden.

Collaboration and coordination are often used as if they were synonymous, but as used in this text, there is a difference between the two. **Collaboration** is the working together, or teamwork, of two or more helpers using a common plan of action. Coordination does not imply a common plan of action; in fact, there may be two or more plans of action. Collaboration and teamwork are two kinds of coordination. In this section, several other methods of coordination are presented.

For coordination to be effective, there must be a spirit of working together toward a desirable end. For example, this end could be a common goal, such as maintaining in the community a person with chronic mental illness. This would require coordination of different services provided by different agencies, such as socialization and vocational rehabilitation services as well as housing services, medical monitoring services, income maintenance services, and the like. Public social services as well as mental health and vocational rehabilitation units and perhaps other agencies would all need to be involved.

In another example, the end may be the common goal of providing a range of services to a particular community to enable it to meet the needs of its aging members. This might involve coordination of the services of the senior citizens' center, the public health nursing agency, public social services, and the variety of other services available in the community. The goal would be not only to help specific older clients but also to enable existing services to more appropriately respond to the needs of all older persons. The common end would be a network of needed services that would be usable by a broad range of older persons.

An important aspect of coordination is the mutual satisfaction of all concerned. The persons or agencies involved need to believe that it is advantageous to coordinate their services with others. This feeling of common benefit leads to open exchange and feelings of satisfaction, which are necessary for productive relationships. Coordination can involve a range of resources broader than those of formal social service agencies. It can involve professionals from a variety of disciplines: service providers of community institutions such as schools and churches; community self-help group leaders; and the informal resources of friends, family, and work colleagues.

Coordination can be carried out through several mechanisms. One is to locate those who serve a similar population in a common setting, often called a multiservice center. This can be done by locating either the agency or the individual service deliverers (e.g., family service worker, a community health nurse, an income maintenance worker) representing a variety of agencies in a common setting close to those needing service. It is assumed not only that this will make services more accessible to clients but also that close proximity will encourage sharing among the professionals.

Another means of linking services has been an information and referral service; this can serve as a coordinative mechanism, depending on its means of functioning and on the capacity of those who staff it. If the emphasis is on providing information about services, the coordinative function will probably not be carried out. If the emphasis is on referral and enabling clients to access needed services, then a coordinative service is enhanced by follow-up and evaluation of the service delivered. Evaluation can also lead to identification of unmet needs and of needed services that are not available and thus to program development. A coordination approach that merits special consideration is case management.

**Case management** has received considerable attention as a coordinative approach to service delivery. It has been found useful in the fields of child welfare, mental health (particularly with the chronically mentally ill), developmental disabilities, and gerontology. Its use is often indicated when a client needs a range of services from several social service or health providers. Provision for such services is supported by federal legislation.[32]

Although the process of case management has been identified in a varying manner from field to field, a common thread has emerged. According to Karen Orloff Kaplan, the process contains five components: (1) case identification; (2) assessment and planning; (3) coordination and referral; (4) implementation of services; and (5) monitoring, evaluation, and reassessment.[33]

In case management, assessment and planning involve consideration not only of client needs but also of the resources available within the informal network of relationships and in the immediate community. Assessment is carried out with maximum client input and involves identifying the needed resources and weaving them into a plan that is congruent with the client's culture, desires, and lifestyle. This weaving together can be described as developing a *complementary resource pattern*. The case manager provides an integration so resources are not duplicated or at cross-purposes, and the client can sense a holistic concern for need fulfillment.

The case manager reaches out to the various resources to obtain their cooperative input and to provide the information needed for coordinating services. The case manager may need to creatively develop a new resource or modify an existing one. Often the case manager or her agency provides a part of the needed service. Regular monitoring is another task of the case manager.

Several case management models have been developed, usually addressing service in a particular field of practice (e.g., child welfare, services to older adults). One developed by Jack Rothman seems to depict the process most thoroughly and clearly. This model begins with access to the agency through outreach or referral and proceeds through intake and assessment, which may have both short- and long-term psychological, social, and medical components to goal setting. From this point, a variety of options are possible: intervention planning, resource identification and indexing, and linking clients to formal agencies or informally to families and others. Counseling, therapy, advocacy, and interagency coordination, including policy considerations, may also be used but are outside the process loop and are used only when needed. Monitoring, reassessment, and outcome evaluation are also within the loop. Rothman noted that the process is meant to be used flexibly and is cyclical in nature.[34]

Two goals are often discussed in relation to case management: continuity of care and maximum level of functioning. *Continuity of care* is important because many of the clients who benefit from the use of this approach need services for an extended period of time, if not for the rest of their lives. This care may need to be provided in a range of different community and institutional settings. A holistic plan for services is considered desirable, and case managers can often provide the desired continuity. *Maximum level of functioning* is important because many clients with whom this approach is used operate at a less-than-independent level of functioning. Because of the multiple needs involved, they may not be functioning at the highest level of which they are capable. A case management approach provides an overview that can lead to planning, which encourages a maximum level of functioning.

Stephen T. Moore noted that case management should be an enabling and facilitating activity. A major thrust is to ensure that formal service complements family care and other informal helping rather than competing with or substituting for such care. This can add to the complexity of the service. The case manager may not only need to consider the current and potential strengths, limitations, and ways of functioning of the informal care system but may also need to develop a potential for help within these systems. She may need to provide support and other services to the informal system to enable it to perform as the needed resource. It is important to be aware of the stresses on the informal system as well as the needs of the helping system.[35]

Case management calls for the social worker to use both direct and indirect approaches. It is truly generalist social work practice in that it weaves together a variety of strategies so that the range of needs of clients with multiple challenges can be met. Coordination is a major concern of the case manager.

## Evaluation and Termination

Evaluation takes place throughout the change process. The worker evaluates the validity and reliability of the the information he has. He evaluates the thoroughness and accuracy of his assessment, the progress toward goals and objectives, and the effectiveness of his practice actions. Evaluation is also used to determine when the work is done and the needs are met. When this occurs, the worker moves toward termination. In actuality, termination can occur at any time and may be planned or unplanned. When termination occurs, the worker reviews the work that has been done and assists the client in carrying this over to her everyday life. A more thorough discussion of evaluation and termination takes place in later chapters.

C A S E   **3.1**

## Social Work in an Assisted Living Facility

Sue is the social worker at Sunnyside Assisted Living Facility. She leads several groups at the facility, including groups for residents and a support group for familiy members. Mrs. Jones is a resident who has been very active in several groups at the facility. Her daughter, Judy, asked to speak with Sue to discuss some concerns. Judy said that she was worried that she would not be able to keep her mother in the facility once her savings were depleted. She was also feeling very guilty about having her mother stay rather than bringing her home to live with her. She explained that she had three young children and that both she and her husband needed to work. In addition, their house was not very big and could not really accommodate a wheelchair if that is what her mother needed. Sue reassured her that it was okay to have her mother stay at Sunnyside. She said that a lot of the families felt the same way. Sue then discussed Medicaid eligibility and the need to spend down assets to become eligible. Judy said that she had heard about that when her mother first entered care, but had hoped the family could avoid having her mother go on welfare. However, now it looks like they will have no choice. Sue tried to reassure her and told her not to be embarrassed. She said that the majority of residents have to use the Medicaid option after two or three years at the facility. She referred Judy to the local Department of Human Services (DHS) to find out more information and to meet with a worker.

Judy called the next day, very upset. She said that she had gone to DHS and after a long wait was told she would have to come back the next day. She took off from work again and met with the worker the next day. The worker told her

about all of the information that she would need to gather to establish her mother's eligibility. Judy said that she already felt overwhelmed with work and her family obligations. She was concerned about taking too much time off, which could jeopardize her job and would also have a negative impact on family finances. However, she wanted to be sure that her mother could stay at Sunnyside. Sue asked if Judy wanted her to contact the worker on her behalf to see what could be done and Judy agreed. Sue also invited Judy to attend the family meetings at the facility. Sue met with Mrs. Jones to explain the situation and obtained releases of information.

Sue contacted the DHS office and spoke with the worker, who explained that with recent cuts in state spending along with early retirements, their office was very short of staff. They discussed various options and Sue offered to help in any way she could. The worker suggested that if Sue helped Mrs. Jones and her daughter with the forms and supporting documentation, then it could speed up the process. Sue agreed. She met with Mrs. Jones and Judy and helped fill out forms and gather documentation. Sue then went with Judy to meet with the worker at DHS. They found that there were a few more items that were needed. Judy said that she could get them in a few days. Later in the week, Sue contacted Judy to make sure that everything was settled. Judy indicated that they had done what they could for now and thanked Sue for her assistance. Judy had attended her first meeting for families and it was a positive experience. She told Sue she felt relieved and it was nice to talk with others who were going through the same thing.

CASE **3.2**

## Crisis Intervention

Mrs. Jones was rushed to the hospital after she complained of severe pain in her hip during a physical therapy session. Sue met her daughter, Judy, at the hospital and they met with the doctor. He said that Mrs. Jones had developed a blood clot and would need emergency surgery. Judy asked what her mother's prognosis was. The doctor said that as long as they could remove the clot her chances were good. However, if it moved or if they found clots in other places, then it might be less positive.

After the doctor left, Judy collapsed in a chair, buried her face, and started sobbing. Sue moved next to her to comfort her. Judy said that she was not sure if she could take much more. She is worried about her mother, but also about her job and her family. Her boss was giving her a hard time about taking off so much time from work. She was worried about losing her job. She also said that she and her husband had been having more arguments and that all of this stress was becoming overwhelming.

Sue said that Judy needed to take one thing at a time instead of trying to deal with everything at once. They talked about her mother's condition and Sue pointed out that Mrs. Jones had been making excellent progress and was starting to walk with some assistance. She had also been noticeably more cheerful and outgoing before this latest setback. Sue felt that the combination of her improved health and mental outlook would help Mrs. Jones to survive this health crisis. Judy said that she hoped that Sue was right. Sue said that at the very least, Judy needed to stop worrying about what might happen and just take this situation one hour at a time until they see the outcome. She pointed out that worrying resulted in living one's life as if the worst things are happening even when they don't happen.

Judy said she never thought of it that way. She stopped crying and said she was still concerned about her job and her marriage. Sue asked her if there was a human resources department or a union where she worked. Judy said there were both. Sue talked with Judy about contacting them to determine what benefits she was entitled to have in terms of time off for family health issues. Then she could ask human resources and/or her union representative to meet with her boss about the situation.

Sue then discussed Judy's relationship with her husband. Judy feels that her feelings of being overwhelmed were probably causing most of the stress in their relationship. She feels that her husband does not know what to say when she gets upset. Sue noted that he had not attended any of the family support group sessions. Judy said he was staying at home to watch the children while she went. Sue indicated that it might be worthwhile to get a sitter and have them both come to the group. This would give them more of a feeling of facing this together. Judy said that she had a neighbor with whom she trades child care time and she thought it might work to have her watch the children so they could go. Perhaps they could stop and eat beforehand or afterward.

Judy was greatly relieved and thanked Sue for her help. Judy's sister arrived as they finished. They talked briefly and then Sue excused herself to return to her office at Sunnyside. She explained that she had a group to meet with in about an hour. She asked Judy and her sister to keep her abreast of their mother's condition and that she would be there to help them with anything that was needed. She asked if they would like to talk with the hospital chaplain or the social worker. They said that either one might be helpful, especially the chaplain. On the way out, Sue stopped by both offices and asked if they could look in on the family.

# Summary

This chapter is a brief summary of the change process as it is used with individual group members. It is adapted from the ninth edition of our companion text, *Social Work Practice: A Generalist Approach*. The phases of the change process include assessment, planning, action, and evaluation and termination.

The assessment involves both content and process. It has five steps: identify the initial concern or need; identify the nature of the concern or need; identify potential strengths and resources in the ecosystem; select and collect information; and analyze the available information. Planning also involves both content and process. A plan should include goals, objectives, units of attention, and tasks. In addition to a common goal and individual goals, groups may also use mutual or shared goals and reciprocal goals. Direct practice actions are actions taken directly with clients. Indirect practices actions involve actions on behalf of clients. The final phase is evaluation and termination.

## QUESTIONS

1. Using the schema in Table 3.1, develop a social history on yourself or someone you know.

2. Set a goal for yourself that you can reach in a week. Write it in outcome terms and identify two objectives that relate to the goal. Identify a task for each objective.

3. Empowerment has been considered of particular importance when working with women, people of color, and populations at risk. Why do you think empowerment is important in such situations?

4. Consider a situation that you are facing and describe a negative thought or feeling that you have about it. Change the thought to a positive one that predicts a successful resolution and describe the feeling that accompanies it. How would acting on the positive thought change your behavior in that situation?

5. Describe the crisis process in a situation in which you have been involved. What was most helpful in the resolution of the crisis?

6. Name some situations in which you believe support is an appropriate action for a social worker to take.

7. Choose an activity that you think will be helpful in a specific situation. How did you go about choosing this activity? How should it be structured and presented?

8. In what kinds of situations would the mediating model be appropriate? When would it not be appropriate?

9. Discuss the strengths and limitations of the various kinds of coordination.

## SUGGESTED READINGS

Johnson, Louise C., and Yanca, Stephen J. *Social Work Practice: A Generalist Approach,* 9th ed. Boston: Allyn & Bacon, 2007 (Chapters 5–13).

Edwards, Richard L., Ed. *Encyclopedia of Social Work,* 19th ed. Washington, DC: NASW Press, 1995 ("Assessment"; "Crisis Intervention: Research Needs"; "Direct Practice Overview"; "Natural Helping Networks"; "Women: Direct Practice").

Miley, Karla Krogsrud, O'Melia, Michael, and DuBois, Brenda L. *Generalist Social Work Practice: An Empowering Approach,* 5th ed. Boston: Allyn & Bacon, 2007.

Saleeby, Dennis. *The Strengths Perspective in Social Work Practices,* 5th ed. Boston: Allyn and Bacon, 2009.

Sheafor, Bradford W., and Horejsi, Charles R. *Techniques and Guidelines for Social Work Practice,* 8th ed. Boston: Allyn & Bacon, 2008.

# 4 The Change Process with Groups

## LEARNING EXPECTATIONS

1. Understanding the importance of the small group in generalist social work practice.
2. Understanding various direct service groups offered within generalist practice.
3. Understanding the use of the change process in generalist practice with groups.
4. Understanding the group process to be able to recognize its various aspects in the functioning of a small group or a family.
5. Understanding how the social worker can facilitate the work and process of any small group.
6. Beginning skill in facilitating small-group interaction.

This chapter provides a foundation for working with groups within a generalist social work practice framework. There are two general categories of groups: those that provide direct services to clients, and task groups that are used to facilitate change in organizations and communities. The first category, referred to as direct service groups, is the focus of this chapter as well as Part Two of the text. The purpose of these groups is to provide a benefit to members. The change process is used in several ways in direct service groups. Assessment and planning occur before the group begins, between group sessions, and during the group. Assessment includes understanding the small group as a social system. Assessment, planning, and direct practice actions are used to facilitate the group and are often taught to group members. Evaluation occurs throughout the life of the group. Termination can be planned and unplanned and can be experienced by the group as a whole or by individual members as they leave the group. Assessment, planning, actions, and evaluation and termination with direct service groups is examined. How these are used during various stages of group development is discussed in Part Two. Most of the material discussed here and in Part Two is also relevant for task groups. Community and organizational change and the use of task groups is examined in greater detail in Part Three of the text.

## Group Purpose

A **group** is a system of clients or a multiclient system. To the extent that the worker works with the group as a whole to facilitate achievement of its purpose, the group can be considered as a system. Direct service groups are a means by which services are delivered to several clients who have common needs or interests. In this discussion of direct service groups, the primary purpose of the group is to serve the needs of its members. The types of group purposes considered here in this text will be (1) growth and skill development, (2) prevention services, (3) support and self help, and (4) counseling or probelm-solving and decision-making groups which we will call change oriented groups. Therapy groups are for those clients who need to overcome major difficulties in social functioning. In this text, we assume that providing therapy is limited to MSWs with advanced training. This topic is beyond the scope of this text.

MSWs and BSW-level social workers under supervision provide group work services aimed at facilitating growth and skill development and providing prevention services, support, and counseling services. Most growth and skill development groups are offered to the general population, although these services can also be provided to people experiencing greater need. Examples of growth and skill development groups are recreation groups, education groups, parenting groups, social skills training, and various youth groups, such as scouting, church groups, and the like. It is assumed that the benefits that are gained from this type of group come from participation.

At the other end of the spectrum are counseling or problem-solving and decision-making groups. Counseling groups are defined as serving the needs of individuals who are faced with important decisions or difficult problems. In this view, counseling groups are for clients who are capable of making and carrying out decisions or solving problems with assistance. In contrast, therapy groups are for clients who need assistance in overcoming major barriers to social functioning before they will be able to participate in growth and skill development activities or make and carry out decisions and solve problems. For example, a child who is exhibiting disruptive behavior or is emotionally unstable may need therapy to overcome these difficulties before he is able to participate in a recreation group. Placing him in a group that is not designed to meet his needs usually leads to scapegoating and other harmful experiences. When offering direct service groups, the worker must be careful to avoid members who exhibit a wide range of social functioning. If there is too much disparity in social functioning, members will have difficulty relating to one another.

Support groups and self-help groups are offered for a wide variety of situations. Typically, members have either already been through a difficult situation and need support, or they need help coping with a situation that is beyond their control. In one type of support group, members need assistance in continuing changes that they made in individual or group counseling. Because managed care programs increasingly are limiting the length of service, these groups are important resources. Support groups are not typically considered to be a reimbursable service, but it is important that agencies offer this type of service so that clients receive support after counseling ends. The second type of support group is designed to help clients and family members cope with situations such as coping with cancer or incurable conditions, bereavement, and the like. Coping with these situations can be especially difficult because of feelings of helplessness and hopelessness. Giving and receiving support from others in similar circumstances can be a powerful aid in facing these challenges. Self-help groups are included here under the umbrella of support groups because a major value of these groups is also giving and receiving support to members.

Prevention groups are designed to serve the needs of those who are at risk of experiencing difficulties in social functioning. Prevention groups may follow a specially designed curriculum, or they may use growth and skill development activities or decision-making and problem-solving processes, or both. The difference here is that membership is limited to those who are identified as being at risk. For example, a drug prevention group would be appropriate for youth who have a family member who has abused drugs or alcohol or for youth who live in an area where drugs are prevalent. This type of group could use a curriculum that educates its members about drugs and offers strategies for avoidance. Recreation or outings could be offered as rewards for attendance and participation. Skill development and decision making can help encourage members to refuse drugs.

The purpose of the group influences decisions about membership. Age, gender, developmental stage, and social functioning are important considerations. The purpose of the group also dictates the role of the worker and the types of services rendered. Group purpose must be understood and incorporated into every facet of the work to facilitate success for the group as a whole and to ensure maximum benefit for members.

## Assessment with Small Groups

There are two major types of assessment needed for small groups: product and process. Assessment as *product* includes collecting and organizing data on each potential group member prior to beginning the group. This is mainly done with counseling and with certain prevention groups. It involves utilizing the steps in the Johnson/Yanca model of generalist practice described in Chapters 2 and 3. The emphasis for data collected is on assessing the individual's "fit" with both the group's purpose and other potential members, and on ensuring that the group is appropriate for meeting the needs of members. The worker who is forming a small group should conduct an individual assessment by asking two questions: (1) What are the issues, needs, concerns, and strengths of the individual being interviewed? (2) How would this individual fit with the other potential group members and the overall purpose of the group?

*Process* refers to the interactions within the group and what those interactions mean or represent. The worker needs to understand the significance of group interactions and group dynamics. Understanding group process means understanding the meaning behind members' verbal and nonverbal behaviors. This understanding is not only about individual members but also about the group as a whole. Understanding process includes understanding the stages of group development and how individual and group behavior represents various stages. It also means understanding when individual or group behavior is inconsistent with the stage of development.[1]

Although the purpose of the group will influence member selection, it is generally desirable to have members who are somewhat similar in socioeconomic status, age, and level of concern regarding the group's purpose. An ethnic, cultural, and gender balance can also be important, again depending on the group's overall goals. Because in small groups, members learn from and use each other's strengths, diversity in this area can be an asset for group functioning. Diversity in members' experiences can be helpful if the disparity is not too great because members can learn from one another about how to deal with situations relevant to the purpose of the group. It is important to determine how potential members might interact with others in a group setting and what role they might be expected to assume. Communication skills, social skills, and developmental level must also be assessed in light of potential group membership.

In some instances, commonalities rather than diversity, or diversity rather than commonalities, are preferred. For example, a group for people who have been sexually abused would probably function better if all members are of the same sex. A group for people who are dealing with the death of a family member, however, may benefit from members who are in various stages of the grieving process. Again, the purpose of the group determines the composition.

Table 3.1 presents a schema for developing an individual social history. Depending on the purpose of the group and the setting, an individual social history or assessment either may already be available or one may be desirable in order to ensure a good fit between individual members and the group and to ensure that individual needs are met within the group. This is most often used with therapy and counseling groups. Occasionally, it may be needed or required for prevention groups. It is not usually used for the other groups being studied here. The schema includes information that is typically gathered. Various settings may require greater emphasis on certain areas, while assessments in other settings may contain additional information.

Once the group has begun, group assessment skills may include utilization of the tools described in Table 4.1 and the sociogram depicted in Figure 4.1. These provide information about the group at a particular point in time and may contribute to an understanding of group dynamics or indicate when the group leader should intervene. Ongoing periodic assessment of members' progress and interactions, as well as group dynamics, will also help the worker shape or reshape the structure and intent of the group.

**TABLE 4.1    A Schema for the Study of the Small Group as a Social System**

**I.** Structure
  **A.** Boundary
    **1.** What is the purpose, mission, or task of this group?
    **2.** Identify members of the group. Describe them as persons. (Use appropriate parts of Table 3.1.)
    **3.** What are the factors that separate these persons from other persons? How were the members chosen? Under what circumstances would a person no longer be a member of this group?
    **4.** What is the history of this group? How and why was it formed? How long has it been meeting?
    **5.** What is the position of the worker with this group?
    **6.** What is the influence of the environment on this group and its functioning? Include environmental expectations, impingements, and resources.
    **7.** Describe the open/closed character of the boundary. Include communication and energy exchange and openness to new ideas and ways of functioning.
  **B.** Relationship framework
    **1.** Describe any rating/ranking of group members.
    **2.** Draw a sociogram.
    **3.** Describe the manner in which members fill roles. Are all needed roles filled? Are any roles overfilled? Which members fill several roles?
  **C.** Bond
    **1.** What is it that holds members of the group together? Note common interests and friendships.
    **2.** Describe the climate of the group.
    **3.** What are the goals of the group? Are they explicit and known to, and accepted by, all group members?
    **4.** What are the norms or rules for functioning in this group? How did they develop? Are they known to, and accepted by, all group members?
    **5.** What are the rewards of membership in this group?
    **6.** What priority do members give to the group?

**II.** Functioning

    **A.** Balance/stability

        **1.** How does this group adapt to changing conditions? Consider change both in the environment and within the group.

        **2.** How much time is spent on group maintenance and how much on group task? Is this balance appropriate?

    **B.** Decision making

        **1.** How does this group make decisions about norms, goals, and plans for work?

        **2.** Describe group problem-solving mechanisms. Do any members engage in diversionary or blocking tactics that inhibit problem solving?

        **3.** Describe leadership as it facilitates or inhibits the group's decision making.

        **4.** How do group members influence group decisions?

        **5.** How is conflict resolved? Is it recognized and kept in the open?

    **C.** Communication

        **1.** Describe communication patterns of the group.

        **2.** Does the group have adequate feedback mechanisms? Is attention paid to nonverbal communication?

        **3.** Do all group members have adequate opportunity to communicate? Do any members tend to over-communicate?

        **4.** Are there any content areas that seem to be troublesome when communicating?

        **5.** Is attention paid to communication difficulties that arise from cross-cultural or cross-professional interaction

    **D.** Task implementation

        **1.** Describe the manner in which the group carries out its tasks. Describe the quality of interaction in carrying out tasks.

        **2.** Do any members engage in diversionary or blocking tactics that inhibit carrying out plans?

**III.** Development

    **A.** Identify the stage of development in which the group is operating.

    **B.** Describe any factors that may be inhibiting continued group development.

**IV.** Strengths and Challenges

    **A.** What are the strengths of the group?

    **B.** What are the challenges for the group?

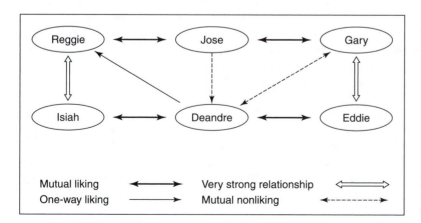

Mutual liking              Very strong relationship

One-way liking           Mutual nonliking

**FIGURE 4.1   Sociogram of a Group of Delinquent Boys in a Group Home.**

# Assessing the Small Group as a Social System

The term *group* is often used in an imprecise, broad sense. The designation of *small group* as a social system places some limitation on the term. As a social system, a **small group** is composed of three or more persons who have something in common and who use face-to-face interaction to share that commonality and work to fulfill needs, their own or those of others. An effective small group allows each person in the group to have an impact on every other person in the group. The group is an entity or system that is identifiable, and it is more than the sum of its parts. For best results, a counseling group should not exceed eight to ten members. The size of other groups should be determined by the types of activities and the age or developmental level of members. A task group may require more members to accomplish its tasks. Support groups may be larger, but membership fluctuates. Groups, like all social systems, have structure (the form of a system at any point in time); a way of functioning or behaving in order to accomplish tasks; and development that takes place in stages over time.[2] (See Table 4.1.) To develop sufficient understanding for effective interaction in and with a small group, a social worker needs to assess all three of these dimensions.

In addition, the group has an ecosystem, and each group member has an ecosystem unique to that member, although certain systems may overlap, such as community systems in which group members share membership. The purpose of most groups is generally to assist members in getting their needs met from their ecosystems and meeting the needs of others in those systems. Members are expected to use what they gain in the group to bring about growth and change in their lives outside the group. In a task group, the purpose is to bring about change in the ecosystem of the group. Thus, the worker needs to develop skills in facilitating the group in accomplishing its goals and objectives, both within and outside of the group.

## Group Structure

Three major dimensions of structure are boundary, relationship framework, and bond. **Boundary,** in a social system, is the point at which the system of interaction around a function no longer has the intensity that the interaction among the members has. Sometimes membership in a group is clearly defined; at other times, the determination of boundary may be difficult to establish. For example, a drop-in group at a community center will have sporadic attendance.

When considering boundary, it is important to take into account who the group members are. All members have a personal history, current needs, and responsibilities toward other systems of which they are a part. These affect each person's functioning in the group. Each group member receives certain rewards for participating in the group, and these need to be identified. The history of the group; how and why it was formed; and any change in focus, membership, or way of functioning as it influences current structure are important for a group assessment.

The worker's role in the group is another component of relationship. Henry Maier has identified three orientations to member–worker interactions. A Type A relationship has a strict boundary between the work of the group and larger life situations. The worker is considered an expert who functions from a position of separation from the rest of the group, yet exercises considerable control over the functioning of the group. In a Type B relationship, the worker is more a part of the group, yet has the distinctive role of facilitator of group functioning. In a Type C relationship, the worker is a member of the group, and there is no role differentiation. The Type C relationship would likely include groups such as community groups or interdisciplinary teams, which will be covered later.[3]

The environment of the group also affects the group's functioning. The environment places expectations on, and furnishes resources for, the group. The boundary may be relatively open or closed. When a group has an open boundary, it is fairly easy for individuals to join the group, and the group is open to new ideas and other communication from the environment. When the boundary is more closed, membership is restricted, as is communication from outside. However, as mentioned earlier, the purpose of the group is either to act on the environment as a group or for members to act on their environment as individuals in order to bring about balance in meeting needs. The boundary helps to define the group, but members continue to have a life outside the group that influences their functioning in the group and that is influenced by their functioning in the group.

The relationships among the members can be examined in several ways, three of which include:

**1.** *The rating-ranking pattern*—In some groups one (or more) member(s) clearly has higher status than the others. When examining relationships from this perspective, it is important to look not only at the status hierarchy but at the reason for members' status as well.

**2.** *The sociogram*—The **sociogram** shows patterns of liking and nonliking.[4] It can also show subgrouping and strength of relationships in a group. Figure 4.1 describes a group of delinquent boys in a group home. Reggie and Isiah have a very strong relationship, as do Gary and Eddie. There are mixed relations among others.

**3.** *The role structure*—Kenneth Benne and Paul Sheats have identified three categories of roles that may develop in groups: group-task roles, group-building (or group maintenance) roles, and individual roles. **Group-task roles** are related to the accomplishment of the function or task of the group. In discussion groups, roles include the initiator or contributor of ideas, the information seeker, the clarifier of ideas, the information giver, the opinion giver, the opinion seeker, and the orienter. **Group-building (group maintenance) roles** are those that focus on the maintenance of the group as a system. Roles that fall into this category include the encourager, the harmonizer, the compromiser, and the gatekeeper. The gatekeeper is the one who controls the flow of communication by allowing, encouraging, and blocking messages from the various group members. The third category is composed of the **individual roles** that satisfy individual need but detract from the work of the group. These roles include the dominator, the special-interest pleader, and the blocker.[5]

Often, leadership is considered to be a role. **Leadership** can be thought of as filling several roles, particularly of those needed for effective group functioning. The identification of who fills which roles, which roles are not being filled, and which members tend to carry many or crucial roles clarifies group structure.

**Bond** is the cohesive quality of the group; it is a "we feeling" as opposed to an "I-he-she feeling." It is expressed in common group goals, in norms for group behavior, and in common values held by group members. In systems terms, steady state is a related concept.

*Steady state* is a particular configuration of parts that is self-maintaining and self-repairing. In other words, it is a state of systems that leads to both stability and adaptability. The functional group needs to maintain stability while still being adaptable to changing conditions and situations.

Description of the bond existing in a group identifies what holds the group together: common interests or tasks, friendships, desire for relationships, and the like. Also important is the identification of group goals, norms, and values as well as the ability of the group to adapt to changing conditions and situations.

The structure of the group is described by identifying the aspects of boundary, relationship structure, and bond. The structure changes as the group interacts and carries out its function over time. The social worker strives to enable the group to develop a structure that enhances the quality of the interaction of its members while also enhancing the group's ability to achieve its purpose. Generally, this involves either balancing the interactions between the group and its ecosystem (as in a task group) or enhancing the ability of members to meet their own needs as well as the needs of their ecosystem (as in counseling or support groups).

## Group Functioning

Group interaction is a complex process influenced by the actions of group members and by the interactions among the various members. These actions and interactions in turn are influenced by group members' needs and responsibilities. The process is also influenced by the needs of the group as an entity accomplishing tasks and maintaining itself. The situation or environment in which the group functions also influences the functioning. This functioning, which is quite complex, is transactional in nature.

One way of describing group functioning is in terms of the *use of energy*. Every system has a limited amount of energy, and there is always a state of tension concerning the way that energy will be used. Tensions may be expressed in terms of energy allotted to group tasks or to group building. They may be expressed in terms of stability versus change or adaptability issues. Each group develops ways of dealing with these energy issues.

Another way to describe group functioning is in how it uses information. Much of the social work endeavor involves the exchange of information. Group members share information within the group and use information from outside the group. They also take information from the group and use it in their interactions with their ecosystem. The bulk of the work in groups involves exchanges of information designed to achieve goals and objectives for the group and its members. Members are expected to use what they learn to either act on the group's ecosystem (task groups) or to act on their own (counseling or support groups). The need for confidentiality can restrict the flow of personal information from the group.

Another aspect of the group's functioning is its *decision-making* and *communication processes*. Groups make decisions about which roles and tasks belong to which members, about how to communicate and implement group decisions, and about the use of energy. Decisions are made in different ways in different groups. Sometimes a rational or problem-solving process is used; sometimes compromise is a method; sometimes one or more group members impose their will on the rest of the group. Often groups merely function on the basis of past experience.

Closely related to decision making are issues of leadership, power, control, and conflict. **Conflict** is often viewed as a negative ingredient of group interaction. Properly managed, however, it can be a force that enhances group creativity and problem solving. Conflict is expected in a situation in which people of varying backgrounds seek to work together. Conflict is the struggle for something that is scarce. In a group this may be attention, power, status, influence, the right to fill a role, and so on. Groups make decisions about how conflicts will be resolved. One of the tasks of a social worker in fostering group interaction is to identify conflict areas and help the group work toward healthy resolution of the conflict.

Communication is the heart of the process of group interaction and thus a most important aspect of its functioning. Information, decisions, and directives are distributed through communication among group members. Communication is the means of forming and modifying opinions and attitudes. The *communication process* is described by focusing on who communicates to whom and about what. Communication is discussed in greater detail in the next chapter.

Another way of describing the group's functioning is to note the *task implementation process,* that is, how the group accomplishes its task. The task implementation process is concerned with who does what and whether or not individuals carry out delegated tasks.

The functioning of the group is simply movement in carrying out the group's function. The structure changes as the movement takes place. This change is related to the development of greater organization, which results in specialization and stabilization. As the worker in and with the group strives to influence the group's interaction, he enables the group to carry out its function and tasks.

## Group Development

As the group functions and the structure changes, it passes through a series of expected, identifiable stages. At each stage, the group has differing group maintenance needs. The capacity for the group to fulfill its function grows as it progresses through the stages of development. Groups develop at different rates. Factors that encourage group development include:

1. The strength of the members' commitment to the group's function, tasks, and goals
2. The satisfaction of the mutual needs of the members
3. The liking or caring that the members feel for one another
4. Reciprocation rather than competition for roles
5. Respect for diversity among group members
6. The amount of time the group spends together
7. Interaction that encourages individual growth
8. A degree of homogeneity that allows group norms and goals to form
9. A degree of heterogeneity that provides different ideas and points of view among the members

The stages of group development may be conceptualized as follows:

**1.** *The orientation stage*—Members come together for the first time, seek similarities in interest, and make an initial commitment to the group. There is also an approach-avoidance mechanism at work. Patterns of functioning around tasks begin to develop. Task roles begin to emerge. Emphasis is on activity and orientation to the situation. Individuals make decisions about the desirability of belonging to the group and whether to become dependent on other group members.

**2.** *The authority stage*—There is challenge to the influence and control of the group by individual members. Conflict develops; members rebel and search for individual autonomy. Power and control are issues; there may be dropouts. Structure and patterns of functioning are revised. Members share ideas and feelings about what the group should do and how the group should function. Norms and values develop through this sharing.

**3.** *The negotiation stage*—The group confronts, differs, and engages in conflict resolution. Goals, roles, and tasks are designated and accepted. Group traditions are stronger, norms develop, personal involvement intensifies. Group cohesion is stronger, and members are freer in sharing information and opinions.

**4.** *The functional stage*—A high level of group integration is reached. There is little conflict about structure, and ways of functioning have been established. Roles are differentially assigned to members and accepted by all. Communication channels are open and functional; goals and norms are known and accepted. The group has the capacity to change and adapt. Conflict and tension are managed with minimal energy use; a problem-solving capacity develops. Members are interdependent. Plans are implemented, tasks are completed, and goals are reached. The group can evaluate itself and its work.

**5.** *The disintegration stage*—At any of the first four stages, a group may begin to disintegrate. Signs of disintegration include the lessening of the bond. There is a reduction in the frequency and strength of group interaction, in common norms or values for group members, and in the group's strength of influence on members. At the same time that this is occurring, members will generally be strengthening and increasing their interaction with their ecosystem outside of the group.

Identifying a group's stage of development allows a worker to respond to that group with greater understanding about the structure and functioning of the group. It also provides an informed response to that group's functioning, which is a means for enhancing the interactional processes of the group.

Understanding the small group as a social system is a prerequisite to effective work as a group member or to working with the multiclient system. This understanding is a guide for the worker's interactions and interventions when working in and with groups.

## Planning with Small Groups

There are four ways that planning is used with small groups. These include (1) planning for a new group, (2) planning for each group session, (3) planning within group sessions, and (4) facilitating the development and use of planning skills by group members. This last use of planning is similar to that used with individuals and will not be repeated here. The worker uses the small-group experience to teach skills in planning and to support the successful completion of goals, objectives, and tasks.

## Planning for a New Group

In starting a new group, the worker needs to formulate a plan or proposal that can be used in working with supervisors, administrators, other staff, and other agencies and in recruiting potential members. Generally, administrators and supervisors will be concerned about efficiency and effectiveness, so these issues should be addressed. Other staff and other agencies will be concerned with why they should refer clients to the group and who would be appropriate. Potential group members will wonder what benefit they could expect from participating.

There are several formats that can be used for constructing a proposal if one has not been developed by the agency. Essentially, the worker should answer the questions why, who, what, where, when, and how. The question why is answered by a thorough discussion of the purpose of the group and the potential benefits for participants. The proposal should include a description of who the members will be and how they will be recruited. It should include a description of what will take place during sessions and over the course of the group. If a curriculum is to be used, a table of contents and a sample of a session is generally attached as an addendum. The plan should describe where and when the group will take place, how long sessions will be, and when the group will end. There should be a description of resources that are needed and how these will be obtained. The cost of these resources may be formulated in a budget format. Examples of recruitment flyers or letters, informed consent forms, and other materials should also be attached. In addition, the process for evaluating the group should be described. A schema for planning a new group and a case example of a proposal for a group is provided in Chapter 6.

## Planning for Group Sessions

The worker's role in planning group sessions can vary considerably. Factors include group membership, the structure of sessions, the type of group, and coleadership. Groups with younger members or members with developmental delays or a significant impairment (such as mental retardation or mental illness) generally require more planning and direction from the worker. Members with lower social functioning need structure to ensure successful completion of tasks. Usually, sessions of these types of groups are structured around the use of discussion and activity. The most common structure is discussion-activity-discussion, or DAD. The worker leads a discussion of events during the week and of the activity for the session. The group engages in the activity. This is followed by a discussion of the activity itself, including any benefits, and its use in everyday life. Planning for the next session may also be discussed. Other combinations of discussion and activity may also be used to organize sessions.

Growth and skill development groups generally require considerable planning and preparation. Education groups require the most preparation, since the worker often assumes the role of teacher or presenter. Skill development groups usually use a curriculum that has structured activities involving more preparation by the worker. In addition to becoming familiar with the activity, the worker is responsible for securing supplies and facilitating participation. Prevention groups often use a curriculum or structured activities. Support groups for older adolescents and adults are usually less structured. Planning for support groups generally requires providing resources such as information, speakers, videos, and similar materials. Counseling groups are the least structured and require less planning ahead of time, but planning is used more within the group process.

In using coleadership, the workers must use planning before and after each session to coordinate their roles and activities so that they complement each other. Workers need to be consistent and avoid contradictions and confusion. Maintaining consistency is difficult but important to avoid sending mixed messages to group members.

### Planning within Group Sessions

The use of planning within group sessions may involve engaging the group in planning for activities that will take place during group sessions, between sessions, or in the future outside of regular sessions. In addition, planning is used within groups that are intended to assist members in learning to use the change process, decision making, or problem solving. Members use the group to develop goals, objectives, and tasks designed to make changes in their daily lives. Various types of goals are covered in Chapter 3.

In groups using a DAD structure with higher-functioning members, either discussion phase may include planning for future activities. The ending phase often includes planning for the next session. Groups that live together in group homes, residential programs, and institutional settings generally use group sessions to plan activities that will take place between sessions or in the future. Since these members are living together, they also need to use groups to manage their daily living activities and resolve problems that arise. The change process is used to facilitate decision making and problem solving. Planning is an important phase in these activities. These groups may be used for long-term planning for group activities and projects such as community service activities, outings, and field trips.

In counseling groups, members use the group to assist in decision making and problem solving. The change process facilitates these activities. Members use the group to help assess the situation and develop a plan. The group provides support for carrying out the plan. In the course of making decisions and solving problems for themselves and with one another, members gain knowledge and skills in the use of the change process for the future.

## Direct Practice Actions with Small Groups

Working with the small group as a multiclient system means that the worker facilitates the group in terms of structure, functioning, and development while ensuring that members obtain maximum benefit from their experiences in the group. Thus, group work involves a constant process of balancing the needs of the group in maintaining itself as a group and the needs of individual members. This discussion of practice actions is mainly used with change-oriented groups. Specific actions for various groups is discussed in Part Two.

Since the needs of individual members are important, all of the direct practice actions and strategies that are identified in Chapter 3 can be used in working with small groups. In addition, interaction skills that are covered in Chapter 5 are vital to working with groups. These include actions related to relationship building, the change process, resources, empowering and enabling, crisis resolution, support, activity, and mediation. Practice actions are used to facilitate completion of the plan, removal of barriers to the plan, and the functioning of both the system and individual members. These practice actions will not be repeated here, but the reader should review this material before proceeding and include them in her work with small groups. This section focuses on actions to facilitate group development and functioning, including actions taken to (1) facilitate group formation, (2) facilitate discussion leadership, (3) resolve conflict, (4) enhance group interaction, (5) facilitate group development, and (6) structure group activities.

Indirect practice actions may be needed on behalf of individuals in the group or on behalf of the group as a whole. In instances when influencing the environment or environmental change is needed, the worker should make every effort to either support the group in acting on its own behalf or include the group in actions the worker takes.

## Actions to Facilitate Group Formation

Although social workers sometimes work with already formed systems or groups, at times it is necessary to form a group. People considered for group membership may not be acquainted with one another. The handling of the formation process is an important factor in whether the group will be able to function to meet its goals. There are four stages in the formation of a group: (1) establishing the group's purpose, (2) selecting members, (3) making the first contacts with prospective members, and (4) holding the first meeting of the group.

The group's purpose may develop from client request or from an agency's staff decision that there is a need that can be met through developing a group. Some of the reasons for forming a group are the following: (1) when several people facing similar situations can benefit from sharing their experiences; (2) when group influence on individuals is great, such as during the teenage years; (3) when the target for change is in the environment, such as the development of a new community service; (4) when a natural group exists; (5) to improve relationships with others; (6) to aid those experiencing social isolation; (7) to provide opportunities for growth and skill development; (8) to provide support; and (9) to prevent the development of problems for at risk populations. The group is an excellent vehicle to use for reality testing, for it is a social microcosm of the larger society. Groups should not be used to save workers' time when a common goal or purpose does not exist, when an individual is in danger of being overwhelmed by the group, when there is insufficient commonality for a cohesive climate to develop, or when the environment impinges on the group's functioning or prevents it from reaching its goals. Groups can work together on individual needs, on interests and activities shared by members, on relationships within or outside of the group, on decision making or task achievement, or on targeting for change in the larger community.

For a group to be functional, group members must have some commonality (in part, the purpose and function provide the commonality). At this stage of the formation process, the worker and agency identify a common need and translate the need to the purpose for the prospective group. The worker formulates tentative group goals. Based on the purpose and the tentative goals, the worker begins the selection of members. Consideration is given to how many people should be in the group. When members have good interactional skills, the number can go as high as ten or twelve and still allow for interaction among all members. For clients with little interactional capacity, the size of the group should be limited to five or six persons.

Group commonality is in part based on the attractiveness prospective members have for one another. People are attracted to other people because they admire them, hold common values with them, respect them, or support their functioning in some way. People feel most comfortable with those who are similar to themselves. For a group to be productive, however, it is necessary for the members to be sufficiently different from one another so that unique contributions can be made by each group member. The worker must determine how much commonality is necessary for the group to be attractive to prospective members and how much difference is necessary to carry out the function of the group.

In choosing prospective members, the worker must evaluate how well these individuals can be expected to function in the group and what their contributions might be. The choice of prospective members is based on multiple factors that relate to the need for balance and the individual qualities of these members.

In facilitating group formation, the worker considers the diversity of its members. In most groups, it is generally best that members come from a variety of backgrounds. If only one member has a particular diversity background (such as being the only woman or African American in the group), that person is likely to feel out of place and is at risk of leaving the group. However, if at least one other member shares the same diversity, the chances that both members will stay improve considerably. In terms of the functioning of the group regarding diversity, the worker should facilitate open discussions of the differences that exist among members and help the group see the strengths in others who are different and realize how diversity strengthens the group itself. The worker should not assume that everyone shares his view of valuing diversity. It is likely that the prejudices that are present in society will also be present in the group. The worker's role is to facilitate positive exchanges that will help group members to know one another as human beings. Identifying commonalities is generally the first step in this process. If members can appreciate each other as human beings, they can begin to look at what makes each group member unique and individual, including his or her diversity. Given the prejudice in society toward people of color, women, homosexuals, non-Christians, various ethnic groups, and the like, this work is very delicate and must be undertaken with caution and planning. It is best if ahead of time the worker has developed some degree of competence with respect to the diversity in his group. This can be done in part during screening interviews and by conducting a self-assessment and some research. During the screening interview, the worker uses naturalistic inquiry to discover the prospective member's perceptions regarding her diversity. In the group, the worker models the use of naturalistic inquiry and respect for diversity. If the group can solidify an appreciation for the diversity of its members, the members can learn a great deal from one another, and the group will have access to a wider variety of experiences from which it can draw on as resources.

Other factors in forming a group are the resources and expectations that arise from the prospective group's environment. These factors affect the prospective member's ability to function in the group and also affect the manner in which the group can function.

When the worker has completed the process of choosing prospective members, the next step is an initial contact with each person. During the initial contact, the worker explains the purpose of the group and the reason for considering the person for group membership. Together they explore how the group may function and come to a decision about the prospective member joining the group. In many ways, this session is similar to the worker's initial interview with an individual client. The major purpose of the session is to begin to engage the member in the group and to orient the member to the group.

The first meeting of the group is crucial for group formation. The group function and the way of operating are discussed again. The worker enables members to share their reasons for joining the group and their individual goals with respect to the group. The worker facilitates communication among the members and helps them begin formulating group norms and goals. The group begins to work on the tasks of carrying out the function of the group. Every attempt is made for this first session to be a positive experience for all members.

Adequate group formation is time consuming, but if properly done it actually saves time later. It reduces the chances of having a mismatch of group members and prepares the members for functioning in the group. In this way, the time in the group can be spent on its function and tasks, not on unrelated individual needs.

When the group is ongoing and not time limited, the group must decide how it will add new members. If it is an open group, as are support groups and self-help groups, members can join or leave at any time. For these groups, a certain member or members should be identified who can quickly orient new members to the norms of the group and help introduce them to the group.

In closed groups that are ongoing, new members are usually only added when someone leaves the group. The worker generally takes responsibility for screening prospective members. In groups with voluntary members, the group may be responsible for the decision of whether or not to accept a prospective member after the worker describes the person and her situation, or the worker may have responsibility for making a decision. In nonvoluntary groups, such as the one in the group home from the case study in this chapter, the staff of the agency decide who to accept through an intake process. The worker should ensure that the group has resolved any termination issues and is ready to accept the new member. Termination is discussed in more detail below. In either case, the worker typically will orient the new member prior to the group meeting and then facilitate having the group complete the orientation process during the first session that the new member attends. This orientation should include introductions, a discussion of group rules, and a discussion of what is expected of the new member in terms of participation. Periodic checks should be made with the new member and feedback given for the first few sessions to facilitate having him join in the group process.

## Actions to Facilitate Discussion Leadership

Discussion is the means of communicating within the group. The worker carries the task of enabling the discussion to develop until such time as leadership emerges in the group. This enabling takes place through:

1. *Climate setting*—The worker pays attention to the physical atmosphere. Chairs are placed so that all members can have eye contact and are neither too close nor too far apart. The atmosphere should be warm, friendly, and relaxed.
2. *Stimulating*—The worker encourages the sharing of ideas. The worker also helps group members disagree without developing hostility.
3. *Encouraging mutual respect and understanding*—The worker helps members understand their commonalities and differences. The right of people to be different is considered. The worker demonstrates respect for all members and their ideas. This modeling often helps members respect one another.

4. *Reducing overdependence*—The worker encourages the group to develop its way of functioning. The worker seeks ideas and facts from the members and helps group members fill the essential roles.

5. *Drawing in nonparticipants*—The worker helps a member who is not active in the discussion to contribute by asking questions or asking for information.

6. *Checking overaggressive participants*—The worker points out to the group the need for each member to have an opportunity to participate.

7. *Helping the group define and verbalize goals and needs*—The worker stimulates group thinking and helps the group in making decisions and developing plans.

8. *Helping the group to problem solve*—The worker clarifies issues, analyzes problems, discovers and describes possible solutions, evaluates solutions, and carries out decisions. Also, the worker helps the group focus when it gets off course and summarizes as appropriate.

9. *Helping the group appreciate member diversity*—The worker encourages appropriate exploration of the diversity of its members through the use of naturalistic inquiry. The worker helps the group to value diversity and appreciate the strengths each member possesses from that diversity and the increased strength this brings to the group as a whole.

10. *Helping the group deal with conflict*—The worker points out symptoms of conflict, helps individuals clarify viewpoints and state positions, and seeks commonalities.

In providing discussion leadership to a group, the worker is also teaching members of the group how to take responsibility for their own leadership. The worker needs to help the group avoid placing undue pressure for conformity or dependency on its members, allowing harmful and unsupportive responses to vulnerable members, and tolerating assertive and talkative members to receive all the attention. As soon as group members are able to carry any part of this responsibility, the worker encourages the discussion leadership to begin to rest in the group members and then assumes the enabler role.

## Actions to Resolve Conflict

For many people conflict is frightening. There is a feeling that disagreements can lead to fighting, and the fear of uncontrolled fighting explains, in part, the fear of conflict. Other people believe that conflict can result in nothing positive and thus attempt to avoid it. Conflict does not need to result in uncontrolled fighting. It can lead to the development of new ways of functioning that give rise to new ideas.

Conflict is to be expected when people of different backgrounds and differing experiences interact with one another. Conflict in small groups is not to be avoided; it is to be managed. Differences about what the task and function of the group is, who will fill roles, and what the norms of the group will be should be discussed and negotiated. Negotiation is a process in which all parties to a conflict state their points of view and the reasons for them. These points of view are then examined to discover if there is any faulty thinking and if there are any aspects the parties are willing to accommodate; attempts are then made to reconcile the disagreement. Often, faulty communication is a part of the disagreement. Usually, each point of view has something that can contribute to the work of the group. Conflict is not to be avoided but rather to be brought into the open and dealt with by the group.

Following are some aids to the resolution of conflict:

1. Define the conflict not as one person's problem but as the group's concern.
2. Listen to all points of view and seek to identify similarities as well as differences among them.
3. Seek clarification so that each point of view is fully understood.
4. Try to avoid win-or-lose solutions.
5. Do not ignore cues that conflict exists; check them out.
6. Work for a cooperative rather than a competitive climate.

Because social workers have skills in understanding people and their behavior, the worker can help the group recognize conflict. The recognition of conflict is the first step toward its management and resolution. When conflict is not recognized, it can be most destructive to the group's interaction.

## Actions to Enhance Group Interaction

Four factors are particularly helpful in enhancing interaction to enable the group to reach its goals and to carry out its tasks or functions: (1) member involvement; (2) decision making about norms, goals, and roles; (3) group discussion skills; and (4) structuring of meetings.

*Member involvement* is a prerequisite to effective decision making and problem solving. The climate of the group is a major contributor to member involvement. The ideal group climate encourages participation; is friendly and accepting; and is supportive of, and sensitive to, the needs of individual members. The group climate is one in which effectiveness is expected and self-actualization and innovation are encouraged. There is a stress on inclusion and trust. Members seek to collaborate with one another. The ideal group distributes influence and power among the members rather than relying on an authoritarian power figure. Influence and power rest in the knowledge and skills of the members. Conflict is not suppressed but is dealt with in the discussion process. Members engage in periodic evaluation of the work of the group.

A troublesome area in relation to involvement is bringing a new group member on board. An effective group does this in an organized manner so that the new member understands how the group functions, what its goals are, and what is expected of the new member. The new member needs time to get to know the group and its members, and the group needs time to get to know the new member.

A second contributor to effective functioning is the *decision-making process*. In making decisions about norms, goals, and roles, it is important that all members be involved in the process and that consensus be reached whenever possible. Not all group decisions must be made in this way. An alternative is the democratic process. However, this generally means that a minority will not have their way. For significant decisions or decision making over time, care needs to be taken to include members in decision making so members are not left out. After norms and goals are set, some decisions may be made by individual members with permission from the group.

The process of developing norms is known as **norming**—the process by which implicit norms or expected ways of behaving are made explicit. The norms are examined to discover if they are appropriate to the task. Periodically, the norms should be evaluated to determine their usefulness. Changes are made in the norms as necessary. Norms that are most useful to group functioning are those that allow recognition in decision making and that support individuals and the cohesiveness of the group. Another important norm is that feelings are valid information.

The *development of goals* is another shared responsibility. Goals should be clear to, and accepted by, all group members. Whenever possible, a match should be sought between individual and group goals. Goals should not be imposed on the group. It is helpful if the goals are prioritized.

*Role definition* also belongs to the total group. No member should automatically take on a specific role without permission from the group. Messages should be clear to all members about the acceptability of members filling roles. A conflict over roles—the desire of two or more persons to fill the same role—should be openly negotiated and alternatives sought. Compromise is an appropriate mechanism in resolving role conflict. No one person should have a role overload, that is, be filling too many of the needed roles. One means of encouraging participation is to spread the roles among the members. Periodic evaluation to determine how roles are filled is helpful.

A third characteristic of good group functioning is *group discussion skill*. Group discussion is to the small group what interviewing is to the one-to-one action system: a means of structuring communication. One definition of group discussion is "two or more people talking with one another in order to achieve mutually satisfactory understanding of each other's images or beliefs or a solution to a problem."[6] Cooperative interaction is influenced by each individual's perception of the topic under discussion and the group process. Two factors are particularly important for good group discussion: good communication and the use of the change process as a guide to group thinking.

Good communication calls for skill in sending messages and receiving messages so that all can know what is happening. No one person monopolizes the conversation. The feedback is:

1. Descriptive rather than evaluative
2. Specific rather than general
3. Considerate of the needs of all persons involved
4. Directed toward that which the receiver has control over
5. Well timed

## Actions to Facilitate Group Development

When a social worker works with a group of unrelated people, the focus is on group interaction. Because the system may not have formed, in the early stages the worker may be involved in interaction that enables the group system to form. Again, the interactions are to enable individuals to become part of the group and to function in the group. The major focus is on group interaction, not on worker–individual member interaction; otherwise, the worker is not working with the group system but with individuals in the presence of other individuals.

The worker influences the group process in several ways, including:

**1.** *Acceptance*—The worker accepts individual members with their feelings, attitudes, ideas, and behaviors. Through such acceptance, other members come to see the member's contribution, realize that their feelings can be respected, and appreciate difference. In being accepted by the worker, group members gain strength to carry out their roles in the group.

**2.** *Relationships*—The worker helps each group member relate to other members and gain interactional skill. The worker also uses relationship to help members find their commonalities.

**3.** *Enabling and supporting*—The worker helps members accept themselves and others, express themselves, have a feeling of accomplishment, and involve themselves in the activity and decision making of the group. In addition, the worker helps the group and its members gain understanding of their group process and how it may be modified. The worker contributes facts and understanding that enable the group to function.

**4.** *Limiting behavior*—When behavior of individual members is harmful to themselves or to others or is destructive of property or relationships, the worker helps the group or the individual member to limit such behavior.

**5.** *Guiding*—The worker helps the group by providing guidance for the discussion process, such as helping the group keep on focus or task, and teaching effective decision-making and planning skills. The worker also guides the activity and the movement of the group in its process.

**6.** *Alleviation*—The worker relieves tensions, conflicts, fears, anxiety, or guilt that may be interfering with group functioning.

**7.** *Interpreting*—The worker helps the group understand the function of the agency and of the worker in relation to the group's task. The worker may also interpret the meaning of the feelings or actions of the group or its members.

**8.** *Observation and evaluation*—The worker constantly tries to understand what is happening in the group and why it is happening.

**9.** *Planning and preparation*—The worker plans for the group as needed to enable the group to function and carry out its purposes.[7]

Throughout the process, the worker helps the group members to identify strengths in themselves and in their ecosystem. The worker facilitates the ability of members to assist one another in identifying these strengths. Thus, the role of the worker is to help the members reach out to one another in such a way that they can help one another in meeting their needs or in some way influencing their environment so that group and individual needs are met. Helping the group as a system to carry out its task is the focus of the social worker when working with a multiclient system.

The social worker's role is influenced by the stage of group development and by the stage of individual development of group members. During the orientation stage the worker is very active with the group. The worker helps group members to share their needs and concerns; structures group meetings so the members can get a vision of how the group can function; enables group members to maintain distance while making decisions about the group and their role in the group; and attempts to maintain a comfortable, accepting climate.

As the group moves to the authority stage, the worker allows members to challenge ideas and ways of functioning. The worker helps members recognize and deal with conflict. The worker supports the group and its members as they struggle to find ways to work together.

As the group begins to negotiate differences, the worker supports this negotiation and continues to assist the group in dealing with conflict. The group is helped to identify norms and values, establish goals, and negotiate roles. The worker clarifies feelings and ideas.

In the functional stage, the worker allows the group to function as independently as possible. The worker serves as a resource person and as an observer and helps the group evaluate its process. During this stage the worker's contribution to the group's process and work depends on what will be useful as the group engages in its work together.

When a worker senses the onset of disintegration, a decision should be made with the group about whether the group has served its purpose; then the disintegration should be allowed to progress or an attempt should be made to help the group reverse the disintegration. If the decision is to reverse, the worker's role is to help the group determine the reasons for the disintegration and take the steps needed to restore the group to an appropriate level of functioning. A change process is used with the group. If the group has served its purpose, then the worker helps the group understand what is happening and feel good about the group's accomplishments.

### Actions to Structure Group Activities

The group can be enabled to function through the use of activity. Activity can be tasks the group does together, such as games, crafts, or other program materials, or it can be structured exercises. The way in which a worker structures these activities can affect the group's development. Activity can also give the group data on which to make decisions about its functioning. Another part of structuring is the use of the physical facility and the time and place of the meeting.

When working with the multiperson client, the worker has four primary tools: (1) the worker and the way he uses self, (2) the use of group process, (3) discussion as a means of communication, and (4) structure and activity. Through the use of these tools the worker enables the group to function and carry out the tasks that lead to goal fulfillment.

The generalist social worker's interactive repertoire includes skill in working with small groups as well as in one-to-one interaction. To develop this skill, the worker needs knowledge of group process and means for enabling the functioning of the multiperson client group.

## Evaluation and Termination with Small Groups

Evaluation takes place throughout the work with the group and on completion of either group or individual plans. The evaluation process includes evaluating the functioning of the group and of individual members. In evaluating the functioning of the group, the worker considers the stages of group development to determine if the group is functioning in a manner that reflects the appropriate stage. She evaluates progress toward group and individual goals. In some groups, members leave after completing their work. In these groups, individual evaluation of progress and of completion of plans is necessary. For time-limited groups in which everyone terminates at the same time, the worker asks for feedback about the experience.

Successful termination in small groups depends on whether the group is an ongoing group or one that is time limited. If an individual is leaving, as in the case of an ongoing group, the individual may have ambivalent feelings. He may feel good about achieving his goals but sad at the prospect of leaving those who have assisted him. The degree to which the group has been cohesive represents a bond or a sense of belonging that is now being left behind. This may be similar to what young adults feel when they become emancipated. Termination by an individual is a reminder for everyone in the group that some day they will also leave or that the group may come to an end. Each member wonders when termination will happen for them. Some may be spurred on to achieve their goals. Others may shrink from the prospect and even regress out of fear or anxiety.

Termination for individuals leaving an ongoing group may include some kind of graduation ceremony, certificate, and/or ritual. At the least, a member needs to be able to say his good-byes so that he can go on with his own work. This is also essential for the group to become ready for the new members who will follow. Members should be encouraged to allow for two or three sessions before finalizing their termination from the group. If members drop out without notice or suddenly announce their termination, the remaining members may need time to work out their feelings before they can trust one another again or are ready for a new member.

In time-limited groups, termination is an issue from beginning to end, and members choose how much to invest themselves based on this fact. Those who remain with the group will experience termination together. Often, a celebration or graduation should be planned to mark the occasion and to highlight the success of the group and its members. For some groups, certificates of achievement may be appropriate. At the least, members should be given an opportunity to express their feelings about the group experience.

In both types of groups, members may drop out prematurely. When this occurs, the worker should contact those members to see if they will return to the group. The worker may be called on to help overcome a barrier or to negotiate a problem between the absent member and the group or one of the other members. If a member cannot be convinced to return or if a return is not appropriate, the worker should arrange for alternate services. Since the group has invested time and energy in the absent member, they need feedback after the follow-up contact.

## Summary

Multiperson interaction is an important generalist social work activity. To be effective in multiperson interaction, a social worker should understand the small group as a social system. Understanding the structure, functioning, and development of the group gives the worker direction for effective interaction. The purpose of the group affects the nature of the group, including groups for the purposes of change, growth and skill development, support, and prevention, among others. There are two types of assessment of groups: product and process.

Social workers work with small groups to carry out tasks and to serve clients. They can enable these groups to function by (1) helping all group members participate in the group, (2) clarifying the decision-making process, (3) stimulating the discussion process, and (4) structuring group meetings.

Generalist social workers work with multiperson clients to enable the system to function. In doing this, the social worker helps groups to form and uses group discussion techniques and activities to facilitate group functioning. The direct practice actions that a social worker uses to work with small groups are self, group process, discussion, and activities.

Planning and evaluation and termination are important processes at the beginning and ending of work with groups.

CASE **4.1**

## Session Summary of a Group of Delinquent Boys in a Group Home

January 18: Today was Deandre's first day in group, replacing another member, Frank. While Deandre had met everyone earlier, the group spent some time telling him why they were in placement, what they were working on, and where they were at in terms of progressing through the program. When asked about his situation, he bragged about working as a guard in a drug house and about how he and another boy had shot up a guy's car. Reggie challenged him on this and asked Deandre where that had gotten him. Deandre tried to act tough by saying that it didn't bother him to have to do some time. Jose asked him what would have happened if he had

killed the guy. Deandre admitted that he could have faced life in prison. When asked by Reggie if that would have been worth the twenty dollars the man owed, Deandre was very quiet. He did not say very much for the rest of the session. The group then spent some time discussing their last community service project, which was singing Christmas carols at some nursing homes and at an activity center for developmentally disabled adults. They decided that they wanted to do something at one of the local nursing homes for Easter but would also like to follow up with the developmentally disabled adults, especially when the weather got better.

CASE **4.2**

## Group of Delinquent Boys in a Group Home

I. Structure

  A. Boundary

    1. **Purpose:** The boys in the group have all been placed in the group home by juvenile courts. Each boy has a history of mainly property crimes or involvement with drugs. The purpose of the group is to work on the life skills needed to resolve situations that are barriers to success at home, at school, and in the community. The group plans and carries out community service projects.

    2. **Group members:** There are six members in the group.

      Reggie is a sixteen-year-old African American who has been in the home for eleven months and is nearing discharge. Reggie was living on the street before being sent to the home and had a series of theft and drug possession charges. He claims that his mother's live-in boyfriend was abusive toward him so he left home. He is uncertain where he will go after discharge, but he is hoping that his grandparents might agree to take him.

      Isiah is a fifteen-year-old African American who has been in the home for eleven months and is also nearing discharge. Isiah had a long history of delinquency, including burglary and drugs. He and his two older half-sisters were raised by his grandmother.

      Jose is a sixteen-year-old Mexican American who has been in the home for eight months. He was sent there for assault and car theft, which he committed with members of a gang. His girlfriend was pregnant when he was placed and has since given birth to a boy. Jose wants to marry her when he leaves and get a job.

Gary is a fourteen-year-old Caucasian who has been in the home for three months. He was sent by the court for a series of burglaries, which he committed with a group of friends. His parents are divorced and have married other partners.

Eddie is a fourteen-year-old Caucasian who has been in the home for three months. He is the youngest of six children and was sent to the home for a series of car thefts.

Deandre is a fourteen-year-old African American who has been in the home for a month after he was caught working in a drug house as a guard. Deandre had run away from home after being released on probation from the youth home.

3. **Why these boys constitute a group:** This is a nonvoluntary group that is a part of the boys' rehabilitation program. Failure to complete the program will likely mean placement at the state boys' training school or some restricted setting. The boys will not leave the group until they are discharged.

4. **History of the group:** The group is an ongoing group based on admission and discharge from the program. The group must unanimously recommend members for discharge. Candidates must present a thorough assessment of the difficulties that resulted in their placement, an assessment of their strengths and challenges, and a comprehensive discharge plan that includes a place to live and educational, vocational, and community service plans. The group meets daily Monday through Saturday. The current group membership has been together for a month since Deandre arrived.

5. **Workers and the group:** The workers are two social workers who facilitate the group either jointly or on a rotating basis to cover Saturdays. The workers in this group have a combination of A and B characteristics (see Maier's typology). They are definitely in a professional role, which would be Type A, but they allow the group to do much of the work. They also spend a great deal of time with the boys outside of the group, especially with community service projects, family work, and individual counseling sessions. This makes them more Type B in the group members' view of them.

6. **Environmental influences:** Group members have what amounts to two ecosystems: the one they left when they were removed from their families and the one they share with each other in the group home. Since most of their time is spent together in the group, they share many of the same experiences with the environment. The situation is somewhat different at school, since they attend either the middle school or the high school and have different classes. The group home has been operating for ten years, and the local community has become accustomed to it. The community service projects that the group undertakes have had a very positive influence, but the boys are still seen as outsiders and regarded warily by some parts of the community since they are delinquents. The local Boys and Girls Club has welcomed them, and the group members have established a relationship with the YMCA. Some of the boys participate in athletics and clubs at school.

7. **Meeting arrangements:** The group meets in the living room daily from Monday through Saturday after dinner for ninety minutes.

8. **Openness/closedness:** The group has a closed boundary, since membership is determined by admission and discharge from the program.

B. Relationship framework

1. **Ranking:** There is no rating and ranking in this group. All are seen as equal, and ideas from all are accepted. However, boys who are preparing for discharge are expected to take a positive leadership role to demonstrate their readiness for life outside of the home.

2. **Sociogram:** (See Figure 4.1.) It should be noted that there is a generally positive relationship among all group members but that there is a tendency for the boys to pair up based on race or ethnicity and age.

*(continued)*

C A S E  **4.2**  **Continued**

3. **Roles:** Reggie is the organizer and a natural leader in the group. He is serious and reminds everyone of their responsibilities when they forget and is also most active in organizing community service projects. In the meetings, he is quick to point out unsuccessful behaviors in group members and participates in finding positive alternatives.

Isiah is probably the most popular member. He is very humorous and always seems to have a smile on his face. Sometimes his humor takes the group away from their task, but he is also very adept at pointing out difficulties in a humorous way that seems to put members more at ease in terms of accepting responsibility.

Jose is a listener. He makes his contribution by working on his own agenda but sharing his work with the group for their comments. In some ways he models for the rest of the group the work to be done in that he is making an effort to take the responsibility that parenthood has thrust on him.

Gary is a follower who seems to be willing to go along with whatever the group wants. Recently, however, he has been distracting the group at times from their task by making funny sounds or changing the subject. While this is a blocking activity, it seems like it is a sign that his individuality is coming out. It also seems to relate to subjects with which he may be uncomfortable.

Eddie is a questioner. He often seems to be stalling group discussion, but what he is really doing is asking the group for some direction and at times this helps the group to look at itself and how it is functioning.

Deandre is still being rebellious by challenging positive activities in the group and refusing to accept responsibility for his actions. He has not found a positive role with the group as yet and feels like he is being picked on.

C. Bond

1. **What it is:** The commonality of their situation of being adolescent boys living together in a group home is a major component of the bond. The desire to return home is of major importance. They must have approval from all of the members of the group before a release goes to the staff for approval.

2. **Climate:** The climate is most comfortable when planning a project or an outing in which everyone participates. It is less comfortable when the group is working on life skills, especially when an unsuccessful behavior or attitude has been identified in a member.

3. **Goals of the group:** The group goal is for each member to learn to make successful decisions that result in positive life outcomes. This includes learning life skills such as social skills, conflict resolution, decision making, planning, and personal and social responsibility.

4. **Norms of the group:** Most group norms are explicit in terms of the program and the expectations for individual and group behavior. The norms of the group are that members must attend all meetings, which last an hour and a half; members must be on time; the material discussed is confidential and must not be discussed elsewhere; the group will spend part of the time focusing on individual situations and part of the time planning group projects or outings.

5. **Priority of the group:** Group members give high priority to the group, since it is important to their success in the program and their eventual discharge.

II. Functioning

A. Balance/stability

1. **Adaptation:** Recently, the group has not had a stable environment and stable membership due to turnover. The most recent member, Deandre, took the place of a member who was removed by the court when he eloped, broke into a house, and stole a car. Deandre is having some difficulties in

adjusting to placement. Before that time there had been several successful discharges. The group spent a lot of time discussing its most recent failure, and this seems to have helped it to regain some stability. Most of the boys were able to admit that they had thought of doing the same thing when things got tough or they were homesick. Thus, they seem to have been able to turn a negative into something positive. Members have been very patient with Deandre and seem determined to help him to become part of the group.

    2. **Maintenance vs. task:** During the first meeting with Deandre, the group spent considerable time on maintenance. There was much discussion as to how the group works together. A contract was developed detailing some of the work to be done with Deandre. This is still in progress. For most meetings, minimal time is spent on group maintenance, since the group meets so frequently. At the beginning or end of each meeting, there is some discussion about projects and how well the group is fulfilling its contract with one another. As the group is working well together, the balance is appropriate.

**B.** Decision making

    1. **Method:** Decisions are made by consensus. For example, when discussing projects or outings, members discuss several possibilities and, as a group, decide on the specific plans.

    2. **Problem solving:** Problems tend to relate to a particular group member's struggle to make successful decisions. The pattern is for members to throw out ideas as to possible solutions and then together consider each solution. Group solutions are implemented after consensual decision making.

    3. **Leadership:** Reggie and Isiah tend to share the leadership role. Both tend to be facilitative leaders. At times Jose calls for the worker to take this role by asking the worker to be more directive and tell them what to do.

    4. **Influence on decision making:** Group members all have influence on the decisions through their contributions to discussion. Reggie and Isiah seem to have the most influence because of the quality of their contributions.

    5. **Conflict:** Conflict is either denied by group members or is taken as a challenge. The worker notes that when group members recognize a conflict, they tend to ask for input from him about a decision or task. They refuse to recognize this as a mechanism of avoiding conflict, even when this is pointed out by the worker. However, after this denial, they work as a group in a problem-solving mode to resolve the differences.

**C.** Communication

    1. **Patterns:** The group gives each person an opportunity to discuss each issue. There are some blocks, as mentioned above. Older or more veteran group members are aware of the communication process and of the need for listening as well as talking. Occasionally, newer or younger members will get into a side conversation. Other members will call attention to this, which ends the intrusion into the work of the group.

    2. **Feedback:** The veteran group members often ask each other for feedback. Newer members do not solicit feedback but are given it by veteran members.

    3. **Opportunity:** Each group member is encouraged to add his thinking to the group discussion. If one member gets off on a tangent and holds the floor too long, someone steps in and brings the discussion back to the subject.

    4. **Troublesome content areas:** Personal responsibility is the biggest trouble area for the group. The older, veteran members have come to realize the importance of this area, not only for graduating from the program, but also for life afterward. Newer and younger members are very evasive and much more willing to blame others for any difficulties.

    5. **Cross-cultural factors:** There is a tendency for the group to pair up by race and ethnicity. Much of this has been reduced by sharing experiences with one another. Members seem to have

*(continued)*

CASE **4.2** **Continued**

come to the realization that underneath their skin, they are all human beings. However, there is still some separation that appears in the group.

**D.** Task implementation

    **1. How tasks are carried out:** Projects and outings seem to bring about the most enthusiasm. Discussing personal responsibility is usually met by some denial, with more veteran members moving quickly to acceptance. The group tends to get down to business on its own unless there has been a recent conflict. Discussing chores and daily living concerns generates a lot of complaints initially, but the group tends to find ways of resolving issues without too much intervention from the workers.

    **2. Blocking tactics:** Denial is a primary blocking tactic that all members use at some time. Newer members use it frequently. Deandre's rebelliousness and Gary's distractions are blocking tactics, but are predictable, given their circumstances.

**III.** Development

    **A. Stage:** The group demonstrates elements of various stages depending on the circumstances. With the recent addition of a new member, there has been some orientation and authority stage elements when working with Deandre. Overall, it seems to be primarily in the negotiation and functional stages, with newer members setting goals and veteran members fulfilling goals.

    **B. Inhibiting factors:** Denial and projection have been such basic defense mechanisms for members for so long that it is very difficult to give these up. Veteran members do so fairly quickly, but these responses still occur as an initial reaction to most difficulties.

**IV.** Strengths and challenges

    **A. Strengths:** The group is self-organized with well-focused tasks, especially with projects. The relationship framework, bond, decision-making process, and use of the problem-solving process are all very functional for the group tasks.

    **B. Challenges:** The group itself is functioning well; however, individual members face obstacles to success, especially when they return home. The immaturity of younger members is frustrating for those who are approaching graduation.

---

## QUESTIONS

**1.** Using the schema for study of a small group, describe a group in which you have participated. How does this help you understand what was happening in that group?

**2.** Think about groups of which you are now a part. How do you think you might enable that group to function more effectively?

**3.** Identify a conflict situation in a group with which you are familiar. What was the cause of the conflict? How did the group handle the conflict? Was there a better way to handle the conflict?

**4.** How would you justify to an agency administrator the amount of time needed for good group formation?

# SUGGESTED READINGS

Edwards, Richard L., Ed. *Encyclopedia of Social Work,* 19th ed. Washington, DC: NASW Press, 1995 ("Group Practice Overview").

Gitterman, Alex, and Shulman, Lawrence. *Mutual Aid Groups, Vulnerable and Resilient Populations, and the Life Cycle,* 3rd ed. New York: Columbia University Press, 2005.

Grief, Geoffrey, and Ephross, Paul, Eds. *Group Work with Populations at Risk,* 2nd ed. New York: Oxford University Press, 2005.

Haslett, Diane C. *Group Work Activities in Generalist Practice,* Belmont, CA: Thomson-Brooks/Cole, 2005.

Jacobs, Ed, Masson, Robert, and Harvill, Riley. *Group Counseling Strategies and Skills*, 6th ed. Pacific Grove, CA: Brooks/Cole, 2009.

Johnson, David W., and Johnson, Frank P. *Joining Together: Group Theory and Group Skills*, 9th ed. Boston: Allyn and Bacon, 2006.

Kottler, Jeffery. *Learning Group Leadership: An Experiential Approach*, Boston: Allyn & Bacon, 2001.

Maier, Henry W. "Models of Intervention in Work with Groups: Which One Is Yours?" *Social Work with Groups,* 4 (Fall/Winter 1981): 21–34.

Northern, Helen, and Kurland, Roselle. *Social Work with Groups,* 3rd ed. New York: Columbia University Press, 2001.

Shulman, Lawrence. *The Skills of Helping: Individuals, Families, Groups, and Communities,* 6th ed. Belmont, CA: Thomson-Brooks/Cole, 2009.

Toseland, Ronald W., and Rivas, Robert F. *An Introduction to Group Work Practice,* 6th ed. Boston: Allyn & Bacon, 2009.

# 5 Interaction and Engagement with Groups

## LEARNING EXPECTATIONS

1. Understanding the action system as one context for generalist practice with groups.
2. Understanding the concept of engagement and relationship and of their importance in generalist practice with groups.
3. Understanding the specific characteristics of a professional relationship.
4. Appreciation of the complexity of cross-cultural relationships in generalist practice with groups.
5. Knowledge about conducting group sessions.

Social work practice takes place in an interpersonal interactional process. This interaction is more than an exchange between a worker and group members; the worker also interacts with colleagues, community persons, professionals, and people who are significant to the helping situation (significant others). The interaction can be one-to-one; between the worker and another person; or it can take place in multiperson situations such as a family, a team, or a small group. Although there are similarities between the process of interaction of one individual to another and the process of interaction with multiperson systems, there are also differences. This chapter focuses on the interaction of the social worker with group members and on group interaction. The social work interaction may take place with individual group members or with members of systems in the environment. For learning purposes, the focus is on interactions within problem-solving, decision-making, and counseling groups. Interactions in growth and development, support, prevention, and task groups may be similar but often have a different purpose, may be less intense, or have different content. However, the development of good communication is frequently a primary or secondary purpose in these other groups. In addition, group work relies on good relationship skills and so skill building and facilitating positive interactions are mainstays in working with groups.

In an ecosystems strengths approach with problem-solving, decision-making, and counseling groups, the work that is done by the worker and the group may involve other parts of the group's ecosystem and that of individual group members or the worker's ecosystem. In most cases, the work is done within the group with the expectation that it will be manifested in relationships outside of the group. Thus, in most cases group members use the strengths and resources available in their ecosystem. This approach empowers the group and its members to take control of their lives and get their needs met while meeting the needs of others in the environment. In some cases, the worker may need to assist group members in developing skills. When members are unable to mobilize resources or there is a major obstacle to doing so, the member and the worker may decide that the worker should intervene more directly either with or on behalf of the member. Most of the skills covered in this chapter are important to the functioning of the group and its members both within the group and in interactions outside of the group. Because the interactions within the group make up the core of social work with groups, it receives primary focus; however, interactions with members of the various ecosystems is also discussed. Much of the knowledge base relative to interaction also applies to the interactions that a worker has with other persons.

As discussed in Chapter 2, in an ecosystems approach to working with groups there is an emphasis on the interactions and transactions that take place among systems and subsystems. Figure 5.1 can be used to depict the transactional nature of an ecosystem. Transactions between people and within an ecosystem can influence the feelings, thoughts, and actions of people and systems and can also be influenced by the feelings, thoughts, and actions of other people and systems. In developing an understanding of the environment as an ecosystem, the worker seeks to understand the feelings, thoughts, and actions of people, the human systems in the ecosystem, and the transactions within the ecosystem as well as to understand the effects of diversity on the ecosystem. The group or group members are considered part of the ecosystem, and matter, energy, and information are exchanged among various systems that make up the ecosystem. When there is **congruity** or balance in

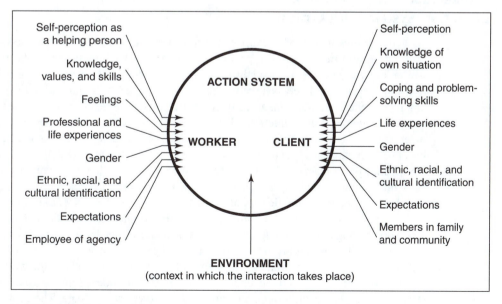

**FIGURE 5.1   Relationship.**

these exchanges, all of the systems function in a manner that results in needs being met for the group and its members and for other systems in their ecosystem. However, when there is an unmet need, there is imbalance or **incongruity** in the ecosystem. The work of the social worker and the group focuses on restoring balance or developing a new balance. This does not necessarily mean that fundamental changes will be needed in group members or in systems in the environment. Instead, the emphasis is on bringing about a change in the interactions and transactions among systems. This approach is more realistic than approaches that hope to restructure or change a persons's personality or change the basic structure and functioning of a system, an organization, or a community.

Much of the work in groups represent exchanges of information. This includes information that flows among group members, from group members to worker, from worker to group members, from group members to other systems in their ecosystem, from worker to other systems in the group's or group member's ecosystems, and from worker to other work-related systems in her ecosystem. The purpose of exchanging information is to influence growth and change in various parts of the ecosystem with the purpose of meeting needs and restoring balance. Much of this process involves changing interactions.

Since the exchange of information is the focus of most of the social work endeavor, especially in groups, issues that are important in understanding interactions are (1) engagement and formation of an action system, (2) the nature of relationship, and (3) communication. Techniques to enhance relationship and communications are also important, as they can improve the quality of interactions. As discussed earlier, the worker striving to become diversity competent uses naturalistic inquiry and inductive learning regarding culture and diversity as she facilitates building relationships within the group and proceeds through the phases of the change process.

## Engagement and Formation of an Action System with Groups

An **action system** is formed because of the work to be done and because the tasks to be carried out require more than one person. In order for an action system to be formed, the worker must engage the group and its members. **Engagement** occurs when a helping relationship is established between the worker and group members and within the group itself among members. In addition, an ecosystem strengths approach is based on the theory that needs are met through interaction. Group members work together to accomplish a task or meet goals or achieve the purpose of the group. The worker collaborates with a colleague because each may have special areas of expertise relative to the work at hand or because the worker may profit from another view of the situation. The worker and group members interact with one another when they have some information needed for helping the group or a member or when they provide support or information about resources to meet needs.

In group interaction, the efforts of all parties are necessary in the helping endeavor. The worker brings to the interaction a professional knowledge base and a professional set of values and skills for helping. The worker also brings the total self, finely tuned, to be used with the group as is appropriate to the needs of the helping situation and the worker's capacity. The worker brings skill in understanding situations, identifying needs, focusing on strengths, facilitating the group, and facilitating growth and change. The group members bring needs, a perception of the situation, life experiences that influence this perception, and capacity for growth and change. Group members also bring motivational forces for work in meeting needs or for bringing about change. In the work to be done, the roles of the worker and of the group and its members emerge from what each brings to the interaction.

The first encounter is crucial in forming the action system, since it determines much that will happen in subsequent sessions. The nature of the interaction, its kind and quality, begins to form at this point. At times, the first encounter takes place between a prospective group member and the worker outside of the group or before the group is formed. At other times, the first encounter occurs during the group. When the group is time limited or is just beginning, the first group session may be the first encounter. At the very least it is generally the first encounter for group members with each other. When the group is ongoing, the new group member may have encountered the worker beforehand, but in some groups this may not be the case. The prospective or new group member will be making decisions about whether the group can provide the needed help, can be trusted, and has the capacity to understand his situation.

Typically the initial contact takes place either as a result of a referral or recruitment. Referrals can come from almost anyone, but most often they come from other professionals either within the agency or from other agencies. Self-referral may also occur. An important task for most group workers is to recruit group members. This can be done either formally or informally. Formal recruitment involves advertising or distributing information about the group. Informal recruitment is mainly by word of mouth. (Recruitment and referral are covered in later chapters under planning for groups.) At some point during the first encounter, either with the worker or the group, prospective or new members will need to decide if they will join the group.

Social workers disagree about whether new workers should read records of a previous worker before meeting the prospective group member. Records may present stereotypes or invalid assumptions that can color the thinking of the new worker. They may focus on problems or deficits rather than strengths and resources. But if records can be read with an open mind and an eye for facts, they can be good preparation for deciding on the appropriateness of group work.

In preparation for the first contact, the worker may decide to collect and review any available information to determine what is known about the prospective or new group member. Consideration of the person's ability to relate and participate are important, as is matching needs with the purpose of the group. Other factors, such as age, developmental level, and diversity, may be important. A general rule to follow when working with voluntary groups is to ask new members at some time during the first group session whether they will return to the group. The worker needs to structure activities that will facilitate a positive answer to this question. (Preparation for the group and considerations regarding membership are covered in later chapters.) If new members return for another session, it is a good sign that they may be engaged and committed. If they return for a third, it is a virtual certainty.

Another type of action system that social workers are often involved in is one made up of a social worker and a person who is not a client or group member. This is a common arrangement when using an ecosystems strengths approach, since mobilizing potential resources and changing interactions and transactions are the focus of the work. The nonclient is generally a member of the family's ecosystem or a significant other in a family member's life, a resource provider, or an individual who is or could be involved in a helping endeavor. In utilizing an ecosystems approach, the worker uses resources in the community and within her work-related ecosystem. In this case, the nonclient might be another service provider, a community influential, a person who is or could be involved in action plans focused on community or organizational change, or a person whom the worker is seeking to educate about some aspect of service delivery or the social welfare system.

Although worker–nonclient relationships are somewhat different, the worker still must pay attention to the formation of the action system. The same principles apply to these systems as apply to worker–client systems. If a worker uses the process of precontact, exploration, negotiation, and agreement, both parties are more aware of the reason for working together and of the responsibility of each party for that work. Nonclient individuals may also display resistance. Exploration of the resistance is a first step in overcoming it and in deciding if it is possible to form a functional action system. A positive, strengths-based approach tends to result in less resistance than an approach that focuses on deficits or problems.

## Relationships and Groups

**Relationship** is the cohesive quality of the group and is the primary means by which groups meet needs and facilitate change or accomplish tasks. It is the product of interaction between two or more persons. *Relationship* is a term of considerable historical significance in social work practice. It has often been expressed as "good rapport" or engagement with the client system when viewed from the perspective of worker–client interaction. The development of a good relationship has been seen as a necessary ingredient of the helping endeavor. Helen Harris Perlman has provided a description of relationship and its importance: "Relationship is a catalyst, an enabling dynamism in the support, nurture and freeing of people's energies and motivation toward problem solving and the use of help."[1] In her view, relationship is an emotional bond and is the means for humanizing help. Further, she stated, "'Good' relationship is held to be so in that it provides stimulus and nurture. . . . [It] respects and nourishes the self-hood of the other. . . . [It] provides a sense of security and at-oneness."[2] These concepts also apply to relationships among group members. In groups in which the purpose is to meet needs through mutual aid, developing relationships is critical to help being given and received. For groups in which the purpose is to gain a benefit through participation, bonding and commonality are established through relationships. This is also a critical factor in support and self-help groups. In task groups, relationships provide the vehicle by which the group accomplishes tasks and achieves its goals.

The social work relationship is both a professional and a helping relationship. A **professional relationship** is one in which there is an agreed-on purpose; one that has a specific time frame; one in which the worker devotes self to the interests of the client system; and one that carries the authority of specialized knowledge, a professional code of ethics, and specialized skill. In addition, a professional relationship is controlled in that the worker attempts to maintain objectivity toward the work at hand and to be aware and in charge of her own feelings, reactions, and impulses.[3]

## The Helping Relationship with Groups

A great deal has been written about the nature of *helping relationships*.[4] The characteristics that appear most often in these discussions include the following:

**1.** *Concern for others*—An attitude that reflects warmth, sincere liking, friendliness, support, and an interest in the client. It communicates a real desire to understand person in situation.

**2.** *Commitment and obligation*—A sense of responsibility for the helping situation. Dependability and consistency are also involved. The worker must have a willingness to enter into the world of others, with its hurts and joys, its frustrations and commitments.

**3.** *Acceptance*—A nonjudgmental, noncritical attitude on the part of the worker, as well as a realistic trust of the client and respect for the client's feelings. Belief that the client can handle her own problems and can take charge of her own life.

**4.** *Empathy*—An ability to communicate to the client that the worker cares, has concern for the client, is hearing what the client is perceiving, wants to understand, and is listening and understanding.

**5.** *Clear communication*—The capacity to communicate to the client in ways that enable the client to fully understand the message being sent.

**6.** *Genuineness*—The worker's honesty about self and his own feelings. An ability to separate the experiences and the feelings of the worker from those of the client. Genuineness on the part of the worker allows the client to become what the client wants to be. It is present when the worker's communication is understood and comfortable for the client. The worker's personal style of helping should not be an inflexible use of technique.

**7.** *Authority and power*—The expectation that the client will work to fulfill needs and responsibilities and will want to resolve the situation. This involves encouraging the client to go beyond the present level of functioning and providing guidance and resources so that goals can be reached. It involves insistence that the client do what she can for herself. The worker's knowledge and skills are a base for authority and power. The client must know that the worker's power and authority are not to be used to dominate or control her but to assist her in having her needs, and those of others around her, met in a positive, mutually beneficial manner.

**8.** *Purpose*—The helping relationship has a purpose known to, and accepted by, both worker and client. According to Beulah Compton and Burt Galaway, this is the most important characteristic of all.[5]

There is some disagreement about the place of advice giving in helping. Traditionally, social workers have thought it unhelpful to give advice; advice was seen as the worker's solution for the client and not the product of mutual problem solving and thus was not useful for the client. Clients, however, often indicate that they expect and are looking for advice.[6] Advice is tangible evidence of help. If advice is given, it should come first from the group. In some instances it may be given selectively by the worker, as a result of mutual problem solving by worker and the group or its members. Advice from the group or the worker should be presented in a nondemanding manner as something that might be tried, leaving the final decision for its use to the group member. When given in this manner, advice may well be a useful tool for helping. However, it is essential that the advice be given by the group or the worker and received by the group member in a way that ensures that the member sees it as one of several options. Generally, it is best to use advice as a last resort, when a group or one of its members is truly stuck or if the group or a member seems headed for a situation that is harmful to themselves or others or if they are overwhelmed by a crisis.

Another characteristic of the helping situation is that help can be given by group members to each other and to the worker. Group members help one another and the worker understand their situation or culture or diversity. This is help and should be recognized as such. When group members evaluate the usefulness or means of help and the appropriateness of goals, this is help. Such a view of help enables group members to see their roles as interdependent rather than as superordinal to subordinal. An interdependent relationship encourages growth rather than dependency and is more helpful.

Biestek's classic seven principles of a casework relationship and the worker's role in using each principle are one way of defining the responsibility of the social worker in a worker–client interaction or action system. His principles included: individualizing the client system; encouraging expression of feelings that is purposeful; responding to the client's feelings in a controlled and purposeful way; communicating acceptance; maintaining a nonjudgmental attitude; respecting the client's right to self determination; and preserving confidentiality.[7]

These principles can also be used to guide the worker in her relationship with the group and its members. They help promote a climate in which the group can work toward fulfilling needs. They can also be used as a model for relationships among members as they seek to establish a system of mutual aid. It is important that groups respect each member as an individual with his or her own thoughts, feelings, actions, values, beliefs, experiences, diversity, and the like. The group should encourage its members to express thoughts, feelings, and ideas and members should be expected to respond appropriately. The group should be a place where members are accepted and respected. Group members should be encouraged to be nonjudgmental as they hear each others' needs, concerns, thoughts, and feelings. The group should respect each person's right to self-determination and should preserve confidentiality for those groups in which personal information is shared within the group.

## Special Influences on the Helping Relationship

Any difference in diversity among group members and between group members and the worker has an influence on the action system's functioning. These include situations in which the worker and the group or its members come from different ethnic or racial backgrounds and those in which the gender of the worker affects the interaction with group members and the environment in which the action takes place.

Several obstacles seem to be prevalent in cross-diversity helping relationships:

**1.** *Mutual unknowingness*—Because of a lack of knowledge about the other's culture or diversity on the part of both the worker and the group, there is a tendency toward stereotyping. Fear of the other is also a result of lack of knowledge and understanding. Inappropriate "good" or "bad" judgments may be made. Social distance that does not allow for the sharing and the trust necessary in the helping endeavor is often present. Of particular importance is lack of knowledge about traditional communication patterns.

**2.** *Attitudes toward the other culture or diversity*—Negative attitudes may have developed from limited knowledge about a different culture or diverse group. These attitudes may also have developed from negative experiences with persons who belong to the same cultural or ethnic or diversity group as the person being interacted with.

**3.** *Availability of different opportunities*—Members of different cultural or diversity groups have different opportunities. When the social worker or group members do not understand this difference of opportunity, they can have unrealistic expectations about how members should use the help offered. This fact can also relate to the use of appropriate resources. Some resources are not usable for a particular diversity group. For example, a culture that does not allow expression of feeling or that uses limited verbal expression and is action oriented will have considerable difficulty with group discussion. Some resources are available to, and traditionally useful for, particular ethnic groups. For example, Native Americans traditionally use the tribe's Shaman or elders as a resource. They also have the support and financial aid resources of the Bureau of Indian Affairs.

**4.** *Conflicts between societal and cultural expectations*—These often are difficult to resolve around the helping situation. Group members may have difficulty in identifying these conflicts, and the worker may not be aware of them.

In addition, group members from various diversity groups may have a low sense of self-worth as a result of chronic and acute oppression and discrimination. This can result in low expectations for resolution of situations, in special relationship needs, and in lack of appreciation of their own diversity. There may be a different worldview, different expectations for the use of time, and different expectations of male and female behavior. These can get in the way of developing working relationships. Group members may have a low level of trust toward persons of other cultures or diversity; this may be the result of past relationships that produced pain and anger. A group member with a low level of trust may use concealment mechanisms that hinder the helping endeavor. Different mechanisms for showing respect can result in misunderstandings. Different mechanisms for expressing ideas and feelings and different communication patterns can be particularly troublesome. Ann Brownlee has identified some of the areas in which communication differences may exist in cross-cultural relationships, including situations appropriate for the communication of specific information; tempo of communication; taboos; norms for confidentiality; ways of expressing emotions, feelings, and appreciation; meaning of silence; form and content of nonverbal communication; and style of persuasion or explanation.[8] In order to work effectively in cross-cultural situations, the worker should develop an understanding of diverse needs, the complexities of cross-cultural communication, and her own biases and prejudices, and must also develop considerable skill in accurate perception and tolerance for difference. In groups, the worker encourages these same understandings within the group among members.

In using an ecosystems strengths approach, it is essential that the worker be diligent, flexible, and creative in uncovering strengths and resources within the group, its members, and their ecosystems. Contrary to its professed belief in freedom and tolerance, the United

States has a history of oppression and discrimination toward minorities, especially people of color. The basis of prejudice and discrimination is viewing other cultures as weak, inferior, and undesirable. Thus, members of the dominant culture, as well as nondominant cultures, are not accustomed to finding strengths in other cultures. In spite of the social worker's efforts to be nonjudgmental, it will be impossible to avoid all prejudice and stereotyping, since these are pervasive and embedded in the dominant culture. Even if the worker has a predisposition toward seeing strengths, it is unlikely that she will thoroughly know these strengths unless she has had considerable exposure to or has conducted research about other cultures. It is also unlikely that group members will be able to identify strengths in other members who are different from them unless they have had considerable exposure to members of that population. Nonetheless, if the worker and the group make a real effort to see strengths and positive opportunities, they can overcome the negative effects of cultural bias.

Gender is another factor that affects relationships. Social work literature contains little discussion of the influence of the worker's gender on the helping endeavor or on group interaction. There seems to be an assumption that a skilled worker should be able to work with both male and female clients. Although this is probably true, social workers should become more aware of gender factors in professional relationships and within the group. One study has found that when male and female workers make assessments about female clients, male workers see these clients as less mature and less intelligent than do female workers. Female workers see women as having greater need for emotional expression and less need of home and family involvement than do male workers.[9] Differences in perceptions between male and female social workers, then, seem to exist. These different perceptions are probably a result of sex-role socialization and can affect professional relationships.

Joanne Mermelstein and Paul Sundet have found differences in client expectations in rural areas because of gender factors. In the female worker–female client situation, the client expects nurturing, mothering, and friendship. In the female worker–male client situation, the client sees taking help from a woman as going counter to his definition of manhood. The interaction is also affected by taboos about what is to be discussed with women. In the situation of male worker and female client, the male worker is seen as performing a traditional female nurturing role. The female client expects the male worker to support her, to give her moral guidance and clear direction. In the male client–male worker situation, the male client expects the male worker to prove his masculinity.[10]

Social workers should examine the expectations for male and female behaviors from the group members' perspective and take these into consideration in developing action systems and in understanding and using relationships within these systems. Attention also must be given to the influence of gender of both worker and group members on practice, that is, on the functioning of the action system. Workers also need to develop an understanding of how their own gender expectations influence their professional relationships.

Other differences that may exist between worker and group are young workers with older group members; unmarried workers with experienced parents; well-educated, middle-class workers with illiterate, poor families; heterosexual workers with homosexual clients, or vice versa; and upright, well-behaved workers with norm violators. These and other differences all influence the functioning of the action system—the helping relationship.

Social workers have given little attention to the understanding of the relationship in an action system that does not involve a client system—for example, relationships with other professionals such as a teacher or a pastor or relationships with community leaders. Yet workers may use this type of action system in working with groups or serving individual group members, especially when using an ecosystems strengths approach. In discussing this type of system from an interactional viewpoint, Yvonne Fraley has suggested that mutual problem solving is more effective if this type of relationship is assessed using these six variables: (1) the position of the worker ("actor one")—that is, the location of actor one in an agency or community system; (2) the goal of actor one in the relationship; (3) the position of the other ("actor two"); (4) the goal of the other; (5) the form of communication being used (verbal, written, nonverbal media, etc.); and (6) the method of influence being used by each actor (problem solving, teacher–learner, helper–helpee, etc.).[11] This kind of analysis points out that in the nonclient action system, there needs to be some reason for the two actors to work together. If the goals of each are compatible, if one actor does not feel threatened by the position of the other, and if the form of communication and the method of influence are carefully chosen, there is a better chance for gaining the desired outcome.

Regardless of the nature of the action system, the characteristics of the actors (worker–group member or member–member or worker/member–other), and the situation in which the interaction is taking place, the relationship is a crucial factor in whether the work together produces the desired outcomes. Each person brings much to the group that can aid in, or detract from, relationships and the work to be done. The social worker must be aware of these factors and use them to further the work by developing functional working relationships with other people. (See Figure 5.1.)

Relationship is not the end-state goal of the helping endeavor or the group action system; it is the glue that holds the group together and so is a necessary ingredient of a well-functioning group action system. It is not a relationship in which there is no conflict and all is happiness and goodwill, nor is it an overly dependent relationship. It is a relationship in which conflict is open and examined and in which there is respect for the position of others. It is a working relationship, and the purpose of the relationship is the accomplishment of tasks needed to fulfill need and promote growth and change.

## Communication within Groups

Because effective communication is such an important ingredient of any functioning action system, it is important for all social workers to develop good communication skills. Communication is the sending and receiving of messages between two or more persons. Effective communication occurs when the persons involved in a situation accurately perceive the messages of the other person and in which the messages are sent in a way that allows the receiver to take action or respond to the sender in ways that facilitate the purposes of the communication. The purposes of communication in the social work interaction include:

1. Gathering information needed for the helping endeavor, including strengths and resources
2. Exploring ideas, feelings, and possible ways to meet need based on the strengths and resources within the group, its members, and the ecosystem

3. Expressing feelings or thoughts
4. Structuring the work of the group
5. Providing support, informing, advising, encouraging, and giving necessary directions

Communication is a process. The *sender* conceptualizes the message and through a *transmitter* (the voice or visual production) sends the message through a *channel* (sensory and modern technological means) to a *receiver* that interprets the message cognitively and affectively. This results in a *response,* another message, and/or an action. The response may result in *feedback,* a means for the sender to evaluate the effectiveness of the message. One other factor of the process is *interference* or noise. Interference consists of those influences from outside the process that affect the message while it is in the channel and cause *distortion* of the message as it reaches the receiver. (See Figure 5.2.)

Each part of the process has a particular function and special problems that can interfere with the effectiveness of the communication. The sender must conceptualize the message in a way that is understandable to the receiver. This requires understanding how the receiver deals with and interprets ideas and information. The transmission of the message takes place not only through verbalization but also through nonverbal means. Nonverbal communication takes place through vocal tone and behaviors, such as gestures, facial expression, and body position. The motivation, needs, feelings, and attitudes of the sender influence the manner in which the message is transmitted. The message has content—the specific words used—and it has meaning—how that content is treated. The choice of words, the order of ideas and words, and the use of humor and silence all contribute to the quality of the message.

Special attention needs to be paid to cultural and personal differences in the meaning of words. Different cultures can have different attitudes, values, and beliefs that influence how words are interpreted and the meaning of nonverbal communication. Beyond the cultural aspect, each of us has unique and individual life experiences. For example, take the word *mother*. For someone who has had a warm, loving relationship with his mother, the word will evoke positive feelings. However, if a person had experienced the death of his mother at an early age, the word *mother* will probably be associated with grief and loss. Even siblings can have different ideas of their mother based on their individual perceptions.

As the message travels through the channel, the possibility of distortion is great. Previous experiences, cultural and societal demands, and attitudes and feelings of the receiver

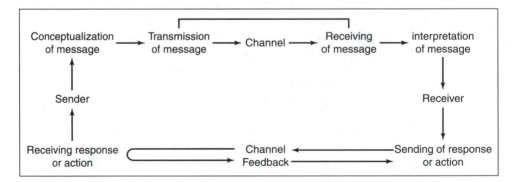

**FIGURE 5.2   Communication.**

can distort the message. Distractions such as additional stimuli, concerns, and responsibilities can distort the message. The recognition of distortion and noise is a recognition of the transactional nature of communication.

The manner in which the message is received also influences the effectiveness of the message. The receiver may perceive or interpret the message in a manner different from the intention of the sender. The receiver may not comprehend the meaning of the message as intended or may receive only a part of the message. These influences can occur between any individuals, but are especially important when communication occurs between two people who are different in terms of diversity. Feedback is the means of ascertaining if the message received and the message intended by the sender are sufficiently similar to make the communication effective. Feedback is sending a message about a received message to the sender of that message. The feedback is also subject to the problems of the original message.

Effective communication is communication in which the outcome is the accomplishment of the purpose intended by the sender. Messages that have the best chance of being effective are those in which:

1. The verbal and nonverbal messages are congruent.
2. The message is simple, specific, and intelligible to the receiver.
3. The receiver can understand what is meant by the sender.
4. There is sufficient repetition for the receiver to sense the importance of this message from among other messages being received simultaneously.
5. There has been sufficient reduction of both psychological and actual noise.
6. Feedback has been solicited from the receiver and sufficient time taken to ensure that the original message was received.

Effectiveness in communication is affected by the credibility and honesty of the sender of the message. The receiver who has reason to trust the competence and reliability of the sender will tend to be receptive to the message and its expectations. Effective communicators tune into and are sensitive to the feelings and situations of those they are communicating with. They are assertive without being overly aggressive or confrontational.

Often communication is not just with the client system but with other professionals, with significant others in the environment, or with people who may in some way be involved in situations that are blocking need fulfillment. These relationships are particularly important when the focus is on organizational or community change. The principles of communication discussed in this section apply to interactions with nonclients even though communication may be of a bargaining or adversarial nature. When social workers find themselves in situations in which the viewpoint of the other may be different from their own, clear communication is imperative. Sometimes the differences can be resolved through clarification of messages. Other times a clear understanding of the differences allows work to progress.

Brett Seabury has identified several problems that confront social workers in their communications with clients and significant others. These can also occur within the group:

1. *Double messages*—Two contradictory messages are received simultaneously or in close succession.

2. *Ambiguous messages*—These messages have little meaning or several possible messages for the receiver.

3. *Referent confusion*—The words have different meanings to each person, or they may be professional jargon not understood by the other person involved in the communication.

4. *Selective attention and interpretation*—This causes distortion of the message or confusion as to meaning.

5. *Overload*—This is the receiving of more messages than a receiver can interpret and respond to at any one time.

6. *Ritual or order incongruence*—This is the failure of the message sequence to follow expected or habitual behavioral patterns.

7. *Regulator incompatibility*—The use of eye contact and patterns of speaking and listening that regulate the communication of one party in the interchange are not known to, used by, or are unacceptable to another party in the interchange.[12]

Other barriers to effective communication are inattentiveness, assuming the understanding of meanings, and using the communication for purposes different from those of others in the interchange (having hidden agendas). Cross-cultural communication is particularly problematic because the structure of messages differs from culture to culture. Even if the same language is used, words are used differently or have different meanings. Each culture has its own idioms and expressions, and the syntax (form) of the language may be different. The differences make it difficult to listen to the messages and make the likelihood of misunderstanding great. The social worker must overcome the barriers to effective communication if the action system is to function to reach its goals. This applies to communication between the worker and individual members, between group members, or between the worker or a member and the group as a whole. The worker needs to facilitate effective communication within the group. In social work, communication is dialogue. The worker and the group openly talk together and seek mutual understanding. Floyd Matson and Ashley Montagu, in the introduction to *The Human Dialogue,* describe communication as not to "command" but to "commune" and that knowledge of the highest order (whether of the world, of oneself, or of other) is to be sought and found not through detachment but through connection, not by objectivity but by intersubjectivity, not in a state of estranged aloofness but in something resembling the act of love.[13]

This is the essence of communication in its most effective form. This kind of communication adds vitality to, nourishes, and sustains the process of working together, the interaction.

## Group Sessions

Group sessions need to have some structure if they are to be productive and conducive to achieving the goals and purpose of the group. Each group worker develops her own style in facilitating various groups. Various groups call for different styles in leading or facilitating the group. In addition, the age and developmental levels of group members affect the structure and the style of leadership or facilitation. Group leadership and facilitation is an art and a skill. A general guide to preparing for group sessions includes preparing for the session, knowing the stages of a session, and developing group facilitation skills.

More specific suggestions for group sessions for various types of groups are presented in Part Two.

Each group session should have a specific purpose or goal. Generally, this purpose is related to the overall purpose of the group and the stage of group development. It will also depend on the agency function and the group or group member's needs and the nature of the situation at hand.

## Preparing for a Group Session

In preparing for any group session the worker has three tasks: (1) planning the environment for the session, (2) planning the content of the session, and (3) "tuning in." Each of these tasks is carried out before the group session.

The worker thinks about the physical conditions of the space where the group meets. The worker arranges the space to encourage the participants to work together. This can be done by giving some thought to the placement of chairs (and tables or other furniture). A room that is comfortable and does not have too many distracting features is ideal. If the room is too small for the group to sit comfortably, the worker arranges to meet in an area that will accommodate the group while maintaining confidentiality. The worker tries to prevent interruptions such as phone calls and knocks on the door. The worker also tries to provide a place for the group where the conversation will not be overheard by others. Attention is given to the time of the interview so that group members will be able to attend regularly. The worker will think about the impact of his dress on the group. In some groups, the type of activity dictates more informal dress. Other groups might expect more formal dress such as business casual.

In planning for the content of the session, the worker will recall the goal and the purpose of the service and will identify the goal for this particular session. The tasks to be accomplished will be considered. Any additional knowledge or information needed will be obtained. The worker might review notes about the previous session if there has been one. The structure of the session and issues to be addressed will be considered. This planning is done to give form and focus to the session, but the worker is prepared to be flexible and make changes if the group or a member has unanticipated needs.

In tuning in, the worker first tries to anticipate the needs and feelings of the group and its members in the session and to think about his own response to those feelings and needs.[14] The worker tries to become aware of his own feelings and attitudes that might interfere with effective communication. Such awareness should minimize the impact of these feelings and attitudes on the group. The worker also needs to prepare to help by dealing with personal needs and any work-related attitudes that might interfere with the work of the group.

Preparation for the group session is one way to promote worker readiness, which communicates to group members that they are important and that the work to be done together is important. Worker readiness prepares the way for effective group facilitation.

## The Stages of a Group Session

All group sessions have three stages: (1) the opening or beginning stage, (2) the middle or working-together stage, and (3) the ending stage. Each stage has a different focus and different tasks. In each session some time is spent in each stage, but the amount of time spent in each stage may differ depending on the work at hand and the stage of group development. In some groups, the stages represent steps in what might be called a "mini" change process.

One way to conceptualize group sessions is to use the stages of group development that are presented in Chapter 4. These stages were the orientation, authority, negotiation, functional, and disorganization stages. Each group session will revisit these stages at least briefly during the session. For time-limited groups, early sessions will be focused on the first three stages, which are essentially stages devoted to group formation. Later on, less time is needed for these stages and more time is devoted to the work of the group, which is characterized by the functional stage. During the later stages of group development, more time will be devoted to disorganization or termination as the group prepares to end its work together.

For ongoing groups, these stages take place during each session but more time may be spent on one or more stages depending on where members are in their work with the group. The introduction of a new member means the group will need to spend time revisiting the first three stages as it orients the new member, reestablishes norms, and reshuffles roles among group members. Once the new member has been accepted and trust is established, the group will spend less time on these stages and more time on the functional stage during each session. When a member or members are preparing to leave the group, the sessions will be focused on disintegration and termination.

In Chapters 3 and 4, we examined the change process. The phases are assessment, planning, action, and evaluation and termination. However, these phases are not limited to the overall process but are included during each contact with groups that use a change process.

The opening, or beginning, stage of a group session corresponds to the relationship-building and assessment phases of the change process or the orientation, authority, and negotiation stages of group development. The middle or working-together stage involves planning, action, and evaluation and corresponds to the functional stage of group development. It includes evaluating success and barriers to success in carrying out the plan, deciding whether to continue with the plan or to modify it, and taking action to continue success or to remove barriers to success. The ending stage involves termination of the session and this corresponds to the disintegration stage of group development.

During the first few sessions with a new group, more emphasis might be needed on the first phases of relationship building and assessment, with planning and action limited to meeting needs that require immediate attention. Likewise, the last few sessions might focus more on termination. However, elements of each phase of the change process should be built into each session with change-oriented groups. Besides helping to maintain a focus on the work to be done, this has the added benefit of reinforcing the steps necessary for successful change.

The beginning stage starts when the worker opens the session by greeting the group. This might be as simple as saying "good evening [or morning or afternoon]." If this is the first session, the worker plans for some kind of activity that will begin the process of group formation. These are typically referred to as *icebreakers*. A popular icebreaker is to have group members introduce themselves and tell the group something about themselves. A variation of this is to have group members pair up and engage in a brief discussion about themselves followed by either self-introductions or having each person introduce the other member whom he interviewed. The worker should also introduce herself even if she knows all the group members. She might do this first to model introductions for the group. A common topic that might be discussed in the introductions is what each member would like to get out of participating in the group.

Diversity issues may be especially prominent during these first few sessions. The worker should communicate a respect for diversity and a valuing of difference while also seeking to learn about diversity from group members. The worker encourages the group to value diversity as an enrichment of the group process and an opportunity to explore and learn from one another.

During the first session, the major question that group members in voluntary groups need to answer is whether they are joining the group and will return. A major influence in answering this question is whether they have made a connection with at least one other person in the group. Using icebreakers that ensure this connection increases the likelihood that more members will return for subsequent sessions.

Once the introductions have been completed, the worker opens the discussion of the group's purpose. The worker should try to incorporate the desires or goals of group members as much as possible. If the group purpose can be related to individual goals, then people are more likely to join the group. This represents the orientation stage. This stage might take the entire first session for some groups. Other groups will need only a brief discussion before proceeding. Most of this is determined by how much of an investment is expected of members. In change-oriented groups, orientation will typically take longer than it will in growth and development groups because there is a much greater personal investment required for the former as opposed to the latter. It may be necessary to repeat introductions for several sessions before members become more acquainted with each other. In groups in which membership changes regularly, introductions should take place whenever there are new members.

As members develop an investment in being in the group, some conflict is likely to arise. This typically will occur during the first few sessions. This represents the authority stage. Managing conflict requires that the group formulate norms regarding how it will function. Norms typically include decision making and roles. This represents the negotiation stage. As with orientation, these two stages can be resolved in the first session for groups with lower levels of investment, but will typically take longer for groups requiring higher levels. For groups with higher levels of investment such as change-oriented groups, these two stages are usually resolved by the third session or so. The worker should be prepared to facilitate group discussion regarding norms and assist the group as needed in negotiating these. If the group has not completed these stages, the worker should raise this as a topic for discussion in subsequent sessions. Periodically, the group may need to revisit these stages as it struggles with new issues.

If this is a session that represents the functional stage of development, then the meeting typically begins with what might be called a *check-in* which is a way of finding if there are any important issues that need to be addressed. Members may experience crises or other significant events that need to be discussed before they will be ready to work. Another form of check-in is to summarize the last session and discuss any work or issues that have occurred during the time elapsed since the last group session. The worker helps the group define the purpose of this session or recall plans made in a previous session. The group is given an opportunity to discuss this purpose and any special needs that group members might have at this time. This is essentially a reorientation process in preparation for continuing the functional or working stage of the group.

In some groups, a decision will need to be made regarding the agenda for the current meeting. This may have already taken place during the last meeting or it might be set by the overall structure of the group such as a curriculum that the group is following. In setting an agenda, the group may revisit the authority and negotiation stages as it decides what work will be done during the session. In change-oriented groups and some support groups, a decision needs to be made regarding who will have the floor for this session. When the worker senses that the group is ready to proceed with the work to be done, the worker changes the focus of the session and facilitates the group as it accomplishes its work. This is covered more thoroughly in Part Two, when we discuss working with various types of groups.

Before the agreed-on time for ending a session is reached, the worker again shifts the focus. In bringing the session to an end, the worker or group members summarize what has happened during the session and how it fits into the overall plan for the group. The worker and the group together plan the next session and discuss work to be done by each group member before the next session. This represents the disorganization or termination stage.

If the worker has been successful in incorporating termination at the end of each session, the group may be well prepared for termination when it comes. However, even if the worker is able to do this, some group members may have difficulty with termination. Termination is covered for various groups in Part Two.

## Skills Used by the Worker During Group Sessions

As a means of guiding and supporting the work together and of promoting relationship and effective communication and facilitating the group, the worker uses six groups of skills during group sessions: inductive learning and naturalistic inquiry skills; climate-setting skills; observation skills; listening skills, especially reflective listening; questioning skills; and focusing, guiding, and interpreting skills. The skill of group facilitation is, in part, skill in selecting and using the appropriate response at the appropriate time. Like all skills, these must be developed through use over a period of time. The student or worker can improve her communication skills by using them in her everyday life. In addition, many exercises have been developed that are useful in beginning to acquire these skills, but it is only in actual client situations and group sessions that skill development reaches the professional level. Each of these skills should be utilized in a way that is sensitive to cultural and individual differences.

### Inductive Learning and Naturalistic Inquiry

These approaches are important to becoming culturally and diversity competent. Inductive learning refers to three important concepts. According to Doman Lum, the worker must first take a lifelong learning approach to becoming culturally competent. This means that learning does not stop but is built into professional development throughout one's career. Second, the worker should use inductive learning as he comes to know each client or group member and he should encourage this within the group. This requires an openness to new knowledge as the worker and the group discover similarities and differences in how each person experiences his or her own diversity and that of others. Similarities serve to confirm earlier observations of members of a diversity group. Observing differences allows new learning to take place. Thus, the worker never closes the door to the possibility of advancing his knowledge about diversity and he seeks to have group members do likewise. The third concept involves having group members assume the role of teacher while the worker and other group members assume the role of learner each time the group encounters diversity. This recognizes that each person is an expert in his or her own diversity and that he or she experiences that diversity in an individual way.[15] Lum suggested the use of the "Essential Question," which is: "What does X mean to you?" where "the symbol X can refer to a social experience, to feelings, beliefs or cultural meanings."[16] Open-ended questions and facilitative communication skills are used to deepen the group member's narrative.[17]

Naturalistic inquiry comes out of *ethnography*. It involves the use of the inductive process to learn about a culture. James W. Leigh described this as beginning with the position that one does not know what one does not know. This is different from traditional social work, which uses a deductive process in which the worker uses prescribed guidelines for gathering knowledge, formulates a hypothesis about the current situation, and then designs a plan based on this hypothesis. The emphasis in traditional social work is on knowing what one does not know and then using this knowledge to guide the process of acquiring knowledge. To not know what one does not know means leaving oneself open to whatever unfolds in the interaction. Knowledge acquisition is not prescribed ahead of time but unfolds from the interactions that take place.[18] The worker asks what Leigh described as global questions designed to uncover the person's experiences.[19] The role of the group member is as "culture guide,"[20] and the role of the worker and other members as "stranger."[21] These approaches fit very well with an ecosystems strengths approach. In fact, Lum pointed out the need to use a strengths approach in becoming culturally competent.[22]

## Climate-Setting Skills

Three attributes have been identified as characteristics of interpersonal situations that seem to produce understanding, openness, and honesty, which are enabling factors in the work of the action system. These three characteristics are empathy, genuineness, and nonpossessive warmth.[23] These characteristics are essential for change-oriented and support and self-help groups. While other climate setting skills may be needed for other types of groups, these three characteristics are likely to produce positive results for any social worker who leads or facilitates groups. They make the worker appear both human and humane and are likely to lead to group members feeling positive feelings toward the worker and to some extent the group. Exhibiting these characteristics and helping the group to function in a way that reflects them will tend to create a very positive atmosphere in almost any group.

Empathy is the capacity to communicate to the others that the worker and group members accept and care for them. Empathy communicates that at this point in time the person's welfare is to be considered before the worker's or the group's. Empathy is expressed by openly receiving and recognizing the feelings of group members, by accurately perceiving the group members' messages, and by providing the group or member with concrete feedback about messages.

Genuineness is the capacity of the worker and group members to communicate to one another that they are trustworthy. It is expressed by getting to know one another as human beings in ways that meet the group's need for such information. It also reflects congruence between verbal and nonverbal messages. In addition, genuineness involves informing group members when the worker or other members disagree with them and when the their behavior and communication are inconsistent. This skill calls for honesty, but honesty communicated in a manner that is sensitive to the group member's feelings and concerns.

Nonpossessive warmth is the capacity to communicate concern for each other as human beings; this allows group members to make decisions, to have negative and positive feelings, and to feel worthwhile. It has qualities of nonblame, closeness, and nondefensiveness. A warmth that is nonpossessive is displayed through positive regard and respect for each other and through thoughtfulness and kindness as well as appreciation for, and pleasure at, growth and well-being of each other. When working with groups, this also has the added benefit of modeling relationships that need to be founded on nonpossessive warmth and acceptance. Relationships in which this is absent pose a great challenge. Relationships that have this quality are stronger and are sources of strength for the work to be done.

These three attributes are tied to social work values. One of the cardinal values of social work is the belief in the value and worth of every human being. This leads the worker to respect each group member as an individual and to encourage the group to do likewise. This does not mean that the worker approves of all of the group member's behavior. Some group members will have done things that are wrong, either morally or legally, or they will act inappropriately in the group. The worker accepts group members as human beings even with their faults and mistakes. When the worker and the group are able to do this, then they can listen to the group member's story without judging her as a person. This helps the worker and other group members put themselves in one anothers' shoes and leads to empathy. A genuine belief in the value and worth of every human being allows the worker to be more genuine in treating group members with dignity and respect. It allows the worker to care about each person as a human being even though he may find things about her that he does not like. In change-oriented and support groups, it is important for the group to develop this as well so that the group can create a safe place to engage in self-disclosure and work on personal issues that need to be resolved.

The climate of all interpersonal endeavors greatly affects the nature of the relationship and the quality of the communication. Skills in developing and maintaining an accepting, growth-producing climate are an important part of the worker's repertoire. These skills are essential for successful group work for the worker and for the group.

The skills used in group sessions can also be used by the worker in less formal social work interactions and by group members in their everyday lives. They are the same skills that encourage relationships to form and to be used and maintained. In the social work endeavor, in the action system, it is the responsibility of the social worker to facilitate the development of relationships with the group and within the group. As relationships are formed, a common ground for communication is established. To do this, the social worker must understand the group and be willing to work with them in meeting their needs and in resolving the situation. It is also important for group members to do this in change-oriented and support groups. Improved communication and relationships are central to success in the ecosystems strengths approach. The focus of growth and change is on the interactions and transactions among group members and between group members and their environment. Success is often determined by the group member's ability to change their interactions with others and their interactions with the worker and the group. Thus, the worker frequently will be in a position to assist group members to acquire these skills in order to bring about growth and change.

## Observation Skills

People give information and express feelings in nonverbal, behavioral ways. They also provide information and express feelings in the way in which other information is given and discussed. Sensitivity to this nonverbal material is useful for tuning in to where the group and its members really are in relation to the material being discussed, for checking the validity of the group member's verbal expression, and for feedback purposes. Workers should observe the following:

1. *Body language*—What is the group member communicating by the way she sits, by behaviors such as thumping on the desk with the fingers, by facial expression?
2. *The content of opening and closing sentences*—These sentences tend to contain particularly significant material. They also may give cues about the group member's attitudes toward self and the environment.
3. *Shifts in conversation*—These shifts, particularly when always related to similar topics, can indicate that a particular topic is painful, taboo, or something the group or group member does not want to discuss.
4. *Association of ideas*—Observing which ideas group members seem to associate with which other ideas can often give the worker an indication of unspoken feelings.
5. *Recurrent references*—When group members continue to bring up a subject, this indicates that it is a subject of importance to them or one with which they would like help.
6. *Inconsistencies or gaps*—When these are present, it is an indication either that the material being discussed is threatening to group members or that they are unwilling to openly share in this area.
7. *Points of stress or conflict*—In cross-cultural action systems, stress and conflict may indicate areas of inadequate knowledge about cultural aspects of the group member's functioning. This may also indicate misunderstanding on the part of group members or areas of group members' bias or prejudice.

## Listening Skills

Listening is of vital importance in any group. The worker listens to what group members have to say and how they respond to questions and responses. Beginning workers often place primary emphasis on what they have to say and on the questions to be asked. Good questioning enables group members to provide necessary information, consider alternatives, and work on the situation at hand. If the worker's listening skills are deficient, the full value of the group session will not be realized. Active listening—being with group members in their struggle to deal with difficulties and problems—is the appropriate response at many points in the session.

Developing listening skills is also important because social workers often communicate with persons whose language expression is somewhat different from their own. In listening, it is important to try to understand what the group member is attempting to communicate. To do this, the worker seeks to understand what the words mean to the group member. The worker maintains focus on what the group member is saying even though there is a tendency to shut out the communication because it seems strange and is difficult to listen to. It is important to note feeling words and how they are expressed. Listening should reflect an attitude of openness and acceptance. Effective listening involves a sense of timing that allows the worker to focus on the group member and what is being said and does not shut off communication by premature evaluation or advice.

It is also essential to facilitate good listening among group members. In order to participate in the group and engage in mutual aid, group members need to tune in to one another and listen. One technique that can be useful in helping group members to improve their listening skills is to have them repeat what other members said before saying what they have to say. This forces members to listen to one another rather than focusing only on their own thoughts and feelings.

It is much easier to obtain cooperation from others if they know that we are paying attention to what they are saying and experiencing. This demonstrates care and concern for others in a way that has real meaning for them. It is not just lip service, but demonstrates interest in a genuine way.

## Questioning Skills

The essence of this group of skills is knowing the various types of questions to ask and the usefulness of each type of question. A first category of questions includes open- and closed-ended questions. A closed-ended question calls for a specific answer, for example, "What is your age?" These questions are used to gain factual information. An open-ended question is one that enables the group member to define, discuss, or answer the question in any way he chooses. An example of one is "What do you think is the reason your child is not behaving the way you want him to behave?" The open-ended question allows expression of feeling and gives the worker and the group the group member's perception of the subject at hand.

There are also leading and responding questions. A leading question is used when it is desirable for a group member to continue to explore the subject at hand. An example is "You have tried to cope with this problem, haven't you?" A responding question follows the lead of the group member's response, for example, when a group member has been discussing how he has tried to cope and the worker or another group member responds, "Could you tell us more about how you went about helping your child?"

In an answer-and-agree question, the group member is expected to answer in such a way as to agree with the worker, for example, "You are feeling much better today, aren't you?" This usually is not a good form of questioning to use because it blocks discussion and imposes the worker's ideas on the group member.

With most situations, it is better to ask questions so that they contain single, rather than several, ideas. A question with several ideas might be used when the worker is attempting to help the group or a member recognize connections between the ideas. Whether to ask very broad questions or very specific ones depends on the work at hand and on the worker's style. Some workers like to gain a broad picture first and then explore details. Other workers believe it is more helpful for group members to consider small parts of the situation and then look at the broader picture later. Questioning is one of the means used by a social worker to enhance relationships and communication.

In general, it is better for the worker and the group to avoid asking too many questions; otherwise, group members may feel bombarded or put on the spot. Questions also tend to set an agenda that is worker centered rather than client centered. In many respects, questions can be used to control the session so that the group can end up talking about what the worker wants to discuss, as opposed to discussing their concerns. In addition, questions tend to be one sided and offer little opportunity for feedback, interaction, or give-and-take in the interchange. There are other ways to provide guidance or focus that do not use questions but incorporate group member's concerns.

## Focusing, Guiding, and Interpreting Skills

This group of skills is used by the worker to enable the group or a member to accomplish the tasks necessary to reach the agreed-on objectives. It includes the capacity to use encouragers, to paraphrase and summarize what has been said, and to reflect feelings, meaning, and ideas. The worker needs to master these skills and should model them and encourage their use by the group. These are skills that incorporate what group members say or do into the worker's or other member's response. Thus, they are centered on group members and can be used to guide or focus the session on what is important to the group or group member and what the worker and the group need to know about the group or group member, their diversity, the environment, and their needs. The capacity to confront and to elaborate are important in terms of moving the work toward difficult areas and reaching an understanding of the situation or the work to be done. The effective use of these skills includes a sense of timing concerning when to listen, when to focus, when to interpret, and when to direct.

Paraphrasing and summarizing often clarify what has been said. Clarification and elaboration enhance understanding. With understanding of issues and facts, the work can progress as a truly joint effort. Summarizing is a good way to open and close group sessions and to transition from one phase of the session to another. Sometimes the worker takes responsibility for this, but in some groups it may be better to have the group do this.

Confrontation and silence are often difficult for the worker and for group members. Confrontation is the bringing out into the open of feelings, issues, and disagreements. It involves looking at these elements and attempting to find ways to deal with them. If feelings, issues, and disagreements remain hidden, they may interfere with the work at hand. Silence may indicate resistance, frustration, or anger, but it also can provide a time for worker and group to be reflective. Instead of being uncomfortable with silence, the worker can attempt to understand the nature of the silence and use it appropriately. Times of reflection are useful in the work together. Silence related to resistance can be used to develop sufficient discomfort on the part of the group or a member so that they will have to do something. This can help in focusing on the work together. The worker who senses frustration and anger can bring it out into the open, confront the group or group member, and thus deal with it so that the work can proceed.

It is the worker's responsibility to guide and facilitate the group but not to control it. The worker takes whatever material and expression of feelings are given by the group members and, by listening, questioning, focusing, guiding, and directing, enables the process of the work together to proceed toward the desired outcome. The worker models these skills for the group and encourages group members to learn and use them within the group and in their relationships outside the group.

## The Importance of Group Process

There is a saying among group workers that process is more important than content. This means that the real significance of what occurs in group sessions is not measured by the content of what group members say and do, but by the meaning that it has for them. For example, in growth and development groups, the most significant benefit is generally gained from participation and feelings of belonging. Therefore, regardless of the activity that the group is engaged in, the real importance comes from everyone feeling that they have been included. Success is not measured so much by whether the group completed the activity or did it well. It is measured by how well the group was able to function and work together and include all of its members.

The importance of group process cannot be overstated. New group workers will typically succumb to the temptation to overfocus on what they say and do in the group and what the group says and does. In doing so, they miss the real benefits that can come from participating in a group.

Tuning in to group process requires the worker to use her nonverbal skills and abilities and to be analytical in her thinking about the group. She needs to be able to observe and interpret what is occurring at different levels. The content of the session is the overt or surface level. The meaning that it has for members and for the group as a whole is more covert or beneath the surface. Assessing group stages of development means assessing group process. The group does not announce what it is doing or what stage of development it is in. It acts it out and the worker needs to be cognizant of what to look for and needs to understand how the group's actions represent the particular stage of development. For example, during the beginning stages of a group, the worker can expect to see evidence of the orientation, authority, and negotiation stages. When group members seek answers about what they will be doing in the group, they are exhibiting behaviors that are consistent with the orientation stage. When they experience conflict or are struggling with developing a decision-making process, they are displaying actions that represent the authority stage. Resolution of the authority stage takes place as the group negotiates norms and roles.

While group process is important to understand for all groups, it is particularly important for problem-solving, decision-making and counseling groups, and, to some extent, support and self-help groups. In these groups, it is essential for the group to function in a way that meets the needs of all of its members. The functioning of the group represents group process. Some of the great benefits from participating in these types of groups comes from members experiencing feelings of not being alone, having other people care about them and their needs, meeting their needs through collective action, feeling supported and validated, giving and receiving help from others, and feeling connected to others. All of these benefits are experienced through group process.

In addition to understanding group process, the worker needs to understand each member of the group on a process level. As members experience the group, the worker needs to be able to assess their experience without having to solicit constant feedback. She does this by observing how members function in the group and by the extent to which the group experience seems to be affecting them both within the group and outside the group. She observes and interprets interactions among group members and notices patterns and what these represent in terms of relationship building or stresses and strains. To some extent, the worker needs to rely on her instincts and her ability to tune in at the nonverbal level when it comes to tuning in and understanding group process. As workers gain experience with various types of groups, their understanding of group process is enhanced and they learn to trust their instincts more.

## Maintaining Records for Groups

One important area of accountability for social workers is in maintaining records and the use of information about clients. Social work has always placed considerable emphasis on recording. This recording has taken many forms. Typically, when working with groups other than task groups, the social worker uses the **summary record.** Although this type of record takes various forms depending on agency policy, for groups it essentially includes entry data, a plan for the group, session summaries describing significant information and actions taken by the worker, and a statement of what was accomplished as the group ends. The summary record is focused more on what happens with group members than on the worker's input and sifts out the important elements, discarding the superfluous.

Summary records are also used in situations in which long-term, ongoing contact with a client and a series of workers may be involved like a day program or residential care. These records provide a picture of what has happened in the past with a particular client. Agency policy often specifies the form and content of such records. This policy reflects the agency's need for information both to protect itself when questions about the handling of a particular case are raised and to provide the specific information needed for accountability purposes. As summary records may be subject to review by several people, questions of how to deal with confidentiality are important. It is usually good practice to include in summary recording only that which is required to be in the record and only verifiable information, not impressions, feelings, or information that can be misinterpreted.

A commonly used kind of recording for individual clients is the **problem-oriented record.** This method is used not just by social workers but also by most health care professionals. This system has advantages when working in an interdisciplinary setting. It is easily translated to computer databases and is succinct and focused. In some settings, such as those offering change-oriented groups, records may be kept on individual clients who are receiving services in a group format. A copy of the group sessions may be entered into the file but care needs to be taken to maintain the confidentiality of other members. There are several ways this might be done. The safest is to record the actions of each member in his or her own file. Another is to give each group member a coded name or number to be used in the overall group record. A third is to black out names of other group members before placing a copy of the group recording in the file. Most agencies will have workers keep a separate set of group notes and enter individual entries for each member in his or her own file. This can be quite tedious and time consuming and is part of the reason groups are not necessarily more efficient.

Problem-oriented records contain four parts. First is a database that contains information pertinent to the client and work with the client. This includes such things as age, sex, marital status, functioning limitations, persons involved (family and other professionals), financial situation, or any test results. Second is a problem list that includes a statement of initial complaints and assessment of the concerned staff. Third are plans and goals related to each identified problem. Fourth are follow-up notes about what was done and the outcome of that activity. This is where group notes or acivities of individual clients in groups are recorded.

The use of the term *problem-oriented record* is inconsistent with an ecosystems strengths approach. However, a similar format is generally used and might be referred to as a *change-oriented record* or *needs-based record* in that it is driven by the identification and meeting of needs. This record should consist of the identification of needs or concerns and an assessment of the person in environment or ecosystem. A plan is developed that is built on the strengths and resources of the ecosystem and designed to meet the needs of the client and the ecosystem. Progress notes are kept that describe the progress toward goals and objectives. Periodic (generally quarterly) reports summarize the progress made and document the need for further service. A termination summary identifies the reasons for ending the service and the outcomes.

Clients need to understand not only the confidential nature of their work with a social worker but the limits of that confidentiality—that is, that information will be discussed with a supervisor or a professional team. In change-oriented groups and those that involve self-disclosure it is essential that confidentiality be maintained, but it cannot be guaranteed and clients need to be aware of this.

Clients should be told what will be recorded, who will have access to their records, and how long these records will be kept. They need to know that records used in agency and program evaluation are depersonalized so that the identity of clients is protected. They need to know what information is shared with whom and why it is shared.

Workers also need to be sure that clients have given informed consent for the use of information in their records. A client should not be asked to give consent when he is desperate for service; at such a time, making an informed decision is difficult. It is wise for the worker to discuss the use of information at several points during the work together. If the client decides not to share information and knows the consequences of not sharing that information, then the worker should respect the client's right to withhold information to protect his privacy.

The sharing of information about clients requires the client's written consent. This consent should be specific; that is, it should state the purpose for the sharing of the information, an expiration date, and the persons with whom the information will be shared. Clients should be helped to understand their rights in signing or not signing such consents for release of information. Usually, it is wise to have someone witness the client's signature.

Because the release of information could become a part of a legal action, the advice of a legal expert should be obtained in developing a form for the release of information.

Workers should monitor the use of client records to see that information contained in records is not used improperly. When they detect improper or questionable use of records, it is their responsibility to alert supervisors or other responsible persons to the situation. They can suggest ways in which the client's rights can be protected, such as depersonalizing information. If the improper use continues, workers must decide what action needs to be taken to prevent unethical use.

Federal and state legislation regulates the use of various kinds of records, including those used for evaluative purposes. This legislation has generated a growing body of interpretation and judicial decisions regarding the application of these laws, which has further complicated issues of record keeping. The Federal Privacy Act of 1974 (PL 93-579) in essence gives the client the right to see any record containing information about that client. It requires that no disclosure of information in any record be made without written consent from the client and that a record be kept indicating any disclosures of information to other persons.

Other laws have been enacted that call for open access to public records. In some cases, these laws have been interpreted to mean that the records of public agencies and, in some cases, of situations in which governmental funds have been involved are a matter of public record and can be disclosed in a variety of situations, including court proceedings. There seems to be a conflict between privacy and open-access laws that has not been fully resolved.

Issues of confidentiality and access to records need to be addressed by ongoing dialogue, creative thinking, and an ever-present sense of the ethics of the profession of social work. These are not the only issues that have or will arise regarding client records. Every social worker should be alert to identify other issues and to engage in discussions to resolve them.

**Process recording**—a narrative report of all that happened during a client contact, including the worker's feelings and thinking about what has happened—is a form that at one time received great emphasis and was frequently used in the educational and supervisory processes. In recent years it has not been used as often, in part probably because it is extremely time consuming. Also, the intensive individual supervision of workers, which was once considered essential to social work and which made extensive use of recording important, is no longer considered desirable in many settings. Process recording, however, is still a technique that has value for students as they and their field supervisors evaluate their work. It is especially useful to the social worker striving to further develop understanding and skill in difficult situations or in situations in which the worker is developing new skills. Process recordings can be used when working with individuals, families, and groups.

The usefulness of process recording depends, to a considerable extent, on the ability of the worker to recall exactly what happened and in what order and to look at the facts in an objective manner to get at underlying feelings and meanings. The worker must be willing to honestly record the actions and communications of both worker and client or group members. When this technique is used in a supervisory process, the worker must have a trusting relationship with the supervisor. Because of its time-consuming nature, process recording probably should be used only occasionally to enhance the worker's development and learning.

When process recording is used, confidentiality must be preserved. The written record must be kept in a secure place and seen only by those directly involved in the situation or supervising the worker. If a record is to be used for other purposes, such as teaching or as a case example, it must be completely disguised so that neither the person nor the situation can be identified. The purpose of process recording is to aid the worker in understanding the situation and to serve as a tool for learning. After it is used, the process recording should be destroyed. It should not be made part of the permanent record.

A technique used for purposes similar to process recording is taping, either in audio or video format, of interviews, group sessions, or other interactional encounters. This technique can allow the worker to see himself in action with the client. Sometimes it is also useful for the client or the group to view what has happened as a means of evaluating behaviors and interactions. Unless the time is taken to evaluate the underlying elements of the situation (the feeling elements and the reasons behind behaviors), some of the learning potential of this technique is lost. When using the taping technique of recording, workers must obtain written permission from clients to tape sessions. Sometimes taping may inhibit the client or the group, and have a negative effect on the work of the session. Again, confidentiality is an important consideration. Tapes should be destroyed or erased after they have served their purpose.

For the most part, change-oriented groups are those that use client records that require summary recording, or change-oriented or needs-based records. Some type of entry into case records might be made in some settings for clients who attend support groups, and some support groups might maintain minutes of their meetings. Typically, self-help groups do not keep records. The same is true for most growth and development and prevention groups, although attendance records might be kept. This might be done to meet funding requirements or to demonstrate the need for the group.

For task groups, the minutes of meetings are used as the record of the activities of the group. Minutes are summaries of the session and are generally limited to the date and time of convening and adjourning, the members present (and perhaps those absent), the topics covered, important points, decisions that were reached, and issues tabled or planned for the next meeting. Minutes are not usually considered as confidential and may very well be the official public record of the organization. They are generally maintained by the secretary of the group and are submitted for approval at the next meeting before they are entered into the official record.

## Summary

The emphasis in this chapter is on interaction and engagement that takes place in an action system and with the group and members of their ecosystem. The formation of the action system requires understanding of the group and skill on the part of the worker. Special consideration must be given in developing action systems with resistant group members.

Relationship is the cohesive quality of the group and the action system. The helping relationship is for the purpose of assisting and facilitating the group. It is influenced by the life experiences of both group members and the worker. Cross-diversity relationships have special characteristics that the worker must understand.

Communication is an important ingredient of the group. The process of communication can become blocked in a variety of ways. Social workers need to be aware of these blocks and of the means for dealing with them.

It is important to prepare for group sessions and to make them goal directed. Each session has three stages: a beginning, a middle, and an ending. Workers use a variety of skills in the session and models these skills so that group members can also use them. These include inductive learning and naturalistic inquiry; climate setting; observation; listening; questioning; and focusing, guiding, and interpreting.

The same principles and skills used in interaction with groups are also used when working with significant persons in the situation, with those who may be able to provide resources for the group or a member, or with a variety of community persons.

Group process is more important than the content of group sessions. Group process is more overt and includes the way in which the group exhibits evidence of various stages of development and how it functions in carrying out its purpose.

## QUESTIONS

1. What are some of the ways to facilitate the development of a helping relationship within a group? Relationships among group members?

2. Why is the development of relationships so essential to working with groups?

3. Why is it difficult to communicate across cultural boundaries? How can social workers facilitate such communication within a group?

4. Discuss the use of each of the skills in this chapter in working with groups.

5. Discuss group process and its importance in working with groups.

## SUGGESTED READINGS

Johnson, Louise C., and Yanca, Stephen J., *Social Work Practice: A Generalist Approach,* 9th ed. Boston: Allyn & Bacon, 2007 (Chapter 8).

Anderson, Joseph, and Carter, Robert Wiggins. *Diversity Perspectives for Social Work Practice,* Boston: Allyn & Bacon, 2003.

Ivey, Allen E., and Ivey, Mary Bradford. *Intentional Interviewing: Facilitating Client Development in a Multicultural Society,* 6th ed. Belmont, CA: Wadsworth, 2007.

Lum, Doman. *Culturally Competent Practice: A Framework for Understanding Diverse Groups and Justice Issues,* 3rd ed. Belmont, CA: Wadsworth, 2007.

Perlman, Helen Harris. *Relationship: The Heart of Helping People.* Chicago: University of Chicago Press, 1979.

Poorman, Paula B. *Microskills and Theoretical Foundations for Professional Helpers,* Boston: Allyn & Bacon, 2003.

Sheafor, Bradford W., and Horejsi, Charles R. *Techniques and Guidelines for Social Work Practice,* 8th ed. Boston: Allyn & Bacon, 2008 (Chapter 8).

Shulman, Lawrence. *The Skills of Helping: Individuals Families, and Groups,* 6th ed. Belmont, CA: Wadsworth, 2009.

# Generalist Social Work Practice with Groups

Part Two examines various types of groups that generalist social workers are likely to facilitate. Our practice experience and research indicate that these groups are the most common in social work practice. Our practice experience was further validated by research that we undertook in preparation for this text. We surveyed students and field instructors to identify various types of groups that were being facilitated in various settings. We followed up with an interview with a sample of these settings. This was followed by a survey of field directors across the country to determine if our findings reflected what was happening in other areas.

The chapters in this part of the text are applications of the Johnson/Yanca generalist social work practice model to the types of groups that we identified in Chapter 1 and that also reflected our experience and research. Instead of offering highly theoretical versions, we have opted to use a more practical practice-based approach to offering these groups. Thus, each chapter is organized around practical steps that social workers might take in assessing, planning, taking actions, and evaluating and terminating with groups during each stage of our model for group development. This model was developed by Louise Johnson in the original edition of our text *Social Work Practice: A Generalist Approach*, which is now in its ninth edition. The model sees group development as proceeding through the stages of orientation, authority, negotiation, function, and disintegration. We include a model for developing and using program material.

Chapter 6 describes group purposes with various types of change-oriented groups. We have categorized these as problem-solving, decision-making, and counseling groups. We have included schema to be used in planning a new group that can also be used in preparing a proposal for a group. Chapter 7 examines support and self-help groups. Self-help groups are included here because we see the primary benefit derived from these groups as coming from support from group members and sponsors. Chapter 8 presents working with growth and development groups, which may include groups designed to promote healthy functioning in biological, psychological, and social areas of life. These groups also include educational groups and those that offer recreation, socialization, and various types of skill building. Chapter 9 covers prevention groups that often combine growth and development activities with support, decision making, and problem solving to assist participants with dealing with situations that may be harmful to them, such as using drugs and alcohol, engaging in illegal activities, joining gangs, and engaging in risky or unhealthy behaviors.

# CHAPTER

# 6

# Change-Oriented Groups

### LEARNING EXPECTATIONS

1. Understanding the importance of change-oriented groups in generalist social work practice.
2. Understanding problem-solving, decision-making, and counseling groups offered within generalist practice.
3. Understanding the use of the change process in problem-solving, decision-making, and counseling groups.
4. Understanding the group process to recognize its various aspects in the functioning of problem solving, decision-making, and counseling groups.
5. Understanding how the social worker can facilitate the work and process of problem-solving, decision-making, and counseling groups.
6. Beginning skill in facilitating small-group interaction in problem-solving, decision-making, and counseling groups.

This chapter examines generalist social work practice with change-oriented groups. While the purpose of most groups is to bring about change in some way or another, the groups in this chapter are focused on helping members bring about specific changes in themselves or their life situation. Other groups that we consider are focused on providing assistance with coping with difficulties, enhancing quality of life, or preventing difficulties from occurring. Thus, we have chosen the term *change-oriented groups* to refer to the groups in this chapter. These groups consist of problem-solving, decision-making, and counseling groups.

## Group Purposes in Change-Oriented Groups

It may seem that the three types of groups being considered in this chapter are the same, and in many respects they are. Most of the differences are subtle at best. In fact, they might be referred to as problem-solving/decision-making/counseling groups. We have included all three titles in order to cover a classification of groups that are often labeled in different ways in practice, but really have very similar purposes. If we had to differentiate the three, we would say that problem-solving groups are designed to resolve difficulties that individual members are experiencing. Some authors and theorists classify problem-solving groups as those that come together to solve a particular problem outside of the group such as an organizational or community problem. We see these groups as task groups and we cover these in Part Three. In our definition, problem-solving groups are oriented toward individual change.

Similarly, we consider decision-making groups as those that are intended to assist individuals in making decisions about themselves or their situation. Some authors and theorists classify these similarly with problem solving. Again, we see their classification of these groups as task groups. Our version sees decision-making groups as focused on individual group members. For us, the primary difference between problem-solving and decision-making groups is that decision-making groups can be focused on bringing about changes that are not necessarily associated with problems. For instance, group members might be engaged in making decisions about their careers or they might be considering enhancing their quality of life or making life choices that will bring them greater satisfaction.

Our view of counseling groups is that they are intended to provide change opportunities for members who feel that they need to make changes in their life and are capable of carrying these out. We see counseling groups as similar to therapy groups, but with two main differences: (1) The membership in therapy groups must overcome major damage or difficulties before they will be able to function and carry out changes. Frequently, the damage and its effects must be reversed before change can occur. (2) Many therapy groups really amount to individual therapy in what might be called a "fish bowl," meaning that most of the interaction takes place between the therapist and an individual group member in front of the rest of the group. Other group members are expected to receive vicarious benefit from observing the work between the therapist and the other member. We do not see this as true group work because the group is only peripherally involved in the therapy. In counseling groups, members are expected to carry out changes and they use the group to assist and facilitate in this process. The group listens and gives feedback or suggestions. The group assists in formulating a plan for change and provides support in carrying it out.

For purpose of simplifying terminology, we refer to these groups as change-oriented groups here, and when we do so we are referring to problem-solving, decision-making, and counseling groups. Differences in these will be noted as needed.

Change-oriented groups are offered in a wide variety of settings. Some are classified as therapy groups and these are generally offered by staff with advanced degrees, such as an MSW along with some advanced training in group therapy. However, in some settings BSWs and generalist MSWs may provide what may be called group therapy. These settings include inpatient psychiatric hospitals or units, partial hospitalization or day treatment programs, residential treatment programs, and inpatient, outpatient, or residential substance abuse treatment settings. Typically, these groups are offered in settings in which there is close supervision readily available and staff receive advanced training in serving the population participating in these groups. In many respects these groups function more like what we call counseling groups. However, participants are clearly more impaired as evidenced by the fact that they are generally in some form of care.

Change-oriented groups are also offered in a wide variety of other settings. Domestic violence shelters and programs offer groups, as do many community mental health programs, family service agencies, and child welfare programs. Young children are typically not able to make and carry out decisions to change and so they are not usually good candidates for these types of groups. Children and young adolescents are very action oriented, and so they generally do not make good candidates for groups that rely primarily on discussion. Working with children and young adolescents usually calls for some type of activity around which some discussion can take place. The activity may be related to an issue they are dealing with such as divorce, making friends, grief, or school success. Adolescents, around fourteen or fifteen years old and older, can participate in change-oriented groups and are included here along with adults.

## Assessment and Planning Before the Group Begins

While there are elements of the change process in every group, in many groups it is the worker who uses the change process in organizing and facilitating the group. As we mentioned above, group work may actually represent part or all of the action phase. However, in change-oriented groups the change process is integral to the work of the group. The worker needs to facilitate learning and using the change process by the group and its members.

The group worker uses assessment and planning skills before the group begins and between each stage of group development as well as within each group session. Assessment and planning before the group begins is discussed here. Assessment and planning within each session and between sessions is discussed as we cover each stage of group development. While groups may occur naturally in the environment, change-oriented groups are formed groups that have specific purposes. They are not natural groups, but are artificial or contrived. In forming a group, the worker generally must seek and obtain approval from her agency. She must also secure participants and take care of the logistical aspects of the endeavor.

A schema for planning a group is provided in Table 6.1, along with a case example. The schema can be used as a proposal to be submitted to administration for approval. As is mentioned in Chapter 4, when planning for a new group the worker needs to answer the questions why, who, what, where, when, and how. The schema is intended to give basic answers to these questions. It can be modified as needed to include other information or aspects that are unique to any particular situation and can be used with any type of group.

As indicated in Table 6.1, the worker needs to think about and present the reason for the group. Consideration should be given to both effectiveness and efficiency. Any proposal to management or administration will need to address these because they are major concerns for anyone at that level of the agency. The purpose of the group should be designed to meet the needs of potential members while also fitting into the mission and services of the agency. The worker should anticipate questions about why group work is needed or would be the best method of delivering services.

Generally, it is best to present the purpose of the group and the basic aspects of it at the beginning of the plan or proposal. This should be fairly detailed and may include research such as a needs survey or, at the very least, a discussion of the need for a group. It may also include information from professional sources on serving the target population in settings similar to that of the agency or community. The target audience should be identified, along with some description of the benefits they can expect to derive from the group.

Consideration should be given to the size of the group. For change-oriented groups, we recommend six to eight members. Groups can be slightly smaller if regular attendance is assured, but they should probably not be larger. The group will need to have enough time

**TABLE 6.1    Schema for Planning a New Group**

---

**I.** Background information
  **A.** Group purpose
    **1.** Describe the purpose of this group being formed.
    **2.** Why is it being formed?
    **3.** Who is the target audience? How many members anticipated?
    **4.** What diversity is desired?
    **5.** Will membership be open ended or closed, time limited or on going.
  **B.** Worker(s) to be involved
    **1.** Desirable qualifications, experience, expertise.
    **2.** Supervision, consultation needed?
  **C.** Group format
    **1.** Will a particular format (curriculum) be used? If so, what adaptations might be needed?
    **2.** What resources are available to support this group format?
    **3.** How might this format need adapting to provide for member input into planning? For expected diversity issues? To make use of member strengths?
  **D.** Sanctioning of group
    **1.** How does this group fit into the agency's purpose, goals, ways of functioning?
    **2.** What kind of interpretation will need to be made within the agency? The larger community?
    **3.** If not within an agency delivery system, how will the group receive sanction?
    **4.** What resources (financial or other) will be available to the worker or the group?

**II.** Description of the group
  **A.** Membership
    **1.** Specifically describe the anticipated members. See I.A.
    **2.** How will they be recruited? Oriented to the purpose and functioning of the group?
    **3.** Specify the program elements of at least the first two or three sessions. How will members be involved in group planning?
  **B.** Time, place, and other elements
    **1.** Where will the group meet? Who is responsible for setting up the space?
    **2.** What is the time frame of the group? Time for meeting, length of meeting, number of meetings anticipated?
    **3.** Other supports, transportation, child care?
  **C.** Program planning specifics
    **1.** What resources will be needed? Equipment, supplies?

**III.** Evaluation mechanisms
  **A.** Outcomes hoped for group, individual
  **B.** What measures will be used to measure outcomes?

---

available to ensure that everyone has an opportunity to participate. Large groups will limit the time that is available and will prove intimidating for many members.

For change-oriented groups it is essential to consider the composition of the group because group dynamics play a vital role in whether members receive help. Members need to establish a sufficient level of trust to engage in self-disclosure. As is mentioned in

Chapter 5, basic elements of a helping relationship are empathy, genuineness, and nonpossessive warmth and acceptance. To establish these in a group, members need to feel that they have something in common with one another. It is important for the worker to ensure that the group is composed of members who are experiencing similar needs or concerns. At the same time, there needs to be enough variation so that the group does not get stuck and a variety of solutions can be generated. The worker should develop a profile of potential members to address these needs and a recruitment strategy that will increase the likelihood of success. In addition, the worker needs to be able to screen potential group members to ensure that they are appropriate for the group.

Diversity can play an important role in considering membership for change-oriented groups. Some cultural groups are less likely to benefit from group work because cultural taboos limit their ability to engage in self-disclosure. Mostly these are cultures with a heavy emphasis on family and those in which privacy is highly valued. Taboos may take the form of not discussing personal or family issues outside of the family. For example, many Asian and Hispanic cultures emphasize the family and the need to maintain family honor. This includes keeping problems within the family system. Members of these cultures are likely to be better candidates for family or individual work; even this work can be difficult because of these taboos.

The degree of acculturation is important. Clients who retain less of their cultural heritage may actually act much more like the dominant culture and so they may be good candidates for group work, even though other members may not be. Generally speaking, the longer the time elapsed since immigration, the greater the likelihood that more acculturation has taken place. Second generations tend to be more acculturated than first. Third are more than second and so on. Marriage outside of the culture usually accelerates acculturation. However, some clients may retain a considerable amount of their cultural heritage, particularly if they were raised and live in cultural enclaves that preserve more of their cultural identity.

Several advantages and disadvantages associated with diversity are identified in Part One. Because establishing trust is so important in change-oriented groups, diversity takes on added importance. Besides cultural factors that reduce clients' ability to self-disclose, bias and prejudice toward various diverse groups also form a factor for many group members. Bias and prejudice held against a diverse group are typically based on ignorance and a lack of understanding or close relationships. It is typical that people who are biased or prejudiced have had little or no contact with those who are the object of their bias and prejudice. Thus, issues associated with diversity in society are likely to enter into the functioning of the group.

At the same time, diversity within change-oriented groups have several great advantages. One advantage is the opportunity for members to become more acquainted with people who are different. When this occurs, people generally find that they share many commonalities. They also find that there are differences. Ideally, they find that these differences enrich life rather than detract from it. In change-oriented groups, diversity can offer different ways of knowing and changing. Diverse members can bring a diversity of perspectives and a diversity of problem-solving approaches and solutions.

As we mentioned earlier, a good general rule to follow is to try to ensure that there is at least one other member who shares the same diversity. For instance, it is not wise to have only one male or female in a group. If the group is mainly white heterosexuals, it is better if there is more than one African American or Hispanic or gay or lesbian member. In addition, the worker should not allow the group to put members on the spot by asking them to act as a spokesperson for their diverse group. Group members need to be able to speak for themselves as individuals.

Age is an important factor in establishing common ground. Typically, adults and children are not placed in the same group in change-oriented groups, unless it is a group of families. The greater the age disparity, the more difficulty the group is likely to experience because of the disparity of issues or needs with which members are dealing. These are typically based on developmental and life stage issues. Adolescents are likely to be dealing with issues of authority, emancipation, and independence. Young adults are more likely to be concerned about establishing and maintaining intimate relationships. Middle-aged adults are frequently concerned about parenting and family issues. Older adults are more likely to be concerned about aging and health issues. For most groups, it is best if all members are from the same generation or life stage.

Most change-oriented groups are not time limited and have closed membership. The main reason these are not usually time limited is to allow members enough time to make whatever changes they need to make. If these groups were time limited, it would almost invariably not allow sufficient time for all members to complete whatever work they need to do. Closed membership means that new members are not able to just drop in and join the group. Membership is set at a certain number and new members are added only when openings occur. The process for adding new members should be established either by the worker ahead of time or by the group in its early sessions. There are several options for doing this, ranging from the worker being entirely responsible for making these decisions to the group being responsible. Generally, it is best to have a combination of worker and group participation. The worker might be responsible for screening potential group members with the group deciding if and when they might join the group. In these instances, the worker makes it clear to potential members that consideration for membership is mutual and may not be in their best interests. The worker meets with potential members and gathers information. If it appears that the person might be a good candidate for the group, the worker obtains written permission to disclose necessary information to the group and discusses the candidate with the group. If the group decides not to accept the candidate, the worker needs to handle this very delicately so there is no sense of rejection. The best approach is to inform the candidate that it does not appear that the situation would be a good fit and it would not be in the candidate's best interests to join the group at this time. The worker should ensure that the candidate is served in another appropriate way, such as another group or individual counseling or the like.

Whenever a group experience is planned, it is important that the leader or facilitator be competent to lead or facilitate the group. Competence is an ethical issue that is part of the National Association of Social Workers (NASW) *Code of Ethics* and every code of ethics for other professionals. The worker must have appropriate credentials, training, and experience. This can be a critical factor in having a proposal approved. It is also important for the recruitment process. Other workers will want to know that they are referring their clients to a group that has competent leadership. The worker should plan for supervision and consultation as needed.

The plan should include a description of the format for the group. Will the group be structured or unstructured? If the group is to be structured, program material or a curriculum is typically used. This might be material developed by the worker or it may be material that is available from other sources. Structured program material from other sources should be adapted for use with a group. It may need to be adapted further by the group as the group has input into planning. Consideration should be given to the resources that are needed and where these might be obtained. Thought should be given to the appropriateness of the program material for various diverse populations and the desirability for diversity in offering the group. In a strengths-based approach, the strengths of group members are incorporated into planning for the group and the format should be built on these strengths. Unstructured groups do not follow a curriculum or program material but are driven by the members. Each session is structured by the group as it decides what will be dealt with or discussed during that session. However, even these groups have some kind of structure for the beginning, functional, and ending stages of each session and deciding how to proceed.

Change-oriented groups should be offered under the sanction or auspices of one or more agencies. This gives the group its credibility. The community and potential members do not typically know who the group worker is, but they may know the agencies. Agencies are sanctioned by the community to provide services to certain populations. The group purpose and the populations being served should be consistent with the mission, goals, and ways of functioning for the agency or agencies who are sponsoring the group. Sometimes a connection is not obvious and needs to be made by the worker. Sometimes the group represents a new service, a new way of serving agency clientele, or a collaboration with other agencies in serving a new or an existing clientele.

The ability to offer the group will also be determined by who sponsors the group and who will facilitate it. Having more than one agency act as a sponsor has advantages and disadvantages. Most of the disadvantages are associated with the need for coordination, including the need to have various aspects approved by more than one agency. A major advantage is that agencies can share resources and can also provide referrals. One of the major reasons groups fail to get off the ground is either the lack of referrals or inappropriate referrals. Just because a worker offers a group does not mean that people will come to it or that other workers will make referrals. However, if their agency is a sponsor and is invested in the success of the group, it is more likely that workers will make referrals.

The issue of inappropriate referrals should be considered. Sometimes this is the result of a misunderstanding or confusion over who would benefit from the group. Unfortunately, some workers may take this opportunity to send clients whom they do not like or who are particularly difficult. This is highly unethical, but it does happen. In some cases, workers have been known to close the case after the referral is made. Workers should bring these situations to the attention of the agency management.

Plans for a group should include a basic description of who will be in the group, how they will be recruited, and how group members will be oriented to the purpose and functioning of the group. We discussed group composition earlier. However, recruiting members for counseling groups can be a delicate task in many ways. The worker needs to be careful to avoid using labels or terminology that might be offensive. In most instances it is better to use a brief description of the situation that potential group members are experiencing. For instance, if the group will be for parents who have been found to be neglectful or abusive, the worker could include this in information to other workers, but in describing to the parents, it is better to use a simple term such as *parenting group*.

A plan or proposal for a new group should contain a description of what the group will do, and some ideas about what will transpire during typical group sessions. If a group will follow program material or a curriculum, then an example should be presented and if possible, a copy of the program material or a summary or outline should be included. Most change-oriented groups have considerably less structure than this, but some groups, for children and younger adolescents, for example, can be offered within this type of structure. There are structured groups offered in settings such as schools. Topics might include divorce, making and keeping friends, and the like. Each topic is covered over a certain number of sessions and may have an activity that provides a stimulus for discussion.[1]

Projected dates, times, and number of sessions should be included to the extent that these are known. At the very least, the worker should identify the length of the sessions, the time of day and day of the week sessions might take place, and the number of sessions if the group is time limited. If an ongoing group is planned, then this should be identified. The place where the group will meet should be discussed in some detail, along with who is responsible for securing it. Many group workers believe that the space where a group meets will dictate what happens in the group. Space typically dictates what can and cannot be done. If physical activity such as role-plays or exercises are part of the plan for a group, then there needs to be sufficient open space. Members need to feel comfortable while also having their confidentiality protected, so the space should be private. Any materials that will be needed should be identified.

Any additional information that may be needed should be identified and addressed in a proposal. It may be necessary to arrange for transportation, child care, or other needs. These should be anticipated and any potential barriers removed.

A mechanism for evaluating the group should be identified. This should include desired group and individual outcomes and how these will be measured. The most common design for evaluating groups is pretest/posttest. Either the worker uses a test that has already been developed and tested such as a depression scale, or she develops her own scale to measure the progress and outcomes for the group. For a parenting group, this might be a set of questions about parenting style or discipline techniques or the like. For a group working through depression, it might be a scale on which participants give a measure of their depression. The same test is given before and after the group. Any differences are assumed to be a result of participating in the group. Evaluation is not only important for determining outcomes, it is often important for demonstrating the effectiveness of the group and may determine whether the group continues or another group is offered. Groups that are funded by external sources or by grants need to have an evaluation to meet funding guidelines and for future funding.

The budget is an important consideration, especially for a proposal. Agencies that are experiencing tight financial constraints will want to know what the cost-benefit analysis is for the group. If the group is expected to generate income, then an estimate should be presented. There might be funding available from a grant or some group members may have insurance that will pay for group services. The agency may have contingency or discretionary funds available. A realistic estimate of the costs or expenses should be presented. Expenses might include materials, snacks, refreshments, rent, salaries, and the like. An estimate of the units of service along with income and expenses will give administrators a basis for deciding if the group is feasible.

Assessment and planning before a group begins can go a long way toward increasing the likelihood of success. It is also necessary in order to develop a proposal to agency administrators so that approval can be obtained. A well-organized and thorough proposal makes a positive impression and can increase the chances that the group will be approved for implementation.

## The Change Process During the Orientation Stage

While some orientation to group purpose and functioning typically takes place prior to the beginning of a change-oriented group or before a new member joins the group, there will still be an orientation process that takes place as the group begins or when a new member attends. In new situations, most people gravitate first toward what is known or familiar to them. Thus, group members will tend to try to find things that they have in common with each other. The worker can facilitate this by structuring icebreaking activities, as is described in Chapter 5. For counseling groups adding new members, the group itself can structure a process for orienting them. The group worker typically provides some orientation during the screening and pregroup assessment and the group then takes responsibility for completing this in the group.

In any new situation, most people will experience some ambivalence. This is called approach–avoidance. People will be curious about the group and will have hopes that the group will meet their needs. At the same time, there is some fear of the unknown and a question about whether to trust that the group will meet their needs. The approach side of the equation motivates people to come to the group and to join and make a commitment. The avoidance side will cause them to limit their involvement or even quit the group and not return. The worker needs to plan for this and recognize it as part of the process that groups will go through. In time-limited groups or a new group, the whole group experiences it together. In ongoing groups, new members will experience it during the first few sessions and the group will revisit this stage as it incorporates new members. Once an initial commitment to the group has been made, the orientation stage is completed.

As the group goes through this stage the worker uses assessment, planning, actions, and evaluation in facilitating the group. The worker becomes familiar with the issues during the orientation stage and assesses the needs of the group and the needs of individual members. She does this by assessing the thoughts and feelings expressed and the actions that take place. Both verbal and nonverbal levels are included in this assessment.

All change-oriented groups require that the worker and the group balance the needs of the group itself and the needs of its members. This is a constant concern and it requires that the worker be able to assess group process and be able to identify balances and imbalances. We call this the "I–we" balance. Because change-oriented groups need to benefit all of their members, individual needs and goals are as important as group needs and goals. When there is too much emphasis placed on group needs and goals, then individual needs and goals will suffer. If there is too much emphasis on individual needs and goals, then group needs and goals will suffer and the group is less able to function and will be less helpful to its members. This is the art of group work, the ability to assess these imbalances and intervene to rebalance this equation.[2]

During the orientation stage there is more emphasis on the "I" portion of the "I–we" balance. The new group has not become a group yet. If it is to become a group, the members will need to become a "we." This can occur only if members make a commitment to the group and become dependent on one another to meet needs that are within the purview of the group. The worker plans for this and takes action to facilitate group formation. In addressing the group, the worker needs to be cognizant of her use of terms that emphasize the group. This includes the use of pronouns like *we*, *us*, *our*, and the like. She may say things such as, "As a member of this group, how do you feel about. . . ."

Another way to facilitate group formation is to engage the group in planning. This has the combined benefit of helping the group to come together while beginning the process of experiencing the next two stages of group development. As the group engages in planning, it begins the process of becoming a group while helping members to invest themselves in the group. It also allows them to make the group into what they need the group to be and to take ownership of the group. Planning can take place at the beginning of the group after the introductions. Members might be asked what they would like to get out of the group and how the group might meet their needs. The group can then begin to talk about how they would like to function as a group or what they would like to accomplish for that session and the next.

An ongoing group should experience revisiting the orientation stage as it welcomes new members. The group may try to skip or avoid this and other stages by overemphasizing its cohesion and the "we-ness" of the group. In doing so the group is seeking to protect itself from change at the expense of the new member. The group needs to reach out to the new member and find ways to include him or her by incorporating the new member's input into the group process and redistributing roles. If the worker assesses that the group is overemphasizing its "we-ness," she can take action by pointing this out or seek to rebalance the equation by asking members to speak for themselves as individuals. She might ask them to recall their thoughts and feelings when they first joined the group and then ask them what they wanted the group to do. She could then ask the group to act in a manner that is more consistent with the new member's need to feel welcome and included. This can be done ahead of time before new members join so the group has an opportunity to plan for new members.

Throughout the orientation stage, the worker evaluates the progress of the group and evaluates the extent to which each member is affected. Through observation, the worker notices interactions in the group and evaluates the extent to which these interactions represent positive or negative resolution of the issue of commitment to the group. Are members interacting with one another in a positive way? Do they seem to be involved? Are members beginning to function as a group? Who is included and who is not? Who participates and who does not? When the worker observes that certain members seem less invested, he invites them to talk about their concerns or have their questions answered.

Termination during the orientation stage should be focused on encouraging members to return to the group if it is a voluntary group. For groups in residential settings, members should be encouraged to invest themselves in the group as an avenue for achieving their goals, which in most settings is to return home. There are several ways for the worker to encourage a commitment to the group, including summarizing the common ground that group members have found. This can be done by the worker or by soliciting contributions from the group. The worker can also highlight or have the group decide what they would like to address in the next session. Talking about the next session gives the group more of a sense of continuity and can also give the worker a sense of who intends to return, who does not intend to return, and who is undecided. This gives him an opportunity to address any concerns before the group ends or follow up with concerns after the session is over.

Once members become invested in the group and make an initial commitment to it the orientation stage is completed. However, any group or individual member may revisit this stage at any time. Typically this occurs when new members join, but even in time-limited groups members can experience doubts later on and may need to recommit themselves to the group.

## The Change Process During the Authority Stage

As members make an initial commitment to the group they become invested in what happens in the group. This generates the authority stage which is characterized by issues related to power and control and conflict. To a greater or lesser extent, each member seeks to influence the group to become what he or she wishes it to be. While the group has begun experiencing "we-ness," there is still a lot of "I-ness" in the group. Members compete with each other for power and control. They also challenge the power of the group worker. For the most part the worker has to give control to the group for the group to become a group and for the worker to function as the facilitator. For new group workers this can be very threatening. The idea of giving up control is anathema when one of their greatest fears is losing control. However, reality is that the members of the group have to take ownership of the group before the group can become a group. Therefore, the worker really has little choice but to allow this to occur. What the worker needs to do is to plan for this stage and to use her influence to help the group structure itself in a way that is positive and benefits all of its members while meeting the needs of the group to sustain itself as a group. If the worker assesses and plans for the authority stage, she can maintain enough control to accomplish what needs to be done during this stage without losing complete control. This can be a chaotic time for the group and its members. Nothing is set yet. Norms and roles and ways of functioning have not been established.

Actions that the worker can take during this time are to support the group as it struggles through this. In many groups, the group will initially look to the worker to impose her will on the group as the first signs of a power struggle or a challenge to authority surface. If the worker succumbs to this temptation, members may rebel more strenuously or they might leave or the issues of power, control, and authority may submerge. All of these situations tend to be negative for the survival of the group. Open conflict aimed at the worker does not resolve the need for the group to decide on norms and roles. Leaving the group threatens the survival of the group if enough members opt out. Submerging control issues typically leads to passive-aggressive activities in which the efforts of the worker and the group are sabotaged.

Instead of imposing control over the group, the worker encourages the group to establish its own control over how the group will function. The worker yields control by telling group members that this is their group and they need to decide how it will function. The worker makes suggestions and encourages discussion about how the group will make decisions. This is where power and control really lie. Whoever and however decisions are made determine who is in control. Because decision making is so vital, the worker encourages a process that will include everyone in the group and discourages the group from excluding anyone. This essentially calls for some form of consensus to emerge. Groups are often tempted to use a democratic process in which votes are taken. However, problems can occur if those in the minority are consistently losing their voice in how the group functions. Groups that want to use a democratic style need to find ways of avoiding this especially in change-oriented groups where every member needs to benefit from the group. One way is to vote primarily on the priority or sequence of considering options. That way everyone's concerns are dealt with; the main issue is the sequence of doing so and when it will take place.

In this stage, the "I–we" issue is being sorted out and each member is concerned about whether they can retain individual autonomy while still being accepted and belonging to the group. If members feel controlled by the worker or by other members or the group as a whole, they will not feel free to self-disclose and expose themselves to others. This is where the issue arises. It will be settled in the next stage as the group negotiates ways of functioning that are inclusive and do not exclude members of the group. When the worker senses too much "I-ness," she addresses the group as a whole and calls attention to the need for the group to act collectively. She addresses individuals as members of the group and elicits responses out of that collective conscious. When the worker senses that there is too much "we-ness" or emphasis on the group at the expense of one or more individual members, she points this out and addresses members as individuals to rebalance the group.

Ongoing groups that are adding new members will revisit the authority stage as new members seek to establish whether they can be honest about themselves and their concerns and still be accepted by the group. If the group has established a process for including new members and addressing these issues up front, then it can move more quickly through this stage with little disruption. Groups that have not done this may find themselves struggling each time a new member comes into the group. If groups have found ways to make decisions, establish norms, and redistribute roles and share them during the course of the group, then the process of including new members and redistributing roles when new members join will go much smoother than if members have become entrenched or invested in certain roles.

The worker evaluates the group and individual members as the authority stage progresses. She looks for ways to encourage members to talk about their thoughts and feelings and observes how well the group is able to deal with conflict. Issues that address the need to share power, control, and authority are discussed, but conflict that is destructive toward individual members is confronted and discouraged. The worker evaluates how individual members respond to conflict at this stage. Who talks and who does not? Who speaks for the group and who speaks for themselves? Who seems invested and who does not? As these questions are answered, the worker encourages each member to participate in the discussion and may call on those who are quiet. She supports positive conflict resolution that is respectful and inclusive.

Termination during this stage is very similar to the orientation stage. The worker is concerned with members remaining committed to the group so she is careful to reassure the group that conflict is a normal part of group development and she highlights positive outcomes as the group struggles with finding ways to function that are positive and inclusive. The worker or the group should summarize the session and discuss it. If the worker decides to solicit a summary from the group, she should be prepared to reframe this to cast a positive light on whatever conflict has taken place.

As the group experiences the authority stage, the worker assesses the situation and plans for facilitating the group as it struggles with issues of power and control. She seeks to have the group take responsibility for making decisions in an inclusive way that considers the needs of members and the group as a whole. She evaluates group and individual progress through this stage and terminates sessions with a review of the progress that has been made.

## The Change Process During the Negotiation Stage

The conflict that arises in the authority stage is resolved during the negotiation stage. The group confronts, differs, and engages in conflict resolution. Goals, norms, roles, and tasks are established and the individuals become a group. Members feel positive about the group and there is a high level of group cohesion. The worker assists the group to reach this point during the negotiation stage. In settling on goals, norms, roles, and tasks, the group needs to be inclusive. If members are to feel a commitment to the group, they have to be able to see the group as a place in which they can meet their needs and achieve their goals. They must also have positive feelings about other members. They must feel accepted and free to be themselves to a certain extent.

Change-oriented groups require that members share their inner thoughts and feelings and expose vulnerable parts of themselves including their human flaws and frailties. Members have to feel safe and establish trust. Realistically, this can occur only if the group becomes a reflection of the cardinal values of social work. The first of those values is a belief in the value and worth of every human being, which leads to the requirement that people be treated with dignity and respect. When groups establish norms that reflect this value, members feel more safe in exposing themselves to others. If self-disclosure is met by acceptance and members are treated with dignity and respect, they feel good about receiving help and are encouraged to explore themselves and their situation further. This is what it means to experience intimacy: feeling unconditional acceptance for oneself. As other members see this, they are encouraged to risk.

In terms of the "I–we" balance, the group has reached a point at which both sides of this equation are equally important and members feel that "I" has become a part of the "we." In other words, at least some portion of one's identity as a person includes being a member of the group: "I feel that I belong and I am accepted and valued, just as I accept and value other members of our group." In many respects, in addition to the "I" and the "we" there is now an "I–we" that exists in the group and its members. This might best be described in terms of the feeling that for each individual member there is an individual identity or an "I." There is also a collective identity or a "we." However, for the group and each member there is an "I–we," or an identity that includes being a part of the group.

A second social work value is respecting self-determination, meaning social workers believe that people should have a right to make their own decisions about things that affect them. The group also needs to respect self-determination. The help that is given should not be imposed and group members should be allowed to decide for themselves what they do about their situation. Groups that are successful in establishing this value can become safe places to explore options and make decisions without conditions or limitations. Having a safe, accepting environment is invaluable to members in dealing with needs and concerns. Many group members may need to be in a group because they have not experienced this kind of environment in their personal life. Their families of origin may not have provided a very safe and accepting environment and they may not have been successful in establishing very intimate relationships.

A third cardinal value of social work is the belief that people should have the right to have socially accepted needs met in socially accepted ways. This value reflects basic social contract theory. As applied to society as a whole, it means that if society expects citizens to follow laws or social norms, then it must provide opportunities within the law or social norms for everyone to have their needs met. Similarly, counseling groups need to establish norms that give all of their members opportunities to have their needs met within the group. This is an essential feature of inclusiveness. Everyone needs to be included and no one is left out or left behind. This value also extends to the help that is given by the group. This value means that the group will support members in meeting socially accepted needs in socially accepted ways. The concept of social acceptance is important here. The group is not required to help members meet any and all needs or goals. The group should not help members engage in activities that are harmful to themselves or others. So the help of the group is also tempered by societal expectations.

Throughout his work with any group, the worker must take a mediating position. Mediation between client and environment is covered in Chapter 3. Mediation within the group is similar but is different in that all of the group members are clients. In order to serve any client system that has two or more members, the worker must be able to assume and be given a mediating position. This means that the worker does not take sides. If he were to take sides, then the relationship with other members of the client system is under-mined. In many respects, the worker needs to be seen as acting for the relationships within the client system, in this case the group. Taking sides generates rivalry and resentment. If the worker can be seen as neutral, he can help the group or group members to negotiate their differences and arrive at a mutually agreeable resolution.

As the group proceeds through the negotiation stage, the worker utilizes his skills in group facilitation and the change process. He models negotiation and compromise using a mediating position. Before and during group sessions, he assesses the needs of the group during this stage of development and facilitates movement as necessary. When the group is expressing thoughts and feelings appropriately, he allows the interactions to proceed. If the interactions become negative or destructive, he intervenes to help members get back on track. As the group establishes norms, especially like those related to social work values, the worker can use these to help with other norms, roles, and goals. He can ask questions about how the actions or statements fit with those norms and if they do not, how these could be changed so that they do fit. In a change-oriented group that is functioning well, the group itself takes over most of these actions and it is not necessary for the worker to intervene as much. The worker should model these actions for the group and encourage members to take responsibility for these functions in facilitating change in the group and other members.

Planning before and between sessions during this stage is centered on moving the group through the final stages of group formation and resolving issues related to this. If the worker is cognizant of the issues during this stage and the outcomes necessary to complete it, he can plan activities and interventions that will facilitate this. If this is the first session after the group has moved through the authority stage, he should recognize the fact that the group has struggled with those issues and seems ready to proceed with resolving them. He can summarize this for the group or solicit it from group members.

The worker might plan an opening summary that identifies norms, tasks, and goals that have already been established if this has occurred. Again, he could do this himself or solicit these from the group. The decision about when to create one's own summary and when to solicit this from the group takes some thought and consideration. The worker would like to see a summary that is comprehensive and builds on strengths and accomplishments and that sets the stage for the work to be done during the session. The risk is that this will not occur if group members do it. When this occurs, the worker can remind the group about what was missed or **reframe** negative comments into something more positive. For instance, if a group member stated that there were a lot of arguments during the last session, the worker should take this statement and reframe it, saying the group was sorting out its differences and looking for ways to resolve them. Probably the best strategy to use is for the worker to do the first couple of summaries to provide a model. Then he can do a partial summary and have the group fill in the rest, reframing negative contributions into issues related to the group's stage of development. As group members are able to hone these skills, the worker can turn more of it over to them. Generally, even when the group does the summary, the worker will pull it together and fill in any gaps. The worker also facilitates planning within the group session. He does this by helping the group set an agenda for the session and helping the group identify what needs to be done in the next session.

The worker's actions during this stage are focused on development of goals, norms, tasks, and roles. The worker helps the group to focus on these issues, especially as they relate to commonality and differences. He allows the group to negotiate and make suggestions. If necessary he models how to do this. For instance, he might ask the group to identify areas that they all agree on. He could then ask members to identify an area of disagreement. He asks members what it would take for them to be satisfied and then asks other members if they would be willing to do that. At times, he might negotiate reciprocal agreements. These involve each party agreeing to do something in exchange for the other parties doing something in return. This creates an atmosphere of give-and-take, which is usually necessary when individuals come together in a group.

The worker may need to ask questions or make suggestions during this time. He might ask what the group or its members would like to accomplish. He can ask how the group wants to function or what it needs to do and who has suggestions about how to do these things. If the group is stuck, the worker might allow silence to occur for a period of time to see if members will come forward. During a silence, the worker can still facilitate the group by labeling possible thoughts and feelings, such as, "This is hard to talk about," or "It is tough coming up with a solution for this," or similar observations.

If the worker needs to make suggestions to get the group unstuck, it is important that these be couched in terms of choices that the group might make and that it is clear that the worker is not making choices for the group. The worker can say, "Here is something for the group to consider." After making a suggestion, the worker should ask if anyone has any other ideas. This gives the group the message that various options are possible and that the worker does not expect his suggestions to be the only ones that are considered.

As the session unfolds, the worker evaluates the group and each member in a similar fashion as for the previous two stages. He needs to evaluate where the group is in moving through the negotiation stage. He needs to evaluate how each member participates or does not participate. He tries to draw more reluctant members into expressing their desires for the group and into the process of making decisions that are vital to group formation. Members must feel that they have ownership of the group if they are to become full participants.

Termination of sessions during this stage is also similar to the previous two stages except that it is focused on agreements that have been reached regarding goals, norms, and tasks. Unfinished business is identified and a plan is developed or an agreement reached to work on this during the next session. The process can be similar to opening and closing previous sessions in which the summary is offered by the worker, solicited from the group, or some combination of these.

As the group moves through the negotiation stage, it is completing the process of becoming a group and preparing for the work that needs to be done to achieve its purpose. Movement through this stage can be as brief as one session or a portion of a session to two or three sessions. Most of the time one or two sessions is sufficient. For new change-oriented groups and for time-limited ones, this process will generally take longer than for well-functioning, ongoing groups. Groups may need to revisit this and earlier stages of group development, especially ongoing groups. Of course, ongoing groups will visit this stage as it seeks to reconstitute itself when members leave and new ones join. Ongoing groups may also be similar to the previous stage in that groups that share roles and are accustomed to negotiating goals, norms, and tasks will be more likely to reestablish these quickly and smoothly when new members join than is the case for groups in which people are entrenched in roles and highly invested in certain norms.

## The Change Process During the Functional Stage

The functional stage represents the stage during which the work of the group in accomplishing its purpose occurs. Earlier stages are characterized by the group spending time and energy becoming a group. These earlier stages are important and necessary, otherwise the group will not be fully formed and will not be able to accomplish its purpose. Instead of acting on its own, the group would be excessively reliant on the worker carrying the load in accomplishing its purpose. There are times when this will happen with groups. The worker feels like he is doing all the work. Even groups that are well formed may lapse back into earlier stages of group formation. When groups lapse back or revisit these earlier stages, they typically need to proceed through subsequent stages before they are ready to fully benefit from the functional stage. Unfinished business from earlier stages will return and will undermine group functioning in the interim.

In terms of the "I–we" balance, highly functioning groups will tend to maintain this balance during this stage as group members balance the need for the group to maintain itself while also accomplishing its purpose of meeting the needs of its members. Members are very aware of their own needs while also being very sensitive to the needs of each other.

However, even the best groups will have moments when they are out of balance. It may be that one member is dominating the attention of the group and there is too much "I-ness," or the group ignores certain issues that may lead to conflict and there is too much "we-ness." When this occurs and no one comes forth to point it out, the worker may need to intervene and do so. He does this by first pointing it out to see if the group will deal with it. If not, he then addresses the issue using the opposite perspective. Too much "I-ness" means the worker asks the group as a whole (we) or individuals as members (I–we) to discuss their thoughts and feelings about the situation. Too much "we-ness" calls for the worker to ask members to speak for themselves as individuals (I) and express their individual thoughts and feelings.

In change-oriented groups, the functional stage is the point at which members are working on the issues that brought them into service and into the group. Goals have been established or are reestablished and more or less progress is occurring. This is when the benefits of being in a group are being felt. Group formation is typically not very much fun for the worker or the group. Some of it may be tedious, if not downright unpleasant. In fact, it is during the stages of group formation that members are typically at the highest risk of dropping out. Thus, it is important for the worker to be upbeat and reassuring as the group struggles with these stages. Once the group has been formed and a bond among group members established, the pleasures of being a part of the group can be felt. The reason for being in the group is taking place. Of course, not everything is pleasant. In fact, in change-oriented groups, members are typically dealing with the unpleasant parts of themselves and their lives. But the feelings of belonging and closeness with each other and the hope that their lives will improve give group members a sense that great things can be accomplished. Members experience their own progress and observe others working toward their goals. Members are giving and receiving help. The group is humming along and accomplishing its purpose.

The worker continues to engage in assessment and planning before and between groups sessions. He assesses group functioning and identifies work that has been done and work that needs to be done by the group and each of its members. He assesses strengths and challenges for the group as a whole and for each member. In ongoing groups, each member will typically be at a different point in reaching his or her goals. The worker assesses this for each member and seeks to understand how he might facilitate the group in a way that can be of greatest benefit to each member.

As the worker assesses each member and the group, he plans for ways to maximize the benefits of being in the group. Having thought about assessment and planning for the group and each member, the worker can look for opportunities to facilitate changes that are necessary to meet the needs of the group and its members and to assist them in accomplishing goals for the group and each member. Without this, the worker is merely "flying by the seat of his pants" instead of engaging in professional practice. To work with groups means to constantly assess, plan, and act before, during, and after each group session. The worker needs to understand what is helpful and what is not, what is needed and what is not, when the group and members are working and when they are not. Not only does the worker need to understand this, but he also needs to understand what the group and each member need from each other to make the group experience work. This is both art and science. Some of it comes from training, using supervision, and being able to analyze the complex situations that arise during group counseling. Some of it comes from experience, practice wisdom, and learning to develop and trust one's instincts about what is occurring in the group and what it means.

Thus, assessment and planning in group work involves both content and process. The worker observes and thinks about the content of each session. He also analyzes the content to uncover the underlying meaning that it has for the group as a whole and for each member. He observes both verbal and nonverbal behavior. He watches for consistency and **incongruities** or inconsistencies. Ivey has identified six areas of incongruity that can occur. We have added a seventh. These include:

1. Incongruities between two verbals
2. Incongruities between two nonverbals
3. Incongruities between verbal and nonverbal
4. Incongruities between verbal and behavior
5. Incongruities between two people
6. Incongruities between person and situation
7. Incongruities between person and environment[3]

In applying these to working with groups, the first three incongruities are inconsistencies that the worker might observe as group members interact with one another and with the worker. Members say something and then later, or sometimes even in the same sentence, say something different or even contradictory. For example, a member might say, "I love my mother, but I get angry with her because she wants to know everything I do." As an example of incongruity between two nonverbals, the member might be smiling while also clenching her teeth as she says this. Incongruities between verbal and nonverbal occur when a member's verbal and nonverbal behavior do not match. For instance, stating that one is angry while also smiling gives an inconsistent message.

The last three incongruities are situations outside of the group that represent much of what social workers deal with as they work with clients. Incongruities between person and situation are really about need. The person needs to have something occur or stop and instead it is not occurring or will not stop. The person needs to obtain something but is not receiving it. For example, someone who is starving needs food, but the situation that he is in does not result in his receiving enough food. This is really what defines need. Incongruities between two people indicate conflict or disagreement and are a special type of need. Incongruities between person and environment are indications of stressors in the environment that represent challenges to having needs met.

Incongruities that are experienced outside the group can manifest themselves in both the content of what is said or described by group members and by how they act in the group. In other words, members will describe incongruities in their lives that can be categorized in one or more of the last three incongruities. They will also act these out as they manifest the first three incongruities. If the worker or the group is able to observe and assess these incongruities, they can point them out and the group can help resolve them.

The fourth incongruity is about inconsistency between what a member says and what she does. This is the bridge between what is occurring in the group and what is occurring outside of the group. In working on needs and concerns, members set goals. In reaching these goals, members need to achieve objectives and work on tasks either within the group or outside of the group or both. An incongruity occurs when a member states something or makes a commitment to do something, but she does not follow through. She said she would do something, but she did not do it. Or, she said she would not do something, but she did it anyway.

The worker observes incongruities and assesses their meaning and significance. He might wait to see if they recur. If they do not, they are probably not very significant or do not represent barriers or challenges. Those that recur generally represent areas in which members are stuck and may need assistance in dealing with the situation. This leads to work within the group.

The worker takes action to resolve recurring incongruities when the group does not notice them or does not act to resolve them. Incongruities can be handled in a variety of ways. Those that represent situations that are needs outside of the group (the last three) should be clarified so that they can be understood and worked on. Typically, a paraphrase will accomplish this, such as, "So what I hear you saying is that you love your mother, but you are also angry with her because she wants to know everything that you are doing. Is that right?" Incongruities within the group (the first three) can be pointed out, or confronted if pointing them out does not result in working on them. This is not a personal confrontation, but one that points out the incongruity and asks the person to explain it. Pointing out the incongruity might be as follows: "On one hand you say you love your mother, but on the other hand you say that she makes you angry. Is that accurate?" Asking the member to explain it means substituting the question "Is that accurate?" with something such as, "Can you explain this?" or "How do you put these together?" or something similar. These latter questions constitute a confrontation.

Generally, incongruities between what a member says and what she does calls for the group or the worker to confront the member, especially when this represents a failure to follow through with working on her goals and objectives. Again, this is not personal but is either pointing out the inconsistency or asking the member to explain the inconsistency.

In addition to these actions, the worker also uses actions that are described in Chapters 3, 4, and 5. These include actions that can be taken within and outside of the group to facilitate completion of the plan, removal of barriers to the plan, and the functioning of both the group and individual members. These skills are related to relationship building, learning to use the change process, learning to use resources, empowering and enabling, crisis resolution, support, activity, and mediation. In addition, the worker engages in actions to facilitate group formation, facilitate discussion, resolve conflict, enhance group interaction, facilitate group development, and structure group activities. These practice actions will not be repeated here, but will be summarized as they relate to working with change-oriented groups. The reader should review this material before proceeding and include them in her work with change-oriented groups.

In change-oriented groups, relationships are central to the functioning of the group and they are frequently directly or indirectly related to the reasons members are in the group. Successful relationships are built on the ability to communicate, solve problems and make decisions, and resolve conflict in a constructive manner. These are also critical skills for change-oriented groups to acquire. Thus, as group functioning improves, members derive direct and indirect benefits. They improve their own relationship skills while also observing better relationship skills in others. This is one of the great things about groups.

As the group is formed and members learn to relate to one another, they are learning relationship skills that can be used outside of the group.

Similarly, in change-oriented groups members need to learn how to use the change process. The worker facilitates this from the very beginning and throughout the group. As the group uses the change process and members use it within the group, they are also learning how to use it in their lives outside of the group. This is a somewhat simplified version of the change process used by the worker. In essence, the group and its members need to learn to assess the need and the situation, develop a plan, act on it, and evaluate progress and the results. In simple terms, it is assess, plan, act, and evaluate.

During the functional stage in change-oriented groups, the actual changes that members need to make are occurring, and the group is helping to make this happen. The group explores situations with members and seeks to gain an understanding. It helps members to develop plans by brainstorming and making suggestions. It identifies and carries out actions that the group and the members need to take to be successful and helps members monitor their progress by checking in with one another on a regular basis. It provides motivation and support for the changes that need to occur.

In change-oriented groups, members need to learn about resources and how to use them. It is naive to think that the group or the worker will be able to meet all of the needs of the members. However, the group can be a place in which members learn about resources and how to use them. Some of this learning comes from one another and some may need to be provided by the worker. At the very least, the worker should be familiar with the resources in the community and the formal mechanisms for receiving those resources, such as eligibility, referral, application, and similar processes for obtaining resources. Individual members may have anecdotal information about resources that worked or did not work for them. As the group unfolds and the need for resources from outside the group is noted, group members and the worker can share their formal and informal information about accessing those resources. From this, the group can assist members in constructing a plan to obtain necessary resources to meet various needs. Not only do members learn about obtaining tangible resources, but they also learn about the process for doing so.

Often, the group may need to encourage members to be assertive and to advocate for themselves in obtaining resources. Members can practice assertive actions within the group through role-plays and similar activities. In addition, the worker may need to engage in advocacy for group members who are denied services for which they seem to be qualified.

Empowering and enabling are fundamental actions for change-oriented groups. They are covered in greater detail in Chapter 3. These are the primary means, along with support, by which groups bring about change. Change occurs when people are empowered and enabled. While empowering and enabling are used by the social worker in working with individuals and families, nowhere are these actions more powerful than they are in groups. The very experience of being in a group and feeling a sense of belonging is in itself very empowering. Receiving support from the group for change efforts is empowering and enabling. In fact, it is typically more empowering and enabling than when it comes only from the worker and not from a group. Learning assertiveness and advocacy skills is an example of empowerment. As the worker facilitates the group, he assists the group to develop an environment and a process that empowers members and enables them to use various skills. This includes using and facilitating the development of skills in validating feelings, using positive reinforcement, giving feedback, and cognitive and behavioral change.

Crisis intervention is used whenever a crisis or an emergency arises within or outside of the group. This is covered in greater detail in Chapter 3. Crisis intervention within the group typically takes place when a member is overwhelmed by a situation. It may be one that is related to the reason for being in the group or it can be a situation that arises outside of the group during the course of the member's work with the group. Any crisis can make it difficult if not impossible for members to work and derive any benefit from the work. So, crises need to be dealt with whenever they occur. The group is a good place to work on crisis management and resolution. In fact, some settings have what they call crisis groups. When people are in crisis they need support, mobilization of problem-solving efforts, access to resources, and shoring up their **coping** skills. The group is an excellent place to receive these. The group members receive the added benefits of learning to deal with and resolve crises and feeling good about helping someone who is overwhelmed.

Support is another primary means that groups use to bring about change. It is invaluable for change-oriented groups. Support is discussed in greater detail in Chapter 3 and support groups are covered in Chapter 7. The process of receiving support not only benefits the recipient, it also benefits the giver. People feel better about their situation, but they also feel good about themselves because they feel that someone cares about them. In addition, giving support makes one feel positive. Part of the use of support in change-oriented groups is helping the group to establish support for change. In support groups, members are typically coping with a situation that is either beyond their control or cannot be changed, such as coping with cancer or dementia or the death of a loved one. In change-oriented groups, support can be given for efforts to change situations that are under some control of the members. Change can be very intimidating because we do not know what to expect or we might fear failure. Receiving support can be the difference between trying something new and staying put. In fact, often members are motivated to change out of a desire to receive approval from the group and avoid disappointing them.

Most groups use some form of activity in assisting members to make changes. Within the group, there may be role-plays or similar activities. Some groups may benefit from program activities to gain information, develop insight, or generate discussion. The use of program activities is discussed in Chapter 8.

Another activity that is essential in change-oriented groups is for members to work on homework assignments. One of the major blocks to any change effort is carryover. Clients may learn new skills, make decisions, and make commitments to change, but these do not mean that change in their life outside of group or individual sessions will actually occur. Clients may not follow through or may do so only partially. They may try, but fail. The best way to ensure some level of carryover is to have members engage in change-oriented activities outside of the group. These efforts can be discussed in group, where the members receive support and feedback and can problem solve any barriers or failures. Desires to receive approval from the group and avoid disappointing them are powerful motivators for most group members.

Mediating between a member and a system in her environment typically occurs outside of the group. However, members can learn valuable skills by observing this skill directly or indirectly. Most of the time this is indirect observation, unless the group member is a part of the situation. Indirect experiences are ones in which the member and the worker share experiences with this type of mediation with the group and it is discussed. Mediation is also a skill that is used within the group by the worker. This gives members an opportunity to experience this more directly. Maintaining a neutral position can be quite difficult. Learning to give and take, negotiate and compromise is often the key to maintaining good relationships.

The worker engages in actions that are designed to facilitate the development of the group through each stage of development including taking actions to facilitate group formation, facilitate discussion, resolve conflict, enhance group interaction, facilitate group development, and structure group activities. These are described in Chapter 4 and are imbedded in much of what is described in Chapter 5 and in this chapter, and is not repeated here. However, we discuss these actions with respect to facilitating group process, which is what these skills are designed to accomplish. In change-oriented groups, the purpose of the group cannot be achieved unless the group is able to function in a manner that provides members with an environment that supports change.

Groups must also be able to progress through the stages of group development and group members need to interact in a way that supports change. This does not come naturally but needs to be nursed and coached and coaxed and massaged from group members. Much of this is more art than science as the group worker initiates, withdraws, listens, responds, models, encourages, supports, challenges, and shares as he seeks to help the group create the necessary ingredients for change. At times he is like a maestro leading an orchestra. At other times he is like a member of the orchestra making his own music while appreciating the contributions of those around him. Still other times he is like a member of the audience sitting back and enjoying the blending of various notes into a harmony of sound. When groups are coming together and doing their work there is an exhilaration in watching and participating that goes beyond what social workers typically experience in working with individuals. Watching group members help each other is thrilling and gratifying. In groups, the whole is greater than the sum of the parts. The sound of the instruments playing together in harmony in an orchestra is immensely more pleasing than the sounds of the individual instruments playing separately.

As with other stages of group development, the worker continuously monitors the progress of the group and each member. However, during the functional stage the emphasis is on making progress toward achieving group and individual goals and meeting group and individual needs. This is the stage during which group members should be accomplishing whatever they need to do within the group. They should be meeting the needs and resolving the situations that caused them to be in the group. The group should be achieving its purpose, which is to assist members to bring about change in their lives. Part of the worker's evaluation at this stage is determining the extent to which the group is effective and understanding why it is or is not. For those members who are making progress or are completing their work, the worker evaluates what has worked and what has not worked so he can help the group to improve its functioning. For members who are not making progress or who are lagging behind, the worker evaluates what might be missing or what might be needed to make the group more effective. In groups that are functioning well, these evaluations are a part of what the group itself does during sessions. The worker may need to prompt this, but group members can share their own experiences and their observations.

Terminating group sessions during this stage can sometimes be difficult in that the group may want to continue for longer periods of time when members are highly invested in the work that is being done. During some sessions, time seems to fly by because a great deal of work gets done. Other sessions may seem longer when very intense work is occurring and members feel tension building, followed by a release of that tension as significant gains are made or barriers to change are reduced. As with earlier stages, there is a summary of the work that has been done and the work that lies ahead. For members it is important to review work that needs to be done between sessions. This is likely to be much more effective if each member identifies what she intends to do between now and the next group session. The worker should give feedback about what has been accomplished and praise the work that has been done.

## The Change Process During the Disintegration Stage

Disintegration can occur at any time during the previous stages or when members are completing the work that brought them to the group. For time-limited groups, disintegration tends to occur as the group approaches the planned ending of group sessions. In these groups, everyone goes through disintegration and termination together unless someone drops out along the way. However, most change-oriented groups are ongoing, which means that termination is more focused on individual members as they either complete their work or drop out of the group. This section focuses on two types of disintegration, when members are progressing toward completing their work and when a group shows signs of disintegration.

First let us review what occurs during this stage. Disintegration is marked by a lessening of bonds within the group. The frequency and strength of group interaction is reduced along with common norms and values among group members and the strength of the influence that the group has on members. At the same time, members are likely to be increasing and strengthening their interaction with their ecosystem outside of the group.

It is expected that disintegration will occur as members complete their work. For one thing, they are no longer as reliant on the group for problem solving, decision making, coping, support, and other things that the group has provided. The needs that brought them to the group are being met so there is much less motivation to be in the group and less investment in the group. Members are preparing to go on with their lives without the group. The termination process is discussed in Chapters 3, and 4 and is not repeated here, but we will consider group process and the worker's actions during termination.

Whenever a member terminates from a change-oriented group it reminds the other members that some day they will also terminate their involvement. This can create anxiety but can also create motivation to complete their own work. It is not unusual to have a situation in which the group goes on for a period of time with a stable membership, but when one member completes his work, it is as if a logjam has broken and several others will do likewise in a relatively short period of time. At the same time that this is occurring, other members may be regressing back to an earlier level of functioning as they flee from the prospect of leaving the group.

When members leave an ongoing group, new members will typically replace them. As this takes place, the group needs to reform itself around this new composition of members. In reality, whenever membership changes the group is a different group. This includes sessions in which a member is absent. Group dynamics are changed and how the group functions changes as well. This is why it is necessary to close membership and stabilize it for change-oriented groups. It is also a reason to stress the need to make a commitment to attend the group regularly unless there is an emergency or illness. Members are unlikely to open up and trust if they do not know who will be there from one session to the next.

Changing membership means reestablishing the group. In order to go through the earlier stages of group formation, the group must disintegrate and become less cohesive for a while. If the group did not do this, then rigidity around norms, roles, and tasks is likely to set in as a response to these changes and resistance to the changes is elevated. New members will not feel welcome and will have difficulty in seeing a place for themselves in the group. So, some disintegration needs to occur so the group can revisit the first three stages of group development and reform itself around the new membership.

During the disintegration stage, the worker assesses the needs of the group and its members. If this is a time-limited group, then the group and its members need to be prepared for ending the group. This should begin about three sessions from the end to give everyone an opportunity to finish their work and for the group to prepare an ending. The worker reminds the group of this. If the worker and the group have been thorough in terminating each session, then the group has already had some preparation for the termination of the group.

If this is an ongoing group, it means that a member or the worker may be terminating, but the group is continuing on. For member terminations, the worker, the group, and the member should plan for the ending. The worker should ensure that the member has completed his work and that the group has also confirmed this and both the member and the group have prepared themselves for disengagement. The member should be demonstrating that his needs or concerns have been met. He should be showing greater investment in his ecosystem and less in the group. The group needs to let go and support the member as he launches himself from the group. After there have been several of these departures, the group should have developed an awareness of what to do in these situations. However, the first few may be difficult. Members might feel a need to hang on to each other and may be reluctant to let go. The group as a whole may feel threatened as the bonds with the member are loosened. They may worry that the group might fall apart. Once they find that this is not the case, the group will feel stronger as it is able to enjoy the successes of its members as they finish their work.

Premature departures may be difficult to predict and to handle. In change-oriented groups, it is essential that the worker follow up whenever a member drops out of the group because of the reasons that the members are in the group. The group experience is intended to help members resolve situations that require assistance. The worker should contact the member to see if he will return to the group. If not, the worker should offer other services either within her agency or, if necessary, with another agency. The worker should report back to the group whether the member will be returning and reassure them that every effort will be made to see to it that services are offered if the member decides not to return. This is done primarily with change-oriented groups because of the close bond that members have with one another. Members become invested in one another and are hurt when someone drops out. Other types of groups do not typically form such close bonds, but then again those groups do not require the same level of trust and self-disclosure.

The group needs to plan for disintegration and termination. The worker may have had something in mind when she began the group, but the group should be involved in deciding how they would like to end the group if it is time limited or their involvement in the group if it is ongoing and members will be leaving the group. Termination may be as simple as going around the room and having members have their last say. Most will wish the departing member well and will also offer thanks for his assistance or fond memories that they will take with them. Some groups might want to celebrate with food, perhaps a potluck or a cake. Some groups will have graduation ceremonies or rituals. This is more common in groups in residential settings where completion of the group coincides with graduating from the program.

Group disintegration can occur before the group is supposed to end. This is less likely for time-limited groups, since the group is scheduled to end at some point anyway. For an ongoing group, it represents a crisis of sorts. The group has regressed to an earlier stage or is at risk of ending prematurely. Work is probably not getting done. Attendance may be sporadic or dropping. The worker needs to decide if she will act to try to save the group from falling apart or if it might be time to let the group end. If the worker decides to act to save the group, she needs to discuss the group with members. Ideally, this is done in the group, but she might need to contact members individually to find out what is happening and if they want to try to keep the group going. Probably the most frequent reasons for a group to have this happen are personal conflicts that have arisen. If these can be resolved, then the group might continue. If the group is not providing a benefit to its members or if a member is not benefiting from the group or if the group or a member or members are saying and doing things that are harmful to other group members, then this needs to be resolved. If it cannot be resolved, then the group may either end or a member or members may be asked to leave. Of course, if the group ends or members are asked to leave, arrangements are made for everyone to receive other services.

In making an effort to resolve any conflicts, the worker maintains a mediating position and refrains from taking sides. She tries to get each party to express their concerns and asks them for their input in how this might be resolved. Ideally, this should be done either in the group or in a face-to-face meeting. If hostility is too great to do this, then the worker may act as the middleman in negotiating with each side.

As the group begins to disintegrate and terminate or a member prepares to leave, the worker evaluates the work that has been done. The group and members should take stock of where they started and what has been accomplished. They should identify what was helpful, what was not helpful, and what might have been helpful. Throughout the group, the worker needs to evaluate the group and its members and try to anticipate any premature departures before they occur. The worker may be able to head these off by discussing any concerns and encouraging actions that would increase the likelihood of success.

When the group is disintegrating because it is ending, the worker encourages members to loosen their bonds with one another and strengthen bonds with their ecosystem. Some members might resist this. The worker should point out that the quality of their relationships is what made the group successful. Members who have been able to establish satisfying relationships in the group can also do so outside of the group. The worker tries to ensure that members take their successes with them by owning their success. She should not let them attribute their successes to the group or the worker.

If the worker is leaving the group, it will likely be at risk of some disintegration. Some groups may end completely. Others may lose some membership. This can usually be avoided if there has been a coleader or if the new worker can meet with the group several times before the worker departs. This should be a very rare occurrence for time-limited groups. The worker should not start a time-limited group if she knows she is leaving and will not be able to finish the group. However, having the worker leave the group can happen with ongoing groups, especially if they have been meeting over an extended period of time. Workers might leave for a wide variety of reasons. The most common are leaving the agency for another position or moving to another position within the agency.

Less common reasons for the worker to leave are lay off, firing, closing the agency or program, and death. These latter reasons are quite traumatic for both the worker and the group. If the group is ending for any of these reasons, an effort needs to be made to help resolve any issues related to the worker leaving or the group ending and arrangements need to be made for members to receive needed alternative services. Typically, the worker's supervisor should step in and do this if the worker is not available.

Whenever a worker leaves the group, she should prepare the group for her departure and for a new worker. She should ask members to express their concerns and reassure them that other workers will be as committed as she has been and can be as helpful. Often clients feel that help that is given by the social worker is personal and that no one else will be able to help them. Of course this is not true. In reality, they are the ones who do the real work, and if they can work with one worker they will be able to work with others. The idea that only this person can help them is magical thinking. After all, if that were the case, think of the odds that out of all of the billions of people in the world, the worker just happened to be at the agency where the client ended up receiving help. What if the worker happened to be some-where else, across town or across the country or across the world? Would that mean the client would never have received help? Of course not; this line of thinking is ludicrous. The worker should not be so vain as to take credit for the work that was done. Besides, in change-oriented groups, it is the group and its members who do the work and help each other.

For some members, finding out that the worker is leaving becomes a motivator to fin-ish their work. Some might feel that they do not want to wait and work with another worker. Others might feel that they do not want to have to tell their story over again. Some might feel abandoned and do not want to form a bond with another worker. Some members may drop out of the group because of these reasons. Other members might want to finish their work as a gift to the departing worker or to receive the worker's approval before she leaves. While some of these reasons are positive, a decline in membership may still threaten the survival of the group and this should be discussed.

New workers with ongoing groups need to allow the group to have feelings about the previous worker. These should be explored, beginning with the first session. If there are joint sessions with the former and the new worker, it should be discussed openly in those sessions and then discussed again when the new worker starts facilitating the group on his own. If there is a coleader it should be discussed before the other worker leaves, after she leaves, and again when a new coleader joins the group. The worker needs to allow for all of the potential feelings that are typically associated with grief and loss: denial, anger, bar-gaining, grief, and resolution. These may be felt for several sessions before the group is ready to move on.

Groups with new workers will almost inevitably need to revisit all of the earlier stages of group development. They will at least need to orient the new worker, and the worker needs to establish a relationship with the members. This can be a time for the group to reexamine itself and make changes that may actually improve the functioning of the group. In the process of doing this, the group will experience some disintegration before it reforms itself. The new worker should expect this and facilitate the process.

The worker uses her knowledge, values, and skills in facilitating change-oriented groups throughout the stages of group development. She uses knowledge and skills in communication and relationships. She uses the change process and helps the group and its members to learn how to use it. The worker ensures that the group reflects the cardinal values of social work. She uses her knowledge and skills in assessment and planning before the group begins and throughout the life of the group. The worker uses practice actions to facilitate the group and she evaluates progress toward achieving goals. She helps the group and its members to terminate. The social worker develops skills in both the art and the science of group work.

# Summary

One type of group in generalist social work practice is the group that is intended to bring about changes in group member's lives. We refer to this kind of group as a change-oriented group. These include problem-solving, decision-making, and counseling groups. A major component of these groups is self-disclosure. For self-disclosure to occur, members need to build trust. This means that most of these types of groups will be ongoing and have a closed membership.

As the worker facilitates change-oriented groups, she uses the change process at each stage of development. She assesses and plans before the group begins, during each session, and between each session. She acts as needed to facilitate movement of the group through each stage. The worker helps the group through group formation by facilitating orientation, understanding and resolving conflict during the authority stage, and helping the group to compromise and reach consensus during the negotiation stage. She encourages and supports the group in accomplishing its purpose during the functional stage. She helps the group to loosen bonds and supports members in consolidating gains as they are leaving the group during the disintegration stage. She also uses her relationship skills and her skills as a social worker.

CASE **6.1**

## Proposal for a Group for Female Victims of Domestic Violence

### I. Background Information

#### A. Group purpose

The proposed group is for women who are victims of domestic violence. The purpose of the group is to assist members in overcoming the social, emotional, and psychological effects of domestic violence. Members will receive support for developing healthy self-esteem, positive relationships, and greater independence. The group is being formed because individual work is not sufficient to provide these outcomes. Victims of domestic violence need to know that they are not alone and that change can occur. In addition, members will feel more empowered as they engage in mutual aid and assistance.

*(continued)*

CASE **6.1** Continued

The target audience is women who are in the domestic violence shelter or who are clients in the TriCounty Domestic Violence Program. It is anticipated that membership will vary in terms of size and diversity. The ideal size is eight members, but there may be more or fewer than this, depending on the demand for services. The group will be ongoing with a somewhat closed membership, in that members will not be able to drop in. However, the group will not be entirely closed in that members may be added and there will not be a specified number of group members. Additional groups will be added when demand is too high for the group to accommodate any more members.

### B. Group worker(s)

The group will be facilitated by two staff members or a staff member and a volunteer. At least one of the group workers will have either a BSW or MSW degree with a minimum of two years' experience in domestic violence and experience or training in facilitating groups. Currently, there are four staff members who meet these degree requirements and three volunteers. Two staff members and two volunteers have the experience in domestic violence and are trained or have experience in facilitating groups. They will be supervised by the case management supervisor who has an MSW and is trained in group work. One of the volunteers has similar qualifications and can serve as a backup for supervision and consultation.

### C. Group format

The group will use a mixture of structured and unstructured formats. During each session, time will be set aside for each. Structured activities will include learning about the cycle of domestic violence and how to break the cycle, assertiveness training, positive parenting skills, and other activities that members indicate they wish to pursue. These will be adapted to the needs and strengths of the group and its members. Members will be involved in planning the types of structured activities they desire and workers will be responsible for researching, preparing, and implementing them. It is expected that variations of activities from feminist practice, Afrocentric approaches, and other diversity approaches will be incorporated according to the diversity composition of the group. The unstructured time will be used to work with group members on improving self-esteem, developing positive relationships, and establishing greater independence.

### D. Sanctioning of group

The group is an obvious fit with the mission and goals of the agency. In the past, the agency has only provided individual counseling for clients with some groups being offered in the shelter program. This proposal will expand the agency's way of functioning to include group work as a major method of providing services. The agency has grown to a point where the size of the client base is sufficient to provide enough group members to make group work feasible.

The group will need to have access to a room at the shelter and will need funding for coffee or beverages, a healthy snack, and program materials. There is no additional expense for the room except for a slight increase in the utility bill for lighting. A local grocery store has agreed to sponsor the group and provide coffee and juice and surplus fruits and vegetables for snacks.

## II. Description of the group

### A. Membership

As indicated in I.A., the anticipated members of the group will be drawn primarily from women who are in the shelter program and those who are clients of the agency and are living in the community. The women currently being served range in age from eighteen to fifty four. Seventy percent are Caucasian, twenty percent are African American, and ten percent are Hispanic. It is expected that the composition of the group will be roughly similar to this. Fliers will be posted around the shelter and given to case managers to give to their clients. In addition, an article will appear in the agency's newsletter.

As potential members are identified, they will be interviewed by the staff identified as workers for the group. The staff will assess their readiness for the group and will provide a basic orientation. The full orientation will occur in the group itself. As new potential members are identified, a similar process will occur, although the orientation by the worker will be more thorough to ease the transition into the group and reduce the amount of time needed to orient new members during the group.

The first group session will be used to facilitate group formation. An icebreaking activity will be used that has members talk in pairs about themselves and then each member will introduce herself. The group will be offered various types of program activities and will be asked to identify which would be preferred or if there were other activities or information that they would find valuable. It is planned that the cycle of violence will be covered during the second session and a more concentrated discussion about breaking the cycle will occur during the third. This will give group members the opportunity to move slowly toward telling their own stories while also giving them a way of structuring their discussion. It is anticipated that assertiveness training will be the next focus, unless the group decides it would prefer another topic.

**B. Time, place, and other elements**

The group will tentatively meet in the conference room at the agency on Tuesdays from 6:00 to 8:00 p.m. A second group will be added during the day if a sufficient number of members can be recruited. As prospective members are identified, they will be asked to indicate the best times and dates for meetings and the schedule will be adjusted accordingly. The group workers and members will work together in setting a schedule for setting up the room, preparing coffee, picking up the juices and fruits and vegetables, and cleaning and preparing the latter for group.

Transportation and child care may be required. The first option will be to have members car pool with each other. Initially this will be part of the orientation with the worker. It will also be incorporated into the first group sessions. Bus tickets will be offered to those who are not able to arrange transportation. Child care will be arranged using volunteers and students. The students will develop and implement activities that are appropriate for the ages of the children.

**C. Program planning specifics**

Equipment needed will be the agency's audio/video equipment to show DVDs and videos. Program material on assertiveness training and other subjects will need to be purchased. It is estimated that the cost of these will be approximately $1,000.00 for the year. Arrangements have been made to check out material from the local community college and university libraries and to borrow items from the child development program at the community college and the social work department at the university.

**III. Evaluation Mechanisms**

The projected outcomes for the group or groups will be that there will be at least two functioning groups by the end of the first year, one in the evening and a second during the day. Each group member will be asked to identify at least two goals, and half of the members will complete at least one goal within six months of joining the group.

The measures used will be a combination of goal monitoring by the workers to track goals and self-anchoring scales developed by each member as they identify goals for themselves.

# QUESTIONS

1. Using Table 6.1, develop a plan or proposal for a change-oriented group.

2. Describe how you would use assessment skills during various stages of the group from Question 1 or another group.

3. Describe how you would use planning during various stages of the group from Question 1 or another group.

4. Describe how you would use direct practice actions during various stages of the group from Question 1 or another group.

5. Describe how you would use group facilitation skills during various stages of the group from Question 1 or another group.

6. Describe how you would use evaluation during various stages of the group from Question 1 or another group.

7. Describe how you would deal with disintegration or termination during various stages of the group from Question 1 or another group.

# SUGGESTED READINGS

Johnson, Louise C., and Yanca, Stephen J., *Social Work Practice: A Generalist Approach*, 9th ed. Boston: Allyn & Bacon, 2007 (Chapter 14).

Edwards, Richard L., Ed. *Encyclopedia of Social Work*, 19th ed. Washington, DC: NASW Press, 1995 ("Group Practice Overview").

Gitterman, Alex, and Shulman, Lawrence. *Mutual Aid Groups, Vulnerable and Resilient Populations, and the Life Cycle,* 3rd ed. New York: Columbia University Press, 2005.

Grief, Geoffrey, and Ephross, Paul, Eds. *Group Work with Populations at Risk,* 2nd ed. New York: Oxford University Press, 2005.

Jacobs, Ed, Masson, Robert, and Harvill, Riley. *Group Counseling Strategies and Skills,* 5th ed. Pacific Grove, CA: Brooks/Cole, 2006.

Ivey, Allen E., Pederson, Paul B., and Ivey, Mary Bradford. *Intentional Group Counseling: A Microskills Approach.* Belmont, CA: Thomson/Wadsworth, 2001.

Johnson, David W., and Johnson, Frank P. *Joining Together: Group Theory and Group Skills*, 9th ed. Boston: Allyn & Bacon, 2006.

Kottler, Jeffery. *Learning Group Leadership: An Experiential Approach.* Boston: Allyn & Bacon, 2001.

Northern, Helen, and Kurland, Roselle. *Social Work with Groups,* 3rd ed. New York: Columbia University Press, 2001.

Shulman, Lawrence. *The Skills of Helping: Individuals, Families, Groups, and Communities,* 6th ed. Belmont, CA: Thomson-Brooks/Cole, 2009.

Toseland, Ronald W., and Rivas, Robert F. *An Introduction to Group Work Practice,* 6th ed. Boston: Allyn & Bacon, 2009.

# 7 Support and Self-Help Groups

## LEARNING EXPECTATIONS

1. Understanding the importance of support and self-help groups in generalist social work practice.
2. Understanding support and self-help groups offered within generalist practice.
3. Understanding the use of the change process in support and self-help groups.
4. Understanding of group process so as to be able to recognize its various aspects in the functioning of support and self-help groups.
5. Understanding of how the social worker can facilitate the work and process of support and self-help groups.
6. Beginning skill in facilitating small-group interaction in support and self-help groups.

This chapter examines generalist social work practice with support and self-help groups. There has been a substantial increase in these types of groups over the past few decades. Support and self-help groups are focused on providing assistance with coping with difficulties and bringing about change through self-disclosure and support. Thus, we have chosen to cover these two types of groups together because we see the value of both types as coming mainly from the use of support. We begin this chapter by identifying the basic elements of support.

In Chapter 3, we identified Florence Hollis's description of sustainment as one of the procedures of social work practice and very close to the notion of support. Sustainment is primarily expressed by nonverbal means. If we apply Hollis's concepts to support provided in groups we could expect to see group members sustaining or supporting one another by focusing on abilities, competencies, and strengths; showing interest in each other and a desire to help; expressing an understanding of the situation and feelings about the situation; and providing encouragement and reassurance. Reassurance would be realistic and the emphasis would be on the feeling component and support for the acceptability of having feelings about the situation.[1]

We also described Judith Nelson's definition of supportive procedures. Using Nelson's classification we could expect to see the worker and the group providing members with (1) *protection* by giving advice and helping to structure tasks that are necessary to cope with the situation; (2) *acceptance* by empathizing with one another, confirming the value and worth of one another, and expressing an understanding of the situation and feelings about the situation; (3) *validation* by identifying areas of effectiveness and competence, giving feedback and hope, praising, and encouraging coping efforts; and (4) *education* about coping and resources, learning new roles, and developing insight.[2]

So we should see these elements occurring during the functional stage of group development in support and self-help groups. We should also see group members supporting one another in engaging in healthy, growth-producing activities. Deciding on what to support and how to provide support is very important. To some extent the group needs to hear from its members what they need from the group. In addition, the worker needs to facilitate the development of positive approaches to dealing with the situation at hand rather than merely listening to the negative aspects of it. Initially this may need to come from the worker. Gradually, the group should take over as it grows, develops, and learns to share positive coping strategies. Positive coping will typically involve thoughts, feelings, and actions. Listening to stories of woe is depressing. Listening to stories of finding peace and solace and at times overcoming the odds can be uplifting. Meeting spiritual needs at these times is important for many people. Finding respite and engaging in activities that relieve stress are positive approaches to coping. To get to the functional stage, groups need to go through stages of group formation. These stages are made up of what we call orientation, authority, and negotiation. The final stage is disorganization, which signals the end of either the group or the departure of a member from the group.

## Group Purposes in Support and Self-Help Groups

It may seem that the two types of groups being considered in this chapter are different from each other and so they should be examined separately. However, we believe that the differences are much more associated with how these groups are structured rather than how they function. We believe that support from fellow group members is the primary mechanism by which both of these types of groups benefit their members. Let us first look at how support and self-help groups are different. In support groups, typically there is a professional who serves as host, resource person, facilitator, and the convener of the group. Sometimes the professional also offers support, but the most valuable source of support comes from other members of the group. Most self-help groups do not include a professional as a member of the group, although a professional may serve as a host who provides a place for the group to meet and perhaps some resources. There are exceptions when self-help groups are led by professionals, such as residential programs that treat substance abuse disorders.

Most self-help groups have a change aspect to them that makes them somewhat different from support groups. Thus, to some extent the purpose of self-help groups is different and perhaps more closely associated with change-oriented groups. Members of support groups are typically coping with something that cannot be changed or is beyond their control. For example, a support group for parents of children who have died helps parents cope with their loss. Support groups for cancer patients or for their families are intended to provide support as people face this devastating disease. In the first example, members are coping with something that cannot be changed. In the second, they are coping with something that may change, but they do not have control over it. They cannot decide not to have cancer. Members receive support during the group, and in an ideal support group, members exchange contact information and provide support to each other outside of the group.

Many self-help groups are based on a model that is similar to Alcoholics Anonymous (AA). In this model, members engage in self-disclosure and work on a twelve-step program of recovery. The twelve steps based on the description of the founders of AA are as follows:

1. We admit we are powerless over alcohol—that our lives have become unmanageable.
2. We believe that a Power greater than ourselves can restore us to sanity.
3. We have made a decision to turn our will and our lives over to the care of God *as we understand Him*.
4. We have made a searching and fearless moral inventory of ourselves.
5. We admit to God, to ourselves, and to another human being the exact nature of our wrongs.
6. We are entirely ready to have God remove all these defects of character.
7. We humbly ask Him to remove our shortcomings.
8. We have made a list of all persons we have harmed, and are willing to make amends to them all.
9. We have made direct amends to such people wherever possible, except when to do so would injure them or others.
10. We continue to take personal inventory and when we are wrong promptly admit it.
11. We seek through prayer and meditation to improve our conscious contact with God, *as we understand Him*, praying only for knowledge of His will for us and the power to carry that out.
12. Having had a spiritual awakening as the result of these steps, we try to carry this message to alcoholics, and to practice these principles in all our affairs.[3]

The group provides support throughout the process and eventually those in more advanced stages of recovery become sponsors for others who are in earlier stages. Sponsors are available around the clock to assist with resisting temptations to lapse. The change-oriented aspect to self-help groups is what makes them different from support groups and more similar to problem-solving and decision-making groups, but without the presence of a professional worker. There are some self-help groups that have a professional who serves similar functions as those in a support group. One example is Parents Anonymous, a self-help group for parents who have or are at risk of abusing or neglecting their children.

We believe that support is the primary mechanism that makes self help-groups successful. As members self-disclose about their addiction, they receive support from other members. As they move through the twelve steps, they receive more support. When they have a sponsor, they are able to receive support whenever they need it from the same person. This level of support cannot be offered by professional workers who must have time away from their work in order to be able to provide quality services. Agencies can and do provide around the clock crisis intervention, but the staff is typically different from those providing service or the responsibility is rotated on an on call basis.

Self-help groups arose in part because of the lack of success in treating most addictions in therapy groups. The belief in most models of self-help groups is that real change can come only from receiving help from others who have or are going through the same thing. We agree that the group needs to be the primary mechanism for assisting members in bringing about change.

Some people can receive all the help they need in self-help groups and so they do not need professional services. However, we believe that most people need both and some may need to be in a group that is facilitated by a professional. Thus, we view self-help groups as a valuable resource for assisting clients who experience serious addictions or habits, or who need ongoing help to maintain their recovery.

Support and self-help groups are offered in a wide variety of settings to a wide variety of clientele by a wide variety of professionals, including BSWs and MSWs. These settings include hospitals, clinics, and other medical settings; outpatient mental health and family service agencies; organizations intended to serve people experiencing various diseases and conditions (cancer, dementia, addictions, to name a few); and inpatient, outpatient, or residential substance abuse treatment settings. Typically, these groups are offered in settings where there are clients, patients, family members, and/or caregivers who are in need of services that go beyond that which the organization provides on a day to day basis. These groups are typically in need of support for coping with their situation or support for changing it in the case of self-help groups.

As with change-oriented groups, young children are typically not good candidates for these types of groups. Children and young adolescents are very action oriented so they generally do not make good candidates for groups that rely primarily on discussion. There are also some limitations on the extent to which they might be able to provide the supportive aspects required in these types of groups. Usually working with children and young adolescents calls for some type of activity around which some discussion can take place. The activity may be related to an issue they are dealing with such as divorce, making friends, grief, or school success. However, adolescents around fourteen or fifteen years old and older, can participate in support and self-help groups and are included here along with adults.

## Assessment and Planning Before the Group Begins

As with change-oriented groups, the worker uses the change process in organizing and facilitating the group. Often, group work actually represents part or all of the action phase. In the case of support or self-help groups, participation in the group may be the means by which the action phase is carried out. It may also be a supplement to other actions of the client and the worker. In addition, support and self-help groups can be used to provide ongoing assistance after formal services are delivered when support is still needed.

The expansion of managed care has limited the amount of service available from professionals in many settings including health care, mental health, and substance abuse. The most dramatic area where limitations have occurred is in the provision of support. Professionals in these settings no longer have the time to do this and it is often not reimbursed. Thus, support and self-help groups can provide a very valuable service that is no longer readily available from professional workers. Because the number of sessions with a professional is usually limited, workers need to plan for ongoing services immediately and should see to it that clients are connected to those services from the very beginning. Thus, the use of support and self-help groups should be a part of most plans that require ongoing or long-term assistance. The ideal situation is for agencies to coordinate their efforts so that a wide array of support and self-help groups are available while avoiding duplicating efforts. Linking clients with support and self-help groups has the potential to shorten the time clients need services from professionals. It also can decrease difficulties with transferring to a group after termination because clients are involved in a group from the start.

With all groups, the worker assesses and plans before the group begins and between each stage of group development as well as between sessions and within each group session. Assessment and planning within each session and between sessions will be discussed as we cover each stage of group development. Some groups that provide support may occur naturally in the environment and support may come from others in the client's ecosystem. However, support and self-help groups are formed groups that have specific purposes. As such, they are not natural groups but are artificial or contrived.

In forming a group, the worker generally must seek and obtain approval from her agency as she would with change-oriented groups as described in Chapter 6. She must also secure participants and take care of the logistical aspects of the endeavor. A schema for planning a group is provided in Table 6.1 and the same schema can be used for support and self-help groups. The schema can be used as a proposal to be submitted to administration for approval. As we mentioned in Chapters 4, and 6, when planning for a new group the worker needs to answer the questions why, who, what, where, when, and how. The schema is intended to give basic answers to these questions. It can be modified as needed to include other information or aspects that are unique to any particular situation and can be used with any type of group.

As indicated in Table 6.1, the worker thinks about and presents the reason for the group. She considers both effectiveness and efficiency. Support and self-help groups are not typically reimbursed by insurance, nor are members generally charged a fee. They are typically provided free of charge. So, any proposal to management or administration must address the need for such groups that will justify the use of resources because this will be a major concern for agency management. The purpose of the group should meet the needs of potential members while also being consistent with the mission and services of the agency. The worker answers questions about why a support or self-help group is needed and why the agency should provide this service. Building a coalition of agencies that provide a variety of these types of groups can be helpful in overcoming resistance in some agencies. These types of coalitions can have a band wagon effect in which administrators may not want their agency to be left out.

As with change-oriented groups it is best to present the purpose and basic aspects of the group at the beginning of the plan or proposal. This should be detailed because the worker needs to justify the use of agency resources without an expectation of reimbursement. The worker should include research such as a needs survey or, at the very least, a discussion of the need for this type of group. She should also include information from professional sources on serving the target population in settings similar to that of the agency or community. Potential group members should be identified, along with a description of the benefits to members and to the agency and the community if the agency hosts such a group.

It is important to consider the size of the group. For change-oriented groups, we recommend six to eight members, but support and self-help groups are typically much larger because regular attendance cannot be assured. Members will probably come and go and will drop in and drop out or may attend only sporadically. The worker needs to plan for this to ensure a sufficient number of members are attending on a consistent basis. At the same time, the group should not be too large to ensure that the group will have enough time available to give everyone an opportunity to participate. Large groups limit the time that is available to listen to everyone's concerns and may be intimidating for some members. In an ideal group, a small cadre of regular members is needed to provide ongoing support on a consistent basis so the group can function in the face of a fluctuating membership.

For support and self-help groups, the composition of the group influences group dynamics and is a factor in whether members receive help and support. Members need to be able to trust in order to engage in self-disclosure about the situation they are facing and their thoughts and feelings about it. In addition, the typical mechanism for receiving help comes from those who have already experienced at least some aspect of the process of learning to cope with the situation. So veteran members tend to help those who are at earlier stages of coping.

As we mentioned in Chapter 5, basic elements of a helping relationship include empathy, genuineness, and nonpossessive warmth and acceptance. In order to establish these in a support or self-help group, members need to feel that they have something in common. It is important that the group be composed of members who have similar experiences as well as similar needs or concerns. Members need to have enough in common with one another so that empathy can develop. Thus, they should be dealing with similar challenges. At the same time, there needs to be enough variation so the group does not get stuck. In a support or self-help group, variation is provided in part by having members who are at different stages of coping or recovery. The worker should develop a profile of potential members and a recruitment strategy that will increase the likelihood of success. Support and self-help groups are typically open to anyone who wishes to join, so new members may join the group without a formal referral or invitation. Thus, the worker may not be able to screen potential group members to ensure that they are appropriate for the group. However, this is typically only necessary when the worker is beginning a new group. After that, some members will be recruited by other members of the group and the worker can work with other professionals to ensure that appropriate referrals are made.

As with all groups, diversity should be considered in planning for support and self-help groups. As with change-oriented groups, some cultural groups may not benefit from group work because cultural taboos limit their ability to engage in self-disclosure. These are typically cultures with a heavy emphasis on keeping issues within the family and those in which privacy is highly valued. There may be taboos regarding discussing personal or family issues outside of the family.

As with change-oriented groups, the degree of acculturation is important. Clients who are more acculturated into the dominant culture may actually act much more like the dominant culture and so they may be good candidates for group work. Others may retain a considerable amount of their cultural heritage and be less able to use the group.

There are advantages and disadvantages associated with diversity in groups. Establishing trust is important in support and self-help groups, and diversity can affect the ability to trust. Cultural factors may reduce the ability to self-disclose. In addition, bias and prejudice toward various diverse groups may be a factor for some group members. These same issues regarding diversity that we see in the larger society can be factors in the functioning of the group.

At the same time, diversity can have several advantages. One is the opportunity for members to become better acquainted with people who are different. Generally, as people become more acquainted, they find that they have a lot in common. They also may find that their differences actually enrich life rather than detract from it. Just as in change-oriented groups, diversity in support and self-help groups can offer different ways of knowing and supporting. There is a diversity of perspectives and more diversity of sources of support, giving and receiving support, and problem-solving approaches and solutions.

It is better if at least two members share the same diversity. Often this can be resolved in support groups by members bringing other family members or friends with them to the group. This is not as easy for self-help groups in which members need to experience similar problems or addictions. However, in these groups members may still have acquaintances who share their diversity as well as their difficulty and who may be recruited to join the group. There is the added benefit of having these members support each other outside of the group. However, it also carries the additional risk that one of them might undermine the other if they are not successful in maintaining their recovery.

In support and self-help groups, age is still an important factor in establishing common ground. Typically, adults, teens, and children do not participate together unless it is a group for families who need support in dealing with a situation involving a family member or relative. Even then, large disparities in age are not advisable. It is better to have more than one support group, organized along age or generational lines.

Most support and self-help groups are ongoing as opposed to time limited and have open membership. Some self-help groups are closed in the sense that new members cannot drop in but need to attend an open group for a period of time before they are able to join a closed group. For support groups and open self-help groups, new members can drop in and join the group. Membership is not set at a certain number and members may attend as they are able or when they need support. The process for welcoming and orienting new members should be established by the group ahead of time in its early sessions.

As with change-oriented groups, it is important that the facilitator be competent to facilitate the group. The worker should have appropriate credentials, training, and experience. This can be a critical factor in having a proposal approved and in being successful in recruiting new members. Professionals want to know that they are referring their clients to a group that has competent leadership and that the group will be of benefit to those who are referred. The worker should arrange for appropriate supervision and consultation as needed. However, there tends to be lower expectations for credentials and training for support and self-help groups as opposed to change-oriented groups. This is because change-oriented groups typically involve more complicated processes, such as problem solving and decision making, as well as providing support for change. The worker needs to be familiar with various theories about facilitating change, such as cognitive-behavioral approaches. In self-help groups, the professional is likely to be a host and not a participant. At the same time, the worker needs to be knowledgeable about the issues that members face and the resources that will assist the group in providing support and assistance.

The plan includes a description of the format for the group. Both support and self-help groups tend to be loosely structured. Support groups do not typically use program material or a curriculum. However, some self-help groups use program material including many that use a twelve-step program. These typically use some program materials in informing and guiding members through the steps. Resources such as speakers, videos, books, and the like should be made available and may be a part of some sessions. The worker should identify the resources that are needed and where these might be obtained. In a strengths-based approach, the strengths of group members are incorporated into planning for the group and the format should be built on these strengths. Giving and receiving support and overcoming challenges are important strengths that can also inspire other members of the group. In terms of planning during sessions, each session may be structured by the group as it decides what will be dealt with or discussed during that session and the next. Support and self-help groups generally develop some kind of structure for beginning and ending each session and for planning and deciding how to proceed with the focus for the current session and for the next.

Just as with change-oriented groups, support and self-help groups should be offered under the sanction or auspices of one or more agencies, which gives the group its credibility. However, this sanction is less likely for self-help groups. Instead of an agency sanction, most of these groups receive their sanction from a national organization with which it is affiliated, such as AA. The agency typically provides a site to meet and serves as host. Agencies receive their sanction from the community to provide services to certain populations. The group purpose and the populations being served should fit with with the purpose, goals, and ways of functioning for the agency or agencies who are sponsoring the group. The group may represent a new way of serving agency clientele or a collaboration with other agencies in serving new or existing clientele. Many groups will meet at more neutral sites, such as churches and community centers, particularly self-help groups.

As with change-oriented groups, the ability to offer the group will also be influenced by who sponsors the group and who will facilitate it. There are advantages and disadvantages to having more than one agency as a sponsor. Disadvantages include the need for greater coordination and the need to negotiate with other agencies when there are disagreements. Coordination may include having a variety of agencies provide a variety of support groups or host a variety of self-help groups. Agencies that serve certain clientele should be assigned to provide support or self-help groups that are likely to be needed by their clientele. A major advantage in having multiple sponsors or an array of groups offered by various agencies is that agencies can share resources and can also provide referrals. Lack of referrals is a major reason groups fail to get off the ground or dwindle over time. Offering a support or self-help group does not guarantee that people will come to it or that other workers will make referrals. However, if an agency is a sponsor or part of a consortium and is invested in the success of the group, it is more likely that the agency's workers will make referrals.

A plan or proposal for support and self-help groups should include a basic description of potential membership, how they will be recruited, and how group members will benefit from the group. Recruiting members for support groups is a matter of establishing the need and getting the word out to prospective members and agency personnel who are likely to be in contact with them. Recruiting members for self-help groups can be a delicate matter, similar to that of change-oriented groups. Once again, the worker needs to be careful to avoid using labels or terminology that might be offensive, so it is better to use a brief description of the situation that potential group members are experiencing. For example, if the group will be a self-help group for people who are addicted to drugs, the worker could include this in information in communicating with other workers, but for recruiting potential members directly, it would be better to use the name of the group, such as Narcotics Anonymous. Quite often there is pressure from family or a court system in getting people into self-help groups, whereas support groups are almost entirely voluntary.

A plan or proposal for new support and self-help groups should contain a description of what the group will be doing, including what might occur in typical group sessions. If there are program materials available, such as a twelve-step program, this should be presented and if possible a copy of the program material or a summary or outline should be included, usually in an appendix or attachment. Potential topics and resources for support groups should be identified.

The worker should present projected dates and times for the group to the extent that these are known. At the very least, the proposal should include the planned length of the sessions and the time of day and day of the week sessions might take place. In most cases the group will be ongoing, so this should be mentioned. The frequency of sessions can vary considerably. For support groups, sessions are typically scheduled monthly or twice a month. Some support groups might meet weekly. Self-help groups typically meet at least once a week with those in residential settings usually meeting daily. The place where the group will meet should be discussed in some detail, along with who will be responsible for setting this up. The space typically dictates what can and cannot be done in the group. There needs to be sufficient open space if physical activity is part of the plan. Members need to be able to feel comfortable both physically and with respect to confidentiality and privacy. People outside of the group should not be able to listen in on sessions. The proposal should identify any materials that will be needed.

As with change-oriented groups, the proposal should identify any additional information that may be needed. Transportation, child care, elder care, or other needs may be addressed. These should be anticipated and any potential barriers to attending meetings be removed.

The proposal should include a process for evaluating the group, including group and individual outcomes that are desired and how these will be measured. Evaluation in these types of groups tends to be much more informal and also more elusive than is the case for change-oriented groups, in which membership is more stable. Pretest/posttest is the most common design for evaluating groups. However, with support and self-help groups, membership is more fluid. The worker may need to use some form of follow-up evaluation and contact members after they leave the group if a formal evaluation is needed. Typically, formal evaluation is not needed because these groups are not offered under the auspices of funding sources such as grants. As a way of incorporating evaluation and planning into a support group, the worker could design a feedback form that members could fill out at the end of each session that would identify what was helpful and what was not helpful or could be more helpful. It could ask about the members' satisfaction and also solicit ideas about future sessions. Evaluation is not only important for determining outcomes, it may be particularly important in ensuring the group continues or determining if another group is offered. This is especially true for support and self-help groups, which do not typically bring financial resources into the agency, but resources must be used to offer these groups.

Typically, the voluntary nature of support groups means that most agency administrators will be satisfied with attendance figures that will then be used to determine if the groups seem worthwhile. The assumption is that if people are attending, the group must be meeting a need.

There tends to be little if any evaluation of self-help groups as such. In fact, this is often one of the criticisms of these groups. It also tends to make it difficult to measure any claims of effectiveness. Instead, most of the claims of effectiveness tend to be anecdotal in which individuals give testimonials regarding the help they have received.

The budget is an important consideration for a proposal for support or self-help groups, especially because they require the use of resources without bringing in additional funds in most cases. Tight financial constraints for agencies will lead management to consider what the cost-benefit analysis is for the group. Since reimbursement will not typically be available, the emphasis will need to be on the benefit to clientele of the agency and the recognition or prestige that sponsoring a group might bring. The agency may have contingency or discretionary funds available to assist with resources, or donations may be solicited from attendees or people interested in supporting the type of group being offered. The proposal should include a realistic estimate of the costs or expenses, including materials, refreshments, rent, and salaries. Estimating the units of service along with expenses will give a basis for deciding if the group is feasible.

Assessment and planning before any group begins increase the likelihood of success. The worker should develop a proposal to agency administrators so that approval can be obtained. As with change-oriented groups, a well-organized and thorough proposal makes a positive impression and can increase the chances that the support or self-help group will be approved for implementation.

Self-help groups tend to function more like change-oriented groups, only without the benefit of a professional facilitator. This is especially true for closed self-help groups. Conversely, open self-help groups look more like support groups in many ways, including fluctuating membership from session to session, primary reliance on support, and having new and veteran members share their stories. Although, every group is different, open and closed self-help groups will generally operate in a similar fashion to support and change-oriented groups, respectively. At the same time, members of support and self-help groups may not be as invested in the group and may not be able to develop as much trust as change-oriented groups because of their very nature. The fluctuating membership represents much less member commitment to the group and makes it very difficult for a high level of trust to develop. Also, the absence of professional help will tend to limit the extent to which self-help groups will be able to help their members. These groups will be limited by the experiences of their members and by the lack of formal training in the use of a change process that a professional social worker would be able to offer.

## The Change Process During the Orientation Stage

The first three stages of group development tend to be different for support and self-help groups as opposed to change-oriented groups. The main differences for support and open self-help groups is related to the fluctuating membership. This actually produces a new group every time new members join or veterans leave or miss a session. As a result, at the beginning of each session the group needs to go through the process of reforming itself by revisiting each stage of development. Change-oriented groups will also go through stages of development during each session, but the stages of group formation that represent the first three tend to be relatively brief as members check in and deal with any business associated with norms and roles and the like. Closed self-help groups will tend to act in the same way. For support and open self-help groups, these stages need to be more formally structured into how the group reforms itself for each session.

Orientation before the group begins may be somewhat similar to change-oriented groups in that the worker might provide information for new members prior to the first meeting for the group. After that, the worker might do this for new members whom he is aware of prior to their coming to the group. In addition, other workers who are familiar with these groups will inform clients whom they are referring. Referrals tend to be very informal and most support and self-help groups do not require any exchange of information between workers or agencies, or even a notice that a client might join the group. In fact, potential members may self-refer or be referred by other members. It is assumed that people who wish to join the group will be those who feel the need for support or who want to help themselves to overcome the challenges on which the group is intended to focus. Some workers will mention that they have referred clients, mostly as a professional courtesy as opposed to a requirement as it would be with other types of groups we will consider.

There is typically an orientation process that takes place as group sessions begin for support and self-help groups, especially when a new member attends. The process for welcoming new members should be established by the group in its early sessions. Members may volunteer to do this or a rotation can be established among veteran members. Typically, these members will introduce themselves to a new attendee and give them information about what to expect in the group before the group begins. Then they either introduce the new members or have them introduce themselves. In both support and self-help groups, new members will typically be asked to share their story. Confidentiality issues are discussed. Generally, the norm is that what is shared in the group, stays in the group. In support groups, the story is about the situation they are facing. For self-help groups, it is about their addiction, habit, or challenge that they face. Other members briefly share their stories as well. This establishes a common ground for everyone. In new situations, most people gravitate first toward what is known or familiar to them. Thus, in any group, members will tend to try to find things that they have in common with each other.

As with any new situation, most new members will experience some ambivalence about being there. With change-oriented groups we referred to this as approach–avoidance. New members will be curious about the group and will have hopes that the group will meet their need for support. At the same time, they will experience fear of the unknown and will wonder whether to trust that the group will meet their needs. The approach side motivates people to come to the group, to join, and make a commitment. The avoidance side may cause them to limit their involvement or even quit the group and not return. The worker recognizes this as part of the process that people will go through when they attend a group and plans for ways of supporting the approach side of the equation while reducing the avoidance side. At the beginning of a new group, the whole group experiences these feelings together. In ongoing support and self-help groups, new members will experience these feelings during the first session, and the group will likely revisit this stage every time it meets in some form or another but especially as it incorporates new members. The orientation stage is completed for an individual member once an initial commitment to the group has been made. However, the group as a whole will still need to undertake an orientation process at each session when there is a new member.

As a support group goes through the orientation stage, the worker uses assessment, planning, actions, and evaluation in facilitating the group. Workers will also use these with self-help groups that they facilitate. The worker should prepare himself ahead of time by researching the issues members are facing. During the orientation stage, he becomes more familiar with these issues as members describe their situation. The worker assesses the needs of the group and the needs of individual members. He analyzes the extent to which the group will be able to meet the needs of its members. He does this by assessing the thoughts and feelings that are expressed and the actions that take place within and outside of the group. Both verbal and nonverbal levels are included.

Successful self-help groups will use some variation of the change process in their work together. This tends to be less formalized for those groups that are not facilitated by professionally trained social workers but by members themselves. In using the change process, some form of assessing the situation takes place, followed by the development of a plan. Often this is self-perpetuated within the structure of a twelve-step system. As members return for subsequent sessions they will typically report on the successes and failures experienced in acting on their plans. The group evaluates this and gives feedback or suggestions for other approaches to the situation.

In group work, the worker and the group should balance the needs of the group and the needs of its members. This is still a concern in support and self-help groups. In support groups, the urgency of this is somewhat reduced because in groups that are functioning well, support will carry over from group sessions to the interim periods between groups as members have contact with each other outside of the group. However, the worker should assess group process and be able to identify balances and imbalances. We have called this the "I–we" balance. There are times when an individual might dominate the session and the worker or the group will need to balance that individual's needs with those of other members and the group as a whole. Setting an agenda tends to help with this. The agenda can be used to move the meeting along. Other times the group may not be tuned in to the needs of a certain member or members. When this occurs, the worker should focus the group's attention on this. Self-help groups without professional facilitation are literally on their own with this. Most use some sort of an informal agenda to help them to structure the group.

During the orientation stage of most new groups, there is likely to be more emphasis on the "I" portion of the "I–we" balance as members decide whether they will commit themselves to the group. The newly formed group has not become a functional group and will need to become a "we" in order to do so. This occurs when members make a commitment to the group and begin to rely on each other to meet needs for support or self help. The worker develops a plan to facilitate group formation. In addressing the group, the worker uses terms that emphasize the group by using pronouns like *we, us, our,* and the like, and asking questions that emphasize group membership.

As with change-oriented groups, group planning will generally hasten group formation. This helps the group to come together while moving the group toward the next two stages of group development. Planning helps members to invest themselves in the group by allowing them to make the group into what they need the group to be and having them take ownership of the group. Planning typically takes place at the beginning of the group after the introductions. Members are asked to identify what they would like to get out of the group and how the group might meet their needs. The group begins to solidify itself when members discuss how they would like to function as a group or what they would like to accomplish for that session and the next.

Ongoing groups should revisit the orientation stage when they orient new members. Open groups will have new members joining and some veterans attending sporadically. This reduces the intensity of the commitment to the group and the extent to which members self disclose and invest in the group. In fact, every session with new members will require the group to go through the first three stages of group formation before real work can be done. Thus, open groups need to establish a routine that will at least orient new members to the group. This will typically include orienting them to the norms and the structure of group meetings. The group needs to reach out to new members and find ways to quickly include them in the group. This is usually accomplished by new members telling their stories and veterans giving a synopsis of theirs.

Throughout the orientation stage, the worker evaluates the progress of the group by noticing interactions in the group and evaluating the extent to which these interactions represent the development of a supportive atmosphere. Are members engaged in positive interactions? Do they seem to be enjoying themselves? Do they seem to feel supported? Is the group beginning to function as a group? Who is included and who is not? Who participates and who does not? Who gives support and who does not? Who receives support and who does not? If certain members seem less involved, the worker invites them to talk about their concerns and encourages the group to offer support.

Premature termination during the orientation stage can be reduced by encouraging members to return to the group. The worker should explore any barriers to doing so. Often with support groups, the very issue that causes people to need support also creates barriers to attending a support group. For example, cancer patients may not feel well or may experience physical impairments that make it difficult to attend. Caregivers will need to arrange for alternative care while they attend.

As with change-oriented groups, there are ways for the worker to encourage a commitment to the group. He should summarize the common ground that group members have found. The worker can do this or he can solicit contributions from the group. The worker should have the group decide what they would like to address in the next session. Discussing the next session gives more of a sense of continuity. It can also give a sense of who intends to return, who does not intend to return, and who is uncertain. The worker can then address any concerns before the group ends or follow up with members after the session is over.

Once members become invested in the group and make an initial commitment to it, the orientation stage is completed for them. This will be repeated at the beginning of group sessions as new members join the group.

## The Change Process During the Authority Stage

When members make an initial commitment to the group, they become invested in what happens in the group, which generates the authority stage. This stage deals with issues related to power, control, and conflict. This is generally most intense for a forming group, but as the group establishes itself and develops a routine, it is typically not as much of an issue. The intensity of conflict at this stage may be lessened in support and open self-help groups than in change-oriented groups because members may be less invested, especially when there are fluctuations in membership. Changing membership makes it more difficult for members to trust and tends to reduce the degree of self-disclosure. In addition, in support groups members are not typically looking to the group for resolution of their difficulties as is the case in change-oriented groups. However, to some extent, each member will seek to influence the group to become what he or she wishes it to be. During the authority stage, the group has begun experiencing "we-ness," but there is still a lot of "I-ness" in the group. There is typically some competition for power and control. In support groups, members might challenge the power of the group worker, but it may be less likely to occur than in change-oriented groups if members do not see as much at stake. Conversely, issues of power and control can arise fairly often and be quite serious in self-help groups, especially those that have closed membership. Most self-help groups have members serve in leadership positions as opposed to having a professional facilitating the group. While there may be a mechanism in place for sharing this role, these groups are at a much higher risk of experiencing turmoil over authority issues. Without a worker to mediate, the group will have to find a way to resolve these issues or little or no work will get done.

As with change-oriented groups, the worker in a support group has to give control to the group in order for the group to become a group and function as a source of support. Members of the group have to take ownership of the group and give one another support so that the group can become a source of support. The worker should plan for this stage. She uses her influence to help the group discuss how it can structure itself in a positive way that ensures that members receive the support they need while allowing the group to sustain itself as a group. Norms, roles, and ways of functioning for a group have not been established during this stage. For self-help groups, these issues can become a real struggle. It is better if the group can establish norms for sharing roles to reduce the possibility of members becoming entrenched in certain roles.

For support groups, the worker will usually provide some structure for the new group during the initial stages. She gradually turns much of this over to the group as soon as possible. There may be times she will have to step in and provide more structure again as members come and go. However, the worker should be cognizant of the fact that the real authority in the group needs to lie with the members and she needs to encourage this. The worker encourages the group to establish its own control over how the group will function. She tells group members that this is their group and they need to decide how it will function. She makes suggestions and encourages discussion about how the group will make decisions, which is the greatest source of power and control. The worker encourages consensus so that everyone is included in the group. Support groups can use a democratic style in deciding what they would like to do for the next session or a future session, but they need to find ways of including every member so that no one is left out and everyone's needs are met. The voting should be primarily on the priority or sequence of considering options so everyone's needs are met over time.

In the authority stage, the "I–we" issue has not been resolved and members are concerned about retaining their individual autonomy (I) while still being accepted by the group (we). As with change-oriented groups, if members feel controlled by the worker or by other members or the group as a whole, they will not feel free to trust enough to self disclose and expose themselves. The issues that arise during this stage will be resolved at least temporarily in the next stage as the group negotiates ways of functioning that are inclusive. Whenever the worker senses too much "I-ness," she can establish more "we-ness" by addressing the group as a whole and calling attention to the need for the group to act collectively. When the worker senses that there is too much "we-ness" or emphasis on the group at the expense of individual members, she points this out and addresses members as individuals to rebalance the "I–we" aspect of the group.

As new members join support and self-help groups, the group may revisit the authority stage. In support groups, this tends to be focused on the group itself and not so much on the worker provided she has relinquished authority and control to the group. New members will want to know if it is safe to reveal things about themselves and still be accepted by the group. Some of this is alleviated by the fact that support and self-help groups are made up of members who share some specified common experience with which they are coping or seeking to change. Generally, having members share their stories helps with this process. In support and open self-help groups, the process for including new members needs to be established because new people can drop in at any time. If these issues are addressed up front, then the group can move more quickly through this stage with less disruption and get to the work that needs to be done for that session. Groups that have not done this may find themselves struggling each time a new member comes into the group. There will be the inevitable awkward moments and hesitation. It is important for these groups to find ways to make decisions, establish norms, and redistribute roles and share them during the course of the group. For these groups, the process of including new members and redistributing roles when new members join will go much smoother than for groups in which members are invested in certain roles.

As the authority stage progresses, the worker evaluates the group and individual members in a similar manner as change-oriented groups. He encourages members to talk about their situations and to share their thoughts and feelings, and observes how well the group is able to deal with any conflict that might arise. The worker evaluates how individual members act during this stage. Who talks and who does not? Who speaks for the group and who speaks for themselves? Who seems invested and who does not? As these questions are answered, the worker encourages participation in the discussion and may encourage those who are quiet. For the group as a whole, he supports positive conflict resolution that is respectful and inclusive.

Termination during this stage is very similar to the orientation stage and similar to what we discussed for change-oriented groups. In developing groups or with new members, the worker encourages members to remain committed to the group so she reassures the group that disagreement is a normal part of group development and differences are to be expected and respected. She highlights positive outcomes as the group finds ways to function that are positive and inclusive. At the end of each session, the worker or the group should summarize the session and discuss it.

As a developing group experiences the authority stage or when new members join and the group revisits this stage, the worker assesses the situation and plans for facilitating the group as issues related to authority arise. She encourages the group to take responsibility for making decisions in an inclusive way that considers the needs of members and the group as a whole. She evaluates group and individual progress through this stage. She terminates sessions with a review of the progress that has been made.

One of the potential difficulties with many self-help groups is that they need to find their own way through the stages of development and become helpful or at least not be harmful to their members. Assistance with this process is generally not available directly from a professional. However, these groups can receive assistance with difficulties, either directly or indirectly. A direct way of doing this is for the group to call on a professional worker to meet with the group and assist with mediating, problem solving, and finding a solution if they are stuck. An indirect way is for a group member or members to consult with a professional about the situation without disclosing any names and brainstorm about what they might do about the situation. It is not known if or how frequently self-help groups might use any professional assistance such as this. It appears that this would be unlikely. It is more likely that these groups will continue to struggle through these issues until something is eventually resolved. However, social workers should be prepared to give assistance to these groups, especially if they have agreed to sponsor or host such groups.

## The Change Process During the Negotiation Stage

Conflict or disagreements that arise in the authority stage are resolved during the negotiation stage. Most support groups will not experience a great deal of conflict, but they still must resolve authority issues and settle on norms and roles. Conversely, self-help groups are more likely to look like change-oriented groups and conflict may even be a regular issue. As the group progresses, it may confront, differ, and engage in conflict resolution. With or without conflict, goals, norms, roles, and tasks are established and the group becomes a functioning group. At the conclusion of the negotiation stage, members feel positive about the group and there is a high level of group cohesion. The worker assists the group to reach this point. He encourages the group to establish goals, norms, roles, and tasks in ways that are inclusive. The commitment of members to the group is directly related to their ability to see the group as a place where they can meet their needs and achieve their goals. It is important for members to have positive feelings about one another and the group experience. They do not need to like everything about one another, but they generally need to find something positive. Often their common experiences will generate at least enough empathy to give and receive support. Members need to feel accepted and free to be themselves to a certain extent.

Support and self-help groups require that members share their experiences and at least some of their inner thoughts and feelings and in this respect, they are somewhat similar to change-oriented groups. However, there are some differences. Members of support and self-help groups are not as likely to expose certain vulnerable parts of themselves including their human flaws and frailties. Instead, the thoughts and feelings are typically about the situation that they find themselves in, at least this is more likely with support groups. Members of self-help groups, especially those that are closed, may delve into these areas as they relate to the addiction or issue that is the focus of the group. For example, poor self-esteem typically accompanies and is integrated with addiction. Thus, in the process of recovering from addiction, members need to deal with and resolve their low self-esteem. Poor self-esteem can make people more vulnerable to becoming at least dependent if not addicted. Societal attitudes toward addiction tend to reinforce poor self-esteem. It is also not unusual to find that many addicts were physically or sexually abused as children. Thus, these members will need to work on issues related to the abuse.

Members need to feel safe and be able to trust enough to talk about their situation. As with any group, the group experience needs to be consistent with the cardinal values of social work. As discussed above, social workers believe in the value and worth of every human being, which leads to the expectation that people be treated with dignity and respect. Groups that are facilitated or sponsored by social workers and social work agencies must reflect this value. In those that do, members will feel more safe in disclosing their thoughts, feelings, and experiences. If their self-disclosures are met by acceptance and members are treated with dignity and respect, they feel supported and are encouraged to explore their situation further. Giving and receiving support in a caring, accepting atmosphere is a form of intimacy. Members feel accepted for themselves without conditions and in spite of the situation with which they are dealing. As other members see this, they are encouraged to risk being vulnerable.

At this point, members begin to feel that "I" has become a part of the "we." At least some portion of a member's identity includes being a member of this group. Members feel they belong and are accepted and valued and they accept and value other members of the group. Each member has an individual identity or an "I," a collective identity or a "we," and an "I–we" or an identity that includes being a part of the group.

Social workers value and respect everyone's right to self-determination. People should have a right to make their own decisions about things that affect them. The group also needs to respect this and allow members to decide for themselves what they should do about their situation. Groups need to establish this so the group becomes a safe place to talk about needs and concerns without conditions or limitations. This is invaluable to members in dealing with situations in which they need support. This may not be readily available to them in their personal life. Their ecosystem may not be able to provide support or respite.

Social workers believe that people should have the right to have socially accepted needs met in socially accepted ways. The need for support is certainly a socially accepted need. The group needs to establish norms that give all of the members opportunities to have their needs for support met within the group. This is an important part of what it means to be inclusive. This value means that the group will support members in meeting socially accepted needs in socially accepted ways. If these needs cannot be met within the group, members receive assistance from the group and from the worker in meeting those needs from other sources outside of the group.

During this stage with a support group, the worker should take a mediating position. This means that the worker does not take sides or impose his own ideas on the group. The worker needs to be seen as acting for the development of positive, supportive relationships within the group. The worker needs to be neutral, so he can assist the group to negotiate any disagreements and arrive at a mutually agreeable resolution.

The worker uses skills in group facilitation as the group proceeds through the negotiation stage. He models negotiation and compromise using a mediating position as needed. Before and during group sessions, he assesses the needs of the group during this stage of development and facilitates movement as necessary. When the group is expressing thoughts and feelings appropriately and is supportive, he allows the interactions to proceed without interuption. If the interactions become negative or destructive, or the group or a member are stuck, he intervenes to help the group get back on track. He encourages the group to establish norms that reflect social work values.

Planning before and between sessions for developing groups during this stage is focused on moving the group toward group formation and resolving related issues. The worker plans activities and interventions that will facilitate this. He helps the group formulate mutually acceptable goals, norms, roles, and tasks. He can summarize this for the group or ask the group to do so.

The worker typically plans to begin the sessions during this stage with an opening summary that identifies norms, tasks, and goals that need to be established or have already been established. He may do this himself or ask the group to do so. The worker models or encourages a summary that is comprehensive and builds on strengths and accomplishments, setting the stage for the work to be done during the session. If members are unable to do this, the worker can remind the group about what has been accomplished or reframe any negative comments into something more positive. Probably the best strategy to use is the one identified for change-oriented groups. The worker does the first couple of summaries to provide a model. Then he does a partial summary and has the group fill in the rest, reframing negative contributions into issues related to the stage of development. As members are able to hone these skills, the worker turns more of it over to them. Generally, even when the group does the summary, the worker summarizes what was said and fills in any gaps. The worker facilitates planning within the group session by helping the group set an agenda for the session and helping the group identify what needs to be done in the next session.

The worker's actions during this stage with a new group are designed to facilitate the development of goals, norms, tasks, and roles. If new members are joining the group, then they will need to be informed about how the group operates and can be given an opportunity to join in a task or make some type of contribution to the work of the group. This may not come right away but can be offered as appropriate. The worker helps the group to focus on these issues and encourages members to negotiate and make suggestions.

As with change-oriented groups, the worker may need to ask questions or make suggestions. He might ask what members would like to accomplish. He can ask how the group wants to function and who has suggestions. If the worker needs to make suggestions to get the group unstuck, it should be clear that these are choices that the group might make and that the worker is not making choices for the group. After making a suggestion, the worker should ask what the group thinks about it and if anyone has any other ideas. This gives the group the message that other options are possible and that it is not expected that the worker's suggestions are the only ones to be considered.

As the session progresses, the worker evaluates the progress of the group through the negotiation stage. He evaluates how each member participates or does not participate. He encourages reluctant members to express their needs and their desires for the group. Members need to feel that they have ownership of the group so they can become full participants.

Termination of sessions during this stage is focused on agreements that have been reached regarding goals, norms, and tasks. Unfinished business is identified and an agreement reached to work on this during the next session. The process is usually similar to opening and closing previous sessions with a summary by the worker or one that is solicited from the group or some combination of these.

As a developing group moves through the negotiation stage, it is becoming a group and is preparing for the work that needs to be done to achieve its purpose. In support groups, this stage typically requires only a portion of a session. Self-help groups may struggle with this for several sessions and may find that the same issues arise periodically. Support groups may need to revisit this and earlier stages of group development. Self-help groups are likely to do so. In general, ongoing groups will visit this stage at least briefly when members leave and new ones join. Successful closed self-help groups will probably find a way to share roles and to negotiate goals, norms, and tasks. These groups will be more likely to reestablish these quickly and smoothly when new members join.

## The Change Process During the Functional Stage

For support and self-help groups, the functional stage represents the stage during which support is being given and received and the group is accomplishing its purpose. During earlier stages, the group is becoming a group. These earlier stages are necessary for the group to become fully formed and ready to accomplish its purpose. Groups that are not fully formed tend to rely on the worker to provide the support. The worker needs to resist the temptation to be the source of support for group members. This would be an overwhelming task and one that would set the worker up for exhaustion and failure. The support is much stronger when it is received from peers, especially from those who experience similar circumstances. New groups may try to rely on the worker for support. Even groups that are well formed may do this. They might also lapse back into earlier stages of group formation. When this occurs, the group typically will need to proceed through subsequent stages before they are ready to proceed with the functional stage. Unfinished business from earlier stages will tend to return and will affect group functioning.

For a developing support group, the stages of group formation may be accomplished fairly quickly during the first session and the group can provide support more immediately. However, the issues related to group formation may arise again over the next few sessions before these are more fully resolved and the group settles into more of a routine. Sometimes, most of the first session may be taken up with group formation and the worker should plan for this. It is important that at least some level of support be received so that members do not feel that they are wasting their time and decide not to return. Usually an icebreaker that calls for people to break into pairs and discuss their situation will suffice to provide at least some support. As members share information about themselves during introductions, the worker can model giving support and solicit reactions. He should summarize their descriptions of their situations, emphasizing common experiences. Before the group ends, he should check in with members and ask if anyone has anything that they need from the group before they adjourn. These actions will be helpful in ensuring that at least some aspects of the functional stage are experienced, even if the group has not been fully formed.

Highly functioning groups will tend to maintain a good healthy balance of "I-ness" and "we-ness" during the functional stage as group members balance the need for the group to maintain itself while also providing support for its members. Members are very aware of their own need for support. They are also very sensitive to the needs of each other. However, even the best groups will have moments when group and individual needs are out of balance. One member may dominate the attention of the group or the group may not be very supportive with a member. When this occurs, the worker may need to intervene and point this out. If there is too much "I-ness," the worker asks the group as a whole (we) or individuals as members (I–we) to discuss their thoughts and feelings about the situation. If there is too much we-ness the worker asks members to speak for themselves as individuals (I) and express their thoughts and feelings.

The worker continues assessing and planning before and between group sessions. He assesses how well the group is functioning and the amount of support that seems to be shared within and outside the group. He assesses strengths and challenges for the group as a whole and for each member in giving and receiving support. In ongoing groups, each member will typically be at a different point in coping with the situation. Often members who are in later stages of coping will provide support to those who are going through what they went through. The worker assesses the level of support for each member and seeks to understand group dynamics in order to facilitate the development of support in the group.

As the worker assesses each member and the group, he plans for ways to facilitate maximum functioning of the group to maximize the benefits of being in the group. The professional group worker is constantly assessing, planning, and acting before, during, and after each group session. The worker needs to understand what is supportive and what is not, what is needed and what is not, when the group and members are receiving the support they need and when they are not. He needs to understand what it will take for the group to provide support for each member and how members can give support to and receive support from one another. The worker uses training and supervision to understand the need for support from the group members' perspective. He needs to read, listen, and learn about the experience of coping with the situation that the members are experiencing.

Assessment and planning in any type of group work involves both content and process. The worker makes observations during and after each session and thinks about the content and the process. He analyzes the session to understand what seemed to be supportive and what was not and what might be needed. He observes both verbal and nonverbal behavior and watches for consistency and incongruities or inconsistencies, as shown in Chapter 6. Incongruities outside the group are typically areas that are stressors for group members. They represent situations in which support may be needed. They may also represent situations in which part of the ecosystem should or could provide support but is not. Incongruities among verbal and nonverbal behaviors within the group will usually be an indication of some form of stress that may need to be addressed. The worker encourages the group to provide support that is needed in these areas of the member's life.

In addition to these actions, the worker also uses actions described in Chapters 3, 4, and 5, including actions that can be taken within and outside of the group to facilitate completion of plans that are designed to increase coping abilities, remove barriers to the plan and to coping, and increase functioning and coping skills of both the group and individual members. The worker uses skills in relationship building, providing support, learning the change process, learning to use resources, empowering and enabling, resolving crises, activities that can be used to cope or generate support, and mediation. In addition, the worker acts to facilitate group formation, discussion, conflict resolution, interaction, group development, and group activities. These practice actions will not be repeated here, but will be summarized as they relate to working with support groups and providing assistance to self-help groups. The reader should review this material before proceeding and include them in her work with these groups.

In all groups, relationships are central to the functioning of the group. Successful relationships include good communication, problem solving and decision making, and the ability to resolve conflict in a constructive manner. These skills are important in developing coping skills and in giving and receiving support within and outside of the group. Relationships are the means by which support is given and received.

Providing support is the primary purpose of support and self-help groups. Support is discussed in Chapter 3. Group members need to develop positive strategies for coping with the situation. For some, this may be spiritual or based on religious beliefs and prayer. For others it might include stress-reduction techniques and engaging in activities that are outlets for stress such as exercise. Still others need to change negative thinking into more positive thoughts. It may be hard to be optimistic in the face of a situation that cannot be controlled or changed, but pessimism certainly will not help. At the very least, changing negative self-talk to something positive or neutral can be beneficial.

The process of giving and receiving support benefits the recipient and other group members as well. Group members feel better about their situation and good about themselves because they feel that someone cares about them and understands their situation. Giving support also makes members feel positive. In support groups, support is used to cope with situations that cannot be changed or are beyond the members' control. In self-help groups, the group provides support for change. Receiving support can be the difference between trying something new and staying put. Members of self-help groups may be motivated to change out of a desire to receive approval from the group and avoid disappointing them.

Support and self-help group members need to learn how to use the change process. While members of support groups typically cannot change the situation that they are facing, they can change how they cope and can also change other aspects of their ecosystem that is bringing additional stress. The worker facilitates learning the change process whenever needs, concerns, or issues are presented in group. One of the criticisms of some support groups is that the only message members hear at meetings are negative stories that are depressing. These are known as "war stories." Without some kind of resolution or action, members can feel that the group is more of a negative than a positive experience. The response to stories about group members' situations needs to be focused on coping strategies that are or might be successful in helping them deal with the situation. The change process can help with this.

As the group uses the change process and members use it within the group, they are also learning how to use it in their lives outside of the group. When people are coping with a stressful situation, they continue to experience stress in other areas of their lives. Learning and using the change process can help to alleviate some of these other stressors and reduce the overall stress. This change process is a somewhat simplified version of the change process used by the worker. The group and its members learn to assess the need and the situation, develop a plan, act on it, and evaluate progress and the results. In simple terms, members learn to assess, plan, act, and evaluate.

During the functional stage in support and self-help groups, members are receiving support. The group explores the situation with the member and seeks to gain an understanding of it. Other group members share their experiences that are or were similar. Group members help to develop a plan by brainstorming and making suggestions about ways of coping. Members identify and carry out actions that will increase their ability to cope with the situation. In well-functioning groups, this will typically include members sharing contact information with one another so that they can provide assistance outside of the group. Members who are further along or may have already resolved their situation reach out to those who are at the beginning or in the middle of theirs. Everyone has good and bad days. Those having better days can help those who are having difficulty coping. In caregiver support groups, members may provide respite for one another or share the costs of respite and even socialize together to experience some relief from the stresses of caregiving. Members monitor each other's progress by checking in with one another on a regular basis.

Members of support and self-help groups need to learn about resources and how to use them, especially those that can be helpful in coping with the situation. They also need to be able to use resources that will reduce other stressors. Typically, the group and the worker will not be able to meet all of the needs of the members. The group can be a place where members learn about resources and how to use them. Some of this comes from one another and some is provided by the worker. The worker should be familiar with the resources in the community, especially those that are relevant for the types of situations that members of the support group are likely to experience. The worker should be familiar with the formal mechanisms for obtaining resources such as eligibility, referral, application, and similar processes. Individual members may share anecdotal information about resources that they have used. The group and the worker share their formal and informal information about accessing resources. The group assists members in constructing a plan to obtain necessary resources to meet needs associated with the situation at hand or with other stressors.

The group can be helpful in encouraging members to be assertive and to advocate for themselves in obtaining resources. Sometimes the situation that requires support also involves learning to negotiate systems that are involved in treatment such as cancer or other health conditions. Persistence may be needed in dealing with insurance companies and the medical system. Members can practice assertive actions within the group through role-plays and similar activities. The worker may need to engage in advocacy for group members who are denied services for which they seem to be qualified.

Empowering and enabling are actions that can be helpful for members of support groups. For members of self-help groups these actions are fundamental to changing the situation at hand. These actions are covered in greater detail in Chapter 3. When people are empowered and enabled, they are able to cope much better. For self-help groups, members need to feel empowered and enabled or they are unlikely to change themselves or their situation. As with change-oriented groups, these actions can be more powerful in groups than anywhere else. The experience of being in a group and having a sense of belonging is very empowering. Receiving support from the group is empowering and enabling. Learning assertiveness and advocacy skills is empowering. The worker assists the group to develop an environment and a process that empowers members and enables them to use various skills including skills in validating feelings, using positive reinforcement, giving feedback, and making cognitive and behavioral changes that increase coping skills.

Self-help groups may be able to support the development of skills in empowering and enabling, but this may be limited by the absence of a professional worker. To some extent, members can benefit from the group in similar ways as those identified for support groups. Feelings of empowerment and enabling can come from being a member of the group and receiving support from other members. However, the professional training and practice experience of the professional social worker in facilitating the development of these skills is typically not directly available to the group unless it is a self-help group that is facilitated by a social worker.

Crisis intervention is frequently necessary when facilitating support groups. Crisis intervention is covered in greater detail in Chapter 3. Crisis intervention within the group takes place when a member is overwhelmed by a situation. This may be related to the reason for being in the group or it can be a situation that arises outside of the group that is not related. Any crisis will make it difficult for members to cope. It will also be difficult if not impossible for members to work on any issues and to give support. Typically, the member in crisis will need additional support from the group and will probably need assistance from the worker both within and outside of the group. Crises need to be dealt with whenever they occur. The group is a good place to work on crisis management and resolution. People in crisis need support, mobilization of problem-solving efforts, access to resources, and strengthening of their coping skills. The group is an excellent place to receive these, but additional assistance will likely be needed from the worker. Other group members can receive added benefit by learning to deal with and resolve crises. They can also feel good about helping someone who is overwhelmed.

Activity is not typically used in the same way in support groups as it is with change-oriented groups. An important aspect of many support groups are educational activities. These may include speakers, videos, presentations by members or the worker, and the like. Typically, these are related to the situation with which members are coping. Some support groups set aside time for these types of activities at every session. Other groups will do this intermittently as topical areas come up during their sessions. The worker may be primarily responsible for arranging these activities even to the point of researching a topic and developing a presentation for the group. The worker might need to contact a speaker. He may need to arrange for a video to be shown, including locating the video and arranging for equipment. Members may take responsibility for arranging some of these activities as well. Self-help groups may also use educational activities. Some of this may be connected with the specific national organization to which the group belongs. As with support groups, the worker may need to be the resource person for this or it may fall to members to do some or all of it.

In learning new coping skills, members need to take what they learn in the group and apply it to their everyday lives. If the group is the only place where they receive support and use new coping skills, then they will not experience very much benefit from being in the group. This is true for both support and self-help groups. As with change-oriented groups, carryover needs to take place. Members need to use what they learn in the group. They also need to establish a network outside the group from which they can receive support. Some of this network should be in their ecosystem and some may come from members of the group with whom they have established a relationship outside of the group. The best way to ensure some level of carryover is to have members engage in activities that will expand their support system outside of the group. These efforts can be discussed in the group, where the members receive support and feedback and can problem solve any barriers. The desire to receive approval from the group and avoid disappointing them is a powerful motivator for most group members.

Members of self-help groups typically need to make changes not only in themselves, but in the ecosystem as well. Most addictions or habits have a strong environmental influence that has been built up over time that tends to support continuing the addiction or habit.

This is commonly known in these groups as *enabling*. Members of the ecosystem who are enablers either need to change their behavior or the member needs to change her interaction with them, including terminating unhealthy relationships that impede her recovery. This is very difficult to do in most cases and is often the greatest barrier to recovering or maintaining one's recovery. In essence, members of self-help groups usually have to build a new support system in their ecosystem if they hope to make any permanent changes in their life. This requires a great deal of effort on their part and also requires considerable support from the group in carrying this out. Sometimes members of self-help groups will combine attending meetings with professional intervention that can help with their recovery and with building a new support system.

Mediating between a member and a system in the environment typically occurs outside of the group. This is generally the first choice of actions by the worker before advocacy. Social workers use mediation by remaining neutral and bringing a client and a system in the environment together and to reach agreement about service delivery. Members can learn valuable skills in negotiation and compromise by observing mediation directly or indirectly. As with change-oriented groups, most of the time this is indirect unless the group member is a part of the situation. Indirect experiences are ones in which the member and the worker share experiences with this type of mediation with the group. Mediation may not be used as much by the worker within a support group because conflict is not as likely to occur in these types of groups. However, it can arise during the early stages of group development or when group members take responsibility for leading or facilitating the group. When this occurs and the worker has to step in and mediate, members have an opportunity to experience this more directly. Learning to give and take and to negotiate and compromise is a key aspect of good relationships. While support groups have the advantage of having a professional worker who is knowledgeable about mediation, this is not the case for self-help groups that do not have a professional worker unless one or more of the members have acquired this skill.

The worker engages in actions that are designed to facilitate group formation, discussion, conflict resolution, interaction, group development, and activities. These are described in Chapter 4 and are aspects of much of what is described in Chapters 5 and 6 and in this chapter and so will not be repeated here. However, we discuss these actions with respect to facilitating group process for support groups. The purpose of the group cannot be achieved unless the group is able to provide meaningful support for its members in a safe and positive environment.

Groups need to be able to progress through the stages of group development and group members need to interact in a way that is supportive. Support is a skill that most members have learned in their life outside of the group. However, some may be uncertain about giving and receiving support within the group and this needs to be nurtured and facilitated by the worker. When members look to him for support, the worker needs to resist the temptation to respond, and gently steer this toward the group. He does this by asking other members of the group if they have experienced or felt something similar. He asks how they coped with this. He asks how members feel as they hear the story that has been told. As group members respond, he encourages them to interact with one another. He asks them to tell one another what they think and how they feel rather than telling this to him. As the group begins to interact, group process develops and the worker becomes a facilitator for the group rather than the provider of support.

The worker might model some support at times but over time this needs to come from the group. The worker focuses on abilities and strengths, shows interest and a desire to help, expresses an understanding of the situation and feelings about the situation, and provides encouragement and reassurance, as Hollis described.[4] Using Nelson's approach, he models protection, acceptance, validation, and education.[5] However, he is constantly aware of the need to encourage the group members to be the main source of support for one another. Thus, as he models these skills he moves from the process level to the content level by raising the level of discussion to address what he did, how the group felt about it, and how group members can do likewise. As group members display these skills, even at a rudimentary level, he calls this to the attention of the group and uses the group to reinforce it by asking members to share their reactions. As members build these skills the worker steps into the background and allows the group to take over providing support. Probably the ideal support group is one in which the worker comes in and turns on the lights, calls the meeting to order, adjourns the group, and turns off the lights. In fact, he might be able to get it down to turning the lights on and off. In most self-help groups, this is likely to be his basic responsibility.

During the functional stage, the emphasis is on providing the support that is needed. This is the stage during which group members should be getting their need for support met from one another within and outside of the group. The group should be achieving its purpose of providing support to one another. Part of the worker's evaluation at this stage is determining the extent to which the group is effective and understanding why it is or is not. For those members who are making progress in coping with their situation and seem to be lessening their need for support from the group, the worker evaluates what has been helpful and what has not so he can help the group to improve its ability to give support. For members who are not making progress in coping or who are still overwhelmed by their situation, the worker evaluates what might be missing or what might be needed to make the group more effective. In groups that are functioning well, these evaluations are a part of what the group itself does during sessions as it identifies what is effective by members giving feedback to one another. The worker may need to prompt this, but group members share their own experiences and their observations.

Most self-help groups do not have a worker to evaluate the group or its members. Some groups will incorporate some type of evaluation into each session. Typically, this occurs as the group is ending and everyone shares their thoughts and feelings about their experiences in the group. This can also be structured into support group sessions. It can be highly effective, especially when members share with other members appreciation for the support they received. This can serve as a powerful reinforcement for providing support within the group.

# The Change Process During
# the Disintegration Stage

Disintegration can occur during the early stages of the group or later on if there is insufficient membership to sustain the group. These types of groups tend to rely primarily on word of mouth and referrals from organizations that are likely to see people who would be good candidates for the group. Support groups and some self-help groups tend to need periodic or even ongoing recruitment efforts to ensure a steady membership. For most groups, members will recruit new members by sharing their experiences with people with whom they come into contact. More formal recruitment generally is done by the worker or the organization that sponsors the group. This can be done by sending information to other organizations who have clients or patients who need this type of group, or by advertising in local newspapers and public service announcements on radio and television and on cable channels devoted to public access. Placing fliers or brochures in waiting rooms or offices where potential members receive services can also be effective. However, the most power-ful forces in getting new members to join is for a doctor or other professional to recom-mend it, or for current and former members to tell others about their experiences. Many professionals are reluctant to make referrals unless they are confident that their clients or patients will have a positive experience. Thus, word of mouth from satisfied customers will increase the likelihood that other professionals will refer to the group.

Most support and self-help groups are ongoing, which means that termination is more focused on individual members as they reach a point at which they do not need sup-port from the group or drop out of the group. As with change-oriented groups, we will focus on two types of disintegration. One type is when members are completing their work and do not need the group, and the other is when a group shows signs of disintegration.

Disintegration is marked by a lessening of bonds within the group. Support groups may not have bonds that are as strong as change-oriented groups if the self-disclosure and trust have been limited to the situation at hand. However, their bonds tend to be stronger than many other types of groups because they share such serious challenges. In fact, the bonds might be quite strong among members who have been with the group for some time and those who have developed a supportive relationship outside of the group. Self-help groups can have bonds that are similar to change-oriented groups, especially closed self-help groups. During disintegration, the frequency and strength of group inter-action are reduced, along with common norms and values among group members and the strength of the influence that the group has on members. At the same time, members should be increasing and strengthening their interaction with their ecosystem outside of the group.

It is expected that disintegration will occur as members complete their work in self-help groups, although many twelve-step programs emphasize that if a member is an alco-holic (or addicted to narcotics, gambling, etc.), then they are alcoholics for life. They are either wet or dry, but will continue to be at risk of having their addiction interfere with their functioning. Thus, many of these groups discourage members from leaving. Instead, they are expected to take on leadership roles and become sponsors for those who are in recovery.

In support groups, members may find that their situation is resolved or they are coping better and no longer feel a need to attend the group. One unique feature of many support groups is that some members who no longer need the group may stay on to provide support for others who are going through what they went through. However, some members may linger because they have not been able to move on with their life outside the group, perhaps as a result of unresolved grief and loss. When this occurs, it is important the group assist with the process of resolving the grief or the worker may need to facilitate this either within the group or in separate sessions. Members who stay to help others should do so as part of a healthy growth experience in which they continue to derive some benefit from the group.

As members complete their work and are better able to cope, they are less reliant on the group for support. The needs that brought them to the group are being met so there is much less motivation to be in the group and less investment in the group. Members are preparing to go on with their lives without the group. The termination process is discussed in Chapters 3 and 4 and will not be repeated here, but we will consider group process and the worker's actions during termination.

Changing membership means reestablishing the group. In order to go through the earlier stages of group formation more quickly, support and open self-help groups will have at least some structure to quickly incorporate new members. To some extent, the group must disintegrate and become less cohesive as it goes through this process. Ideally there will be enough structure for the group to maintain its norms, roles, and tasks while allowing new members to feel welcome and see a place for themselves in the group. So, some disintegration needs to occur so the group can revisit the first three stages of group development and reform itself around the new membership.

During the disintegration stage, the worker assesses the needs of the group and each member. In an ongoing group, a member or the worker may be terminating, but the group is continuing on. Members may or may not announce that they are ending their involvement with the group. Because other members may miss them or be hurt by not seeing them or being able to say good-bye, some groups will adopt a norm that expects members to let one another know when they intend to leave the group. It is not unusual for members to attend only sporadically as they transition out of the group. As with change-oriented groups, the group needs to let go and support the member as he leaves the group. After there have been several of these departures, the group should be more aware of what to do in these situations. However, the first few may be difficult, as will the departure of long-term members. Members may be reluctant to let go. The group may feel threatened as the bonds are loosened and may worry that the group might fall apart. Once the members find that this is not the case, the group will feel stronger as it is able to enjoy the support that was given to the member and received from him.

In some support groups, the departure of members is caused by death. This might be the death of a member or the death of a family member whose condition was the reason for the need for support. In these groups, it is essential that the grief process be allowed to run its course. When members die, group members need to mourn their loss. When a member has a loved one die, they need to be supported as they mourn. The worker should be aware of the stages of the grief process and should facilitate the group and members progressing through those stages.

Premature departures are generally difficult to predict in these groups. In self-help groups, it may be important for the worker to follow up when a member drops out because of the reasons members are in the group. As with change-oriented groups, the group experience with self-help groups is intended to help members resolve situations that require assistance. The worker should contact the member to see if he will return to the group or if other services are needed. In either case, the worker should offer other services within her agency or with another agency. The worker should report back to the group whether the member will be returning. She reassures the group that other services are available if the member decides not to return. Similar steps should be taken to ensure that former members of support groups either no longer need the support or are coping adequately with the situation.

The group will generally need some type of closure when long-term members leave the group. This typically means going around the room and allowing members to have their last say. Most will wish the departing member well and will also offer thanks for his assistance or fond memories that they will take with them.

Group disintegration can occur for a group that is intended to be an ongoing group. When this occurs, it represents a crisis. The group has regressed to an earlier stage or has not progressed to the point of being functional or is at risk of ending prematurely. Work is probably not getting done and support is minimal. Attendance is usually sporadic or dropping. The worker needs to decide if she will act to try to save the group or if it is time to let the group end. It is relatively rare for support or self-help groups to no longer to be needed. Typically, the reasons for the group to exist have not disappeared. As is the case with change-oriented groups, if the worker decides to act to save the group, she needs to discuss this with members. She does so in the group and by contacting members individually to find out what is happening and if they want the group to continue. Most of the time, more aggressive recruitment will be needed to bring new members on board.

Sometimes a group will begin to disintegrate because there are personal conflicts that have arisen. If these conflicts can be resolved, then the group might continue. The group may not be providing a benefit to its members. A member may not be benefiting from the group. The group or a member or members may be saying and doing things that are harmful to other group members. These situations need to be resolved as soon as possible. If they cannot be resolved, then the group may end or a member or members may be asked to leave. Of course, if this happens, arrangements are made for members to receive other services.

As in any circumstance in which there is conflict within the group, the worker maintains a mediating position and refrains from taking sides. She tries to get both parties to express their concerns. She asks them for their input in how problems might be resolved. Ideally, this is done in the group or in a face-to-face meeting. If hostility is too great, then the worker may act as the mediator in negotiating with each side separate from each other.

As the group begins to disintegrate and terminate or a member prepares to leave, the worker solicits an evaluation of the experience. The group and its members should review where they started and what has been accomplished. They should be asked to identify what was helpful or supportive, what was not, and what might have been helpful or supportive. Throughout the group, the worker evaluates the group and its members and tries to anticipate any premature disintegration. When membership lags or attendance becomes sporadic, she tries to reenergize the group and recruit new members.

If the worker is leaving a support group, it may be at risk of disintegration. Some groups may end completely unless another worker is available to take it over. Others may lose some membership. This can usually be avoided if there has been a solid effort to ensure that support comes primarily from the group. If the new worker can meet with the group several times before the worker departs it will help to reduce the loss. Having the worker leave the group is fairly common for ongoing groups, especially if they have been meeting over an extended period of time. Workers might leave for a wide variety of reasons, the most common of which are leaving the agency for another position or moving to another position within the agency.

Less common reasons for the worker to leave any group are lay off, firing, closing the agency or program, illness, disability, and even death. For support groups and self-help groups facilitated by the worker, these situations can be traumatic for both the worker and the group and will require some intervention. If the group is ending for any of these reasons, an effort needs to be made to help resolve any issues related to the worker leaving or the group ending and arrangements need to be made for members to receive alternative services. Typically, the worker's supervisor should do this if the worker is not available. For self-help groups that do not have a professional worker but are hosted by a worker who is leaving, another worker or agency needs to take over hosting the group. The worker or his supervisor should ensure that this is available to the group.

Whenever a worker leaves a group, she prepares the group for her departure and for a new worker. As with change-oriented groups, the worker asks members to express their concerns. She should reassure them that other workers will be as committed as she has been and can be as helpful. If she has been successful in establishing a group in which members provide most of the support, the group should generally be able to sustain itself after she leaves and a new worker takes over.

New workers need to allow the group to express feelings about the previous worker. These should be explored during the first session. If there are joint sessions with the former and the new worker, issues should be discussed openly in those sessions. They should be discussed again when the new worker starts facilitating the group on his own. If there is a coleader, they should be discussed before the worker leaves, after she leaves, and again when a new coleader joins the group. The worker needs to allow for all of the feelings typically associated with grief and loss, including denial, anger, bargaining, and resolution. These may not be as intense if the group has been the primary means of support. However, if the reason for the group is to cope with death or a terminal illness, then any loss will tend to provoke more intense reactions of grief.

Groups with new workers will probably need to revisit all of the earlier stages of group development. They will need to orient the new worker and establish a relationship with him. In the process of doing this, the group will likely experience some disintegration and then reform itself. The new worker should facilitate this process.

Terminating support group sessions can sometimes be difficult in that group members may want to stay longer to enjoy the support they have received and perhaps avoid having to face the situation they are in without the group. The session should end with a summary of the work that has been done and what lies ahead for the next session. The group should spend some time planning for the next session if there are any educational or special arrangements that are needed. For members, it is important to identify support that may be needed between sessions. The worker should give feedback about what has been accomplished and praise the work that has been done.

## Summary

The worker uses the change process at each stage of development in facilitating support and self-help groups. She engages in assessment and planning before the group begins. She also does this during each session and between each session. She facilitates the group's progress through each stage of development. The worker facilitates the group in accomplishing its purpose during the functional stage. She helps the group to provide support in coping with the situations in which members find themselves. The worker provides information and helps members to learn how to use it in their daily lives. She helps members to consolidate gains as the group is ending during the disintegration stage. The worker uses her relationship skills and her skills as a social worker to facilitate the group and make it a positive, supportive experience. She develops skills in both the art and the science of facilitating support and self-help groups.

CASE **7.1**

# Hospice Support Group

Gwen is employed in a hospice program that includes a support group for family members. The group meets every week because of the difficult situations the families are facing. Members make it when they can. The families are thankful that the group meets every week because they know that no matter what is happening, they can find some temporary solace and support at least once each week. Other support groups meet monthly, but these are mainly for situations that are long term. While it is depressing sometimes to hear about the death of a loved one in one of the families, it is uplifting to know that the person was kept comfortable and they were allowed to die with dignity.

Gwen is primarily responsible for facilitating the support group. Members have chosen to begin the group with a moment of silence for those who are dying or have died. Family members typically update one another about their situations. Most of the current members have been together for two or three months, so they are well acquainted with each other and well aware of the situations that bring them together. Members have exchanged telephone numbers and contact one another regularly. Some have socialized together after arranging to have volunteers provide respite for them at the same time.

At this meeting there are a total of eight members from five families. Because the group is well developed, the group moves quickly through the first three stages of reforming itself. The updates represent the orientation stage, and establishing the agenda is the authority and negotiation stages of the session. As the group moves into the functional stage, members begin sharing some of their thoughts and feelings. Some cry as they talk about their loved one, but most of the time the group shares fond memories of past experiences. They also share some information about services they have discovered and things that have helped them to cope.

For this session, Gwen agreed to develop a presentation on the use of music, progressive relaxation, and guided imagery to relieve stress. She had attended a workshop on this as part of meeting the continuing education requirements for her social work license. The workshop was on pain and pain management. The use of these techniques in managing pain and stress was introduced and Gwen thought it might be useful for members of the support group. Some of these techniques might also be helpful in relieving pain for their loved ones.

Gwen began the session by turning down the lights and asking everyone to get comfortable and close their eyes. She turned on some harp music and asked everyone to take three cleansing breaths. This involves inhaling deeply through the nose and then exhaling slowly through the mouth by blowing as if one were trying to make a candle flicker without blowing it out. This was followed by the progressive muscle relaxation exercise. Gwen instructed members to tense, hold, and relax each muscle group (i.e., feet, legs, buttocks, stomach, back, hands, arms, chest, neck, face, and head) in the body three times. They had to hold the tension for five seconds and then she asked them to gradually relax the muscles and imagine the tension flowing out of their body through their toes, fingertips, and by their breathing. She asked them to silently tell themselves three times, "I am relaxed and calm."

Once all of the muscle groups were covered, Gwen had them imagine they were at a sunny resort. They were coming down the elevator. She counted down from ten to one. She then described walking out on a warm, white sand beach. She took them for a walk on the beach and had them imagine lying down on the warm sand, feeling the warmth of the sand and the sun, and hearing the rhythmic sound of the surf. She told them when they were ready they could open their eyes and return to the room. As members opened their eyes, they were amazed at how relaxed they felt. Some described how they did not want to "come back." Gwen described how they could practice these techniques every day for several weeks and learn to find tension and release it at any time. They could also learn to relax no matter where they were just by training themselves to relax.

As the group was coming to an end, members asked Gwen if she could tell them where they might purchase the CD of the harp music. They also asked if she might make a CD for them to listen to and learn the relaxation techniques she had taught them. She told them she would look into it for them. As the group adjourned (disintegration), members discussed plans for the following week. At an earlier session, the group had asked if a medical professional could come and talk about the use of medica-

tion in pain management. Gwen announced that she had met some local nurses at the workshop and they agreed to help her to find a physician or nurse practitioner to speak to the group. She offered to make arrangements for the next session and they agreed. The meeting was adjourned.

## QUESTIONS

1. Using Table 6.1, develop a plan for a support group.

2. Describe how you would use assessment skills during various stages of the group from Question 1 or another group.

3. Describe how you would use planning during various stages of the group from Question 1 or another group.

4. Describe how you would use direct practice actions during various stages of the group from Question 1 or another group.

5. Describe how you would use group facilitation skills during various stages of the group from Question 1 or another group.

6. Describe how you would use evaluation during various stages of the group from Question 1 or another group.

7. Describe how you would deal with disintegration or termination during various stages of the group from Question 1 or another group.

## SUGGESTED READINGS

Johnson, Louise C. and Yanca, Stephen J., *Social Work Practice: A Generalist Approach*, 9th ed. Boston: Allyn & Bacon, 2007 (Chapter 14).

Edwards, Richard L., Ed. *Encyclopedia of Social Work*, 19th ed. Washington, DC: NASW Press, 1995 ("Group Practice Overview").

Gitterman, Alex, and Shulman, Lawrence. *Mutual Aid Groups, Vulnerable and Resilient Populations, and the Life Cycle*, 3rd ed. New York: Columbia University Press, 2005.

Grief, Geoffrey, and Ephross, Paul, Eds. *Group Work with Populations at Risk*, 2nd ed. New York: Oxford University Press, 2005.

Jacobs, Ed, Masson, Robert, and Harvill, Riley. *Group Counseling Strategies and Skills*. 5th ed. Pacific Grove, CA: Brooks/Cole, 2006.

Ivey, Allen E., Pederson, Paul B., and Ivey, Mary Bradford. *Intentional Group Counseling: A Microskills Approach*. Belmont, CA: Thomson/ Wadsworth, 2001.

Johnson, David W. and Johnson, Frank P. *Joining Together: Group Theory and Group Skills*, 9th ed. Boston: Allyn & Bacon, 2006.

Kottler, Jeffery. *Learning Group Leadership: An Experiential Approach*. Boston: Allyn & Bacon, 2001.

Northern, Helen, and Kurland, Roselle. *Social Work with Groups*, 3rd ed. New York: Columbia University Press, 2001.

Shulman, Lawrence. *The Skills of Helping: Individuals, Families, Groups, and Communities*, 6th ed. Belmont, CA: Thomson-Brooks/Cole, 2009.

Toseland, Ronald W., and Rivas, Robert F. *An Introduction to Group Work Practice*, 6th ed. Boston: Allyn & Bacon, 2009.

# 8 Growth and Development Groups

## LEARNING EXPECTATIONS

1. Understanding the importance of growth and development groups in generalist social work practice.
2. Understanding growth and development groups offered within generalist practice.
3. Understanding the use of the change process in growth and development groups.
4. Understanding the group process to be able to recognize its various aspects in the functioning of growth and development groups.
5. Understanding how the social worker can facilitate the work and process of growth and development groups.
6. Beginning skill in facilitating small-group interaction in growth and development groups.

This chapter considers generalist social work practice with growth and development groups. These are the most common types of groups to which people belong. These groups are not limited to those that are offered by generalist practice social workers. There are a wide variety of professionals, paraprofessionals, and nonprofessionals who facilitate these types of groups in a wide variety of settings. In addition to providing these types of groups, social workers may supervise others in doing so or may operate programs that provide these types of experiences.

Growth and development groups focus on promoting a healthy, positive quality of life in every sphere of human life, including biological, psychological, and social aspects. The biological aspects include health and wellness, and physical growth and development across the life span. Psychological aspects include mental health, and cognitive and spiritual growth and development across the life span. Social aspects include relationships, social skills, and socialization across the life span. These groups can include nearly every aspect of people's lives. The majority of these groups are offered to the general population based on their interests. However, the topics covered by them are also needed by populations served by social workers. Thus, we find generalist social workers providing group experiences that fall under this area of group work to their clients and to others. Sometimes it is necessary for the worker to provide these experiences to clients because those clients would not fare as well in a group with the general population. An example of this is a client who is mentally ill. Sometimes these types of groups are facilitated by social workers in certain settings such as day activity and residential programs for various client groups. In this chapter, we discuss growth and development groups offered by social workers to clients and to the general population.

As we pointed out in Chapter 1, group work came out of the settlement houses and a variety of agencies serving groups including YMCAs, YWCAs, and the Boy and Girl Scout movements, and other youth-serving, recreation, and informal education agencies. Most of the groups in settlement houses and many other settings were facilitated by what we would consider to be early generalist social workers. These were not therapy groups or even change-oriented groups, rather, they were groups that were intended to provide the knowledge and skills necessary to adjust to life in urban America. Some groups included recreation and socialization. They had the added benefit of providing opportunities to learn new social skills and relationship skills.

# Group Purposes in Growth and Development Groups

Growth and development groups are different from change-oriented and support and self-help groups in that anyone can benefit from these experiences. Most growth and development groups are not typically offered specifically for the purpose of bringing about change or assisting in coping with a certain situation. Their primary purpose is to develop or enhance skills and abilities or assist in fulfilling developmental needs and tasks. That is not to say that some of these groups are not used to change behavior or replace skills that are deficient or inappropriate, but this is not their primary purpose or focus.

Let us examine some of these growth and development groups. We define these groups as being any group whose primary purpose is to promote healthy functioning in the biological, psychological, or social aspects of people's lives through group experiences or the acquisition or enhancement of skills and abilities. These groups can range from those that provide recreation to those that are educational in nature. A sports team is an example of a recreation group. Every class in a school is a growth and development group. Community education programs are examples of growth and development groups. Social workers facilitate recreation groups with adults and youth in schools, residential settings, and community centers. They facilitate life skills and social skills groups in these same settings and in family service agencies and child welfare settings with youth who are in foster care or independent living. Social workers provide parenting groups in almost any setting serving youth and families. Social workers provide activities and socialization for people who are older in senior citizen centers, day activity programs, and residential settings, including assisted living facilities and nursing homes. Recreation, life skills, and social skills groups are offered by social workers in mental health settings, domestic violence shelters, substance abuse settings, and other programs. Thus, growth and development groups are offered in a wide variety of settings to a wide variety of clientele by a wide variety of professionals, including BSWs and MSWs.

Unlike change-oriented and support groups, young children are good candidates for many of these groups. Because children and young adolescents are very action oriented, they generally do well in those groups that provide recreational activities and in others that have a more active approach. Sometimes recreation is combined with other types of skill development.

## Assessment and Planning Before the Group Begins

As with any type of group, the worker uses the change process in organizing and facilitating the group. However, unlike change-oriented and support and self-help groups, growth and development groups do not typically use the change process within the group itself. There are exceptions to this, such as some parenting groups that may use the change process in developing approaches to parenting and also life skills groups that should include learning problem-solving and decision-making skills. For some clients, participating in a growth and development group may represent the primary portion of the action phase. However, for most clients it is an important supplement to it. For instance, social skills or parenting skills or even recreation may be included in a service plan along with various change-oriented services. Thus, these groups are intended to supplement the actions of the worker and the client as they work on other changes. In addition, growth and development groups can be used to provide follow up services after formal services are delivered or as an additional service while formal services are being received.

The group worker uses assessment and planning skills before the group begins, between and during each session, and between each stage of group development. Assessment and planning within each session and between sessions are discussed as we cover each stage of group development. While some of these types of groups may occur naturally in the environment, such as recreation groups, growth and development groups are generally formed groups that have specific purposes. Thus, they are mainly artificial or contrived. In forming a group, the worker needs to obtain approval from her agency as she would with any other groups that we have described. She must also recruit participants and coordinate the logistical aspects of forming a group.

A schema for planning a group is provided in Table 6.1 and the same schema can be used for growth and development groups. The schema can be used as a guide for developing a proposal to her administration. As we mentioned, when planning for a new group, the proposal needs to answer the questions why, who, what, where, when, and how. The schema gives basic answers to these questions and can be modified as needed to include other information or aspects that are unique to any particular situation.

As indicated in Table 6.1, the worker needs to consider the reason for the group and present this in the proposal. It should address both effectiveness and efficiency. Growth and development groups are not typically reimbursed by insurance. Members may be charged a fee in some settings, but often the groups are provided free of charge. However, many of these types of groups that are facilitated by social workers are offered in settings in which they are part of a larger program, such as a school, an activity program, a residential care setting, a foster care program, or a senior center. Proposals will need to address the need for such groups that will justify the use of resources because this will be a major concern for management or administration. The purpose of the group should be designed to meet the needs of potential members and also fit into the mission and services of the agency and the goals of the program where they are located. The worker should anticipate being asked why a growth and development group is needed and why the agency should provide this service.

As with other groups, it is best to present the purpose of the group and the basic aspects of it at the beginning of the plan or proposal. This needs to be detailed because in most cases the worker must justify the use of agency resources without an expectation of reimbursement. The worker should include research and a discussion of the need for this type of group.

She should also include information from professional sources on serving the target population in settings similar to that of the agency or community. Potential group members should be identified, along with some description of the benefits they can expect to derive from the group, and benefits to the agency and the community of sponsoring such a group.

The worker should project the size of the group. Growth and development groups may be much larger than change-oriented and support groups. The size of the group will depend on the types of activities, the age and developmental levels of the membership, and the space that is available. The groups need to be large enough to engage in certain activities such as recreation or small-group projects, but not too large that face-to-face interaction is impossible.

For most growth and development groups, the composition of the group is not as important as it was with change-oriented and support groups. Generally, it is assumed that anyone who participates will derive whatever benefits they need merely by their participation in the group and whatever activities the group offers. Members are not expected to engage in much self-disclosure. The exceptions to this may include groups such as parenting groups, in which parents discuss their parenting experiences. However, group dynamics can still play an important role in how much members enjoy their experience and in some groups how well the group does in having a successful outcome. Trust is not as important in most growth and development groups. However, members need to be capable of engaging in relationships and demonstrating skills and abilities that are within a reasonable range of the rest of their group. Otherwise, there is a risk that these members will be left out or even scapegoated or ostracized.

The worker needs to consider what kind of mixture of individuals is best to meet the needs of the group and its members. In some cases, only certain client populations may be eligible. In other cases, the group may be open to anyone who wishes to join. Still other groups may have a mixture of clients and people from the general population. Much of this is dictated by the purpose of the group, the setting, and the types of activities.

Many growth and development groups are open to the general population and anyone who is interested may join. Even so, the worker should develop a profile of potential members and a recruitment strategy that will increase the likelihood of success. Unless the group is restricted to a certain client population, new members may join the group without a formal referral or invitation. Thus, the worker may not be able to screen potential group members to ensure that they are appropriate for the group. However, this is typically only necessary when the group has a specific purpose or a particular composition that might be appropriate for only certain types of members. For example, a life skills group for youth in foster care would not be open to the general population. On the other hand, some parenting groups for parents with children in foster care may be restricted to this population but others may include nonclient members in order to provide clients with healthier alternative forms of parenting.

Diversity may play an important role in considering membership for growth and development groups, but this tends to be less important than it is in change-oriented groups. Unlike change-oriented and support groups, cultural groups are less likely to shy away from growth and development groups because of cultural taboos, because most of these groups do not require members to engage in self-disclosure. There may be some taboos related to the types of activities in which the group engages. As with other groups, the degree of acculturation may be important in this regard. Clients who are more acculturated into the dominant culture may act much more like the dominant culture and so may not be affected by cultural taboos, while others may retain a considerable amount of their cultural heritage and be less likely to join the group.

Several advantages and disadvantages associated with diversity have been identified throughout the text. Because establishing trust is not as important in growth and development groups, diversity tends to be less important. However, that does not mean that the there will not be bias and prejudice toward various diverse groups. Issues associated with diversity in society can enter into the functioning of these groups as well.

As with other types of groups, diversity can have several advantages, such as having the opportunity to become more acquainted with people who are different. Growth and development groups are often good places for this to occur because in many of these groups, the goals of the group and its members tend to be related to accepted developmental concerns. Enjoying the group and its activities can break down some of the barriers between diverse groups that we see in the larger society. Many times sports and recreation teams are made up of members of diverse groups. Working togther as a team affords members the opportunity to know one another in a positive way. Generally, as people become more acquainted, they find that they have a lot in common.

As with other groups, it is generally better to have at least one other member who shares the same diversity. This is more difficult to control with growth and development groups, especially those that are open to the general population. At the same time, members may resolve this by bringing other family members or friends with them to the group. Members may have acquaintances who share their diversity as well as an interest in joining the group. In fact, it is not unusual to have members who are friends or relatives accompany each other in joining these types of groups.

As with other groups, age is still an important factor in establishing common ground. Typically, adults and children are not mixed with each other in growth and development groups unless activities are designed to be intergenerational. Generally, it is best for group members to be somewhat close in age or at least be of the same generation.

Many growth and development groups are time limited. Some are ongoing and have closed membership such as those in day or residential programs. Those that are time limited will typically be closed after the first session or at some point after the group has begun.

As with all groups, it is important that the leader or facilitator be competent to lead or facilitate the group. Competence is part of the NASW *Code of Ethics* and every code of ethics for professionals. Appropriate credentials, training, and experience are needed. Some of these types of groups do not necessarily require a great deal of advanced professional training. Other types may require expertise in specific areas such as groups that have an educational purpose, parenting groups, and social skills groups. The competence of the worker may be a critical factor in having a proposal approved and in the recruitment process. Other workers will want to know that there is competent leadership before referring their clients to a group. Supervision and consultation may be needed, especially when difficult situations arise.

The proposal should include a description of the format for the group. Growth and development groups can range from being loosely structured to those that are highly structured. Recreation groups themselves may range from those with formal competitive events complete with leagues, standings, and championships to informal drop-in recreation programs in community centers. Some groups may use program material or a curriculum, for example, a parenting group that is designed to teach a specific parenting approach.

However, even these groups will typically require modification of the program materials to meet the needs of members.

Resources such as speakers, videos, books, and the like may be part of the group experience and may be a part of some sessions. Consideration should be given to the resources that are needed and where these might be obtained. In a strengths-based approach, the strengths of group members are incorporated into planning for the group and the format should be built on these strengths.

Just as with any other types of groups that social workers facilitate, growth and development groups should be offered under the sanction or auspices of one or more organization. This gives the worker and the group credibility. The organization typically provides a site to meet and serves as the sponsor for the group. As we indicated, organizations are sanctioned by the community to provide services to certain populations. The group purpose and the populations being served should be consistent with the purpose, goals, and functioning of the sponsoring organizations. Sometimes providing or sponsoring the group represents a new service, a new way of serving clients, or a collaboration with other organizations in serving a new or an existing clientele.

The ability to offer a growth and development group will likely be determined by who sponsors the group and who facilitates it. Having more than one organization act as a sponsor has advantages such as sharing resources and providing referrals. Most of the disadvantages are related to greater coordination and the need for approval from more than one organization.

As with other groups, plans or proposals for growth and development groups should include a basic description of group membership, recruitment, and benefits from being in the group. (Group composition is discussed earlier). Recruitment in residential settings is not necessary. In these settings, referrals are made by agencies or individuals and an intake process is used to screen applicants to the program. Recruiting members for community-based groups is a matter of establishing the need and getting the word out to prospective members and agency personnel who are likely to be in contact with them. Those groups that are restricted to human services clientele require both recruitment directed at workers who are serving those clients and a screening process to ensure that referrals are appropriate. For groups that are offered to the general public, an advertising campaign is usually needed to secure prospective members. This may include developing and distributing fliers or brochures, advertising in local newspapers and newsletters, running public service announcements on radio and television as well as public access cable channels. The costs of these activities should be included in the budget for the group.

A plan or proposal for new growth and development groups should contain a description of what the group will be doing, including some ideas about what will transpire during typical group sessions. If there are program materials available, this should be presented and if possible a copy of the program material or a summary or outline should be included. Potential topics and resources for the group should be identified.

Projected dates and times should be included to the extent that these are known. The worker should identify the length of the sessions and the time of day and days of the week sessions might take place. In most cases, the group will be time limited, so possible start and end dates should be identified. The frequency of sessions can vary a great deal. For growth and development groups, sessions are most often scheduled at least once a week, but this may vary. Groups in day activity and residential programs might meet every day during the week or two or three times on certain days of the week. The place where the group will meet should be discussed in some detail, along with who is responsible for making any arrangements. As with other groups, the space where a group meets will dictate what happens in the group and what can and cannot be done. Because physical activity is part of many growth and development groups, there needs to be sufficient open space and members need to be able to feel comfortable. Confidentiality and privacy are not usually an issue unless the group is discussing more personal issues such as parenting. In some cases, it may be more important that the noise from the group does not disturb others who are not in the group. Any materials or special equipment that will be needed should be identified.

Additional information that may be needed should be identified and addressed in a proposal, including such things as the availability or need for transportation, child care or elder care, or other needs. These should be anticipated and any potential barriers addressed.

A mechanism for evaluating the group should be identified that includes group and individual outcomes that are desired and how these will be measured. As with support and self-help groups, evaluation in growth and development groups tends to be much more informal and also more elusive than is the case for change-oriented groups where membership is more stable. The most common design for evaluating groups in general is pretest/posttest. Often, the measurement is more along the lines of determining how satisfied members were with the group, usually through some form of postgroup survey. As with support and self-help groups, formal evaluation may not be needed because these groups are not typically offered under the auspices of funding sources such as grants and the like. However, the worker may need to provide evidence to management that the group was effective and worth the time and expense involved. For groups that involve the acquisition of certain knowledge or skills, a pre- and posttest may be designed and given. In some cases, only the posttest is necessary if the organization is only interested in ensuring that members have a certain level of knowledge or skills (or satisfaction) and the actual change in skill level is not an issue.

As a way of incorporating evaluation and planning into a growth and development group, the worker could design a feedback form that members fill out at the end of each session or periodically that would identify what was helpful or enjoyable, what was not helpful or not enjoyable, and what could be more helpful or enjoyable. It could ask about the members' satisfaction and solicit ideas for future sessions. Evaluation is important for determining outcomes and for demonstrating the effectiveness of the group and may be vital in determining whether the group continues or is offered in the future. For voluntary growth and development groups, most agency administrators will be satisfied with attendance figures, assuming that if people are attending, they must find it worthwhile.

The budget is an important consideration for a proposal for growth and development groups. Organizations will want to know what the cost-benefit analysis is for the group, especially those that are experiencing tight financial constraints. Chances are that reimbursement will not be available or it may not be enough to cover the full costs of the group. Charging members for a group will tend to limit membership, but growth and development groups may be sufficiently attractive that they generate some income from charging fees. Generally, the higher the cost, the fewer the number of people will be who might consider joining the group. The emphasis in a cost-benefit analysis may need to be on the benefit to clientele of the organization and the recognition or prestige that sponsoring a group might bring. The organization may have contingency or discretionary funds available to assist with resources, or donations may be solicited from attendees or people interested in supporting the type of activity or the population being served. Some organizations may have a budget for offering these types of groups because it is within their purview to provide these services. A realistic estimate of the costs or expenses should be presented, including materials, refreshments, rent, salaries, transportation, equipment, and the like. An estimate of the units of service along with expenses will give some basis for deciding if the group is feasible.

Assessment and planning before any group begins increase the likelihood of success. The worker should develop a proposal to management so that approval can be obtained. As with other groups, a well-organized and thorough proposal creates a positive impression that can increase the likelihood that the group will be approved.

## The Change Process During the Orientation Stage

The first three stages of group development tend to be somewhat different for growth and development groups as opposed to change-oriented and support and self-help groups. The main differences tend to be associated with differences in needs and in investment for many group members. The primary benefits of most growth and development groups are derived from participation and socialization. Change-oriented groups resolve issues that create unmet needs. For support groups, the primary need is to cope with a difficult situation. For self-help groups, it is to overcome an addiction or similar challenge. People in change-oriented and support and self-help groups tend to have a high level of need to resolve or cope with their situation. There is a wider range of members in most growth and development groups so there is likely to be a wider range of need. This includes members who do not feel as great a need to be in the group. Also, the level of investment in the group may be different when the need that is being met is different. Meeting basic needs tends to be seen as more important than meeting higher-order needs. This is not to say that some members will not be highly invested, especially those who have unspoken needs. But for many members of growth and development groups there is generally much less at stake. For instance, a recreation group will typically not generate the same level of investment for most members as a counseling or a support group. People can choose other ways of getting their needs for recreation met. The need for recreation may not be felt as intensely as the need to have certain psychological needs met, to cope with a difficult situation, or to overcome an addiction. However, some members may be very competitive and so they may be much more highly invested in a recreation group.

Because there may be less at stake, attraction to the group may also be lessened, especially for members who are recruited from the general public. Members of the general public may simply choose to spend their time differently if the group does not provide a sufficient level of enjoyment or meet a particular need. Groups in residential settings and some day programs may represent a captive audience of sorts. But even these groups can vary in levels of participation. In some of these settings, participation in this part of the program may be entirely voluntary, which means that the group will need to attract members. Even in those settings in which participation is required, the actual participation and level of enthusiasm for activities will be affected by how much members are invested in the group as well as the activity. For those groups that do not have closed membership and allow new members to join at any time, each session needs to begin with the group undergoing the process of reforming itself by revisiting each stage of development. Time-limited groups with closed membership will also go through the first three stages of development during each session, but these tend to be relatively brief as members check in and any business associated with norms, roles, and the like arise.

Orientation before the group begins may be somewhat similar to other groups in that the worker might provide information for new members prior to the first meeting of the group. After that, the worker might do this for new members during the enrollment period if it is a closed group or for any new members she is aware of prior to joining the group if membership is open. In addition, other workers who are familiar with these groups will inform clients who they are referring. Referrals tend to be very informal and most growth and development groups do not require any exchange of information between workers or organizations or even a notice that a client might join the group. In fact, in many groups, potential members may self-refer or be referred by other members. It is assumed that people who wish to join the group will be those who are interested and want to participate. Members may join and have needs that may not be readily revealed and may be unspoken. Sometimes these needs cannot be met by the group. The worker should make an effort to discover unspoken personal needs that would be met by another group or a different service. The worker should refer these members to other services or should consult with a referring worker if there is one. As with support or self-help groups, some workers will mention that they have referred clients, mostly as a professional courtesy as opposed to a requirement, as it would be with change-oriented groups.

There is typically an orientation process that takes place as the group begins for closed, time-limited groups. For open groups, this will occur at the beginning of a session when a new member attends. For open groups, the process for welcoming new members should be established by the group in its early sessions. Similar to support and self-help groups that are open, members may volunteer to do this or a rotation can be established among veteran members. Typically, these members will introduce themselves to new attendees and give them information about what to expect in the group before the group begins. Then they either introduce the new members or have them introduce themselves. In most growth and development groups that are time limited and closed, after either the first session or a set number of sessions, new members cannot join. Generally, they are asked to wait until the next group is scheduled to begin.

As with any new situation, most new members will experience some ambivalence about being there. We have referred to this as approach–avoidance. New members will be curious about the group and will have hopes that the group will welcome them and allow them to participate. At the same time, new members will tend to fear the unknown and will wonder whether the group will accept them as a member and meet their unspoken need. The approach side motivates people to come to the group, to join, and to make a commitment. Avoidance causes them to limit their involvement or even quit the group and not return if they do not see the group as a place in which they feel comfortable. The worker should plan for this and recognize it as part of the process that people will go through when they attend a group. At the beginning of a new group that is ongoing or when a time-limited group begins, the whole group experiences this together. In ongoing groups, new members experience it during the first session and the group will likely revisit this stage every time it meets in some form or another, but especially as it incorporates new members. When an initial commitment to the group has been made, the orientation stage is completed. However, the group as whole will still need to undertake an orientation process to some extent at each session, but especially when there is a new member.

The worker uses assessment, planning, actions, and evaluation in facilitating the group as it goes through the orientation stage. The motivations for members to join many growth and development groups are for enjoyment, acceptance, and acquiring knowledge and skills. The motivation for joining some of these types of groups is almost entirely enjoyment. In any case, the group must be seen as an enjoyable experience or a source of knowledge and skill building or both in order to attract and keep members. This needs to be established in the first meeting or membership may rapidly dwindle. The worker must ensure that members can respond favorably to the question, "Am I coming back?" This needs to be incorporated into the assessment, planning, and actions during the very first group and needs to be maintained throughout the life of the group.

Change-oriented and support and self-help groups have members who are dealing with difficult situations and many have needs that may motivate them to join the group to meet these needs. Growth and development groups may have members who are also motivated to meet these same or similar needs, but there are also likely to be members who are not experiencing difficult situations and who may not be as motivated to join the group, at least not for the same purpose. Thus, the worker may not be able to rely on this kind of motivation to develop and maintain the involvement of members. Instead, growth and development groups generally must have some additional attraction that will bring members to the group and hold them there once they come. This attraction is usually some type of unspoken need such as enjoying the activities of the group, pleasure in belonging and feeling accepted, and the socialization that the group provides.

In some respects, members of change-oriented and support and self-help groups join the group to escape from or resolve an unpleasant situation in their life outside the group. Eventually, it is hoped that they either will be able to change this situation or will cope with it better. In most growth and development groups, it is the pleasantness of the group experience that is most important in determining if members join and stay with the group. The worker needs to assess how to make the group a place in which members will enjoy their experience and acquire the desired knowledge, skills, and acceptance if these are part of the purpose of the group. She should develop a plan that reflects this assessment and take actions that facilitate achieving these outcomes. Finally, the worker evaluates the extent to which this is achieved. Sometimes, this is evident in the actions and interactions in the group. Sometimes, the worker needs to solicit either verbal or written feedback.

Of particular importance in attracting and holding members' interests are icebreaking activities that are planned for the first group meeting. The process of having members introduce themselves or interview and introduce each other may or may not provide this. As a general rule in growth and development groups, it is best to engage right away in activities that the group will be doing throughout the life of the group. In many cases, some sort of team-building exercise is needed. If the group purpose involves everyone working together as a team, then an activity that starts this process should be planned for the first meeting. This can be almost anything in which cooperation is highly valued. Recreation groups typically use drills or a scrimmage. Skill-building groups may use a challenge or a problem-solving activity related to the purpose of the group. For example, a parenting group might be asked to work on a solution to a common parenting problem. If subgroups or smaller groups are beneficial or at least not harmful, then competitive situations can be used to build teamwork within the subgroups. Small groups are a good way for adult learners to acquire knowledge and skills. These do not have to be competitive and can actually be used to demonstrate how skills can be used in a variety of ways.

As we have indicated, all groups require that the worker and the group balance the needs of the group itself and the needs of its members. The worker should assess group process and be able to identify balances and imbalances which we have called the "I–we" balance. It is not beneficial for the group when there is too much focus on an individual or individuals during a session. The worker or the group will need to balance individual's needs with those of other members and the group as a whole. Setting an agenda tends to help with this by serving to move the meeting along. Other times, the group may not include a certain member or members. When this occurs, the worker should focus the group's attention on the need to be inclusive.

During the orientation stage, especially in a new group, there is a tendency for there to be more emphasis on the "I" portion of the "I–we" balance, as members may not have decided to commit themselves to the group. The members have not formed themselves into a group yet or the group may be revisiting an earlier stage of group formation. If it is to become a group or reform itself into a group, the members will need to become a "we." The "we" occurs when members make a commitment to the group and begin to function in a way that meets their collective interests. The worker plans for this and facilitates group formation or reformation. In addressing the group, the worker uses pronouns that emphasize the group like *we*, *us*, *our*, and the like and by emphasizing group membership.

As with other groups, group planning will generally hasten group formation. Planning as a group helps the group to come together while moving the group toward the next two stages of group development. Planning together helps members to invest themselves in the group by allowing them to make the group into what they need the group to be and having them take ownership of the group. In some growth and development groups, group planning may be limited by the purpose of the group. For example, educational and skill development groups may have a more structured format in order to cover the material or learn certain skills. Age and developmental level may limit members' ability to engage in planning. In these cases, the worker can present a plan to the group and then solicit feedback. The worker can also look for opportunities for the group to plan within whatever structure there is. When using program materials or a curriculum, the worker should be prepared to modify it to meet the needs of the group. Initial planning typically takes place at the beginning of the group after the introductions. If the group purpose allows for sufficient flexibility or the group is designed to be one in which sessions are more fluid, members might be asked what they would like to get out of the group and how the group might meet their needs. The group members can then discuss how they would like to function as a group or what they would like to accomplish for that session and the next or for future sessions.

For the initial session of a group, the worker should plan for a brief period of group formation followed by an activity that would solidify this. It is important that at least some type of activity take place that is related to the purpose of the group so that members do not feel that they are wasting their time and decide not to return. Usually, an icebreaker is planned that builds teamwork or calls for people to break into pairs or small groups and discuss some aspect related to the group's purpose. For example, a recreation group might engage in some sort of skill-building activity in pairs or small groups, followed by an activity for the whole group. If members are asked to share information about themselves during introductions, the worker can model doing so first. Afterward, she should summarize this, emphasizing common experiences. Before the group ends, the worker should check in with members and solicit feedback about the session before they adjourn. These actions will be helpful in reinforcing various aspects of the functional stage that will follow later.

Ongoing growth and development groups should experience revisiting the orientation stage as it orients new members. Open groups will have new members joining and may have veterans attending sporadically. This tends to reduce the commitment to the group and the extent to which members invest in the group. Often, growth and development groups will establish a routine. New members are then oriented to the routine that the group has established. Ongoing groups will typically establish a routine for orienting new members to the norms and the structure of group meetings. Ongoing groups need to reach out to new members and find ways to quickly include them in the group.

Throughout the orientation stage, the worker evaluates the progress of the group by noticing interactions in the group and evaluating the extent to which these interactions represent the development of a positive atmosphere. Are members interacting in a positive way? Are there indications that they are enjoying themselves? Are their spoken and unspoken needs being met? Are the individuals beginning to function as a group? Who is included and who is not? Who participates and who does not? When the worker observes that certain members seem less involved, she finds ways for the group to be more inclusive and encourages members to participate.

Termination of sessions during the orientation stage for voluntary groups is focused on encouraging members to return to the group and exploring any barriers to doing so. As with other groups, there are ways for the worker to encourage a commitment to the group. She should summarize what the group has accomplished. The worker can do this or she can solicit contributions from the group. Discussing the next session will give a sense of continuity. It might also give the worker a sense of who intends to return or not and who is ambivalent. She can then address any needs or concerns before the group ends or follow up with these after the session is over.

Once members become invested in the group and make an initial commitment to it, the orientation stage is completed for them. This will be repeated to some extent at the beginning of group sessions and as new members join the group if it is an open group.

## The Change Process During the Authority Stage

As with other groups, when members of growth and development groups make an initial commitment to the group they become invested in what happens in the group, leading to the authority stage, which raises issues related to power and control and increases the possibility of conflict. These issues tend to be less intense for growth and development groups because of the nature of these groups. Groups that are educational or recreational or aimed at skill development tend to not be as intense in general than those whose purpose is to bring about personal change or provide support for difficult life situations. For the most part, the stakes are much higher for members of change-oriented and support and self-help groups than for members of growth and development groups. Generally speaking, the more important the purpose of the group is to members, the more intensity we would expect to see during the authority stage. Usually members of growth and development groups have less invested in the group than members of change-oriented and support and self-help groups.

Typically, issues during the authority stage will be most intense for a developing group. As the group establishes itself and develops a routine, it tends not to be as much of an issue. Most members will try to exert at least some influence on the group to make it what he or she wishes it to be. During this stage there is some "we-ness" in the group, but there is still a lot of "I-ness". This will tend to persist throughout the life of growth and development groups. Members might compete with one another for power and control or challenge the power of the group worker.

As with other groups, the worker in a growth and development group has to give as much control as possible to the group in order for the individuals to become a group. With groups made up of children or members who have limited developmental capacities or who have significant impairments, the worker will retain more authority than in groups whose members are well-functioning adults. Many of the groups in this category require the worker to have specific knowledge or skills that members expect to learn from being in the group. This is especially true for educational and skill-building types of groups. Thus, the worker will need to have a certain level of expertise that will tend to place her in the role of expert. However, members should participate in their learning and be involved in planning for the group. If members are expected to use what they have learned outside of the group, they have to own what they have learned and see it as part of their own expertise. In order for this to happen, as much power and control as possible needs to be shifted from the worker to the group and its members.

Members have to take some ownership of the group and invest enough to work at helping the group accomplish its purpose. The worker should plan for this stage. She influences group structure to ensure that members receive maximum benefit from the group. Norms, roles, and ways of functioning for a new group have not been established yet during this stage. Typically, for growth and development groups with well-functioning adults, the worker will provide the initial structure and gradually turn some of this over to the group as it develops the capacity to do so. However, she will tend to keep at least some control throughout the life of the group depending on how much of her expertise is needed by the group and how much structure is needed to accomplish the group's purpose.

Because growth and development groups typically require more structure and also are likely to be time limited, the worker will tend to make more of the decisions about what occurs during group sessions. Often this has been planned ahead of time. In fact, the entire schedule for the group may be set by the need to accomplish or cover certain material in order to achieve the group's purpose. This schedule may need to be modified by circumstances that arise. In some groups, the worker will introduce certain rules. This might be followed by some discussion of those rules. This is especially important for groups with children or members who are somewhat limited in their development or their social skills. In most groups, the worker can elicit suggestions about other rules that might be helpful in getting the group to function. To the extent that is feasible, the worker encourages the group to establish some control over how the group will function. This is a delicate balance. The worker has ideas about what the group needs to do to accomplish its purpose. However, she also knows that she cannot and should not make people do things that they do not want to do. Thus, she must retain enough control to maintain the structure that the group needs while allowing enough freedom for members to feel that this is their group and not the worker's.

She gives decision-making power to the group within certain parameters that will balance the need to accomplish its purpose with the needs of members to have a say in how that is accomplished. She makes suggestions and encourages discussion about how the group will make decisions within those parameters. She encourages consensus so that everyone is included in the group. Some growth and development groups may use a democratic style in deciding what they would like to do for the next session or a future session within parameters that will still allow it to accomplish its purpose. However, the group needs to find ways of including every member. If the group votes, it should limit voting to primarily establishing the priority or sequence of options so everyone's ideas are included over time.

As with other groups, during the authority stage the "I–we" issue has not been resolved and members are concerned about retaining their individuality while still being part of the group. If members feel controlled by the worker or other members or the group as a whole, some may rebel or resent that control. The issues that arise during this stage will be resolved at least temporarily in the next stage as the group negotiates ways of functioning that are inclusive. When the worker senses too much "I-ness," she can establish more "we-ness" by addressing the group as a whole and calling attention to the need for the group to act collectively. For recreation groups this might come in the form of emphasizing teamwork. When the worker senses that there is too much "we-ness" or emphasis on the group at the expense of individual members, she points this out and addresses members as individuals to create a better balance in the "I–we" aspect of the group.

If the group is open, it will likely revisit the authority stage when new members join. New members will want to know if they will be accepted by the group and if there is place for them in participating in the group's activities. If new members can drop in at any time, then some type of routine needs to be established to accomplish their inclusion. Groups that have not done this may find themselves struggling each time a new member comes into the group. It is important for the worker and the group to find ways to make decisions, establish norms, and redistribute roles and share them during the course of the group. For these groups, the process of including new members and redistributing roles when new members join will go much smoother than for groups in which members have become invested in certain roles.

The worker evaluates the group and individual members throughout the group as well as during the authority stage progresses. The worker evaluates how individual members respond to this stage. Who participates and who does not? Who speaks for the group and who speaks for themselves? Who seems invested and who does not? As answers to these questions occur, the worker encourages each member to participate in the group's activities and tries to provide opportunities for each member to experience success and to contribute to the success of the group. She supports positive conflict resolution that is respectful and inclusive. By this time, the worker should have at least some sense of the unspoken need of some group members. She should evaluate if and how these unspoken needs are being met. At some point, the worker must decide whether these needs should remain private or should be shared with the group. If they should be shared, then the worker helps the member to share.

As we identified with other types of groups, termination of sessions during this stage is very similar to the orientation stage. In new groups or with new members, the worker is concerned with members remaining committed to the group and returning. If disagreements have taken place, she is careful to reassure the group that this is a normal part of group development and that it shows that people care about the group. She emphasizes that differences are to be expected and respected. The worker highlights positive outcomes as the group finds ways to function that are positive and inclusive. The worker or the group should summarize the session.

As a new group experiences the authority stage or when new members join and the group revisits this stage, the worker assesses the situation. She plans for facilitating the group when issues related to authority arise. She helps the group establish basic rules and assists in having the group add other appropriate rules. To the extent that it is feasible, she encourages the group to take responsibility for making decisions. She ensures that decisions are made in an inclusive way that considers the needs and interests of members and the group as a whole. She evaluates group and individual progress through this stage and terminates sessions with a review of the progress that has been made.

## The Change Process During the Negotiation Stage

Conflict or disagreements that may arise in the authority stage in growth and development groups are resolved during the negotiation stage. Growth and development groups must resolve authority issues and settle on norms and roles. There may be overt conflicts or disagreements or they may be covert or hidden. If they are hidden, the worker needs to identify them and help the group deal with these issues. The worker may need to be much more active in at least establishing basic rules for the group. There may need to be rules that the worker presents to the group from the very beginning. As the group progresses, it may experience confrontation and disagreements that require conflict resolution. With or without conflict, goals, norms, roles, and tasks are established and the group becomes a group. At the conclusion of the negotiation stage, members feel positive about the group and there is a high level of group cohesion. The worker assists the group to reach this point. She encourages the group to establish goals, norms, roles, and tasks in a way that is inclusive. To a great extent, the overall goals of the group are inherent in the purpose of the group. Education groups are formed so that members can acquire certain knowledge. Recreation groups serve to provide members with opportunities to enjoy various activities and to meet socialization needs. Skill development groups provide opportunities to learn new skills. However, the commitment of individual members to the group is directly related to their ability to see the group as a place where they can also meet their individual needs and achieve their individual goals. It is important for members to have positive feelings about the group experience. In growth and development groups, it is assumed that needs will be met and goals will be achieved by participating in the group and its activities. Generally, it is also assumed that if everyone is given an opportunity to participate, members will meet their individual needs and achieve their individual goals at whatever level is satisfactory for them.

Most growth and development groups do not require that members share their experiences and their inner thoughts and feelings. The exceptions are parenting groups and some social skills groups. However, members are not expected to expose vulnerable parts of themselves including their human flaws and frailties. Instead, the thoughts and feelings are typically about the situation that they find themselves in. Thus, self-disclosure is minimal in some types of groups and not expected at all in most growth and development groups.

As with any group that is facilitated by a social worker, the group experience needs to be consistent with the cardinal values of social work. The belief in the value and worth of every human being leads to treating people with dignity and respect. Groups that are facilitated or sponsored by social workers and social work agencies must reflect this in everything that the groups do. This applies to growth and development groups as well as change-oriented and support and self-help groups. This value should be reflected in the basic rules that the group establishes. There is an expectation that the worker and all members will exhibit this in their interactions. Members need to feel accepted unconditionally and they need an equal opportunity to participate and have their participation valued by the group.

As the negotiation stage progresses, members begin to feel that "I" have become a part of the "we." At least some portion of their identity includes being members of this group. Members feel they belong. They are accepted and valued. They accept and value other members of the group. Each member has an individual identity or an "I," a collective identity or a "we," and an "I–we" or an identity that includes being a part of the group.

Social workers value and respect self-determination. People have a right to make their own decisions about things that affect them. In growth and development groups, this typically means that members should be able to participate in planning in the group and to choose whether they participate in any of the group's activities. The group needs to respect this and allow members to decide for themselves what they will and will not do. Groups need to establish this so the group does not coerce members into doing things that they do not want to do.

Social workers believe that people should have the right to have socially accepted needs met in socially accepted ways. The needs being addressed by growth and development groups should be socially accepted needs. The group needs to establish norms that give all of their members opportunities to have the needs that are consistent with the group's purpose met within the group. This is an important part of what it means to be inclusive. Members may receive assistance from the worker in meeting needs that cannot be met within the group. Typically, needs are met in growth and development groups through participation.

During the negotiation stage, the worker uses her skills in group facilitation. Typically, she presents basic rules that are necessary for the group to function, discusses these with the group, and negotiates any additional rules that the group might suggest. Before, during, and between group sessions, she assesses the needs of the group during this stage of development and facilitates movement as necessary. Because growth and development groups do not deal with deeply personal matters and so group members may not be as invested in the group, members will generally accord some authority to the worker and it is not usually too difficult to negotiate a resolution to the negotiation stage.

Planning before and between sessions for new groups during this stage is centered on moving the group toward group formation and resolving issues that are raised in doing so. The worker plans activities that will facilitate this. She uses activities that will bring the group together in preparation for the functional stage. She helps the group formulate goals, norms, roles, and tasks. She usually summarizes this for the group, but may solicit a summary or contributions from group members.

For the first several sessions, the worker might plan an opening summary that identifies norms, tasks, and goals that have been established to remind group members. She could do this herself or solicit these from the group.

The worker's actions during the negotiation stage with a developing group are aimed at facilitating the development of goals, norms, tasks, and roles. If new members are still joining the group or this is an open group, then new members will need to be informed about how the group operates. They should be given an opportunity to join in an activity to make them feel welcome and a part of the group.

As with other groups, the worker should ask what members would like to accomplish, even if the purpose of the group is clear. Finding common ground is important in having the group develop cohesion so that members can work together during the functional stage. At the same time, the worker needs to know if members have other ideas about what they might get from being in the group. If it is possible for these to be achieved in the group, the worker incorporates them into the group. If they are not, then this is an opportunity to direct members to other ways of meeting their needs.

As the session unfolds, the worker evaluates progress through the negotiation stage. She evaluates how each member participates. She encourages reluctant members to express their needs and their desires for the group and to become involved in activities and discussions. Members need to feel that they are a part of the group so they can become full participants.

Termination of sessions during this stage is focused on reinforcing goals, norms, and tasks. Unfinished business is identified and placed on the agenda for the next session. The process is similar to opening and closing most sessions with a summary by the worker or one that is solicited from the group or some combination of these.

During the negotiation stage, the individuals are becoming a group and are preparing for engaging in activities to achieve the group's purpose. In growth and development groups, this stage typically only requires a portion of a session. Some groups may need to revisit this and earlier stages of group development especially if they are open groups with new members joining. As with other groups, ongoing groups will visit this stage at least briefly when members leave and new ones join.

## The Change Process During the Functional Stage

For growth and development groups, the functional stage represents the stage during which activities are occurring that reflect the purpose of the group. During earlier stages, the group spent time and energy becoming a group. As with other groups, these earlier stages are important and necessary for the group to be formed in order to accomplish its purpose. In groups that are not fully formed, members tend to rely on the worker too much and members do not fully benefit from the group experience. While many growth and development groups will rely heavily on the worker for knowledge and skill development, the worker should plan for ways that the group can be part of the learning process. Role-plays, practicing, and group discussions are common ways to do this.

For developing growth and development groups, the stages of group formation may be accomplished fairly quickly during the first session and the group can proceed to the functional stage almost immediately. However, issues related to group formation may arise again over the next few sessions or later in the group. Sometimes, most of the first session may be taken up with group formation.

Highly functioning groups will tend to maintain a good healthy balance of "I-ness" and "we–ness" during this stage, as group members balance the need for the group to maintain itself and accomplish its purpose while also providing opportunities for members to participate. Members are aware of the need to include everyone in group activities. However, even the best groups can have moments when this is out of balance. One or more members may seek to dominate the group or the group may not be as inclusive with a member or may even seek to exclude someone from the group. When this occurs, the worker needs to intervene and point this out. If there is too much "I–ness," the worker asks the group as a whole (we) or individuals as members (I–we) to discuss their thoughts and feelings about the situation. If there is too much "we–ness," the worker asks members to speak for themselves as individuals (I) and express their thoughts and feelings about how they would feel if the group was not including them or was trying to exclude them.

The worker continues to engage in assessment and planning before, during, and between group sessions. He assesses group functioning and cohesion and progress toward achieving the purpose of the group. He assesses strengths and challenges for the group as a whole and for each member in reaching group and individual goals. The worker assesses group process and functioning and seeks to understand group dynamics to facilitate progress and ensure appropriate levels of participation for all members.

As the worker assesses group and individual progress, he plans for ways to maximize group cohesion and participation in group activities. The worker is constantly assessing, planning, and acting before, during, and after each group session. It is important that members be put in situations in which they can be successful as individuals and acquire knowledge or build skills while also making a contribution to the success of the group. The worker needs to have expertise in the area of knowledge or skill development while also having skills in facilitating groups.

As with other types of groups, assessment and planning involve both content and process. The worker plans the content for each session based on group input and needs. He analyzes the session to understand what seemed to be effective and what was not and what might be needed to be more effective. He observes both verbal and nonverbal behavior and interactions as well as the results of each session. The worker considers the progress the group has made while also understanding how this was accomplished. He plans activities that will continue the growth and development of the group and its members and incorporates group involvement in planning to the extent possible.

In addition to these actions, the worker also uses some of the actions that are described in Chapters 3, 4, and 5, including actions that can be taken within and outside of the group to facilitate completion of plans that are designed to increase growth and development. The worker primarily uses skills related to relationship building and activity. In some groups, he might also use skills related to learning to use resources, empowering and enabling, crisis resolution, and support. In working with growth and development groups, the worker mainly engages in actions to facilitate group formation, discussion, conflict resolution, interaction, group development, and structured group activities. These practice actions are not repeated here, but are summarized as they relate to working with growth and development groups. The reader should review this material before proceeding and include them in her work with these groups as indicated.

In groups, relationships are central to the functioning of the group. This also applies to growth and development groups. However, some groups, recreation groups, for example, emphasize physical activity as opposed to oral communication. As we have indicated, successful relationships include the ability to communicate, problem solve and make decisions, and resolve conflict in a constructive manner. The skill that is most likely to be used in growth and development groups is communication skills. In fact, some growth and development groups, such as social skills groups and some socialization groups, have this as a primary skill to be developed within the group. Problem-solving and decision-making skills can also be learned in growth and development groups. These skills may also be needed in helping some of these groups to achieve the group's purpose. Similarly, conflict resolution skills might be the focus of some of these groups. These skills may also be needed by the worker in resolving conflicts among members in some of these groups. For instance, recreation and team sports can lead to situations in which competition results in conflict. The worker needs to be able to use mediation and conflict resolution skills when this occurs.

Providing opportunities to grow and develop physically, emotionally, psychologically, or socially are the primary purposes of growth and development groups. Participation and acquisition of knowledge and skills are the main means of benefiting from these groups. Group members feel good about themselves when they feel that they belong to groups. In fact, this might be the unspoken need for some members. The sense of connectedness and belonging is important for healthy social and emotional well-being. Acquiring new knowledge and learning new skills are in themselves important for people to feel that they are growing and developing as human beings. It is also important for self-actualization, which is one of the needs identified by Maslow.[1]

Along with relationship skills, activities are generally the focus of growth and development groups and are the means by which most of these types of groups achieve their purposes. During the functional stage, the group is typically engaging in activities that achieve its purpose and members are meeting their needs and achieving their goals. In recreation groups, members are provided an opportunity to engage in recreational activities and to build skills. In education groups, members are acquiring knowledge and skills in the areas that are consistent with the group's purpose. In life skills groups, members are learning skills in cooking, shopping, budgeting, working, and other skills that are needed to be successful in life on a day-to-day basis. In social skills groups, members are learning relationship skills. In parenting groups, parents are learning new or different ways of rearing their children. In an activity group, members may be engaged in a wide range of activities that are commensurate with their age and level of development. In some socialization groups, members are provided with opportunities to socialize with others who are in their own age group. Other socialization groups may be designed to socialize young people into learning more socially acceptable behaviors. Other growth and development groups offer opportunities for a wide variety of activities to almost any population in almost any setting.

In nearly all of these groups, the worker is primarily responsible for planning with the group and arranging activities. In some groups, members may take some or all of this responsibility either as part of their learning or because this fits within the purpose of the group or the worker and the group decide that it is appropriate for members to do this. In some groups, program materials or a curriculum may be used. Whenever this is the case, the worker needs to be prepared to alter or modify this material to meet the needs of the specific group that she is facilitating. Most workers will not use standardized material exactly as it is designed. They will change how it is used or add material from other sources or design their own material either to supplement parts or to replace them. Table 8.1 is a schema for developing and using program materials and can also be used as a guide for developing and using activities in groups.[2] The worker should have skills in using a variety of activities, including a wide variety of games, various arts and crafts, trips into the community, and use of audiovisual materials, to name a few. This is especially important in working with groups of children and young adolescents. Some of these may also be important in working with groups of people who are older.

**TABLE 8.1   Schema for Program Planning in Social Group Work
(Use of Activity and other Resources)**

---

I.  What is the concern, need to be addressed?
   A.  Development of interactional skills
      1.  Development of relationships with others
      2.  Opportunity to make and carry out decisions
      3.  Providing patterns for dealing with conflict
      4.  Modification of interests and development of new interests
      5.  Opportunity to express feelings
      6.  Developing of patterns and disciplines which limit and influence behavior
   B.  Provision for need fulfillment
      1.  Acceptable release of emotions
      2.  Intellectual stimulation
      3.  Opportunity to gain acceptance and status through skill
      4.  Physical growth or control
      5.  Provides intellectual stimulation, understanding, or growth
      6.  Provides acceptable release of emotion
      7.  Is known to meet recognized needs of group members
   C.  Provision of assessment material (Specify any available resources.)
   D.  Interest determination
      1.  Desires and skills as stated by group member(s)
      2.  Usual interests of age, gender, and diversity group
      3.  Consideration of fun, pleasant experience
      4.  Builds on strengths of group members (skills)

II.  Criteria for good program
   A.  Grows out of the needs and interests of the group members
   B.  Takes into account such factors as age, diversity, and ecosystem expectations
   C.  Provides experiences and opportunities to make decisions, develop new skills, understandings, and interests, and opportunities to work with others
   D.  Is varied and flexible
   E.  Evolves from simple to complex
   F.  Adheres to agency policy

III.  Program planning process
   A.  Determine need and interests of group members.
   B.  Select beginning point or level of program considering:
      1.  Attention span and frustration level
      2.  Socialization and intellectual characteristics of group members
      3.  Physical coordination and skill
      4.  Emotional factors: handling of aggression, judgement, and developmental
   C.  Decide on the activity considering A. and B
      1.  Review any resource material available
      2.  Set goals and means for evaluation
      3.  Try out activity
      4.  Adapt as seems desirable
   D.  Determine what is needed to carry out the activity.
      1.  Staff, equipment, supplies, and space

*(Continued)*

**TABLE 8.1   (Continued)**

    **E.** Allocate responsibility for specific tasks.
        **1.** Staff, members, others
    **F.** Carry out activity (role of worker).
        **1.** Present activity to the group.
            **a.** Use a positive approach, show rather than tell, move from simple to complex, set limits
        **2.** During activity
            **a.** Help individuals participate.
            **b.** Attend to group process, influence interaction and group development.
            **c.** Influence group decision process.
            **d.** Observe behavior and relationships, maintain limits previously set.
    **G.** Evaluation
        **1.** Seek individual and group response.
            **a.** Did it meet a need? Was it enjoyable? Likes and dislikes, etc.
        **2.** Worker evaluation
            **a.** Was activity appropriate to meet needs and interests of the group?
            **b.** Were the set goals met?
            **c.** Was preparation sufficient? How might this activity be modified?

*Source:* Based on updated material developed by Louise Johnson in the late 1960s. Published in Harleigh Trecker, *Social Group Work: Principles and Practices*, New York Association Press, 1972, pp. 247–249.

        Part I of the schema in Table 8.1 refers to various areas of concern or need that might be addressed by the activity or program material. This can be expanded beyond what is listed in the schema. Part II of the schema considers the criteria for a good program. The first requirement is that program materials should grow out of the needs and interests of the group. Sometimes workers may be tempted to try new techniques just because they are new. They may have attended a workshop or training program or read about it and are eager to try it. This is not appropriate and really amounts to using the material as a gimmick rather than carefully considering its use as an integral part of the group work. As members express or show interest in a particular topic, the worker can look for ways to enhance the group experience through the use of activities and program materials. Another approach could be one in which the group is designed around particular program materials, such as a parenting approach. Members are recruited who are interested in or could benefit from learning about this approach. However, even in these situations, the worker needs to be prepared to modify the material or modify how it is used in order to fit the needs of the group members.

        Another criteria relates to the demographics of group members. Activities and program materials need to be age appropriate and sensitive to variations in diversity, background, and environment that members have. The material should provide opportunities to gain new knowledge and skills in areas of interest to group members. Flexibility in using the material is important so that it can be used by a variety of groups and tailored to meet the needs of each unique group. In most cases, as people gain new knowledge and skills, the approach needs to evolve from more simple tasks to those that are more complex. In a sense, a building block approach should be used so that new learning is based on previous learning, especially for more complex skills. Finally, activities and program materials need to be consistent with the mission and policies of the agency.

Using activities and program materials follows an organized process that is similar to the change process. The worker uses assessment, planning, action, and evaluation. The first step is to assess the needs and interests of group members. In selecting the level of complexity, the worker considers attention span, social abilities, intellectual level, physical abilities, and emotional factors of group members. The worker reviews resource materials and selects those that are appropriate with these factors in mind. Goals are set along with a means for evaluating the activity or program material. The activity or material is tested before it is used in the group and is adapted as necessary. The worker may try it himself or use colleagues to get feedback on its use. The worker plans for various needs such as staff, equipment, supplies, space, and the like. Responsibilities for various tasks are allocated if this goes beyond the worker.

The action phase is characterized by carrying out the activity or using the program material in the group. The worker begins by presenting the activity or material to the group using a positive approach. He shows members what to do, moving from simple to complex and setting limits. Some adaptation may take place at this point before implementation as members raise questions or concerns. During the activity or implementation of the program material, the worker assists members in participating. He is aware of group process and influences interactions among members and facilitates group development as necessary. He observes the group, noting behavior and relationships and he helps the group maintain the limits that were set.

Use of the material is evaluated throughout the implementation and upon completion to ensure that it is effective, helpful, and not harmful. The worker seeks both individual and group responses to the activity or material. He asks members to give feedback about the extent to which it met their needs and was enjoyable. The worker also uses his own professional evaluation of the experience. He asks himself if it seemed to meet the needs of the group. He evaluates the extent to which the goals that were set were met. He also evaluates the preparation for the activity or material and considers possible modifications if it is used in the future.

Learning to use the change process can be the focus of some growth and development groups, such as life skills groups. This can also be a byproduct of experiences in some of these groups. However, it is not typically part of the purpose of most growth and development groups, but the change process might be used within and outside of the group by the worker, especially if individual members are experiencing difficulties that are outside of the purview of the group. Using the change process with individual group members is covered in Chapter 3. The worker uses the change process in working with groups in terms of assessing the needs of the group and the members, and planning activities that help the group achieve its purpose and meet the needs of the group and the members. He takes actions to implement the plan and to remove barriers that might arise. He evaluates the progress of the group and the members and facilitates termination at the end of each session and when the group ends or a member leaves.

In some growth and development groups, members may want or need to learn about resources and how to use them so they might either add to the knowledge and skills they are learning in the group or continue with their growth and development after the group ends. Sometimes it may be useful to take field trips into the community. The worker may also need to use this in helping individual group members access resources that are not related to the group purpose, but are important for their well-being or to address a situation that comes to light as they are participating in the group. This latter situation should be dealt with outside of the group because it is not part of the purpose of the group. The worker uses the process for doing this that is identified in Chapter 3. The worker may need to engage in mediation or advocacy for group members who are denied services for which they seem to be qualified.

The group worker's use of actions that are empowering and enabling may not be initially apparent in considering the purposes of growth and development groups. However, empowering and enabling are underlying mechanisms in most of what the worker is seeking to accomplish in these groups. Essentially, the goal of the worker is to provide opportunities for group members to acquire new knowledge and skills. In order to use these, members will need to be empowered and enabled. Much of this is achieved within the group by discussing and practicing these skills. When people are empowered and enabled, they have much more confidence in their skills and abilities. Most people are unlikely to try something new unless they are empowered to do so. The group experience in growth and development groups can help to make this possible. As members hear and observe one another and practice skills, they are more likely to gain the confidence that is needed to try these skills in their everyday lives. The experience of being in a group and having a sense of belonging is very empowering. Receiving support from the group for trying new skills and abilities is empowering and enabling.

Crisis intervention as such is not frequently necessary in growth and development groups. Crisis intervention is covered in Chapter 3. However, members of the group may experience crises and the worker may need to provide this service or refer the member to a service that will address their needs. This is typically done outside of the group on an individual basis. A type of crisis that can occur in growth and development groups are injuries or other health crises, such as a heart attack. This is especially true for groups that involve physical activity. Ideally, the worker should be trained in basic first aid and cardiopulmonary resuscitation (CPR) or have someone on hand who is trained. For water activities, knowledge of water rescue and revival capabilities and CPR are a must. Many human service organizations are beginning to develop risk management plans and these types of certifications will likely be required by management for these types of activities. Another type of crisis occurs when groups lose members because of death or disability, especially among groups of people who are older, who are particularly vulnerable to experiencing this.

In acquiring new knowledge and skills, members need to be able to take what they learn in the group and apply it to their everyday lives. If the group is the only place in which they use their new skills then they will not experience much benefit from being in the group. Carryover needs to take place. Members need to use what they learn in the group in their life outside of the group. The best way for the worker to facilitate this is to provide knowledge and activities that can be related to people's everyday lives. This means modifying activities and program materials and using examples that are relevant for members of the group. It means soliciting feedback about the relevance of these for group members.

Mediating between a member and a system in her environment typically occurs outside of the group. This is generally the first choice of action by the worker before advocacy. Social workers use mediation by remaining neutral and bringing a client and a system in the environment together and to reach agreement about service delivery. Mediation by the worker with members of growth and development groups may be needed when conflicts arise in the group. During the early stages of group development or when group members have a fight or an argument or a disagreement, the worker has to step in and mediate. This can be fairly common in groups with children and adolescents and is not unheard of even in adult groups. Learning to give and take and negotiate and compromise is a key aspect of good relationships and may be an important lesson for group members to learn.

The worker engages in actions that are designed to facilitate group formation, discussion, conflict resolution, interaction, group development, and structured group activities. These are described in Chapters 4 and 5, and in this chapter and earlier chapters in Part Two and will not be repeated here, but will be discussed with respect to facilitating group process for growth and development groups. Along with relationship skills and using activities, these group facilitation skills form the core of what group workers do in most growth and development groups.

Groups need to be able to progress through the stages of group development and group members need to interact in a way that supports the success of the group in achieving its purpose. The worker facilitates the group in a way that ensures maximum benefit for group members. Thus, group process is important in growth and development groups, as is the content of group sessions. It is important that the worker understand the meaning behind group actions and interactions of members in the group. These will indicate what stage of development the group is in at any point in time and will also be indications of the progress toward achieving the purpose of the group. In addition, understanding group process gives the worker insight into variations in participation that may be the result of relationships and social considerations. For example, some members may seek to exclude certain members. The worker needs to understand the social construction of the group and how this might play into the actions of various group members. This can give the worker some ideas about how he should handle this situation.

In groups that are open, new members may join at any time and members may attend sporadically. For these groups, each session will have elements of all of the stages of group development, especially when there are new members. For closed groups, members usually become accustomed to a routine that moves the group through the stages of group formation as quickly as possible so that they can reach the functional stage. During the functional stage the group should be accomplishing its purpose and members should be participating and getting their needs met. Part of the worker's evaluation at this stage is determining the extent to which the group is effective and understanding why it is or is not. If the group appears to be effective, the worker continues to facilitate activities that continue this. If it appears that the group is not effective or is less effective than it should be, the worker modifies or plans other activities that might be more successful. The worker may need to solicit feedback in doing this if it is not obvious what is working or not working.

## The Change Process During the Disintegration Stage

Disintegration can occur at any time, especially during the early stages of the group or later on if there is insufficient membership to sustain the group. Growth and development groups for clients tend to rely primarily on recruitment within the organization and referrals from organizations that are likely to see people who would be good candidates for the group. Growth and development groups that include members of the general public require extensive advertising. Ongoing groups tend to need periodic or even ongoing recruitment efforts to ensure a steady membership unless they are part of a residential program. Formal recruitment generally is done by the worker or the organization that sponsors the group by sending information to other organizations who have clients or patients who need this type of group or by advertising in local newspapers and by public service announcements on radio, television, and cable channels devoted to public access. Distributing fliers or brochures, especially in waiting rooms or offices in which potential members receive services, can also be effective.

Most growth and development groups are time limited, which means that everyone knows when termination is scheduled to take place and everyone goes through it together. In ongoing groups, termination is more focused on individual members as they reach a point at which they are ready to leave the group. We focus on three types of disintegration. When time-limited groups end; when members of ongoing groups are completing their work and do not need the group; and when a group shows signs of disintegration.

As with other types of groups, disintegration is marked by a lessening of bonds within the group. Some growth and development groups may not have bonds that are as strong as those of other groups. During disintegration, the frequency and strength of group cohesion are reduced along with interaction, common norms and values among group members, and the strength of the influence that the group has on members. At the same time, members are typically increasing and strengthening their interaction with their ecosystem outside of the group.

In time-limited groups, members tend to hold back from investing too much of themselves in the group because of the time limitation. Self-disclosure may be limited and tends to be associated with more positive aspects of members' lives that are related to areas of growth and development as opposed to engaging in problem solving or coping with difficult situations. That is not to say that members do not invest at all or that some may invest very heavily in the group. However, this tends to be more the exception than the rule for time-limited growth and development groups. Thus, the bonds in these types of groups may not be very close.

These factors combine to make disintegration less intense, but also more likely to occur. Actually, a time limit itself tends to help the group stay together as long as it is relatively brief. If a group is scheduled to meet for ten weeks, members are more likely to stay with the group because they know that their commitment is limited to those ten weeks. But time limits also tend to produce looser bonds because the group will last for only ten weeks. Some attrition is still likely to occur and it tends to occur during the first half of the time period, as some individuals may not see a value for them in the group. Before the group begins or at the first session, the worker should secure a commitment from group members to follow through with the group for the time that it is scheduled to meet. This can reduce attrition, but may not eliminate it.

In time-limited groups that retain membership, everyone goes through disintegration together. The worker should remind members of the ending periodically throughout the life of the group. The tasks during this time are the same as any situation in which termination takes place. The group needs to encourage consolidation of gains that members have made, facilitate the transition from meeting to ending the group, and help members to feel good about the experience while also accepting some sadness or mild grief. Typically, some sort of celebration is planned that highlights the positive aspects of the group experience and the progress that has been achieved. This can range from a mini-graduation ceremony with certificates to a little party with sweets and refreshments. A potluck is another example. If none of these is planned, the group should at least debrief their experience and say their good-byes.

It is expected that some disintegration will occur as members complete their work in ongoing groups. Since most of these are in residential or day activity programs, leaving the group occurs when members are leaving the program. It is hoped that most members are leaving because they are graduating from the program. However, some members will leave because they have flunked out of the program or have achieved a maximum benefit. In programs for adolescents, some will leave because they are too old. Sometimes members elope from the program and will either be missing for a period of time and then return or they may be dismissed or they are withdrawn by their sponsoring organization, typically a court system. In groups of people who are older, some members will be moving to a higher level of care.

Members of ongoing groups who are completing their work have achieved their goals and received what they needed from the group. The needs that brought them to the group are being met so there is much less motivation to be in the group and less investment in the group. Members are preparing to go on with their lives without the group. The termination process is discussed in Chapters 3 and 4 and is not repeated here.

In open ongoing groups, there is a constant change in membership as new members join or potential members drop in and out and others leave the group. Whenever membership changes, the group is a different group. As this takes place, the group needs to reconstitute itself around this new composition of members. Sometimes this will take place at every meeting. Group dynamics change and how the group functions changes. Changing membership makes it more difficult for the group to achieve anything beyond the most basic goals. The bonds in these groups tend to be less strong than bonds in closed time-limited groups. However, the bonds might be quite strong among members who have been with the group for some time.

Changing membership requires reestablishing the group. Some structure is needed to incorporate new members and help the group move quickly through reformation to the functional stage. To some extent, the group must become less cohesive and disintegrate as it goes through this process. Ideally, there will be enough structure for the group to maintain itself while helping new members to feel welcome and find a place for themselves in the group. Some disintegration will occur so the group can revisit the first three stages of group development and reform itself around the new membership.

As with other groups, during the disintegration stage the worker assesses the needs of the group and its members. In an ongoing group, a member or the worker may be terminating, but the group is continuing on. Members may or may not announce that they are ending their involvement with the group, although ongoing growth and development groups that are in residential or day activity programs may limit this. Of course, when members elope from the program, they do not announce this in the group. Ongoing growth and development groups in the community should adopt norms that expect members to let one another know when they intend to leave the group. It is not unusual for members in ongoing community groups to attend only sporadically as they transition out of the group. As with other groups, the group needs to let go and support the member as he leaves the group. After several of these departures, the group should be aware of what to do in these situations. The departure of long-term members may be difficult, but overall lower investment in these types of groups tends to make departures less of an issue. Some members may be reluctant to let go. The group as a whole may feel threatened as the bonds are loosened and they may be concerned that the group might entirely disintegrate. Once they find that this is not the case, the group will carry on without those who have left the group.

In groups for people who are older, the departure of members may be caused by death. This might also occur in other groups as well. Most of the time for groups with younger members, this is from a sudden, unexpected occurrence such as an accident. When members die, group members need to mourn their loss. The worker facilitates the group and members in progressing through the stages of the grief process. At the very least, there should be a moment of silence and perhaps some reminiscing about the member who has died.

Premature departures are typically difficult to predict in these groups. In some groups, it may be important for the worker to follow up when a member drops out because of the reasons members are in the group. Generally, this should be done routinely for a client group. If it is a member of the general public, it is usually optional although advisable to let the group know if he will be returning. If the member is a client, the worker should contact him to see if he will return to the group. If not, the worker should offer other services either within her agency or another agency.

The group will generally need some type of closure when leaving the group or when the group ends. This typically means going around the group and having members have their last say and reviewing experiences and accomplishments. Most will wish one another or the departing member well and recall memories that they will take with them.

As with other groups, disintegration can occur for a group that is intended to be an ongoing group. When this occurs, it is a crisis, at least in terms of the continuation of the group. Typically, the group has regressed to an earlier stage, has not progressed to the point of being functional, or is at risk of ending prematurely. Attendance is probably sporadic or dropping. The worker needs to decide if she will try to save the group or if it might be time to let the group end. If the worker decides to try to save the group, she needs to discuss the group with members either in the group or by contacting members individually to find out what is happening and if they want to try to keep the group going. Most of the time, more aggressive recruitment will be needed to bring new members on board if it is an ongoing group. For time-limited groups, the worker needs to determine what changes are needed to keep the group together and if these will be worthwhile attempting. Sometimes workers will offer a group and no one comes. Other times people come but they do not stay. Most group workers will have these types of experiences some time in their careers if they work with groups long enough.

As with other types of groups, a group might begin to disintegrate because there are personal conflicts. Resolving these are important so that the group can continue and will function effectively. Sometimes changing activities or seating arrangements or the like will accomplish this. Other times a more direct action is needed and the worker needs to mediate the conflict. It is better if this can take place within the group itself and the group is able to participate in the process. If the group is not able to do this or if the situation is too volatile, it may be necessary to mediate the situation either outside of the group or at least away from it. This might be after the group session, outside of the room, or off to the side while the rest of the group is involved in an activity. As in any circumstance in which there is conflict, the worker maintains a mediating position and refrains from taking sides. She asks both parties to express their concerns and asks them for their input in how this might be resolved. If it cannot be resolved, then the group may be threatened or a member or members may be asked to leave. Of course, if the group is made up of clients and it ends or members are asked to leave, arrangements are made for everyone to receive other services.

As the group begins to disintegrate and terminate or a member prepares to leave, the worker evaluates the situation and helps the group to evaluate the experience. The group and members should review where they started and what has been accomplished. They should identify what was positive, what was not, and what might have been more positive regarding the experience. Throughout the group, the worker evaluates the group and its members and tries to anticipate any premature disintegration or departures. When membership lags or attendance becomes sporadic, she tries to reenergize the group, and if this is an ongoing group she recruits new members.

As with other groups, if the worker is leaving an ongoing growth and development group or a time-limited one with a longer time period, it may be at risk of disintegration. This should not occur with time-limited groups unless the time period is longer than usual, such as a semester for a group in a school or when students end their field placement but the group continues on afterward. Generally, workers should not start a time-limited group unless they plan on completing the group. Some groups may end completely when the worker leaves unless another worker is available to take it over, and even then it may lose some membership unless it is a residential or day activity program. It will help to reduce the loss if the new worker can meet with the group several times before the worker departs. Having the worker leave the group is not uncommon for ongoing groups, especially if they have been meeting over an extended period of time. Workers leave for a variety of reasons, the most common being another position, either within or outside of the agency.

Less common reasons for the worker to leave any group include being laid off or fired, the agency or program closing, or dying or becoming ill or disabled. These situations are quite traumatic for both the worker and the group and will require some intervention either by the worker if she is available or by another worker or the supervisor. If the group is ending for any of these reasons, an effort needs to be made to help resolve any issues related to the worker leaving or the group ending. For members who are clients, arrangements need to be made for them to receive alternative services.

Whenever a worker leaves an ongoing group, she prepares the group for her departure and for a new worker. As with other groups, she asks members to express their concerns and reassures them that the group will be able to go on. However, some members may be upset, especially if they have been together for a period of time.

As with other ongoing groups, new workers need to allow the group to express feelings about the previous worker. The worker should explore these feelings, beginning with his first session. If there are joint sessions with former and new workers, feelings should be discussed in those sessions and then discussed again when the new worker starts facilitating the group. If there is a coleader, feelings should be discussed before the other worker leaves, after she leaves, and again when a new coleader joins the group. The worker needs to allow for all of the feelings that are typically associated with grief and loss, including denial, anger, bargaining, grief, and resolution. If the worker's departure is sudden or due to death, then this type of loss will tend to provoke more intense grief reactions.

When new workers join a group, the group will need to revisit all of the earlier stages of group development. The new worker will need to be oriented and he needs to establish a relationship with the members. In the process of doing this, the group will experience some disintegration before it reforms itself. The new worker should expect this and should facilitate this process.

Terminating growth and development group sessions can sometimes be difficult, especially if members are enjoying the experience. They may want to stay longer and may not want the session to end. Sessions should end with a summary of what has taken place and what lies ahead for the next session. Groups might spend time planning for the next session or the worker may give a preview of what is planned.

# Summary

As with other groups, the worker uses the change process at each stage of development in facilitating growth and development groups and provides space and resources. She engages in assessment and planning before the group begins, during each session, and between each session. The worker facilitates the group's progress through each stage of development. Most growth and development groups are closed and time limited. She helps open groups to establish a routine for efficiently incorporating new members. The worker provides videos, speakers, and other resources as needed that will facilitate the group in accomplishing its purpose during the functional stage. She helps the group to engage in activities or interests that brought them to the group. She helps members to consolidate gains as they make progress and when they are leaving the group during the disintegration stage. The worker uses her relationship skills and her skills as a social worker to facilitate the group and make it a positive, enjoyable experience. The social worker develops skills in both the art and the science of facilitating growth and development groups.

C A S E  **8.1**

## An Independent-Living Skills Group

Sylvester and Myra are social work students who are placed at a family service agency. Sylvester is in his first year of an MSW program and Myra is a BSW student. One of their assignments is to facilitate an independent living skills group for teens in foster care who are preparing for independence. The group consists of five males and three females who are fifteen to seventeen years old and are not expected to return home to their biological families before leaving foster care. Most of them will be eligible for the agency's independent living program if they so choose and they receive approval from the state. There are two African American males (Jerrod, seventeen, and Darvin, sixteen) one Hispanic male (Jesse, sixteen) and two Caucasian males (Tim and Bill, both fifteen). There is one female African American (Felicity, sixteen), one Hispanic (Maria, fifteen), and one Caucasian (Emily, seventeen). Sylvester himself is African American and Myra is Caucasian.

Other social work students have been placed with the agency in the past and have conducted similar groups. So there are quite a few resources available to assist in developing activities for the group. Sylvester and Myra have met to plan for the group and decided to catalogue what was available. They researched and found some additional material that was available that might prove useful. They decided

that they would emphasize the "independence" in independent living by having the group decide on what activities would suit their needs. They expected that the group might not consider some skills and so they prepared a list of things that they had to know or learn when they left home. They decided to ask the group what the members thought would be important before suggesting items from the list they had compiled. Sylvester and Myra knew from their social work practice courses that the group members would need to take ownership of the group in order for the individuals to become a group. They felt that this would be the best way to facilitate that process. They expected that some members might be less enthusiastic about being in the group or they might not think that it was "cool." Other members might also be in denial about the fact that they would have to leave care and be on their own. So resistance was to be expected.

At the first meeting, the students used an icebreaker to get started. After brief introductions, they decided to have each member write down on a piece of paper what they were most proud of or what they felt good about themselves. Then they read each one and the group tried to guess who had written it. Initially, some of the members thought this was silly, but after a few times everyone joined

## CASE 8.1 Continued

in and seemed to enjoy the game. Afterward, each member added to their description of positives. This seemed to get the group off on the right foot. Most of the members were quite talkative. The younger ones did not see much point in learning independent living skills, but the older members were quite serious about it. The girls and one of the boys were interested in learning about cooking, but four of the boys did not see any point to it because they figured that they would just eat out. It was decided that the first activity would be budgeting, followed by a comparison of cooking versus eating out. The budget exercise was implemented during the rest of the meeting. Half of the group was asked to go out and price some specific meals during the week. The other half agreed to price the cost of foods that would be used to prepare those same meals at home. They would do this by looking at the price of various foods in their foster home or by going to the grocery store and checking prices. The group ended with a snack and some refreshments. The initial orientation stage seemed to be achieved.

The following week the group met and there was a considerable amount of chatter before the group began. Sylvester and Myra took this as an indication that the group was beginning to gel somewhat, although there was an obvious split between older and younger members of the group. As the group began, the members began to discuss what they had found. Tim and Bill started to crack jokes about the situation. Jerrod was obviously irritated with this and confronted them. He said that this was serious business and that he thought they were acting like fools and wasting his time. The girls agreed. The group got quiet and most of the members looked at Sylvester and Myra. Both remained silent for a moment. Then Sylvester stated that this was their group and they would need to decide how they were going to operate and what they were going to get out of it. Jesse asked if that meant they did not have to come. Myra said that was between them and their workers. Jerrod said he was there because he was going to show everyone that he could be a man and take care of himself. Emily and Felicity agreed that they wanted to be independent adults. Darvin said he was anxious to get a job so he could be on his own. Jesse agreed

that it would be worthwhile attending if he could do this too, but he felt that cooking and taking care of the house was women's work. The three females all chimed in at once when he said this. Sylvester pointed out that there was more to life than getting a job. Everyone would need to learn how to budget and take care of themselves if they were going to be truly independent. He asked Jesse if he planned to move in with a woman when he left home. Jesse said no. Emily asked Jesse who would do his laundry, cook his meals, and clean the dishes. Jesse was silent and then grudgingly admitted that he would have to do this.

The group began sorting out how they were going to proceed. Tim and Bill were obviously the least invested. The rest of the group confronted them and said that they thought that the two of them were too immature to be in the group. They both took this as a challenge and said that they were old enough to start being on the own. The group challenged them to prove it by participating in the group like they were adults instead of acting like they were in junior high. They were silent for a time as the group moved on and eventually joined in the exercise. The group compared eating out with cooking at home and were shocked at how much more it cost to eat out. They then looked at these options in terms of the budgets that they had prepared. It was obvious that eating out was a budget buster. Sylvester and Myra took the events during the group as evidence of the authority and negotiation stages. They encouraged the group to set aside time for fun and time for serious business. The members decided they would take the exercises seriously and use snack time to have fun and joke around.

As the group progressed, the members were able to cover all of the basic skills needed to live independently. These included all of the household tasks, finances, and employment. Each week the group would plan for future sessions and Sylvester and Myra would help to develop exercises and field trips to facilitate their learning. Sometimes they incorporated speakers. Other times they would prepare an exercise from their resources or would develop their own and add them to the manual. As much as possible they let the group members construct their own activities or participate in securing resources to do so.

# QUESTIONS

1. Using Table 6.1, develop a plan for a growth and development group.

2. Describe how you would use assessment skills during various stages of the group from Question 1 or another group.

3. Describe how you would use planning during various stages of the group from Question 1 or another group.

4. Describe how you would use direct practice actions during various stages of the group from Question 1 or another group.

5. Describe how you would use group facilitation skills during various stages of the group from Question 1 or another group.

6. Describe how you would use evaluation during various stages of the group from Question 1 or another group.

7. Describe how you would deal with disintegration or termination during various stages of the group from Question 1 or another group.

# SUGGESTED READINGS

Johnson, Louise C., and Yanca, Stephen J. *Social Work Practice: A Generalist Approach*, 9th ed. Boston: Allyn & Bacon, 2007 (Chapter 14).

Edwards, Richard L., Ed. *Encyclopedia of Social Work,* 19th ed. Washington, DC: NASW Press, 1995 ("Group Practice Overview").

Gitterman, Alex, and Shulman, Lawrence. *Mutual Aid Groups, Vulnerable and Resilient Populations, and the Life Cycle,* 3rd ed. New York: Columbia University Press, 2005.

Grief, Geoffrey, and Ephross, Paul, Eds. *Group Work with Populations at Risk.* 2nd ed. New York: Oxford University Press, 2005.

Ivey, Allen E., Pederson, Paul B., and Ivey, Mary Bradford. *Intentional Group Counseling: A Microskills Approach.* Belmont, CA: Thomson/Wadsworth, 2001.

Jacobs, Ed, Masson, Robert, and Harvill, Riley. *Group Counseling Strategies and Skills.* 5th ed. Pacific Grove, CA: Brooks/Cole, 2006.

Johnson, David W., and Johnson, Frank P. *Joining Together: Group Theory and Group Skills*, 9th ed. Boston: Allyn & Bacon, 2006.

Kottler, Jeffery. *Learning Group Leadership: An Experiential Approach.* Boston: Allyn & Bacon, 2001.

Northern, Helen, and Kurland, Roselle. *Social Work with Groups,* 3rd ed. New York: Columbia University Press, 2001.

Shulman, Lawrence. *The Skills of Helping: Individuals, Families, Groups, and Communities,* 6th ed. Belmont, CA: Thomson-Brooks/Cole, 2009.

Toseland, Ronald W., and Rivas, Robert F. *An Introduction to Group Work Practice,* 6th ed. Boston: Allyn & Bacon, 2009.

# 9

# Prevention Groups

## LEARNING EXPECTATIONS

1. Understanding the importance of prevention groups in generalist social work practice.
2. Understanding prevention groups offered within generalist practice.
3. Understanding the use of the change process in prevention groups.
4. Understanding group process to be able to recognize its various aspects in the functioning of prevention groups.
5. Understanding how the social worker can facilitate the work and process of prevention groups.
6. Beginning skill in facilitating small-group interaction in prevention groups.

This chapter describes generalist social work practice with prevention groups. Like growth and development groups, prevention groups are not limited to those that are offered by generalist practice social workers. A wide variety of professionals, paraprofessionals, and nonprofessionals facilitate these types of groups in a wide variety of settings. In addition to providing these types of groups, social workers may supervise others in doing so or may operate programs that provide these types of experiences.

Generally speaking, it is not easy to obtain or maintain funding for prevention activities, especially from governmental sources. The fundamental approach to social problems in the United States has been residual rather than preventive. A residual approach requires that recipients of services demonstrate that they are experiencing difficulty before they are eligible to receive services. Often some form of means testing accompanies this eligibility determination. This is in contrast to most of Western Europe, where countries provide many services to prevent further difficulty or to prevent them from arising at all. For example, of the major industrialized countries of the world, the United States is the only one that does not provide universal child care. Other countries provide free or inexpensive child care based on need, not income. These countries see child care as part of ensuring that the next generation is raised in a way that will make them good citizens and contributing workers. Quality child care is considered a utility that is an important part of economic activity, just like electricity or gas. In the United States, parents either must secure and pay for care themselves or must prove that they are eligible for subsidized care. Quality care is not guaranteed and not well regulated.

An additional challenge faced by prevention programs is that they tend to be under-funded and are often the first to be cut when there are financial limitations. This serves to reinforce the general attitude in U.S. society that seems to favor a residual approach to social problems. Part of the challenge for prevention programs is that it is more difficult to prove that something was prevented and that the prevention activity contributed to preventing it from occurring.

While prevention programs face these challenges in the United States, providing prevention services in groups tends to be favored for many types of programs. For some, prevention groups are seen as a more efficient use of limited resources. Others see the influence of the group as being an important source of reinforcement for members engaged in prevention behaviors.

## Group Purposes in Prevention Groups

An argument could be made that some growth and development groups are also prevention groups, especially those that are designed for character building for youth. In fact, many prevention groups use the same material and the same approach as growth and development groups. The main differences are the composition of the group, the purpose of the group, and the blending of some of the elements of change-oriented and support groups.

Prevention groups are made up of members who have been identified as being *at risk*. The question is: "At risk of what?" The answer to this question lies in part in the previous chapters of Part Two. Typically, members are at risk of experiencing the kind of difficulties that will result in needing therapy, counseling, or support or that will lead to incarceration, substance abuse, residential or foster care, hospitalization, and the like. All of these are very expensive when it comes to providing services, so it behooves society to prevent people from reaching a point at which they require them.

Prevention groups have considerable overlap with change-oriented, support and self-help, and growth and development groups. The main difference is the purpose of the group. Change-oriented and support groups are aimed at bringing about change or assisting in coping with a situation. The primary purpose of growth and development groups is to develop or enhance skills and abilities or assist in fulfilling developmental needs and tasks. Prevention groups are intended to prevent the development of situations that require major interventions. Prevention groups use the change process, support, and growth and development activities to accomplish this.

Let us look at some of the groups that we include under prevention groups. Our definition for **prevention groups** are any group whose primary purpose is to prevent the development of unhealthy functioning in the biological, psychological, or social aspects of the lives of an at risk population by promoting healthy functioning through group experiences or the acquisition or enhancement of skills and abilities. These groups may include those that are intended to prevent the development of health related conditions such as obesity, diabetes, cancer, and the like. Many prevention groups are aimed at preventing the use of drugs or alcohol. Other groups are used to reduce the temptation to engage in delinquent behavior or to join gangs.

Most prevention groups use some aspect of each of the other types of groups we have studied. Quite often, growth and development activities are used to attract and hold group members' attention. Support from peers in the group is used to resist temptations to use drugs or alcohol, join a gang, or engage in delinquency. Support from peers may be used to get members to engage in healthy lifestyles or alternatives to these temptations. Decision-making and problem-solving skills are used to learn effective ways of declining or resisting the temptation to take part in negative activities and making decisions to participate in positive alternatives. These skills are also practiced in the group.

Prevention groups are offered in a wide variety of settings to a wide variety of clientele by a wide variety of professionals, including BSWs and MSWs. However, most groups, other than health-related groups, are targeted at children and youth, as these groups represent the future at which most prevention groups are aimed.

Unlike change-oriented and support groups, younger children may be good candidates for some prevention groups. Because children and young adolescents are very action oriented, they generally do well in those groups that provide activities and use a more active approach. However, sometimes the message may be lost and they may not understand very much about what drugs, alcohol, or gangs are. Thus, prevention groups for younger children will need to be geared toward their particular age, circumstances, and level of understanding. Prevention groups for younger children are also much more effective if they are geared toward encouraging positive behaviors than if they are only aimed at avoiding negative behaviors. Messages about avoiding negative behaviors can easily become mixed messages. Telling children not to use drugs may actually give them the message that they are expected to do so, but don't do it. Adolescents can better understand the idea of avoiding certain behaviors, but they too may get a mixed message. Besides, messages about what not to do tend to be ineffective. In general, prevention groups need to provide strong messages about what to do.

## Assessment and Planning Before the Group Begins

As with any type of group, the worker uses the change process in organizing and facilitating the group. And like change-oriented groups, prevention groups typically use aspects of the change process within the group itself. This is similar to what is described under decision-making and problem-solving groups in Chapter 6. We will see how these are blended in later in the chapter. Members may be clients, but more often they are at risk of becoming clients. Prevention groups for clients are intended to prevent certain situations that clients may be at risk of developing because they are clients or the purpose is to prevent a situation from getting worse.

The group worker uses her assessment and planning skills before the group begins, within each session, between sessions, and during each stage of group development. Assessment and planning before the group begins is discussed here. Assessment and planning within each session and between sessions will be discussed as we cover each stage of group development. As we discussed with most other groups, prevention groups are mainly artificial or contrived. In forming a prevention group, the worker needs approval from her agency. Participants will need to be identified and recruited and the worker will need to make sure that the logistical aspects are addressed.

Prevention groups are usually made up of some of the more elusive members of any of the groups we have studied. Members may not be told that they have been selected because they are at risk. To do so would make it nearly impossible to carry on prevention activities. In general, people might find the label offensive at worst and unattractive at best.

Instead, there are eligibility criteria that are established and the group is offered to those that fit the criteria. Unless the group experience is highly interesting and attractive, recruiting members may be quite difficult, as is retention. Attendance is likely to be sporadic as members have issues in their lives that draw their attention or they simply forget to come. Many at risk populations live a day-to-day existence, and so keeping appointments is not always as important to them. It is best if the worker plans a strong recruiting campaign and also plans on a high attrition rate. In addition, a system for reminding members about the group may be needed, at least during the initial stages before regular attendance is likely to take place. Advertising may need to include methods other than the mainstream press and television. Local papers, especially those that are free, neighborhood centers, church bulletins, and the like tend to be good places to recruit.

In the end, direct recruitment is often the best strategy. The worker needs to contact schools, community centers, and human service agencies that are located in or serve neighborhoods where prospective group members live. The worker typically needs either to make direct contact with potential members or to have contact with human service providers who are.

The schema for planning a group that is provided in Table 6.1 can also be used for prevention groups. The schema can be used as a proposal to administration to secure approval for a prevention group. Planning for a new group requires that the worker answer the questions why, who, what, where, when, and how. The schema gives a framework for answering these questions and can be modified as needed to include other information that is needed.

The first item in Table 6.1 is a description of the reasons for the group. This is an extremely important part of the proposal. As we mentioned earlier, prevention groups are not easily funded and there is a tendency to raise doubts about their effectiveness because it is usually hard to prove that the prevention activities were responsible for preventing what they were designed to prevent. The worker may need to do research on the frequency of the particular situation that the group is intended to prevent and compare this with the frequency of its occurrence in the community from which members will be drawn. In some cases, a high frequency is already common knowledge so this may not be necessary. Instead, some evidence may need to be presented on the effectiveness of the particular approach with the target population.

The worker should address both effectiveness and efficiency in the proposal. Prevention groups are not usually reimbursed by insurance. The groups are generally provided free of charge. If funding is available, it will usually come from a grant or a contract that specifies the population to be served and may include establishing need and measuring certain outcomes. If there is no external funding available, the proposal will need to address the need for a prevention group that will justify the use of resources. This will be a major concern for management or administration. As with proposals for other groups, the purpose of the group should be designed to meet the needs of potential members and also fit into the mission and services of the agency and the goals of the program where it is located. The worker should anticipate questions about why a prevention group is needed and why the agency should provide this service.

The purpose of the group and the basic aspects of it are presented at the beginning of the plan or proposal. The worker should provide some detail to justify the use of agency resources without an expectation of reimbursement. The proposal should include information from professional sources on serving the at risk population in settings similar to that of the agency or community. The at risk population should be identified, along with some description of how the group will accomplish its purpose. The benefits derived from the group by members should be identified, along with benefits to the agency and the community.

Prevention groups are usually about the same size as growth and development groups and may be much larger than change-oriented and support groups. As with growth and development groups, the size of the group depends on the types of activities, the age and developmental levels of the membership, and the space that is available. The groups need to be large enough to engage in certain activities such as recreation or small-group projects, but not too large that members miss out on opportunities to participate.

For prevention groups, the composition of the group is very important because the group needs to be made up of members who have been identified as being at risk of whatever the group is intended to prevent. The credibility of the group and any claims of success will be based on evidence that members are indeed at risk. Recruitment and screening are therefore important considerations. Sometimes the purpose of the group or the pervasiveness of the issue is sufficient so that anyone could benefit from the group. An example of this are drug prevention programs. The widespread use of drugs and alcohol in U.S. society makes it less likely that a substance abuse or drug prevention program will need to be justified. It also makes it that much more challenging to be successful over the long term.

Generally, it is assumed that if members are carefully selected, they will derive benefits from participating in the group and the activities the group offers. Members may be expected to engage in some self-disclosure, particularly around their exposure to situations that place them at risk. They may also be asked if they have engaged in at risk behaviors or activities, or if they have been tempted to do so. If they have resisted, they are usually asked to share this within the group to help others in resisting the temptation to engage in these behaviors. Activities and group dynamics can be important in how much members enjoy their experience and how well the group does in having a successful outcome. Trust is somewhat important, at least to the extent that members feel free to share their involvement or exposure to at risk behaviors. They need to know that such revelations will not result in negative judgments about them or that they will not get into trouble for these self-disclosures. Members will need to be capable of engaging in relationships and participating in group activities. Otherwise, these members are likely to feel left out.

Because most prevention groups are intended to serve a particular population, a screening process will be needed. Eligibility may be determined on an individual basis or it may be determined much more broadly, by membership in a certain population, by living in a certain area, or other similar circumstances. Any form of eligibility criteria will usually require some type of process for ensuring that the target population is being served. In addition, a recruitment process will typically be necessary because prevention groups are primarily voluntary groups that are offered to people residing in the community as opposed to those in residential settings.

Diversity may play an important role in considering membership for prevention groups, as it does in other groups similar to change-oriented groups. This is usually determined by the amount of self-disclosure that is expected. Some groups expect little or no self-disclosure, so cultural taboos are less likely to play a role in reducing participation. However, there may be some taboos related to the activities planned for the group. As with other groups, members who are more acculturated into the dominant culture may act much more like the dominant culture and so they may not be affected by cultural taboos, while other members may retain a considerable amount of their cultural heritage. As we identified with other groups, the same biases and prejudices toward various diverse groups that exist in the larger society can affect the functioning of any group.

Like other types of groups, diversity can provide opportunities for members to become more acquainted with people who are different. Enjoying the group and its activities can break down some of the barriers between diverse groups. Working together affords members the opportunity to know one another in a positive way. Generally, as people spend time together in positive pursuits and become better acquainted, they find that they have a lot in common. These factors are especially relevant for children who are impressionable and may be more accepting of differences than those who are older and who have solidified various negative attitudes and stereotypes.

As with other groups, it is generally better to have at least two members in the group who share the same diversity. For some forms of diversity, such as gender, this similarity may need to be closer to half of the group. For younger children, this may not be as important. However, in general younger adolescents should be separated into same-sex groups because they tend to prefer this arrangement, especially young adolescent males. This can be difficult to control with prevention groups, but the worker needs to consider diversity as she recruits and screens members for the group.

Age is still an important factor in establishing common ground in prevention groups. Typically, adults and children are not mixed with each other in these groups. Generally, it is best for members to be somewhat close in age or at least be of the same generation. Because of the nature of prevention groups, many of these types of groups are targeted at children and youth. It is best if these groups are made up of members who are within one to two years of each other (for instance, ten and eleven years old). Some groups can handle three years (such as ten to twelve), but the majority of members should be the age that is in the middle. Prevention groups for adults may include parenting groups that also are designed to affect children and youth. Prevention groups for adults may include those aimed at substance abuse or various health issues.

Like growth and development groups, most prevention groups are time limited. Some may be ongoing and have open membership. In these instances, there is usually a series of activities that are rotated and do not build on each other so that members can join at any point and stay or return until they complete the series. Those prevention groups that are time limited will typically be closed after the first session or a certain period of time after the group begins.

As with all groups, the leader or facilitator should be competent to lead or facilitate the group. Every code of ethics for professionals addresses competence. Appropriate credentials, training, and experience are needed. Most prevention groups do not necessarily require a great deal of advanced professional training. For most, the worker needs to have expertise in specific areas that relate to the content that is being offered and the techniques that will facilitate the group process. The competence of the worker is likely to be an issue in having a proposal approved and in the recruitment process. Other workers will want to know the level of competence of the worker to ensure that their clients will receive good services. Supervision and consultation tend to be less important for prevention groups than for change-oriented groups, but these are identified in the proposal and used as needed.

The plan for the group should include a description of the format. Prevention groups can be loosely structured, but many are moderately to highly structured. These groups will often use program material or a curriculum that is designed to prevent a specific social problem from occurring. The worker should still be prepared to modify program materials to meet the needs of members. The use of resources such as speakers, videos, books, and the like may be part of the group experience. The proposal should describe the resources that are needed and how these will be obtained.

As with any other type of groups, prevention groups should be offered under the sanction or auspices of one or more organizations, which gives the group its credibility. The organization serves as the sponsor for the group and typically provides a site to meet. Organizations are themselves sanctioned by the community to provide services to certain populations. The mission, goals and ways of functioning for the organizations sponsoring the group should be consistent with purpose of the group and the populations being served. Sometimes, a connection is not obvious and needs to be made or justified. Sometimes providing or sponsoring the group represents a new service, a new way of serving clients, or a collaboration with other organizations in serving a new or an existing clientele.

The ability to offer a prevention group will likely be determined by the agency or organizations that sponsor the group and by the worker or workers who will facilitate it. Having more than one organization act as a sponsor has advantages, such as sharing resources and providing referrals. Most of the disadvantages are related to the need for more coordination and obtaining approval from more than one organization.

As with other groups, proposals for prevention groups should include a basic description of potential group membership, how members will be recruited, and how they will benefit from the group. Recruitment in residential settings is not necessary. Recruiting members in the community requires getting the word out to prospective members and agency personnel who are likely to be in contact with them. Prevention groups require both recruitment directed at workers who are serving those populations that are identified as being at risk and a screening process to ensure that referrals are appropriate. An advertising campaign is usually needed to secure prospective members. Advertising may include developing and distributing fliers or brochures, advertising in local newspapers and newsletters, and running public service announcements on radio and television as well as public access cable channels. The costs of these activities should be included in the budget for the group.

A plan or proposal for prevention groups should contain a description of group activities over the course of the group and during typical group sessions. If there are program materials, they should be described and should be included in an appendix to the proposal, if possible. Potential topics and resources for the group should be identified.

Projected dates and times should be included in the proposal. It should identify the length of the sessions and the time of day and days of the week sessions might take place. In most cases, the group will be a time-limited group, so possible start and end dates should be identified. Most prevention groups are scheduled at least once a week. The place where the group will meet should be described in some detail, along with who is responsible for arranging this. Space dictates what can and cannot be done in the group. Because activities are part of many prevention groups, there needs to be sufficient open space and members need to be comfortable. Confidentiality and privacy are issues if the group is engaging in some form of self-disclosure. Like growth and development groups, it may be more important that the noise from the group does not disturb others who are not in the group. Materials or special equipment that will be needed should be identified.

Like other groups, additional information that may be needed should be addressed in a proposal, including transportation or other needs. These should be anticipated and any potential barriers removed. For groups with children and youth, in most cases written permission will be needed for participation and a sample of the form should be included in the appendix.

A mechanism for evaluating the group should be included in the proposal. This should include desired outcomes for the group and individual members and how these will be measured. As with support and self-help groups and growth and development groups, evalaution tends to be much more informal and more elusive than for change-oriented groups, in which membership is more stable and needs or concerns can be identified along with the ability to determine if these have been addressed. Certainly, proving that anything was prevented may not even take place for years, if at all. Most of the time, evaluation of prevention groups is either an increase in knowledge or a change in attitude that will make it less likely that participants will engage in behaviors that place them at risk. The most common design for evaluating most groups is pretest/posttest. This is typically the preferred design when measuring change. Usually, the pretest is given at the beginning of the first group and the posttest is administered at the end of the last session. For some prevention groups, a pretest is given at the beginning of each session and a posttest at the end. Sometimes only a posttest is necessary if it is determined that the outcome only needs to be a certain level of knowledge or a certain attitude. If the measurement is how satisfied members were with the group, then only a post-group survey is needed. The worker may use an evaluation form at the end of the group or conduct a follow-up by contacting members after they leave the group. Longer term follow up contact is ideal. Evaluation is important for determining outcomes and for demonstrating the effectiveness of the group. It can be especially important for prevention groups in determining whether the group continues or another group is offered. Those prevention groups that receive funding often do so under a grant. Most grants require a description of the evaluation process and a sample of the evaluation instrument.

The budget is an important consideration for a proposal for prevention groups. Since prevention is hard to prove, particularly on a short-term basis, it is difficult to do a cost-benefit analysis. Organizations will still want to have some type of cost-benefit analysis. However, this is typically limited to calculating the cost per unit of service. The proposal should still highlight the benefit to group participants and the recognition or prestige that sponsoring a group might bring to the organization. Some organizations may have a budget for offering these types of groups because it is within their mission to provide these services. An estimate of the expenses should be presented, including materials, refreshments, rent, salaries, transportation, equipment, and the like. An estimate of the units of service along with expenses will give administrators a basis for deciding if the group is feasible.

Assessment and planning before the group begins will increase the likelihood that the proposal will be approved and the group will be successful. A well-organized and thorough proposal makes a positive impression regarding the competence of the worker and increases the chances that the group will be approved.

## The Change Process During the Orientation Stage

The first three stages of group development for prevention groups tend to be similar to those of growth and development groups. The immediate benefits of most prevention groups are derived from participation as opposed to personal issues as is the case with change-oriented and support and self-help groups. As a result, the level of investment in the group may be less intense. However, some members may become highly invested even though there is generally much less at stake. As we described with growth and development groups, attraction to the group may also be lessened. Therefore, the worker needs to plan activities that will attract members to the group and hold their interest during the course of the group. Groups that do not have closed membership and allow new members to join at any time will go through the process of reforming themselves by revisiting each stage of development at the beginning of each session. Time-limited groups with closed membership will also go through the first three stages of development during each session, but this tends to be relatively brief and generally takes the form of checking in and reviewing individual and group progress.

Orientation before the group begins may be somewhat similar to other groups that we discussed. The worker might provide information for new members prior to the first meeting or during the enrollment period or prior to new members joining the group if membership is open. In addition, other workers may inform potential participants who are being referred. Prevention groups may require an exchange of some information between workers or organizations regarding eligibility, so referrals tend to be more formal than is the case for support and growth and development groups.

There is typically an orientation process that takes place during the first session for closed time-limited groups. For open groups, orientation occurs at the beginning of a session when a new member joins the group. For open groups, a process for welcoming new members needs to be established as early as possible. Similar to other open groups, members may volunteer to do this, a rotation can be established among veteran members, or the worker will assume this role especially for groups with younger children. Typically, the new attendee will need information about what to expect in the group before the group begins or at the beginning of the session. The worker may have already done some of this beforehand in the process of determining eligibility. New members introduce themselves or are introduced by members who have welcomed them prior to the meeting or by the worker. Most prevention groups are time limited and closed, so after the first session or a set number of sessions, new members cannot join. Generally, they are put on a waiting list until the next group is scheduled to begin.

Most new members will experience some of the same ambivalence or approach–avoidance, about being there, which we described for other groups. New members who are joining or members of a new group will experience a certain amount of these feelings just because the situation is new. For those groups that do not expect much self-disclosure, these feelings may be less intense. Once members make an initial commitment to the group, the initial orientation stage is completed. The group will still need to undertake an orientation process to some extent at the beginning of each session before work begins and also when there is a new member.

The worker uses assessment, planning, actions, and evaluation in facilitating the group as it progresses through the orientation stage. Members of prevention groups will typically join the group primarily for enjoyment much like growth and development groups. Some may wish to acquire knowledge and skills. They do not usually see themselves as fulfilling a need. Thus, the group needs to be seen as an enjoyable experience in order to attract and keep members. If this is not established in the first meeting, membership is likely to rapidly dwindle. The worker needs to ensure that members will want to return to the group. As we discussed earlier, change-oriented and support and self-help groups have members who have needs outside the group that will propel them toward using the group to meet those needs. Prevention groups, like growth and development groups, typically cannot rely on this to get members involved in the group. Instead, prevention and growth and development groups need to be attractive enough to lure members to the group and hold them there once they come. Food and fun tend to be important elements in accomplishing this, especially for children and youth.

In most prevention groups, the group experience will determine if members join and stay with the group. If members find the experience enjoyable and worthwhile, they will continue to attend. The worker needs to constantly assess this so that the group can maintain itself. She should develop a plan that incorporates this assessment and take actions that facilitate achieving a positive environment in the group. The worker regularly evaluates the extent to which this is achieved. Typically, this is evident in the atmosphere in the group. However, the worker should solicit verbal or written feedback to ensure that the members are satisfied with their experience.

It is very important that activities that are fun or interesting take place at the first session of most prevention groups. Because it is the group experience that will attract and hold most members to the group, some type of enjoyment in being in the group needs to be the priority. Once this has been established, activities can be introduced that are related to the purpose of the group. Generally, the worker is more invested in prevention, at least initially, than are the members. Eventually, members may value it as well. It is assumed that ultimately they will be better off if they prevent, avoid, or escape from situations that place them at risk.

Icebreaking activities are important for the first group session. Because the group is what tends to be the greatest attraction for prevention groups, an icebreaker should be planned that builds some sort of teamwork, creates enjoyment, or encourages some bonding. For children and youth, games tend to be quite attractive. Introductions can be cursory followed by a fun activity that builds group cohesion. Subgroups may be formed and some type of competition, either physical or mental, takes place. For example, some form of trivia game can be developed in which teams compete to answer questions related to prevention activities. This can be structured like a sport such as baseball in which teams are credited with hits if they answer correctly and outs if they do not. Runs are scored and tallied. For basketball, each correct answer can count as a basket and an incorrect is a miss and a turnover. For football, each correct answer can move the ball down the field toward a touchdown.

All groups need to balance the needs of the group and the needs of its members. We have called this the "I–we" balance. In prevention groups, the needs of members take on some added importance over growth and development groups because members have been identified as being at risk. The worker and the group need to balance an individual's needs with those of other members and the group as a whole.

During the orientation stage, there is usually more emphasis on the "I" portion of the "I–we" balance. Members have not committed themselves to the group. If the group is to become a group, members will need to commit themselves and become a "we." Members need to value one another and the group experience. The worker plans for this. She facilitates group formation or reformation if the group is revisiting the orientation stage. The worker should use pronouns that emphasize the group and ask members to speak as a member of the group as opposed to speaking as an individual.

Group planning tends to hasten group formation. This helps the group to come together and moves it toward the next two stages of group development. Planning together gets members invested in the group and allows them to shape the group into what they want the group to be. This helps members to take ownership of the group. It also helps members to articulate unspoken needs that might be met in the group. However, in some cases the opportunities for group planning may be limited. There may be a prescribed curriculum or set of program materials that need to be covered. Age and developmental levels may limit members' ability to engage in planning. In these cases, the worker should still discuss the plan for the group with the group and solicit feedback. The worker looks for ways the group can plan within whatever structure there is. When using program materials or a curriculum, the worker modifies the material to meet the needs of the group and incorporates group planning into this process.

Throughout the orientation stage, the worker evaluates the progress of the group. She notes the interactions in the group and evaluates the degree to which a positive atmosphere has developed. She evaluates whether members interact with one another in a positive way. She looks for signs that members are enjoying themselves. She evaluates whether the group is beginning to function as a group. She notes who is included and who is not and who participates and who does not. She finds ways for the group to be more inclusive and encourages members to participate.

Termination during the orientation stage of prevention groups is focused on encouraging members to return to the group and exploring any barriers to doing so. The worker should summarize the session and solicit contributions from the group. Discussing the next session gives a sense of continuity and may give some indication about who intends to return. The worker should address any needs or concerns before the group ends or follow up with these after the session is over.

Once members make an initial commitment to the group and become invested in it, the orientation stage is completed for them. The elements of the orientation stage may be repeated to some extent at the beginning of group sessions as members transition from their life outside the group to experiencing the group. Of course the orientation stage will be revisited as new members join the group if it is an open group.

## The Change Process During the Authority Stage

When members of the group make an initial commitment to the group, they become invested in what happens in the group, leading to the authority stage. Power and control issues arise and the possibility of conflict increases. The authority issue may actually be more intense because of the membership of some of these groups. The fact that members have been identified as being at risk may also mean that they are drawn from populations that have been marginalized by society. They may be poor and come from neighborhoods that have high rates of crime, delinquency, and drug activity. These might be the very circumstances that lead to their membership in the group and place them at risk. Issues regarding authority, power, and control may be salient in their everyday lives and if so, they will bring these to the group and act them out. They may be more inclined to challenge authority and more aggressive in resisting control. They may have less invested in the norms of society, so they may be less invested in developing certain norms within the group. In fact, they may be inclined to develop norms that would be considered deviant by the dominant society. All of this needs to be considered by the worker as she plans for the group. She needs to be prepared to handle situations that are somewhat different and possibly more intense than those that she would expect to encounter in a growth and development group that has a membership that is made up of the general public.

Typically, issues during the authority stage will be most intense for a new group, but with some populations who are members of prevention groups, the intensity of the authority stage may continue to exist just below the surface throughout the group. As a result, the authority stage may not be fully resolved and can erupt rather suddenly. In the course of engaging in various activities, conflicts can arise that threaten the group or some of its members. The group may need to revisit this stage and the negotiation stage on a regular basis. During this stage, there is some "we-ness" in the group, but there is still a lot of "I-ness". In fact, for some groups, members may never really achieve very much cohesion. Members might continuously compete with one another for authority, power, and control or challenge the power of the group or the worker.

As with other groups, the worker in a prevention group needs to give at least some control to the group for the individuals to become a group, but this can be a very delicate matter when working with some populations. Some prevention groups are made up of members who have negative experiences with authority and authority figures or who see power being used in a detrimental way in their life outside of the group. Power and authority may be seen as tools to be used to exploit others. Being in a group may be seen as similar to being in a gang. The task for the worker in working with members who have had these types of experiences is to help them to see positive ways of exercising authority and power. He needs to help them to experience the group as a positive force rather than a tool for exploitation. This can be very challenging work.

For the most part, when the worker has a prevention group that presents these types of challenges, she needs to help the group to develop a consensus approach to decision making that is inclusive and benefits everyone. She may need to start out with some highly structured decision-making activities. She cannot expect members to know how to use authority appropriately if they have little or no experience with this in their everyday lives. As the group is able to make decisions and carry them out in a manner that respects each other's needs, then the worker can turn more control over to the group.

As with other groups, those that are made up of children or members who have limited developmental capacities or significant impairments, the worker will retain more authority than in groups whose members are higher functioning adolescents or adults. However, members will need to learn to use what they learn and in order for this to happen a certain level of authority and power and control needs to be shifted from the worker to the group and its members.

Members have to take some ownership of the group and invest enough to work at accomplishing the group's purpose. For some prevention groups, a substantial amount of effort will need to go into developing and maintaining the group. The tenuousness of member commitment, along with authority issues, may mean that the positive functioning of the group is marginal at best. The worker should plan for this, especially if she knows that the members of the group do not have many positive influences or experiences in their lives that would make it natural for them to create positive experiences within the group. They will need to learn how to do this.

The worker influences group structure to ensure that members receive maximum benefit from the group. Norms, roles, and ways of functioning have not been established yet during this stage in a new group that is just forming. In growth and development groups made up of high-functioning adults, the worker provides the initial structure and gradually turns some or most of this over to the group as it develops the capacity to do so. However, with most prevention groups, she will probably need to retain much more control throughout the life of the group and will need to help the group maintain a sufficient amount of structure for the group to accomplish its purpose.

Prevention groups typically require more structure and are likely to be time limited, so the worker usually makes most of the decisions about what occurs during group sessions, especially during initial sessions. Usually this has been planned ahead of time. There may need to be a set schedule for the group to cover certain material to achieve the group's purpose. This schedule will almost invariably need to be modified by circumstances that arise in prevention groups. While most groups are unpredictable, prevention groups tend to be much more so because of the nature of their membership. It is also very challenging for the worker to maintain enough interest to sustain the group. It can be like walking a tightrope, in that the worker must maintain enough structure to ensure that the group remains positive and accomplishes its purpose while still making the group experience interesting enough to hold the attention of the members and make them want to return. One incentive that can be very effective in accomplishing this is food. Having refreshments at the end of each session can be a powerful reward for attending the group and maintaining appropriate behavior. This is especially true for groups of children and youth. Refreshments may be particularly attractive for members of all ages who are poor or underprivileged and do not have these readily available in their everyday lives.

In most prevention groups, the worker will introduce certain rules. This should be followed by a discussion of those rules. The introduction of rules is likely to lead to the authority stage. A discussion of the rules can help the group move toward the negotiation stage. Having the worker introduce basic rules is especially important for groups with children or members who are somewhat limited in their development or their social skills. The worker may ask for suggestions about other rules that might be useful in helping the group to function. The worker encourages the group to establish control over how the group will function to the extent that is feasible. This is also a delicate balance. The worker has ideas about what the group needs to do to accomplish its purpose, but she also knows that members need to take ownership of the group. The group needs enough structure to accomplish its purpose while allowing enough freedom for members to feel that this is their group and not the worker's. She helps the group make decisions within certain parameters. A balance is needed between the need for the group to accomplish its purpose and the needs of members to have a say in how that is accomplished. The worker makes suggestions and encourages discussion about how the group will make decisions within those parameters. Consensus is encouraged so that everyone is included. Sometimes the group may use a democratic style in deciding what members would like to do. However, every member needs to be included. If voting occurs, it should not be used to exclude anyone. Instead, voting is best used to establish the priority or sequence of options so everyone's needs or desires are addressed over time.

During the authority stage, the "I–we" issue is still tipped toward the "I" side of the equation. Members are concerned about maintaining their individuality, but they have also begun to be concerned about being accepted by the group. Some members may rebel or resent control by the worker or the group, especially for certain at risk populations. The issues that arise during the authority stage are resolved at least temporarily in the negotiation stage. When the worker senses too much individuality, she can establish more group cohesion by addressing the group as a whole and emphasizing the group. When the worker senses that there is too much emphasis on the group at the expense of individual members, she addresses members as individuals to create a better balance between individual needs and group needs.

In open groups, the group will revisit the authority stage when new members join. New members will struggle with the issue of individuality and acceptance by the group. This is particularly intense when there is an established group and new members wonder if the group will be open to creating a place for them in the group. In prevention groups, usually the worker establishes how new members are incorporated into the group as part of the plan for the group and then reviews this with the group. If new members can join any time, then a routine needs to be established to include new members.

The worker evaluates the group and individual members during the authority stage. She evaluates the level of participation for each member, their investment in the group, and the degree to which the group accepts members. She encourages each member to participate and tries to provide opportunities for everyone to experience success and to contribute to the success of the group. She uses positive conflict resolution that is respectful and inclusive.

Termination during this stage is very similar to that in the orientation stage. In new groups or with new members, the worker is concerned with members investing themselves in the group and returning. If disagreements have taken place, she emphasizes that differences are to be expected and respected. The worker highlights positive experiences and summarizes the session.

Throughout the authority stage, the worker assesses the situation. She plans for issues of power and control to arise and helps the group reach a positive resolution. For most prevention groups, especially those for children, the worker establishes basic rules for the group and assists the group in establishing other appropriate rules. To the extent that it is feasible, she helps the group to take responsibility for making decisions as well as helping it to make responsible decisions. Her goal is for decisions to be made in an inclusive way that considers the needs of members and the group. She evaluates group and individual progress and terminates sessions with a review of the progress that has been made.

## The Change Process During the Negotiation Stage

Most of the conflict or disagreements that arise in the authority stage in prevention groups are at least temporarily resolved during the negotiation stage. However, the nature of the membership of many of these groups means that authority issues, norms, and roles may continue to arise throughout the group. Generally, the worker is much more active in establishing basic rules for the group. These basic rules will typically be related to maintaining appropriate behaviors in the group. For instance, in groups of children or youth, the worker may need to say that hitting will not be allowed. When the group is discussing something, only one person at a time can talk. Profanity and other forms of disrespect are not allowed. As the group progresses, it will typically experience some confrontations and disagreements that require conflict resolution. The worker will need to mediate these and get the group back on track. At some point when members become sufficiently invested in having the group function, goals, norms, roles, and tasks are established and the individuals becomes a group.

At the conclusion of the negotiation stage, members feel positive about the group and there is enough group cohesion to proceed with the main work of the group. To reach this point, the worker helps the group to establish goals, norms, roles, and tasks. He ensures that this is done in a way that is inclusive. While the overall goals of prevention groups are somewhat elusive, the intermediate goals can typically be identified by the types of activities in which the group will engage. Education involves acquiring certain knowledge. Recreation provides opportunities to enjoy various activities. Skill development promotes learning new skills. The commitment of individual members to the group is directly related to their ability to see the group as a place in which they can also meet their individual needs and achieve their individual goals. It is essential that members have positive feelings about the group experience. The worker cannot make the same assumptions as he made with growth and development groups regarding meeting members' needs. While participating in the group and its activities are important, members who are at risk are usually dealing with circumstances that make it difficult for them to get their needs met. The worker needs to be certain that everyone is given an opportunity to participate and that members have their individual needs met to the greatest extent possible.

Most prevention groups require some discussion of members' experiences within and outside of the group. Members are not usually required to disclose their deeper thoughts and feelings, but are typically asked about thoughts, feelings, and behaviors related to whatever the group is designed to prevent. Members are not expected to expose vulnerable parts of themselves such as their human flaws and frailties. Discussing thoughts, feelings, and actions is usually related to developing resistance to succumbing to some type of negative behavior or engaging in alternative behaviors. For instance, in a drug prevention group, members may be asked about their drug use and experiences with being offered drugs. The group can then explore ways of resisting the temptation to use drugs by engaging in certain thoughts, feelings, and actions. There might also be a discussion of other ways of feeling good and having fun that do not include using drugs or alcohol. Thus, some self-disclosure may be expected in many of these types of groups.

Any group that is facilitated by a social worker needs to be consistent with the cardinal values of social work. Social workers believe in the value and worth of every human being, which means treating people with dignity and respect. This is reflected in the basic rules that the worker establishes with the group. Members need to feel accepted. They need an opportunity to participate and have their participation valued by the group.

As the negotiation stage progresses, some members of prevention groups may begin to feel that "I" have become a part of the "we." For these members, at least some portion of their identity includes being members of this group and they feel they belong. Not everyone in the group will experience this and those that do will not necessarily experience it in the same way or to the same degree. This variation is due in large part to the situations that lead to members being identified as being at risk and in need of prevention services. Some members may be able to transcend the negative experiences that have placed them at risk. Others will remain more guarded and suspicious with lower levels of trust toward others and toward authority figures in general.

Social workers value and respect self-determination. People should have the right to make their own decisions about things that affect them. In any group, this means that members should be able to choose whether they participate in any of the group's activities. The group needs to respect this and allow members to decide this for themselves without fear of retribution or any negative consequences. Members should not be coerced into doing things that they do not want to do.

Another social work value is the belief that people should have the right to have socially accepted needs met in socially accepted ways. Group norms need to be established that give all of their members opportunities to have the needs that are consistent with the group's purpose met within the group. Some members may need assistance from the worker outside of the group in meeting needs that cannot be met within the group.

The worker uses his skills in group facilitation during the negotiation stage. He presents basic rules that are necessary for the group to function. He discusses these with the group and negotiates any additional rules that the group might suggest. He continuously assesses the needs of the group and facilitates movement as necessary. Because prevention groups will typically have members who face major challenges in their life outside of the group, there are often challenges to be faced in working with them in the group. The worker can expect that some members may have difficulty in accepting his or the group's authority. It may be difficult to negotiate a resolution to the negotiation stage, especially one that will hold up throughout the life of the group. Instead, the worker needs to understand that norms, rules, and roles may be somewhat fluid and will need regular attention as the group proceeds.

Planning before, during, and between sessions for new groups during the negotiation stage is focused on group formation with the realization that this might be tenuous at best. The worker plans activities that will facilitate moving the group through the negotiation stage. He helps them to formulate goals, norms, roles, and tasks by using activities that will bring the group together to decide on these. The worker summarizes this for the group, but may ask for contributions from group members in higher functioning groups.

For the first several sessions, the worker should plan an opening summary that identifies norms, tasks, and goals that have been established as a reminder for group members. This is especially true for groups with children and younger adolescents, those with lower functioning members, and those with members who are prone to or at risk of engaging in negative behaviors. He should be prepared to stop the group when norms are being violated and take time to reestablish and reinforce them.

The worker's actions during the negotiation stage with a new group facilitate the development of goals, norms, tasks, and roles. The worker introduces this as a topic for discussion during this stage. The goal is to find enough common ground for the group to develop cohesion so they can work together during the functional stage.

As the session unfolds, the worker evaluates progress for individual members and the group as a whole through the negotiation stage. He evaluates participation and encourages reluctant members to join in activities and discussions. Members need to feel that they are a part of the group so they can become full participants.

The termination process is similar to closing most sessions with a summary by the worker or one that is solicited from the group or some combination of these.

During the negotiation stage, the group is being formed and is preparing for the activities that will achieve its purpose. In prevention groups, this stage may require a longer period of time than in other groups and the resolution may need to be revisited regularly throughout the life of the group.

## The Change Process During the Functional Stage

For prevention groups, the functional stage is when activities are occurring that reflect the purpose of the group. The members spent time and energy during earlier stages becoming a group, which is important and necessary for group formation to occur so that the group can accomplish its purpose. In groups that are not fully formed, members tend to rely on the worker and so members do not fully benefit from the group experience when this occurs. Role-plays, practicing, games, group activities, and group discussions are common ways to help the members to move toward relying on one another.

During the functional stage, most prevention groups will use a combination of what we have outlined for the three types of groups described earlier in Part Two. For most groups, the worker will plan activities that are similar to those for growth and development groups. At least some of these activities are designed to make the group enjoyable and attractive for members. Without this, it would be difficult to offer a prevention group to at risk populations because most of these groups are voluntary. There are some exceptions to this, for example, groups offered in schools such as Drug Abuse Resistance Education (D.A.R.E.) or other substance abuse prevention programs.

In addition to growth and development activities, most prevention groups will also have a blending of change and support. Typically, members are encouraged to engage in problem solving and decision making related to the situations that the group is intended to prevent. Role-plays and practicing activities are focused on these types of situations. Members are encouraged to find ways to resolve situations that they may face in a positive way that avoids the negative consequences associated with what is intended to be prevented. For instance, a drug prevention group for youth typically includes role-playing situations in which the youth is offered drugs. They practice ways of resisting the temptation or influence to use drugs.

Support comes into play in having the group be a place where members receive support for alternative ways of dealing with situations that place them at risk. For example, in a drug prevention group, youth receive support for not using drugs and resisting the pressure to use. They may also receive support for engaging in alternative, positive activities. For youth who live in areas with high rates of drug activity, their ecosystem has many influences that support the use of drugs. These may include peers, neighbors, friends, and even family or relatives. The group provides support for alternatives to these influences.

For new prevention groups, the stages of group formation may take some time to accomplish or may be tenuous or incomplete throughout the life of the group. This is one of the main reasons that many prevention groups use more structured experiences such as program materials or curricula. These help in moving the group into activities related to the functional stage, even though group cohesion may be limited. In any case, when the group proceeds to the functional stage it has begun to accomplish its purpose. Usually, issues related to group formation will arise again over the next few sessions and may occur even later in the group. Often most of the first session may be taken up with group formation. For the initial session of a group, the worker should plan for a brief period of group formation followed by an activity that would solidify this. It is especially important to provide an activity that is enjoyable so that members will be motivated to return. In some groups, the highlight may be the snack. The worker should not be discouraged by this or by indications that members are coming to have fun or eat. In prevention groups, the important thing is to get them there.

Some groups that are higher functioning may be able to achieve a good healthy balance of "I-ness" and "we-ness" during this stage as group members balance the need for the group to maintain itself and accomplish its purpose while also providing opportunities for members to participate. Members in higher functioning groups are aware of the need to include everyone in group activities. However, even the best groups can have moments when this is out of balance. What is more likely to be the case in prevention groups is for the "I-we" to be out of balance. One or more members may seek to dominate the group because that is what they have learned to do in their natural environment or they may be so needy that the need for attention is overwhelming. On the other hand, the group may not be as inclusive with a member or members and may even seek to exclude someone from the group. This might be a carryover from conflicts outside of the group or it may be competition for power and control or it may be scapegoating or other negative motivation. When this occurs, the worker needs to intervene and point out norms or rules that reinforce inclusion. When there is too much emphasis on individuality, the worker addresses the group as a whole or asks individuals to discuss their thoughts and feelings about the situation as members of the group. If there is too much emphasis on the group at the expense of individual needs, the worker asks members to speak for themselves as individuals and express their thoughts and feelings about how they would feel if the group was trying to exclude them or not include them.

The worker continuously engages in assessment and planning before, during, and between group sessions. She assesses how the group is functioning and the level of cohesion. She assesses whatever progress is evident in achieving the purpose of the group. She assesses strengths and challenges for the group as a whole and for each member. The worker assesses group process and functioning. She seeks to understand group dynamics to facilitate progress and ensures appropriate levels of participation for all members.

The worker plans for activities that will maximize group cohesion and participation in group activities. She assesses, plans, and takes actions before, during, and after each group session. It is important for members to feel good about their experiences and to benefit from participating in the group.

With any group, assessment and planning involve both content and process. The worker plans the content for each session in many prevention groups, especially those for children. She analyzes each session and seeks to understand what seemed to be effective and what was not. She plans activities that are enjoyable and effective in helping members to deal with circumstances that place them at risk. She observes verbal and nonverbal behavior and interactions during each session. The worker analyzes the stage of development of the group and the progress it has made. She plans activities that maintain interest in the group while also accomplishing the group's purpose. She supports group involvement in planning to the extent possible.

In addition to these actions, the worker also uses some of the actions that are described in Chapters 3, 4, and 5, including actions that can be taken within and outside of the group to facilitate completion of plan. As with growth and development groups, the worker primarily uses skills related to relationship building and activity. She may also help group members in learning to use resources, empowering and enabling, crisis resolution, and support. She engages in actions to facilitate group formation, facilitate discussion, resolve conflict, enhance group interaction, facilitate group development, and structure group activities. These practice actions are not repeated here, but are summarized as they relate to working with prevention groups. The reader is encouraged to review this material before proceeding and include them as indicated.

Relationships are central to the functioning of the group. Successful relationships include good communication, the ability to problem solve and make decisions, and resolve conflict in a constructive manner. These skills are used in prevention groups to help members deal with situations that place them at risk. In addition, these skills may be needed by the worker in resolving conflicts among members in some of these groups. The worker needs to be able to use mediation and conflict resolution skills when this occurs.

Along with relationship skills, activities are generally used in prevention groups to hold members' interest and may also serve to help them in dealing with circumstances that place them at risk. During the functional stage, the group is typically engaging in activities that achieve its purpose and members are learning new skills and techniques in dealing with their circumstances. For example, in drug prevention groups, members learn about the effects of drugs and how to resist offers to use drugs. In groups designed to prevent delinquency, members learn alternative ways to meet their needs or resist getting into situations that will lead to trouble. In prevention groups for parents, parents are learning new or different ways of raising their children. In health prevention groups, members may be engaged in a wide range of activities that lead to healthier ways of living.

In most prevention groups, the worker is primarily responsible for planning and arranging activities. In some groups, members are asked to provide examples of situations that place them at risk and this forms the content for prevention activities. In many prevention groups, program materials or a curriculum is used. Whenever the worker uses this type of material, she needs to be prepared to alter or modify it to meet the needs of the specific group that she is facilitating. Most workers do not use standardized material exactly as it is designed, but will change how it is used or add material from other sources or use parts of it combined with other material or design their own material to supplement part of the material. In Table 8.1 and the discussion that accompanies it in Chapter 8, we present a schema for developing and using program materials as a guide for developing and using activities in groups.

The challenge for workers with prevention groups is ensuring that the use of the material will hold the interests of group members while also providing them with what they need in dealing with their circumstances. In essence, activities need to be relevant to the interests of members and to their circumstances outside of the group. Thus, an important criteria in using program materials in prevention groups relates to the demographics of group members. Activities and program materials need to be age appropriate and especially sensitive to variations in member diversity, background, and environment. Flexibility in using the material is essential so that it can be used by a variety of groups and tailored to meet the needs of each unique group.

Activities in prevention groups can actually be used in two different ways and in different patterns. Activities are often the central mechanism by which the group accomplishes its purpose. In other words, engaging in the activity is the way that members learn to deal with their circumstances. In addition, activities can be used as an incentive or reward. After the group accomplishes the purpose of the session, members may be rewarded by participating in activities that are highly enjoyable. For example, a portion of a group session with youth might include playing basketball or another game or sport.

Using activities and program materials with prevention groups follows an organized process that is similar to the change process including assessment, planning, action, and evaluation. The worker assesses the needs and interests of group members in planning for the group and throughout the process of implementing the group. In selecting the level of complexity of activities, the worker considers attention span, social skills, intellect, physical abilities, and emotional factors of members. The worker reviews resource materials and considers these factors in selecting the types of materials or activities. Sometimes the materials are designed specifically for certain types of prevention groups. Other times the worker will adapt material to suit this purpose. The activity or material is tested before it is used in the group and is adapted as necessary as described in Chapter 8.

As we described with growth and development groups, the action phase with most prevention groups is characterized by carrying out the program material or activity in the group. The worker presents the activity or material to the group in a positive way. She demonstrates what they will be doing and sets limits. She may need to adapt the material at this point before implementation as members raise questions or concerns. During the activity, the worker assists members in participating. She is aware of group process and facilitates the group as necessary.

Use of the material is evaluated throughout implementation and upon completion. It is essential that the worker ensures that the material is effective, helpful, and not harmful. Evaluation is done at both the individual and group level. The worker seeks feedback and uses her own professional evaluation of the experience.

Learning to use the change process is frequently an aspect of prevention groups. Because problem solving and decision making are important elements in prevention, learning these skills as they apply to situations that place members at risk is part of most prevention groups. The change process may not be specifically taught to the group but role-playing and practicing situations related to the prevention goal leads to learning problem-solving and decision-making skills that are related to the change process.

The change process is used by the worker within and outside of the group. Using the change process with individual group members is covered in Chapter 3. The worker uses the change process in working with groups in terms of assessing the group and its members, planning activities, taking actions to implement the activities, evaluating the results, and facilitating termination at the end of each session and when the group ends.

In many prevention groups, members need to learn about resources that will alleviate their situation or will provide alternatives to the circumstances that they face. As with other groups, the worker may also need to use this in helping individual group members address situations outside of the group. The worker uses the process for doing this that is identified in Chapter 3. The worker should be prepared to use mediation or advocacy when group members are denied services for which they seem to be qualified.

The group worker's use of actions that are empowering and enabling are especially relevant for prevention groups. Empowerment and enabling are typically necessary if members are to overcome the situations that they face that place them at risk. Identifying members as being at risk is likely to mean that they are members of populations who are not empowered. Essentially, prevention activities are designed to provide opportunities for group members to acquire new knowledge and skills that will empower them in dealing with their circumstances and enable them to overcome or transcend those circumstances. For example, in a drug prevention group for youth who live in areas with elevated drug activity, members need to be empowered to resist using drugs and enabled to use new or strengthened skills in doing so. It is hoped that these youth will be able to avoid using drugs in spite of all the influences in their environment that would make it more likely that they would. This takes a considerable amount of empowerment. It is hoped that by discussing and practicing these skills in the group, members will be empowered and enabled in using them outside of the group. Group members need to be empowered and enabled so they have more confidence in their skills and abilities in dealing with these situations. At the very least, they will be exposed to alternative ways of dealing with them. People are not likely to try something new unless they are empowered to do so. The group experience can help to build confidence in using new skills and techniques as members hear each other and observe each other and practice skills. Members may gain enough confidence to try these skills in their everyday lives. Belonging to a group is very empowering, along with receiving support from the group for trying new skills and abilities.

As with growth and development groups, crisis intervention is not used very often in prevention groups. However, in any group, members may experience crises and the worker may need to provide this service or refer the member to a service that will address their needs. This is typically done outside of the group for individual members who are identified as needing assistance with situations that have overwhelmed them. Crisis intervention is covered in Chapter 3. However, the same types of crises that we discussed with growth and development groups can occur in prevention groups as the groups engage in various activities. These include injuries or other health crises. In addition, by virtue of being a member of an at risk population, most members will experience many forms of crises in their life outside of the group. Thus, the worker needs to be prepared to use crisis intervention when the situation requires this type of action.

In groups that involve physical activity, the worker should be trained in basic first aid and CPR or have someone on hand who is trained. Water rescue, revival, and CPR are required for water activities. The sponsoring organization should have policies and procedures and risk management plans that will cover these types of activities if staff are expected to use them in their work.

Acquiring new knowledge and skills includes learning to apply these in group members' everyday lives. If the group is the only place in which members use their new skills, then they will not gain much benefit from being in the group. Members need to use what they learn in the group to deal with situations outside of the group. To facilitate this, the worker needs to ensure that activities can be related to people's everyday lives. This requires modifying activities and program materials and using situations that are relevant for members. It also means facilitating the group in providing support for members in using their skills outside of the group.

The worker uses mediation in assisting members to overcome barriers to needed services. This typically occurs outside of the group and is generally the first choice of action by the worker before advocacy. In mediation, the worker remains neutral and brings the group member and a system in the environment together and to reach agreement about service delivery. In advocacy, the worker takes the group member's side and uses influence to obtain services. Mediation is also used when conflicts arise in the group. When conflicts arise during the early stages of group development or when group members have a fight, argument, or disagreement, the worker needs to intervene and mediate. This is fairly common in groups of children and adolescents, especially those made up of certain at risk populations where conflict is a part of their everyday lives. Learning to give and take, to negotiate and compromise is key to helping members to control their behavior within and outside of the group.

The worker engages in actions to facilitate group formation, facilitate discussion, resolve conflict, enhance group interaction, facilitate group development, and structure group activities. These are described in Chapter 4 and are embedded in much of what we describe in this chapter and in earlier chapters in Part Two. These are not repeated here, but their application to prevention groups are discussed.

Groups typically progress through the stages of group development. As they do, members need to interact in a way that helps the group in achieving its purpose. The worker facilitates the group in a way that maximizes success and ensures maximum benefit for group members. Thus, both content and process are important in all types of groups. Group process is not highlighted much in professional literature on prevention groups. It is important that the worker understand group process and the meaning behind group actions and interactions of members in the group. The worker uses her understanding to identify the stage of development that the group is in at any point in time. It is also an indication of the progress toward achieving the purpose of the group. In addition, understanding group process gives the worker insight into group dynamics that may be constructive or destructive for the group or certain members For example, some members may seek to use the group for their own benefit. They may try to retaliate for incidents within or outside of the group or seek to exclude certain members. Understanding group process can give the worker some ideas about how to handle these situations.

During the functional stage, the group should be accomplishing its purpose and members should be participating. The worker evaluates the extent to which the group is effective and tries to understand why it is or is not. The worker continues to facilitate activities that appear to be effective and modifies or plans other activities when they are not. The worker solicits feedback and uses it to improve the functioning of the group and its members.

## The Change Process During the Disintegration Stage

Disintegration with prevention groups can occur at any time, especially during the early stages of the group. It can occur any time there is insufficient membership to sustain the group. Group members of prevention groups tend to be quite elusive and may not be very reliable in attendance. High attrition can be expected unless there is a ready pool of members, as in a school or neighborhood or community center. Ongoing groups will probably need ongoing recruitment efforts to ensure a steady membership. Direct recruitment of potential members or contact with human service providers who have clients who would benefit is usually best. Members who enjoy the group are likely to be a strong source for new members. High visibility and frequent reminders are helpful in maintaining membership.

Most prevention groups are time limited, everyone knows when termination is scheduled to take place and the group goes through it together. In most ongoing groups, termination is more focused on individual members who reach a point at which they are ready to leave the group. For prevention groups, members tend to drop out without warning rather than announcing their departure. If they do announce it, this typically takes place at their last meeting, perhaps even at the end of it.

While disintegration is marked by a lessening of bonds within the group, for prevention groups the bonds may not be that strong to begin with or members may know one another outside of the group so the bonds within the group are not remarkably different from bonds outside of the group. During disintegration, the frequency and strength of group cohesion are reduced, along with interaction, common norms and values among group members, and the strength of the influence that the group has on members. At the same time, members should be increasing their interaction with their ecosystem outside of the group.

In time-limited groups, members tend to hold back from investing too much of themselves in the group because of the time limitation. In addition, prevention groups may be characterized by a much lower level of investment to begin with because members may not have particularly positive experiences with relationships and may even have serious issues with feelings of abandonment. The circumstances that make them at risk may also make them less likely to emotionally invest in others. Some members may invest, but not necessarily in the group. They may bond with a smaller circle of friends in the group or they might have a stronger bond with the worker than with the group. The bonds in these types of groups may not be very close. These factors may make disintegration more likely to occur.

In time-limited groups that retain membership, the group goes through disintegration together. The tasks are the same as any situation in which termination takes place. The worker and the group need to recognize gains members have made and help members to feel good about the experience. The worker reminds the group of the ending date about three or four sessions before it occurs. Typically, some sort of celebration is planned that highlights the positive aspects of the group experience and the progress that has been achieved. A mini-graduation ceremony with certificates is helpful, as some members may never have received any such recognition.

It is expected that some disintegration will occur as members drop out or leave the group in ongoing groups. Most of these will have some type of rotating series of sessions and do not build on each other so that anyone can join at any point and finish the cycle. Some ongoing groups are themselves drop-ins in which members come and go regularly.

In open, ongoing groups, the constant change in membership changes the group each time membership changes. Group dynamics are changed and how the group functions changes. Changing membership makes it difficult for the group to achieve anything beyond the most basic goals. The bonds in these groups are not very strong unless members know each other well outside of the group.

Changing membership requires some structure to quickly incorporate new members and help the group move quickly through reformation to the functional stage. Typically each session is a stand alone session or a mini-intervention. Ideally, there will be enough structure and enough regular members for the group to maintain itself while helping new members to feel welcome and find a place for themselves in the group. Disintegration occurs at the end of each session.

As with other groups, the worker assesses the needs of the group and its members during the disintegration stage. In an ongoing group, a member or the worker may be terminating, but the group will continue. Members may or may not announce that they are leaving. For the rare ongoing prevention group in the community, the group should adopt the norm of expecting members to announce when they intend to leave the group. However, members may not adhere to this norm and will tend to deal with termination in the same way as they do in their life outside of the group. It is not unusual for members in prevention groups to attend only sporadically throughout the group and as they transition out of the group. The group as a whole may feel threatened if membership dwindles and the worker may need to intervene to bolster attendance. Making contact with some of the members who have left or are not attending may be enough to get some of them to return.

Members of prevention groups may be lost due to death. Those who live in high-crime areas or who have high-risk medical conditions may die. When members die, group members need to mourn their loss. It is not unusual for members of prevention groups to know one another outside of the group; while the bonds in the group may not be very strong, members may have relationships outside of the group that are. The worker facilitates the group and members in progressing through the stages of the grief process as appropriate. At the very least, the worker should lead the group in a moment of silence and perhaps help them to reminisce about the member who has died.

Premature departures are likely to take place in most prevention groups, although this may not be readily predictable for individual members. Because the group is made up of members who are at risk and because low attendance can easily be a threat to the survival of the group, it is generally important for the worker to follow up when a member drops out or does not attend.

The group will generally need some type of closure when the group ends, which typically means going around the group, having members have their last say, and reviewing their experiences. Members should be encouraged to wish one another well and recall positive activities that they will take with them as memories. The worker will typically need to model this for the group by being the first to recall something uplifting.

As with other groups, disintegration can occur for a group that is intended to be an ongoing group, although ongoing prevention groups are not very common. For those that are ongoing, this represents a crisis, because the continuation of the group is in question. Attendance is probably dropping or sporadic. The worker needs to decide if it might be time to let the group end or if efforts should be made to save the group. If the worker decides to try to save the group, he may need to contact members who are not attending to encourage them to return. Aggressive recruitment will be needed to bring new members on board if it is an ongoing group. For time-limited groups, the worker needs to determine changes that will keep the group going. He needs to decide if it is worthwhile to attempt these changes. Sometimes, workers will offer a group and no one comes or people come but they do not stay. This is especially true for prevention groups because of the nature of the population from which most groups are drawn.

A group might begin to disintegrate because there are personal conflicts. Since many prevention groups have members who know each other outside of the group, conflicts from outside of the group can be brought into the group and conflicts within the group can carry over to relationships outside of the group. Resolving these are important so that the group can function effectively and continue to attract members. Changing activities or seating arrangements or the like might resolve the conflict, but often a more direct action is needed. The worker needs to mediate the conflict or assist the group in doing so. It may be necessary to do this outside of the group, perhaps after the group session. At the very least, the worker may need to do this away from the group, for example, outside of the room or off to the side while the rest of the group is involved in an activity. As in any situation in which there is conflict, the worker should maintain a mediating position and refrain from taking sides. He has both parties express their concerns and asks for their input in resolving the matter. If it cannot be resolved, the group may be threatened or a member or members may be asked to leave. Arrangements should be made for everyone to receive other services.

As the group begins to disintegrate and terminate, the worker evaluates the situation and helps the group to evaluate the experience. Members should review what they have accomplished. They should be asked for feedback about what was helpful and what was not or what they enjoyed. Throughout the group, the worker evaluates the group and the members and tries to anticipate premature disintegration or departures. When membership lags or attendance becomes sporadic, he tries to revitalize the group. In an ongoing group, he recruits new members.

As with other groups, if the worker is leaving an ongoing group or a time-limited one with a longer time period, there is a high risk of disintegration. The worker should not start a time-limited group unless he plans on completing the group. Most prevention groups will end completely when the worker leaves, unless another worker is able to establish a relationship with the group beforehand. The most common reason for the worker to leave is for another position either within or outside of the agency.

As we mentioned earlier, less common reasons for the worker to leave may include being laid off or fired; having the agency or program close; or becoming ill or disabled, or dying; Most prevention groups will not survive these situations and those that do are likely to be seriously depleted. If the group is ending for any of these reasons, an effort needs to be made to help resolve any issues related to the worker leaving or the group ending when members are informed about these circumstances. Typically, the supervisor should handle this if the worker is no longer available. The assumption should be that resolution needs to occur immediately as it is highly unlikely that anyone will return for another session.

Dealing with situations in which a worker leaves an ongoing prevention group and new workers join such groups is quite rare and very similar to what we describe earlier.

Terminating prevention group sessions is not usually very difficult, especially if members are enjoying a snack at the end. Typically, when they are done with the snack they will leave or will take it with them. However, terminating the session before snack time may be somewhat chaotic, especially with children, as they sense the ending and begin to anticipate snack time. The worker should help the group to establish norms around this and a routine that will help to maintain some focus and order.

## Summary

As with other groups, the worker uses the change process at each stage of development in facilitating prevention groups. She engages in assessment and planning before the group begins. She also does this during each session and between each session. She facilitates the group's progress through each stage of development. If it is an open or ongoing group, she helps the group to establish a routine for efficiently incorporating new members. The worker provides activities that facilitate the group in accomplishing its purpose during the functional stage. She helps the group to support members as they consider ways to prevent difficulties that place them at risk. She helps members to consolidate gains as the group is ending or they are leaving the group during the disintegration stage. The worker uses her relationship skills and her skills as a social worker to facilitate the group and make it a positive, enjoyable experience. The social worker develops skills in both the art and the science of facilitating prevention groups.

CASE **9.1**

## Substance Use Prevention Group for Youth

Roshanda and Juan are both employed at a program serving youth. The program offers drop-in recreation; an alternative education program for youth who are suspended from school; and numerous clubs that offer activities such as ceramics, photography, arts and crafts, and the like. Some of the programs that are offered are prevention groups that are aimed at drugs and alcohol use and others on delinquency. Each group is structured for different ages. The age range for the program is nine to eighteen. There are prevention groups for nine to eleven, twelve to fourteen, fifteen and sixteen, and seventeen and eighteen. The older age groups provide mentoring to younger ages as a part of their group experience. The youth come primarily from a mixed racial and ethnic background and are generally of a lower socioeconomic status. Many are from single-parent homes.

Roshanda and Juan are facilitating a mixed group of twelve- to fourteen-year-olds with both males and females. The purpose of the group is to help members to resist using drugs and alcohol. There is a set of program materials that is available and Roshanda and Juan have modified it to fit the needs of this group. The group is voluntary and so they must find ways to attract members to the group. They have found that a combination of using games to get the information across followed by a snack seems to work well. The group meets twice a week on certain dates and times, but the membership tends to fluctuate somewhat as the same members are not always attending the program on the same day. However, there is a small cadre of regulars who seem to be in the building almost every day and are regular attendees.

As the first participants trickle in, they show an intense interest in what the snack is for the day. Roshanda and Juan have heard this before and are not discouraged by the apparent focus on the snack. They are confident that the participants are getting something from the group and the activities as evidenced by the intense competition in the games. Roshanda and Juan use various team sports to get across the material for the day. There is generally a brief presentation, a guest speaker, or a video to start the meeting. This is followed by a question-and-answer game that is used as a stand-in for an actual sport. For example, sometimes the group chooses sides for baseball teams. Correctly answering a question is a hit. An incorrect answer is an out. Runs are scored as base runners are moved around the bases. Games using football, basketball, and hockey are employed in a similar manner, with correct answers representing yardage in football, baskets in basketball, and shots in hockey. For football, everyone starts at the goal line. Every correct answer moves the ball ten yards. Four incorrect answers results in turning the ball over to the other team. For hockey, a variation that is used is allowing the other team to make a save by answering another question correctly. If the answer is not correct, then the shot results in a goal.

Questions include both factual information about drugs and alcohol along with questions about how to avoid or refuse using them. Using these games to get the youth to learn the material has proven to be very successful. When the session is nearing the end, each member takes a brief quiz on the material and they enjoy a snack.

## QUESTIONS

1. Using Table 6.1, develop a plan for a prevention group.

2. Describe how you would use assessment skills during various stages of the group from Question 1 or another group.

3. Describe how you would use planning during various stages of the group from Question 1 or another group.

4. Describe how you would use direct practice actions during various stages of the group from Question 1 or another group.

5. Describe how you would use group facilitation skills during various stages of the group from Question 1 or another group.

6. Describe how you would use evaluation during various stages of the group from Question 1 or another group.

7. Describe how you would deal with disintegration or termination during various stages of the group from Question 1 or another group.

## SUGGESTED READINGS

Johnson, Louise C., and Yanca, Stephen J., *Social Work Practice: A Generalist Approach*, 9th ed. Boston: Allyn & Bacon, 2007 (Chapter 14).

Edwards, Richard L., Ed. *Encyclopedia of Social Work,* 19th ed. Washington, DC: NASW Press, 1995 ("Group Practice Overview").

Gitterman, Alex, and Shulman, Lawrence. *Mutual Aid Groups, Vulnerable and Resilient Populations, and the Life Cycle,* 3rd ed. New York: Columbia University Press, 2005.

Grief, Geoffrey, and Ephross, Paul, Eds. *Group Work with Populations at Risk.* 2nd ed. New York: Oxford University Press, 2005.

Ivey, Allen E., Pederson, Paul B., and Ivey, Mary Bradford. *Intentional Group Counseling: A Microskills Approach.* Belmont, CA: Thomson/Wadsworth, 2001.

Jacobs, Ed, Masson, Robert, and Harvill, Riley. *Group Counseling Strategies and Skills.* 5th ed. Pacific Grove, CA: Brooks/Cole, 2006.

Johnson, David W., and Johnson, Frank P. *Joining Together: Group Theory and Group Skills*, 9th ed. Boston: Allyn & Bacon, 2006.

Kottler, Jeffery. *Learning Group Leadership: An Experiential Approach.* Boston: Allyn and Bacon, 2001.

Northern, Helen, and Kurland, Roselle. *Social Work with Groups,* 3rd ed. New York: Columbia University Press, 2001.

Shulman, Lawrence. *The Skills of Helping: Individuals, Families, Groups, and Communities,* 6th ed. Belmont, CA: Thomson-Brooks/Cole, 2009.

Toseland, Ronald W., and Rivas, Robert F. *An Introduction to Group Work Practice,* 6th ed. Boston: Allyn & Bacon, 2009.

# PART THREE

# Generalist Practice with Organizations and Communities

Generalist practice includes working with organizations and communities to bring about change on behalf of client systems. This is an essential aspect of social work practice with clients at risk of discrimination and oppression. Current and historical attitudes and actions have denied these groups equal access to political, economic, and social power. Although most forms of discrimination are illegal, barriers still exist and prejudice seems firmly embedded in U.S. society. Practice with these groups that only focuses on the person or family and the immediate environment may not bring about real change.

A cardinal value of social work is that people should be able to have socially accepted needs met in socially accepted ways. If people are expected to give up some freedom so that everyone's rights are protected, then they have a right to expect that their rights will be respected as well. A just society is one in which everyone has an equal opportunity to participate in its political, economic, and social benefits. A major concern of social work has been a commitment to promote social justice and to challenge injustice. Most often this takes the form of advocating for clients when they are denied services or resources. It is also embodied in cause advocacy and social action organizing.

It takes courage to fight prejudice and discrimination. We as social workers must adopt the attitude that we will not tolerate intolerance. We must stand up for what is right and just. However, it is not enough for social workers to merely react when social injustice occurs. Taking a proactive approach to organization and community practice is also needed. Social workers must constantly be aware of opportunities to bring about change in their organizations, in other organizations, and in the community that will improve opportunities, especially for groups that have been oppressed. We must have the courage of our convictions in pursuing equitable treatment for all of our citizens. Social workers use their skills on behalf of clients to facilitate needed changes in the agency, the human service network, and the community. They assist in assessing needs, planning programs, and developing resources, and they act to bring about changes that will ensure equal opportunity for everyone. They speak up on behalf of those who are not able to speak for themselves. They practice in a way that empowers and enables those who cannot feel or experience their own power. They use their influence to support these changes. In doing so, they support their professional organizations on a state and national level as well.

Part Three deals with the change process in generalist social work practice with macrosystems. This includes working with organizations and communities. Chapter 10 examines the organization as a social system. It includes a schema for studying a social agency. Chapter 11 describes the change process with organizations, with a focus on groups in organizations. Often, part of the business of organizations takes place in various groups within the organization. The change process within organizations frequently involves the use of task groups. The generalist social worker needs to be knowledgeable about her role in various groups and how to facilitate task groups so she can work within the organizational structure and can advocate for change as needed. Chapter 12 examines the community as a social system. It includes a schema for studying a community. Chapter 13 describes the change process with communities, with a focus on groups that are typically used to bring about community change.

# 10 Generalist Practice with Organizations

1. Understanding the need to work with organizations in generalist practice.
2. Understanding organizations as social systems.
3. Knowledge of organizational structure in generalist practice.
4. Knowledge of organizational management in generalist practice.
5. Understanding working in a bureaucracy as a generalist social worker.
6. Understanding the change process in working with organizations.

This chapter deals with the change process in generalist social work practice with organizations. It is rare for the BSW-level worker or an inexperienced MSW to be called on to work directly with organizations as client systems in bringing about change. However, social workers typically work in organizations and as they do, they are inevitably involved in groups within the organization and at times may represent the organization in groups with representatives of other organizations.

Working within an organization and working with other organizations on behalf of clients require that the worker understand the structure and functioning of organizations. As she works for and with organizations, the worker may become involved with the change process as a member of the agency staff and as a participant in task groups with other organizations. When the social worker engages in these activities, she acts on behalf of clients to ensure that changes that are made at the organizational level benefit clients who are in need of services and resources. The worker brings her knowledge and skill in working with groups and in assessment, planning, direct and indirect practice actions, and evaluation to working with organizations.

This consideration of generalist practice with organizations will be from the point of view of BSW and MSW social workers who are practicing in human service organizations. It is not intended to be comprehensive enough for managers or administrators to use as a tool for managing organizations. It is assumed that more detailed study would be needed that would include education and training specifically designed for this purpose. There are entire textbooks devoted to management. In fact, there are entire books devoted to each individual approach to management. Our purpose here is to educate the beginning generalist social worker on working within organizations.

The first part of the chapter examines the organization as a social system. This is followed by a discussion of organizational structure. Next comes a description of management styles from the worker's perspective. A consideration of working with a bureaucracy follows. Finally, there is an examination of the use of the change process in organizations.

## The Organization as a Social System

Social work is an agency-based profession. The **agency** is the immediate environment of the worker–client interaction. This interaction often takes place in an office or building identified as the agency. The influence of the agency is strong even when the interaction takes place elsewhere in the community. As an employee, the worker is a part of the agency system, and because of this the worker is accountable to the agency. The form and content of the service offered must be within the agency's purview and guidelines. The manner in which the agency is structured and functions greatly influences the nature of the worker–client system interaction. Client systems in agencies are typically made up of individuals, families, or groups. The agency also provides resources for both the worker and client systems. To work in and use the agency in service of client systems, the social worker must first understand the agency and its way of functioning.

Social workers not only need to understand the agency in which they are employed, they also need to be able to understand other social agencies. This is important if the worker is to help clients use the resources and services of other agencies. In addition, where needed resources are not available or usable, an understanding of the agency is a prerequisite to bringing about needed change.

From an ecosystems strengths perspective, the agency is a part of the worker's ecosystem and also becomes a temporary part of the client's ecosystem as the helping process develops. In addition, the agency has an ecosystem that is made up of the community. An important component of the agency's ecosystem is the human service delivery system within the community of which the agency is a part. Understanding the agency as a system and as a part of the larger ecosystem is essential to maximizing access to important resources for growth and change.

Agencies in which social workers are employed vary according to type and organization. Some are exclusively social work agencies. They provide social services delivered by professional social workers (MSW or BSW). A family service agency is an example. The family service agency may, however, have a homemaker service or use nonprofessional workers in other ways. A family service agency is a voluntary agency; that is, it has a governing board of citizens and raises money for its support in the community (either separately or with other agencies). Once voluntary agencies did not use governmental funds, but since public funds have been used to purchase service from private agencies, this is no longer true.

Other social workers are employed by a variety of governmental agencies in what is known as the *public sector*. These agencies are often state and/or federally funded. The worker is regulated by law and by governmental policies and regulations. Other social workers are employed in what is known as *host* or *secondary* settings. In this kind of setting, the primary function of the setting is not social service; social services are used to enhance the primary service. An example of this kind of setting is a social worker in a hospital. In other settings, the social worker is part of an interdisciplinary team. The prime focus may be social service, or it may be some other service. Work in a community mental health center is an example of this kind of setting. Barbara Oberhofer Dane and Barbara L. Simon pointed out that social workers in host settings have predictable issues that they must address. These include value discrepancies between social workers and the primary discipline in an agency, an often marginal status assigned to social work in such settings, devaluing social work as woman's work, and role ambiguity and role strain.[1] Thus, agencies vary with respect to several dimensions: size, means of support and governance, nature of the primary service offered, and range of people who are employed.

Before a worker can effectively deliver service as a professional in a bureaucratic organization, the worker must first understand the organization. A social systems approach, again, is a means for developing that understanding.

The first task in understanding an agency is to define its boundaries. The entity that operates with a great enough degree of autonomy so that a unique structure and ways of functioning have developed—in which the influences within the structure are stronger than those without—might be identified as the agency. In a Veterans Administration hospital, the social services department might be the choice as the primary system for focus if interaction among departments is limited largely to department heads. If the interaction is greater within a team of doctor, nurse, and social worker, then the unit team might be considered the agency. Because both kinds of interaction are important, however, the total institution might be the better choice. None of these answers is completely adequate. Whatever set of boundaries is used, it should be one that defines the entity with the greatest influence on the worker–client interaction.

The second task is to determine environmental factors that influence the structure and functioning of the agency. These influences involve other social systems and broad socioeconomic factors, including those that impact the agency either by providing resources or by placing expectations. Some of the social systems that may need to be considered include the following:

1. Any organization or system of which the agency is a part (e.g., a national membership organization, a statewide organization, or an institution of which the social services department is a part)
2. The community (or communities) from which clients come or that provides support for the agency
3. Professional organizations to which the workers belong
4. Foundations or other sources of support
5. Community planning and funding bodies
6. Governmental bodies that regulate or supply support for the services
7. Colleges and universities that educate for the professions employed
8. Other social agencies
9. Individuals, families, and groups who are clients or potential clients
10. Organizations such as churches and service clubs that may be resources to the agency or its clients

Socioeconomic forces that should be considered include the following:

1. Economic trends
2. Societal trends
3. Community expectations

4. Community need
5. Political forces
6. Governmental policies or regulations
7. Cultural and diversity needs within the community

The third task is to understand the structure and functioning of the agency system. The factors involved include:

1. *The purposes, objectives, and values of the system*—These are spelled out in articles of incorporation, enabling legislation, agency handbooks, mission statements, and other official documents. Also important is how these formal expressions are interpreted and implemented in actual service delivery. The agency's value priorities influence this interpretation and implementation. The history of the agency is important in determining how the purposes, objectives, and values developed.

2. *Agency resources, including financial resources*—Resources include the funds provided by the community, through either gifts or tax money; the building or other physical structures the agency leases or owns; and the people, both paid and volunteer, including professional and support staff.

3. *The traditional ways of working*—Each agency tends to use particular approaches in its service (such as long-term counseling, crisis intervention, provision of specific resources, group work activity). This can also include specific theoretical approaches, such as task centered, psychoanalytic, and so on. Agencies tend to work with particular systems, individuals, families, groups, or communities. They tend to hire workers with particular educational backgrounds for specific tasks (e.g., MSW, BSW, college graduates, persons indigenous to the community). They have particular patterns of work (e.g., case management, teams).

4. *Boards or other governing bodies*—An important consideration is the method of sanctioning the agency (public or private). If public, the laws, policies, and other regulations that govern the agency and the organizational structure of the larger organization of which the agency is a part should be identified. If private, the structure and functioning of the board of directors are the focus. Members of the board and their motivations and needs are also important, as is the relationship of the governing body to the agency and its staff. Another element is the committee structure and functioning. This structure can be one of the board, the staff, or a combination of the two. It is often in committees that new ideas are formulated, that the work of the organization is carried out.

5. *The organizational structure*—This includes both the formal and informal structure, the administrative style, the accepted norms and values, the decision-making and communication processes, and the power and control patterns.

6. *The staff*—Important considerations include who they are as both persons and professionals; the relationships among staff (formal and informal); and the relationship of staff, clients, administration, and governing body. The professional identification and qualifications of staff should also be considered.

7. *The clients*—Often clients are overlooked as a part of the agency system. Without them the agency would have no reason for existence. In an age of consumer advocacy, this

aspect of agency functioning takes on new importance. Consideration should be given to client needs, expectations, and ways of relating to the agency. The status, designation (consumer, patient, student, etc.), and values relating to clients should also be considered.

**8.** *Diversity*—Diversity within the agency and other agencies is an important consideration. Some questions to consider are the following: What are the hiring practices of the agency that assure a diverse staff? Are there appropriate attitudes and stereotypes? How do policies and procedures affect service to diverse groups? Do some groups feel excluded because of expectations for receiving help?

Each of these aspects of the structure and functioning of the agency system may overlap with other aspects. In developing understanding of an agency, workers should be aware of these overlaps and of the relationships and linkages between the various aspects. Workers also need to be aware of any special aspects of their agency that affect its structure and functioning. In order to gather the information needed for understanding an agency, an organized framework is often useful, such as Table 10.1.

## Organizational Structure

There are several ways of viewing organizations. Exploring each of them is beyond the scope of this text. Instead, we present a basic approach to working within organizations with various types of structure. In examining the structure of the organization, the worker needs to consider both vertical and horizontal structure. Vertical structure looks at the layers within the organization. The more layers there are, the more vertical is the organization. Bureaucracies are considered to have a high level of vertical structure. At the other extreme are organizations that are less vertical, or flat. Smaller agencies may have only two levels, an executive director and direct service staff. Horizontal structure refers to the breadth or span of the organization. The primary consideration with horizontal structure is the number of staff and the various programs that an organization has. Organizations with a wide horizontal structure will have more direct service staff or will have more different programs than an organization that is relatively narrow in terms of horizontal structure.

As organizations grow, they tend to become more complex. With growth, there is a need to consider the impact of both horizontal and vertical growth on the functioning of the organization and its staff and on the delivery of services to clients. As organizations add layers and become more bureaucratic, staff at upper levels of the organization get further away from the level at which services are delivered. The risk with this development is that decisions that are made at higher levels will be less relevant to service delivery and may even be harmful. At the same time, the cost of operating the agency may increase as higher paid staff are added to each layer of the organization and the organization adds more layers.

Typically, as organizations grow they add administrative positions in a similar pattern. Increasing the size of a small agency with one administrator generally means adding one or more supervisors. In most organizations, each supervisor should probably be responsible for a maximum of about ten staff. Some agencies may have a higher ratio than this, but the ability of a supervisor to maintain sufficient knowledge of program operations, clients, records, and the like becomes much more difficult. We believe that the ideal maximum size for most organizations is probably about six to eight direct services staff for each supervisor.

The next layer that is usually added is one or more assistant directors. In medium-size agencies, this level will be responsible for overseeing the daily operation of the agency and would typically supervise three to six supervisors. The ideal maximum size before there is a serious loss of hands-on knowledge about the programs will vary, depending on the size of the caseloads, the size of the budgets, the number of supervisors or programs, and the number of geographical locations. The next layer is usually referred to as program directors. This layer would be added between the assistant director level and the supervisor level and would have a similar expected maximum load as an assistant director in a medium-size organization. Some organizations may add program directors before an assistant director is added. In larger agencies, another level may be added, often called division directors. This layer is typically added between assistant director and program director levels.

Ideally, each program director has three or four supervisors. Each division director has three program directors and each assistant director has three division directors. Finally, there should be a maximum of three assistant directors. These sizes may vary somewhat, depending on the services of the agency, the size of the client population, the geographical area covered, and the like. The more geographical locations, the smaller the ratio should be of these layers of administration. Similarly, substantial differences in service delivery require smaller ratios. There is a huge difference between providing oversight to one on-site program with several staff versus several on-site programs that provide a variety of services. There is also a huge difference between an on-site program and having the same program offered at several sites. Oversight becomes even more complex when there is a variety of programs located at a variety of sites.

Some human services organizations have begun using the same terms used in business for upper-level administrators. Instead of calling the top administrator the *executive director*, the title is *president* and assistant directors are referred to as *vice presidents*. Typically, other levels are still called the titles we have discussed above.

Organizations that grow but remain relatively flat also run the risk of losing control or oversight over the functioning of all of their programs. In addition, programs that are located in widely dispersed geographical locations are not likely to receive much supervision from higher-level managers, even in organizations with greater vertical structure let alone those that are relatively flat.

Social workers need to be aware of the structure of their organization as well as other organizations with which they have contact. They need to understand how the structure of organizations affect their functioning. Often, workers express concern over the bureaucratic functioning of their agency and other organizations, so it is particularly important to understand how to work in a bureaucracy.

## Organizational Management

Most BSWs and inexperienced MSWs will not find themselves in a management position, but all workers are affected by the management style of their organization. There are several approaches to management and the reader can consult texts on their specific styles. In addition, most social work texts summarize and compare several of these approaches.

Generally, most approaches take the viewpoint that the reader is a manager or must learn how to be one. We would like to offer a different perspective, that of the worker. From the worker's perspective, the most important factors in the management style of her organization is the degree to which she is able to participate in decisions that affect her as an employee and as a professional social worker and the degree to which she feels supported in delivering services to her clients. Let us look at what it takes to provide this and what kind of barriers or challenges that might arise when it is missing.

First let us identify what we consider to be good management practices. If direct service workers are to feel supported in providing professional services they need to be treated as professionals. It makes no sense to hire workers for their education, experience, and skills and then not use these in managing the organization. Good managers expect the best out of their staff and provide the support necessary to help them achieve this. Good managers realize that their responsibility is to make it easier for their staff to deliver services to clients. Staff are not hired to make it easier for managers to do their jobs.

A fundamental principle of good management is that employees tend to treat clients the same way they are treated by managers. If workers feel valued, they are more likely to value their clients. If workers feel that they are not valued, it affects their morale and is likely to have a negative affect on how well they serve their clients.

Good managers make their expectations clear to their staff and provide appropriate feedback. Good managers give credit and recognition for a job well done. They are available to solve problems and to support staff in working with difficult situations. They provide supervision that enhances the professional growth of staff. They promote teamwork and professional pride. They advocate for resources that are needed and for appropriate policies and procedures that will assist staff in providing quality services to clients.

Organizations that value their staff provide adequate compensation and benefits and construct personnel policies that ensure that staff have the necessary organizational supports to carry out their duties. Staff should be encouraged and supported in engaging in professional development activities. There should be sufficient sick, personal, and vacation leave in place. Health care benefits should be provided, along with disability and unemployment insurance. These are tangible ways that organizations send messages to staff about how much they are valued.

Good managers provide opportunities for staff to make decisions or to offer input. Most organizations and managers will fall along a continuum regarding the degree to which staff at lower levels participate in decision making. At one extreme are organizations and managers that are mainly authoritarian, decisions are made by managers at the top of the organization and staff are expected to carry these out without questioning them. These organizations tend to be more bureaucratic, but even in small agencies some managers may use this style of management. At the other extreme are those organizations and managers who rely on consensus and include staff at all levels of the organization in making decisions. It is easier to do this in smaller organizations than in larger.

Most organizations and managers are probably somewhere toward the midrange of the continuum. Some decisions may be made top down and others may be bottom up. In some organizations, there are either temporary or permanent structures for making decisions that have various levels of inclusion. In smaller organizations, it may be possible to include all of the staff in certain decisions. In larger organizations, groups may be formed that are made up of representatives from the various levels that are affected by the decisions. Frequently, these groups are charged with developing options and making recommendations, but upper-level management makes the final decision.

## Working in a Bureaucracy

With the growth of a service society, many social workers find employment in bureaucratic settings. They are confronted with the conflict between professional and bureaucratic expectations—with human need, human pain, and societal injustices and with agency policy, rules, and regulations. They are confronted with the slowness of change, the seeming unresponsiveness of the system, and demands for accountability by the bureaucratic agency. They are also confronted with the need to find ways to use the agency and its resources to meet the needs of clients. This calls for a set of skills for functioning in a bureaucracy.

Ralph Morgan identified five roles that social workers have adopted in bureaucratic organizations:

**1.** *Functional bureaucrats*—These workers just happen to be working in a bureaucratic organization. Their major orientation and loyalty are to the profession and its values. They look for interaction with, and recognition from, professional peers. There is resistance to interaction in and with the bureaucracy. These workers are usually very competent practitioners whose services are valued by the agency, so that the agency overlooks their lack of bureaucratic loyalty.

**2.** *Service bureaucrats*—These workers are oriented to the client, but also see themselves as part of the bureaucratic structure. They maintain relationships with both professional peers and agency staff. They are ambivalent about their identification with the agency but believe the agency is the means to help clients reach their goals and to obtain needed resources.

**3.** *Specialist bureaucrats*—These workers attempt to reconcile "bureaucracy to humans and humans to the bureaucracy." They use the rules and regulations but are also guided by professional judgment. They understand that the human condition is so complex that it can never be encompassed by rules and regulations. They seek means of using professional discretion to make the system work in the service of the client. They realize that, like all human endeavors, the agency is imperfect. They have a strong professional identification.

**4.** *Executive bureaucrats*—These workers are oriented to the exercise of power. They are innovators, infighters, and risk takers who tend to enforce bureaucratic norms. They like to manage people, money, and materials.

**5.** *Job bureaucrats*—These workers have a considerable investment in a bureaucratic career. They seek job security. Their primary orientation is to the agency. They adhere to rules and regulations. They also live by the agency norms.[2]

When working in a bureaucratic setting, a combination of characteristics of the functional bureaucrat, the service bureaucrat, the specialist bureaucrat, and the executive bureaucrat seems most effective. This combination of characteristics should include a professional loyalty, a client orientation, a mediation stance, a sense of realism, a search for areas of discretionary freedom, a respect for rules and regulations, and an innovative approach to services. This is a tall order for a young, inexperienced worker but one that should be attempted. It would seem, then, that the issue is not professional versus bureaucratic but rather a search for means to combine the best of the professional with the best of the bureaucratic.

Robert Pruger has pointed out the necessity for learning bureaucratic skills at a time when it is increasingly impossible to deliver professional service without being a bureaucrat. He indicated that one can be a "good bureaucrat." A first step to developing these skills is the realization and acceptance of the reality that a career in social work will involve work in and with bureaucracies. He sees the key to being effective in a bureaucracy as maintaining the greatest amount of discretion possible. To maintain this discretionary power, a worker must be self-directive. The worker who expects to be told every move to make soon loses this power. The good bureaucrat also knows how to negotiate stresses, opportunities, and constraints. According to Pruger, the worker does this by:

1. Staying with it, not giving up on the first try
2. Maintaining vitality and independence of thought
3. Being responsible by understanding legitimate authority
4. Conserving energy, working only on some issues, and choosing issues that are worth the effort[3]

The bureaucracy, like all human institutions, is meant to serve society's needs. The social worker who can help the social service bureaucracy meet the needs of people can become a valuable employee. This can give the worker leverage to obtain the needed discretion. Another means of gaining this leverage is to gain the competence the agency sees as important. For example, if the agency is developing the case management approach to working with some clients, then the worker should seek information, go to workshops, and collect material about this way of working with clients. In order to maintain discretionary power, it is important for a social worker to demonstrate good judgment. Part of this good judgment is the ability to make decisions that are in compliance with agency rules and regulations, that do not cause negative community reactions, and that lead to effective service to clients. Another part of good judgment is doing the right thing at the right time. The attributes of self-directedness and good judgment are possible when social workers have a realistic sense of their professional self, when they use a knowledge base in making decisions, and when they develop a repertoire of skills.

Some ways in which workers can enhance their effectiveness are the following:

1. Don't seek blame; rather, spend the energy available on seeking solutions.
2. Learn to do a lot with a little. Be realistic about the resources available and make them stretch as far as possible.
3. Be comfortable with uncertainty, ambiguity, and inconsistency. When these are present, discretion is necessary.
4. Be self-confident, creative, and responsible.

The use of supervision can be an effective means of becoming a good bureaucrat. The supervisor can provide a great deal of information about the agency, what is happening, and what is allowable. The worker can negotiate with the supervisor for a degree of discretion. The supervisor can be a sounding board for new ideas. To use the supervisory process effectively, the worker must take responsibility for bringing questions and problems to the supervisor. The supervisor needs to have some knowledge of the problems that exist for the worker in order to defend him when questions arise from other parts of the system.

Social workers get into difficulty in a bureaucracy when they make unfounded decisions or do not determine the feasibility of plans they make. Problems also develop if their concerns are not focused, but instead take the form of vague complaints. The expectation that change will take place overnight also can cause difficulty. An understanding of what the agency is trying to do and what is expected of the worker is a base on which to develop effective service. A thorough understanding of the agency as a social system is a prerequisite for being a good bureaucrat.

The development of managed care means adding another layer of bureaucracy to the service delivery system. Under these systems, decisions regarding the amount of service are no longer left to the worker and the client but are reviewed by another agency or entity. Managed care also has had an impact on how workers provide services and on how they document their work. Assessments may need to be reviewed prior to approving services, and justification is required if service continues beyond the allotted number of sessions. This means that documentation and service delivery are more closely tied together. The amount of service is usually prescribed by the diagnosis. Social workers in mental health typically have been reluctant to diagnose, since mental health care is based on a disease-based, medical model of service. This reluctance leads many workers to give the most benign diagnosis for the symptoms presented. Under managed care, this generally means briefer service. Thus, it is important to obtain accurate assessment and diagnosis to ensure appropriate services are available.

Social workers are in a good position to adapt to changes brought about by managed care and various forms of limiting services. Their skills in negotiating systems, problem solving, and advocacy are needed by agencies and clients operating within this new environment. Social workers will need to promote the development of prevention approaches and adequate aftercare services to ensure that support for change endures beyond the formal intervention period. Increasingly, managed care companies have employed social workers as service reviewers. Workers employed by companies that are committed to quality service as well as efficiency may find a comfortable niche in facilitating the maximum effective use of limited resources. However, those employed by a company that overemphasizes profits or limiting services will find that ethical dilemmas make it nearly impossible to survive with a commitment to social work values and ethics intact.

The development of managed care and the competition for scarcer resources have added to stress. Workers must account for their decisions and have external and sometimes arbitrary limits placed on the time for providing service. In addition, competition or limits on funding may threaten the survival of the agency. Workers feel stress about job security or how their jobs might change. One phenomenon that has received considerable attention is *worker burnout*. Christina Maslach described this as "helping professionals losing positive feelings, sympathy, and respect for their clients or patients."[4] **Burnout** may be a symptom of stress in the agency system. It interferes with a worker's capacity to interact with clients and others in a professional capacity. Martha Bramhall and Susan Ezell described some of the symptoms of burnout as feeling unappreciated, loss of the ability to laugh, being literally sick and tired (suffering from headaches, backaches, stomachaches), feeling exhausted, dreading going to work, or having trouble sleeping.[5] Some people seem particularly susceptible to burnout. They tend to be people who take on too much for long periods of time, in a very intense manner. They are often young and enthusiastic about their work. Another group susceptible to burnout are those who use relationships in the work situation to compensate for a lack of meaningful relationships in their private lives. Workers who feel they cannot achieve their objectives or believe they lack control over their activities also seem particularly vulnerable to burnout.

Social workers need to be sensitive to their functioning and to symptoms of burnout. If they are developing, they should engage in a plan to overcome the burnout. Although stress within the agency system can be a source of burnout, the worker can develop lifestyle changes that allow the worker to function within the system. Identification of the condition is the first step. Once burnout is identified as the source of the difficulty, the worker should pay attention to personal needs that have been slighted. The worker needs a regimen that includes sufficient rest, exercise, good diet, and other positive self-care tasks. The worker should develop a network of personal resources that can help in meeting personal needs. Having a person who can serve as a sounding board and help in analyzing a work situation is particularly useful.[6]

Prevention of burnout should be a goal for all social workers. Preventive measures include providing time and energy for personal needs—the pacing of oneself to provide a time to work and a time for self is important. Developing the skills of a good bureaucrat is also important. This includes taking responsibility for maintaining and enhancing one's sphere of discretion.

Using the strengths perspective can help in reducing worker stress and the potential for burnout. It is a positive approach to helping clients and assumes that necessary resources to meet client needs can be found or developed within the client and the environment. Instead of focusing on deficits, it looks at assets, abilities, and capacities. Even though the worker may still feel stress, she is relieved from the burden of being an expert who is responsible for having answers to client problems. Instead, the client is recognized as an expert in his own life, and the worker uses her expertise as a resource for assisting the client in meeting his own needs.

## Using the Change Process in Organizations

While the BSW or inexperienced MSW social worker is not very likely to be called on to develop a formal organizational study, she needs to understand her organization and other organizations in the community as she works with individuals, families, and groups. She also needs to be able to function within her organization. Thus, the social worker needs to be knowledgeable about the information outlined in Table 10.1. She needs to be able to understand organizations as social systems. She needs to be able to understand how the change process is used by organizations and how to use the change process as she works with and within organizations.

**TABLE 10.1    A Schema for the Study of a Social Agency**

---

**I.** Organizational structure
 **A.** Identify the boundaries of the organization.
 **B.** Discuss the structure of the organization.
  **1.** Mission goals and objectives
   **a.** The purposes, goals, objectives, and value priorities of the organization
   **b.** The purposes, goals, and objectives of each program
  **2.** Describe the organizational structure (include an organizational chart and narrative description).
  **3.** The organization resources
   **a.** Financial (sources and amount)
   **b.** Physical property
   **c.** Staff (paid and volunteer)
 **C.** Identify the organizational structure of any larger organization of which the agency is a part.

**II.** Organizational functioning
 **A.** The sanctioning of the organization (public or private)
  **1.** If public, identify the laws, policy, and regulations that impact on the organization functioning.
  **2.** If private, describe the structure and functioning of the board of directors.
   **a.** Describe the board (describe members as persons and their positions).
   **b.** Describe the roles and responsibilities of the board (both internal to the board and with the rest of the organization).
   **c.** Describe the committee structure and functioning.
  **3.** Describe the means of citizen involvement and input.
 **B.** Describe formal and informal functioning of the organization.
  **1.** Describe the accepted norms and values of the organization.
  **2.** Describe communication processes of the organization.
  **3.** Describe decision making processes of the organization.
  **4.** Describe power and control aspects of the organization.
 **C.** The staff
  **1.** Describe the staff as persons and as professionals, their relationships, diversity, roles, and ways of working with each other and with clients, administration, and governing boards.
  **2.** Identify formal and informal staff groups and describe their functioning.
 **D.** The clients
  **1.** Describe the clients, their diversity, needs, characteristics, expectations, role, and status.
  **2.** Describe the traditional ways of working with clients.
  **3.** Describe the intake and referral system and how the organization obtains clients.
  **4.** Describe the referral network and the organizations that clients are referred to.

**III.** Development
 **A.** Describe the history of the organization.

**IV.** Strengths and challenges
 **A.** Identify the strengths of the organization in terms of serving clients.
 **B.** Identify the challenges the organization experiences in serving clients.

## Assessment in Organizations

The schema in Table 10.1 gives an outline for the content of a typical agency study. Professional consultants on organizations and organizational change will use a much more detailed version that may include additional areas of study. For the typical social worker, developing an understanding of the content of Table 10.1 is sufficient. The process most workers use for assessing an organization tends to be informal. It is important that the worker gain an understanding when he first begins working in an organization. It is also important to understand other organizations that serve the same clients and are part of the human services network. In understanding his own organization, the worker should begin by reading material on the mission, goals, and objectives of the organization and the goals and objectives of the program in which he works. In private nonprofit organizations this might be found in the articles of incorporation or in policy manuals or brochures that advertise the agency or program. Procedure manuals are used to describe how goals and objectives are implemented and may also contain this information. If the program is funded by a grant, the grant itself will typically describe goals and objectives. In public agencies, a public law forms the basis for operating and expending tax dollars. Administrative rules are promulgated that describe the implementation of the law. Manuals containing formal policies and procedures are required, and typically these are placed in binders so that any changes can be easily added. These are the formal versions of goals, objectives, policies, and procedures for the organization and the program.

The organizational chart gives the worker a picture of the structure of the organization. However, all too often it is out of date. In larger organizations, there may be staff assigned to maintain the organizational chart, such as the human resources department. In medium and small agencies, this may not be the case. Often the chart is not updated unless some external source requires it, such as a licensing or accreditation body. Thus, in many organizations the organizational chart may reflect what existed when the last review took place, making it sometimes years out of date. In fact, field instructors often give their students the assignment of updating or creating an organizational chart.

In addition to understanding the formal aspects of the organization, the worker needs to understand the informal system. Formal written documents describe how the organization should function; however, all organizations also develop informal ways of functioning that may not necessarily reflect what is written. Over time, policies and procedures give way to what is called practice, which reflects interpretations of policies and procedures. It is essential that the worker also become knowledgeable about these practices and the extent to which they are acceptable. Since these are not written down in a formalized manner, the worker acquires this knowledge by listening and observing other staff.

As the worker assesses the organization, she learns how it is structured and how it functions. She discovers how various forms of assessment take place. She considers who is responsible for these forms of assessment. Besides assessments that are made in delivering services to clients, organizations need to assess their own functioning. Data need to be accumulated and analyzed regarding the appropriateness of goals and objectives and the ability of the organization to carry out its mission. This may lead to planning new or improved programs or improving other aspects of the organization. Typically, this also includes an evaluation of the effectiveness of the organization and its efficiency. Various members of the administration are usually responsible for these activities, but line staff may be involved in gathering or contributing data. Some forms of assessment are written into policies and procedures and some are superfluous.

## Planning in Organizations

Organizations also need to engage in planning. Plans should reflect the assessments that take place. Some planning is described in policies and procedures and some of it occurs in less formal ways. Because planning often involves spending time or money, it is often tied to the budget and to the fiscal years for the organization. *Fiscal years* is intentionally plural because there may be several fiscal years in an organization's budget. There is the fiscal year that the organization uses for its overall budget, usually coinciding with the calendar year for private organizations. For public organizations and for private organizations funded by public funds, the fiscal year is different. The federal government's fiscal year begins October 1. States may or may not have fiscal years that coincide. There may be grants that are on different fiscal cycles. Thus, some programs within the organization may have fiscal years that are different, depending on the sources of funding.

Plans may be immediate and cover the current or following fiscal year. Other plans may be longer term. Some plans are aimed at maintaining or improving the effectiveness or efficiency of the program and other plans may be related to expanding services or changing them over time. Planning in many organizations tends to be top down. In other words, administrators at higher levels make plans and staff at lower levels are responsible for carrying them out. Sometimes planning is bottom up. In these cases, planning is done by staff at lower levels, such as line staff and supervisors. Generally, this type of planning requires approval from higher-level administration or even the board of the organization. Some organizations are able to combine these and develop plans that have input from upper and lower levels of the organization. The reader may wonder which is best, and the answer is the proverbial "it depends." Some general rules to follow are that all levels of the organization should be involved in some form of planning, but not all levels need to be involved in all planning. Planning should be as inclusive as possible without becoming cumbersome. Inclusiveness should be determined by who is affected by whatever is being planned.

The social worker identifies the types of planning that take place in the organization along with who participates. The worker is involved in the planning process as appropriate for his responsibilities within the organization. He contributes to the process and may be responsible for facilitating it.

## Practice Actions in Organizations

As plans are implemented, various members of the organization are responsible for various actions that are required. In Chapter 11, we focus more on aspects of these actions as they relate to the use of groups within organizations. In most organizations, groups are used to support service delivery to clients and to carry out other administrative functions.

To some extent, most of the other actions that are described in Chapter 3 and subsequent chapters can also be applied to generalist practice with organizations. These actions are related to relationship building, learning to use the change process, learning to use resources, empowering and enabling, crisis resolution, support, activity, and mediation. In addition, the worker engages in actions to facilitate group formation, facilitate discussion, resolve conflict, enhance group interaction, facilitate group development, and structure group activities. These practice actions related to groups are covered in Chapter 11.

In organizational practice, relationships are central to the functioning of the organization. Successful relationships are built on the ability to communicate, problem solve and make decisions, and resolve conflict in a constructive manner. The more functional the relationships among members of the organization are, the better will be the organization's ability to function. Conversely, dysfunctional, impaired, or damaged relationships will impair the organization's ability to function. Similarly, organizations need to have a functional change process. Those that do will be able to grow and adapt to new challenges. This is another version of the change process used by the worker. In essence, the organization needs to be able to assess needs and situations, develop plans, act to implement plans, and evaluate progress and results.

In organizational practice, members need to learn about resources and how to use them. It is naive to think that one organization or program will be able to meet all of the needs of all clients. Social workers need to learn about resources within the agency and in the community and how to use them so she can share this information with her clients and make appropriate referrals. Some of this learning comes from other workers. Some of it comes as the worker becomes oriented to the agency and the community. At the very least, the worker should be familiar with the resources in the agency and the community typically used by clients and the formal mechanisms for receiving those resources such as eligibility, referral, application, and the like. Empowering and enabling are a part of organizational practice. These are covered in greater detail in Chapter 3 in terms of their use with clients. To empower and enable clients, workers themselves need to be empowered and enabled within their organization. When staff participate in making decisions and have input into the process, they are empowered. They are able to articulate the needs of their clients and are able to identify ways of improving service delivery. They can also articulate their own needs as employees and as professionals. When staff are empowered in this way, they are more likely to support decisions and have some investment in implementing them. When staff are not allowed to participate or their input is not solicited or considered, they have little investment in successful implementation of decisions. Change occurs when people are empowered and enabled.

Crisis intervention is typically thought of as something that workers do with clients. However, organizations can also experience crises. In addition, workers can experience personal crises that can affect their ability to function, along with professional crises that may arise in the course of providing services. Organizational crises are typically associated with funding and with survival of the organization or programs within the organization. Having a sufficient reserve fund can help to soften the blow of funding cuts or can provide gap funding while other sources of revenue are secured. Other measures such as staff reductions may be necessary, or in the extreme case, the agency or a program closes. Sometimes staff may be able to assist with a crisis by voluntarily cutting wages or benefits, working shorter workweeks, taking voluntary layoffs, and the like. Good managers develop emergency plans that save as many positions and as much service as possible. When programs close, they may be able to shift staff to other programs or find positions with other organizations. In some cases, organized advocacy efforts may be successful in having full or partial funding restored. Often, this involves putting pressure on political representatives in an organized campaign.

The ability to assist staff with personal crises is a must for any competent manager. Over time, even the best staff members will experience personal crises that will affect their ability to carry out their responsibilities. This might include the death or disability of family members, illness, separation or divorce, and the like. When this occurs, managers need to respond in a caring and supportive manner that will help the staff member to resolve the situation. Often, this means giving time off or allowing some flexibility in scheduling. It means arranging for case coverage, including the supervisor covering the worker's caseload for a short period of time or temporarily distributing the caseload to other staff until the worker returns. When organizations respond in this manner, they are communicating a loyalty and commitment to the employee that is likely to be returned if the organization needs employees to make sacrifices when there is an organizational crisis.

Professional crises can be related to challenges in serving clients or in difficult relationships with other professionals. Some staff may also experience a career crisis in which they consider changing positions or even changing careers. One of the hard facts of working with people who are depressed is that they may commit suicide. Clients can also commit crimes, including homicide. These are very stressful events for workers. Good supervision provides a relationship in which it is safe to process these events and provide support. Organizations also need to foster support systems among staff members that can assist in these situations. Developing and maintaining good relations among staff members may be challenging at times. Fellow employees or supervisors can assist in resolving these matters which generally requires a mediating approach.

Support is another important aspect of organizational practice. Organizations and managers need to provide both tangible and intangible forms of support in order for staff to provide quality services on a consistent basis over time. Adequate financial support is a vital form of support. There are fundamentally three basic approaches to adequate funding. One is to provide the maximum amount of quality services with the funding that is available. This requires balancing efficiency and effectiveness. However, this approach leaves the agency or program vulnerable to changes in funding, including declining funding or even loss of funding. Some organizations or managers may become complacent or may be quite conservative when it comes to applying for grants and other sources of funding. At the other end of the spectrum is an approach that considers the amount and types of services that are needed and then aggressively searches for ways to fund them. There may still be some financial vulnerability in this approach because the more numerous the sources of funding, the greater the risk of losing funding from any one source. It may mean constantly going through the process of applying for grants or for contracts with local, state, or federal funding sources. A third approach is a blend of these two, in which the organization identifies the amount and types of services needed, maximizes the funding that can be procured, and also uses a combination of efficiency and effectiveness in utilizing the funds at hand. Accumulating a financial reserve can be a critical factor in maintaining programs that are vulnerable to fluctuations in funding.

Tangible support includes providing facilities, furnishings, supplies, and equipment that are necessary to carry out the functions of the organization. The buildings and furnishings of an organization provide an important part of its image. The use of up-to-date technology can increase efficiency dramatically. For example, in addition to their use in program evaluation, computers are used by some agencies to maintain case records. Software has been developed and continues to be refined that allows for an entire case record to be entered into the system, a big advantage over maintaining handwritten paper records. Interactive programs are available that allow the client (with assistance, if necessary) or the worker to answer questions about the situation and the needs or concerns. The program then produces a narrative assessment. Some programs are designed to suggest a plan, complete with goals and objectives. Whatever is selected can be modified or new goals added. The computer will then elicit feedback regarding goals when progress notes are entered and will produce quarterly, annual, and termination summaries. With the development of voice recognition programs that receive dictation and of powerful laptop computers, it is likely that in the future nearly all social workers will be using some form of computerized record keeping. Technology has the potential for considerably increasing worker efficiency in meeting "paperwork" demands, which could leave more time available to work with clients.

Intangible support mainly refers to support that comes in the form of relationships and the overall atmosphere in the organization. Workers need to feel supported by their colleagues, supervisors, and higher-level administration, the reverse is also true. Supervisors need to form supportive relationships with other supervisors both within and outside of the organization. Staff at other levels of the organization need to do likewise. These support networks are vital to carrying out the business of the organization and providing a positive atmosphere within the organization. There is a considerable degree of reciprocity in developing a positive supportive atmosphere within the organization. Staff members who are supportive tend to receive support. Good managers provide positive supervision and consultation that support professional growth and support career and professional development that meets the needs of staff.

Support is particularly important when organizational change takes place. Change can be very intimidating because we do not know what to expect or we might fear failure. Receiving support can be the difference between trying something new and staying put. In fact, staff members can be motivated to change out of a desire to receive approval from their peer group and avoid disappointing them.

Organizations engage in a wide variety of activities in carrying out their functions. Many use various types of groups in doing so. Some of these activities are necessary to maintain the organization and to carry out daily functions. Other activities are intended to bring about change. In Chapter 11, we consider how organizations use various types of groups to accomplish these activities.

A mediating approach is used in a variety of ways within and between organizations. In addition to using a mediating approach with clients and on their behalf, organizations need to resolve conflicts within the organization and in its dealings with other organizations. Good managers learn to use mediation in resolving issues among staff members. Good organizational practice requires a mediating stance in working out issues between organizations. Sometimes a member of the organization acts as a third party in mediating a dispute between two other organizations. At other times, aspects of a mediating approach can be useful in negotiating a compromise with another organization. Attempting to see both sides of an issue and looking at ways in which both organizations can have their needs met requires taking a neutral stance as opposed to merely pushing only for what is best for one's own organization. Learning to give and take and negotiate and compromise is often the key to maintaining good relationships.

## Evaluation in Organizations

Evaluation is a critical element for any organization. Without ongoing evaluation, organizations cannot demonstrate effectiveness or efficiency. If funding sources decide to require evidence of effectiveness as a condition of continued support, the organization needs to have already gathered the information, otherwise, it may be too late. Often, grants and contracts for services have evaluation requirements built into the requirements. Sometimes evidence of units of service is confused with evaluation. Units of service can be used to demonstrate efficiency but are not an indication of effectiveness. To demonstrate effectiveness, the organization needs to gather data about outcomes with clients. This can be difficult for some programs to measure. Client satisfaction surveys may be used if funding sources will accept these as evidence of effectiveness, particularly if they include feedback about achieving goals and alleviating difficulties associated with the request for services. It is best to have the instrument along with the evaluation method and definitions of successful outcomes approved ahead of time so there is an agreement that these are acceptable. Workers are typically involved in gathering data for program evaluations. It is important that the worker understand the process and its purpose so that accurate data can be collected. The worker should also understand how to use the data to improve his own service delivery.

As part of the process of monitoring and improving service delivery, organizations should include evaluation as an integral part of its operations. Planning should be based on accurate data so that new or improved services can be based on reliable information.

# Summary

Generalist social work practice with macrosystems involves understanding organizations as social systems. To function within an organization and work with other organizations, the social worker needs to understand organizational structure and functioning. Good managers should provide the necessary support systems for staff to be able to function within the agency. Learning to work successfully in a bureaucracy is important for the many social workers who do so. There are several different approaches to take. A risk factor for social workers is burnout, which can undermine the worker's ability to function and provide quality services to clients.

The phases of the change process are used in organizational practice for developing and maintaining necessary functions and to bring about necessary changes. Organizations engage in assessment, planning, actions, and evaluation as they work to provide quality services to clients and to plan for new and improved services.

# QUESTION

1. Identify an organization in your community. Use the schema in Table 10.1 to assess the organization as a social system.

2. Describe the management style that characterizes the basic approach that is used by an organization in your community. Describe the management style that you would use if you were a manager.

3. Describe the approach that you would use in working in a bureaucracy.

4. Describe the risk factors for burnout in an organization or program with which you are familiar. Describe how you might avoid burnout.

5. Describe how the organization in Question 1 uses the change process in its functioning.

# SUGGESTED READINGS

Johnson, Louise C., and Yanca, Stephen J., *Social Work Practice: A Generalist Approach*, 9th ed. Boston: Allyn & Bacon, 2007 (Chapters 7, 14, and 15).

Netting, Ellen F., Kettner, Peter M., and McMurtry, Steven L. *Social Work Macro Practice,* 4th ed. New York: Longman, 2008.

Netting, Ellen F., and O'Connor, Mary K. *Organization Practice: A Social Worker's Guide to Understanding Human Services.* Boston: Allyn & Bacon, 2003.

Rae, P. Ann, and Nicholas-Wolosuk, Wanda. *Changing Agency Policy: An Incremental Approach.* Boston: Allyn & Bacon, 2003.

Weinbach, Robert. *The Social Worker as Manager,* 4th ed. Boston: Allyn & Bacon, 2003.

# 11 Task Groups in Organizations

1. Understanding the need to work with organizations in generalist practice.
2. Understanding various forms of group work with organizations.
3. Understanding group work and various methods of organizational practice.
4. Knowledge of facilitating various groups in organizations.
5. Understanding the use of the change process at various stages of group development with task groups.

Most generalist social workers work in organizations. As they do so, the functioning of their organization becomes a focus of attention. Some of this focus is from the perspective of an employee. Some of it is from the perspective of a professional social worker. Some of it is from the perspective of a provider of services to client systems. This latter perspective may also require a focus on the functioning of other organizations. Social workers should be committed to advocating for the needs of clients as these relate to their own and other organizations. They should also be committed to helping organizations deliver effective services in an efficient manner. They should have knowledge and skills in maximizing organizational functioning and in facilitating organizational change.

Historically, consideration of the organization as a target for change has received little attention in social work literature. Yet in working with clients, workers (particularly in the public sector) are well aware that the functioning of the agency (policy, procedures, etc.) often is a source of blockage to client need fulfillment. It follows that social workers should develop a means for influencing agency change. Organizational change as a strategy can be defined as "a means of enhancing the effectiveness of human service organizations in their relations with clients. . . . [It] is a set of interrelated activities . . . for the purpose of modifying the formal policies, programs, procedures, or management practices. . . . The intended outcome . . . [is] to increase the effectiveness of the services provided and/or to remove organizational conditions that are deleterious to the client population served."[1] This strategy focuses on means of change from within the organization and is carried out by those in middle or lower levels of the organization.[2]

This chapter begins with a discussion of task groups in organizations and of changing organizations from within. It continues with an examination of the social worker as a group member. This is followed by a consideration of group development in working with task groups in organizations.

# The Use of Task Groups in Organizations

Organizations use groups in a variety of ways. Fundamentally, these ways can be considered under two basic categories. The first are ways in which organizations use groups on an ongoing basis to maintain themselves and carry out their business. Groups under this category might be classified further into those that are used for administrative or management purposes and those that are related to service delivery. The second way that organizations use groups is to bring about change. These can also be classified into administrative and change-oriented purposes. These types of groups tend to be temporary, but some organizations may have more permanent groups that engage in longer term planning.

Groups are important to the functioning of nearly all organizations. Organizations themselves are groups that share a common mission and goals. In order to achieve these common goals and accomplish the mission of the organization, smaller groups are needed to coordinate the efforts of staff at various levels of the organization. Generally speaking, the larger the organization, the greater the need for coordination and the more groups that are used. As social workers practice within organizations, they will find that at least some of their time will be used to participate in task groups within the organization. Some of these groups will be related to administrative functions, some will be related to service delivery, and some will be devoted to changing the organization.

The most common administrative task groups are board meetings and staff meetings. Board meetings are used by the board of directors or by advisory boards or by committees of the board to conduct business for the organization. While the chief executive officer (CEO) is the primary member of the organization's staff who attends board meetings, other administrative staff may also attend some meetings and occasionally other staff may do so. In addition, the worker may be asked to serve on the board of other organizations in the community. It is important that the worker understand how boards operate so that she can understand her organization as well as other organizations in the community.

The board of directors or board of trustees of a private nonprofit organization is typically composed of members of the community who are responsible for oversight of the organization. Their primary purpose is to ensure that the organization operates within the law and its charter or articles of incorporation and that it meets its fiduciary responsibilities as well as its obligation to serve the community. Board members may be recruited for their power or influence. Some members may have special skills to assist with the organization's functioning such as an attorney or an accountant, and certain business people. Some members are recruited for their strong community service or the fact that they represent certain groups.

Boards have the authority to set organizational policy, approve budgets and the expenditure of funds, and hire and fire the CEO. The board of directors has the ultimate responsibility for governing the organization and is responsible for monitoring its activities. It accomplishes its monitoring duties by receiving reports on service delivery, budget reports, and audits. Boards must approve policies, procedures, and job or position descriptions and any changes in these. When staff are operating within these policies and procedures and the duties described in their job or position descriptions, they have the sanction of the organization to do so.

All organizations that are incorporated must have a set of bylaws that govern the operation of the board. The board must abide by the bylaws and must follow formal procedures for amending them. Typically, this involves advanced notification to all board members and it may include a requirement of more than a simple majority of members, such as a two-thirds majority. Bylaws establish the authority of the board and include a description of a quorum for conducting business, the board officers or executive committee, the establishment of standing committees, terms of office for members, nominating and voting procedures for members and officers, and the like.

Most organizations that employ generalist social workers are either governmental or private nonprofit agencies. Some may be for profit, but if they are incorporated they typically function in a manner similar to nonprofit corporations, unless they are privately owned or are partnerships. Most for-profit organizations are found in clinical, health, substance abuse, and residential or inpatient settings. For-profit organizations have become much more prevalent with the privatization of many types of human services. For example, in the 1960s the overwhelming majority of nursing homes were operated by governmental and nonprofit organizations. Now the majority are operated by for-profit corporations.

Boards of directors typically function in a more formal manner, although some boards may be less formal than others. At the very least, parliamentary procedures apply whenever the board is conducting official business such as approving budgets and expenditures, hiring or firing the CEO, and approving policies and procedures. Typically, boards meet once a month, but some may meet more or less frequently. There is a formal agenda with a call to order, approval of agenda, approval of the minutes of the last meeting, committee and financial reports, old and new business, and adjournment as minimal headings.

Boards also conduct business at committee meetings. Typically, there are two or three standing committees that are established in the bylaws. At minimum there should be a finance committee and a personnel committee, and usually a committee that reviews policies and procedures. Special committees may be set up by the board. These are generally time limited and are intended to serve a specific purpose such as a fund-raising activity or a search committee to hire a CEO.

Governmental organizations function as a result of laws and involve the expenditure of tax dollars. Administrative rules are then promulgated that govern the operations of various government departments. They do not have a board of directors but often have advisory boards to represent the community and recipients of services. Advisory boards do not have policy or fiduciary authority but serve primarily as a feedback mechanism. Governmental organizations that provide human services are located in the executive branch of the government. Usually state government is responsible for providing direct services to citizens, but there are some federal agencies that do so, such as the Department of Veterans Affairs, which operates Veteran's Hospitals and outpatient programs that employ social workers. The executive branch of state government is generally responsible for public mental health, adult and child protective services, public child welfare, public assistance, aging services, and similar services. Some states use local governmental organizations to provide these services or there may be contractual arrangements with private agencies. Subcommittees of the legislature or of county boards also provide oversight for these governmental organizations.

Advisory boards may also be used by programs within private organizations. Typically, they provide feedback and may also engage in activities such as fund-raising. As with governmental organizations, advisory boards have little, if any authority over the organization or program. However, advisory boards may have considerable influence, especially if they have members who are influential. They may also have influence as a result of media attention.

In addition to agency boards, there may be committees set up within the organization to accomplish various purposes. These are used in both public and private organizations. Committees are often used for planning purposes, to develop new programs, or to provide input regarding changes in policies or service delivery. Most committees are temporary and have a charge to accomplish a specific purpose. Once this is accomplished, the committee reports on its activities or makes recommendations and is disbanded.

At every level in organizations, there are groups that meet to assist in accomplishing its purpose. Typically, these are called staff meetings. In larger organizations with division or program directors, staff meetings at the highest levels are what might be described as cabinet meetings similar to what occurs at the highest levels of state and federal government. This is where the heads of various departments meet together, usually with the CEO, and report on their respective departments. They are used to report on activities and program statistics, engage in problem solving and decision making, communicate from top to bottom and from bottom up within the organization, and to make future plans for the organization or specific programs within the organization. Similar types of meetings may take place within each division or program. Most of the time, each of these types of staff meetings at the administrative level are scheduled monthly. Most of these meetings have some type of a formal agenda but they are conducted less formally, because parliamentary procedures are not typically used. The agenda is primarily used to keep the meeting flowing and participants on task.

At lower levels of large organizations or in small organizations, staff meetings are used to oversee service delivery and conduct agency business. In larger or midsize organizations, these are conducted by supervisors. In small organizations, the CEO might meet directly with the staff who provide services. Staff meetings may or may not have a formal agenda, but an agenda should be used to provide a flow and to keep the meeting participants on task. Staff meetings are generally used to discuss administrative and management tasks and issues regarding overall service delivery. They may be used to communicate policy and procedure decisions and their implementation. These can include policies related to personnel matters as well as to service delivery. Staff meetings can be used to give feedback to upper levels of the organization and to monitor the quality and quantity of services. The frequency of staff meetings varies a great deal even within the same organization. Some programs may find it necessary to meet only once a month. Others may meet twice a month or every week. Frequency depends on the need to coordinate activities and conduct agency business.

Other types of groups that are used within organizations are **teams**; case or treatment conferences, and in-service, training, or professional development groups. Because teams are actually multiworker systems, they are discussed separately in this chapter. Case or treatment conferences are designed to assist workers with difficult situations with their clients by bringing together various members of the organization's staff to problem solve and discuss service delivery. Many organizations use staff meetings to accomplish this. Time might be set aside at staff meetings for this purpose or separate meetings can either be regularly scheduled or scheduled as needed. For these meetings, the worker presents his case situation and his supervisor and colleagues brainstorm about how to serve the client in the most effective manner. Sometimes, personnel from other parts of the organization may be invited to participate. This type of meeting may be used to meet requirements of insurance companies for mental health and substance abuse treatment. Staff meet with a physician or psychiatrist and perhaps a psychologist to develop and approve treatment plans. Smaller organizations typically hire private psychiatrists and psychologists on a contractual basis for this purpose.

Large and midsize organizations generally organize and offer various types of professional development activities within the organization. These are usually offered in groups. Some of these may be training activities for new staff. Other activities might be classified as in-services that are intended to augment or increase expertise in some area. Social workers may engage in these activities as a participant or as a presenter.

Every social worker who works in an organization will almost certainly be required to attend and participate in staff meetings. Social workers may be employed at other levels including CEO. They may also serve on agency and advisory boards as well as committees within the organization. Ways of working in organizational groups is discussed separately in this chapter.

## Changing Organizations from Within

As she works in organizations, the social worker participates in activities that include changing the organization. The social worker begins with assessment. Some of the understandings a worker must develop when using a change-from-within strategy include:

1. The agency as a social system (See Table 10.1 for a discussion of a schema for developing this understanding.)
2. The source of the block to need fulfillment (Is it in policy or procedure? Is it due to lack of agency resources? Is it caused by methods used to deliver service?)
3. The forces within the agency and the community that influence the agency functioning in relation to the need
4. The usual processes used to bring about change in the agency
5. The source of decision making in the areas needing to be changed
6. Any influences to which the decision-making source is particularly sensitive
7. The decision maker's receptivity and resistance to the change sought

The assessment process should identify what requires changing if client or other needs are to be fulfilled or the effectiveness or efficiency of the organization is to be improved. It is not sufficient to say that change must take place.

In planning change within an organization, it is important to be inclusive. Often, there is a temptation to bring about change by issuing memos or directives. This can lead to resentment, resistance, and even sabotage by those who are affected by the change. How change occurs is as important as what gets changed. Getting input from those affected ensures greater investment in carrying out the change and helps to avoid barriers. Getting input from clients should be done whenever applicable and feasible. At the least, client needs and concerns should be considered as primary, and proactive advocacy should be used by the social worker. **Proactive advocacy** means advocating for clients before barriers are encountered by avoiding policies that are not in the best interests of clients.

In a small agency, it may be possible to include everyone in the planning process. When major change is planned in larger agencies, it is usually wise to establish a task group made up of representatives from various levels of the agency. The representatives should solicit input from the groups they represent. The task group is generally given responsibility to recommend changes to the executive. Generating several options, along with an analysis of the advantages and disadvantages of each, will allow the administrator to retain her decision-making role while incorporating input from other levels of the agency.

It is important that both the place where the change should take place and the desirable change at that site be specified. The assessment should specify what change is possible and what limitations may exist. There should be some consideration of timing factors that need to be taken into account in planning for change.[3] For example, if management is under stress because of changes being imposed from a central office, the chances that management will be receptive to discussing other changes with line staff is doubtful. However, if management is concerned with a problem of service delivery, it may be receptive to discussing change that could result in better service and also alleviate the problem.

According to Herman Resnick and Rino Patti, the change process contains the following steps:

1. Practitioner's perception of a problem in agency functioning
2. Discussion of problem among practitioner and like-minded colleagues, including an assessment of change potential
3. Commitment to the change effort by persons involved in the assessment
4. Formulation of the goal to be sought
5. Analysis of resistance to change
6. Development of an action system and mobilization of resources (needed persons added and group development takes place)
7. Formulation of a plan of action
8. Submission of proposal to the decision makers; take other action as needed

At this point, the change is either accepted, rejected, or modified. At each step, goals may change as new information or input is gained.[4]

An important consideration is whom to include in the change effort. At least some participants should have a good understanding of the agency functioning. Some should be respected, valued members of the staff. Some should be those who can influence decision makers; some should have skills in negotiation, mediation, and in carrying out the particular change. Agency change can originate from the efforts of one person, but to implement a change-from-within strategy, others who possess the characteristics and skills needed also must be involved.

Several techniques or methods can be used to bring about change in organizations. Patti and Resnick identified eight collaborative and nine adversarial activities. Collaborative activities are to (1) provide information, (2) present alternative courses of action, (3) request support for experimentation, (4) establish a study committee, (5) create new opportunities for interaction, (6) make appeals to conscience or professional ethics, (7) use logical argument and data, and (8) point out negative consequences. Adversarial activities are to (1) submit petitions, (2) confront in open meetings, (3) bring sanctions against the agency, (4) engage in public criticism through use of communication media, (5) encourage noncompliance, (6) strike, (7) picket, (8) litigate, and (9) bargain.[5]

Collaborative activities should always be tried first. The use of adversarial activities should be restricted to situations in which collaborative activities have not worked but change is necessary. Before using adversarial activities, workers should determine if such strategies will bring harm to clients and if they are willing to take the personal risks involved.

Rothman, Erlich, and Teresa identified four means of bringing about change in organizations:

**1.** *Promoting an innovation*—This is carried out by testing a new or modified service with a small group of clients. If it is successful, it may later be adopted for use on a larger scale. An example is using a group approach to deliver a service.

**2.** *Changing an organization's goals*—One way to do this is to change the structure of influence by increasing the power of appropriate groups within the agency. For example, developing a clients' advisory group would increase client input into decision making and provide a new source of information or influence.

**3.** *Fostering participation*—This is a means of encouraging broader participation in the functioning of an agency. For example, a staff group could be involved in the planning for a new program. One means of fostering participation is through providing some kind of benefit for the participation, such as public recognition.

**4.** *Increasing the effectiveness of role performance*—This can be carried out by clarifying the role performance expected of those working in an agency. It can also be carried out by encouraging various kinds of staff development.[6]

In-service training for workers can be used to introduce new service delivery ideas. If the social worker is skillful in the use of group interaction, he can sometimes enable a staff group to examine and adopt a new idea. Sometimes social workers are given the opportunity to lead an in-service session; in doing this, the knowledge from adult education and staff development literature can be useful.[7]

Edward Pawlak pointed out that an ideal time for bringing about change in an organization is when leadership changes. He provided suggestions for workers who wish to engage in organizational change, including influencing the selection of new leadership and altering the manner in which rules are interpreted and enforced. Revising of roles, or role interpretation, is another means for change.[8]

It should be apparent that several approaches and techniques are available for changing organizations. The choice of approach depends on the change being sought and the situation. Two factors must be considered: risk for the worker seeking the change and resistance of other persons within the organization.

Three kinds of risks may be involved when a social worker engages in changing from within: job loss, restricted upward mobility, and strained working relationships.[9] Not all of these risks may be present, but a careful assessment should indicate the extent of the risk.

Each social worker must then make the decision whether he is willing to take the risks involved before using this strategy.

Resistance is almost always present to some degree in change activity. Change upsets the system's functioning and causes uncertainty. Thus, the social worker must be prepared to modify the plan to mitigate resistance. When dealing with resistance, an attitude of compromise is often necessary. Workers who are determined that their plan be accepted are most apt to encounter a negative response. Those who engage in joint consideration of a problem likely will find a solution acceptable to all. Understanding the nature of the resistance and dealing with it are essential skills when using a change-from-within strategy.

Because social work is primarily practiced within organizations, particularly bureaucracies, the change-from-within strategy is important to the social worker's repertoire. The social worker's ethical responsibility is to work toward the humane delivery of social services in a manner that meets client needs. To do this, it is often necessary to bring about change in organizations. The social worker can use the change-from-within strategy to bring about change.

## The Social Worker as a Group Member

The social worker is frequently called on to participate as a member of various groups. These include task groups, teams, and staff meetings. The worker uses his knowledge and skills in use of the change process in working with groups to facilitate successful achievement of group goals and tasks for groups of which he is a member. The change process with these groups involves assessment, planning, action, and evaluation.

Use of the change process in group discussion is a means of structuring group thinking. All members of the group should understand the change process and be aware of which step in the process the group is using. In this way, group thinking can progress from need identification and formulation to analysis of the situation, to identification of possible goals, to analysis of the possibilities, and to choice of a plan. Thus, the plan becomes the property of the group rather than the contribution of an individual member.

Several areas that often give groups difficulty as they attempt to change are the following:

1. Lack of clarity in stating the need
2. Lack of necessary information
3. A critical, evaluative climate
4. Pressure for conformity
5. Premature choice of a goal or plan

If a plan for implementation is a result of group thinking, there is a better chance that it will be carried out.

Some attention should be paid to the structure of group meetings to further enhance the group's capacity. There should be preparation for group meetings, just as there is preparation for an interview. Various members should be responsible for bringing needed information to the meeting. Someone should take the responsibility for ensuring that the meeting room is comfortable and arranged so that each member can have eye contact with every other member. Someone should be responsible for seeing that agendas and other needed printed materials are available and for keeping minutes or recording decisions in some way. The planned agenda should be reviewed and revisions made, if necessary, at the beginning of each meeting. Everyone should know what the meeting is intended to accomplish and what the time limitations are.

The middle part of the meeting is spent on the task of the day. When necessary, the group should deal with any group maintenance issues that seem to be impeding the work at hand. Discussion should focus on tasks or goals or on the process of carrying these out. All members should be urged to participate. Someone should be responsible for keeping the group on task and helping it move through the change process in an orderly manner. Before the allotted time is over, the group should review what has been accomplished at the meeting, and plans should be made for the next meeting.

In helping the group involve members, make decisions, have productive discussions, and structure the discussion, social workers can be a valuable resource for the group. Knowledge of group process and of the problem-solving process and skill in group discussion form the base of effective membership in a group.

Several issues of group participation are of particular concern to social workers when they participate as members of small groups, including (1) the use of the team, particularly the interdisciplinary team, as a means of service; (2) leadership in its delegated form; and (3) conflict management, which is discussed above. Each of these issues confronts the social worker and, if not understood, can block effective group functioning.

## Use of the Team

Although the well-functioning team can be very effective in providing service to clients, there are often problems that cause some social workers and agency administrators to question the team approach. These problems need to be understood and some ways for overcoming them considered.

The team has been defined as "joining the essentially dissimilar skills which colleagues in diverse occupations bring to bear upon different aspects of a common problem."[10] This definition is most applicable to the interdisciplinary team, and it is the interdisciplinary team that presents the greatest hazards for working together. Dissimilarity of backgrounds and work expectations are a major cause of these hazards, as is overlap of the expertise of the various helping professions. This can lead to conflict over turf.

Some of the most frequent problems encountered by teams are the following:

**1.** *The time and energy needed for team building*—The task of the team is to provide service to clients. Often, the immediacy of the need for service and number of clients needing service place expectations on the team that militate against the use of time and energy for team building. These expectations may come from within the team or from the agency within which the team or any of its members operate. Yet, effective team functioning requires time and energy from the team members. The allocation of time and energy for team building can be problematic.

**2.** *Communication*—The use of technical language by any member of the team that is not understood by all other members of the team blocks communication. Persons from different disciplines often use the same terms but with somewhat different meanings. When this happens, there are problems in communication.

**3.** *Decision-making traditions*—Professions and agencies develop traditions about how decisions are made. In bureaucratic organizations, decisions are made from above, and lower-status persons are expected to implement the decisions. A team in such an organization may have a leader appointed by the administration; the appointed leader may assume an authoritative stance. In health care, the doctor, as the high-status professional, has traditionally used this authoritative stance. This is needed in an operating room, but it is not helpful in a protective service situation. Other decision-making models may call for everyone to have equal decision-making power about all aspects of service. All team members may not have equal knowledge or understanding of certain aspects of the team's service. One of the purposes of a team is to accommodate differing types of expertise to be used in service of the client. The decision-making process needs to allow for this diversity of understanding yet facilitate the process so that it is reasonably expedient.

**4.** *Use of the change process*—As with all small groups, goals need to be accepted by all. Differences in goals among team members can arise from inadequate need identification. If team members see the situation differently and do not understand or accept the team goals, hidden agendas can develop. If team members are functioning at different stages of the change process, confusion in planning results.

**5.** *Implementation of plans and carrying out tasks*—Team members usually have other tasks and other influences on how they prioritize their work. This can result in assigned tasks not being carried out, particularly when those tasks are imposed on members.

**6.** *Functioning within a complex organization*—Sometimes organizations institute or sanction the use of the team approach without full understanding of the implications of teamwork. The organization may not allow sufficient time for team functioning, may impose leadership that does not enable team functioning to develop, or may interfere with the team's ability to function in other ways.

Each team is unique and must discover its own way of functioning. Some will function in a cooperative manner in which an integrated approach to client service is the mode. Others will use a collaborative approach in which the team decides on the services needed; appropriate members then provide those services in an autonomous manner. Other teams will use various combinations of the two approaches. Regardless of approach, teams that function best have members who are dedicated, share a common ideal, and have confidence in one another. Members also have a willingness to work together, to learn from one another, and to share clients. They have a cooperative rather than a competitive climate, flexibility, and good communication and problem-solving processes. They also have the support of the agency of which they are a part. Social workers can contribute to the enhancement of the decision-making process by helping the team to identify the issues confronting the team so that it can work for resolution.

## Leadership

Because leadership has differing meanings for different persons, it is often the source of problems in group functioning. Some people perceive a leader as being one who tells everyone else what to do. Others see the leader as one who consults with the other group members but in the end makes the decisions. Still others see the leader as the one who enables the group to function. Some people who carry the title *leader* are appointed, some are elected, and others emerge from the group. Some people resent leadership or leadership by certain people or professions. Others expect the leader to take full responsibility for the group or expect a member of a particular profession to automatically be the leader.

More and more, leadership is being understood as *interpersonal influence*; in this sense, the meaning of leadership, as used here, is captured. Such influence can be exerted in a variety of ways, some of which are more helpful in furthering the functioning of the group than others. The idea that only one person, elected or emergent, carries the entire leadership responsibility is fallacious. If group members understand leadership as a shared responsibility, much interpersonal conflict can be avoided. The group can then use the knowledge and skills of all group members, and the leadership can change, depending on the task at hand.

As a group member, the social worker can influence, or enable, the group to carry out its task and function. Some of the tasks involved in this enabling include:

1. Seeing that decisions are made (but not making them for the group).
2. Being sure the group knows what it is doing: Are there goals that are known to all the members? Does the group know its purpose? Are group norms explicit?
3. Making certain the group knows how it is doing: In what stage of the change process is the group functioning? Are the essential roles in the group being filled? Are all group members' contributions accepted? Is communication open and understood by all?
4. Being sure that when things are not going well or feeling good, the group stops to evaluate what is wrong.

Social workers with a knowledge of group process can carry out these tasks for any group, regardless of their position in the group. To do this, they must use good judgment about how and when to exercise this kind of influence. In this way, they exercise leadership and influence the group's functioning.

### Social Work Tasks

Social workers who are group members are qualified to carry out three tasks that can be very useful for the group in its functioning: consultation, facilitation, and coordination. The *consultation* task calls for the worker to ask for and offer information and suggestions; there is no demand that the suggestions be accepted. Consultation provides an expectation that all group members will examine the information and suggestions in light of their particular perspective and provide feedback on the usefulness and validity of the social worker's contributions. This type of consultation is a means of enabling the group to engage in a joint process of thinking about clients and situations to identify strengths and resources and to develop plans for action. Through consultation, the social worker contributes the expertise she brings to the group. This expertise can be in the area of group functioning, or it can be in the form of contributions to the task of the group.

*Facilitation* is the process of enabling others to function. Facilitation of the group process is one form of the facilitation task. Social workers can carry out this task in a number of ways. They can support helpful behaviors of other group members, model useful behaviors, ask appropriate questions, or provide appropriate observations and feelings about the group. They can teach other group members about group process and functioning. Other means of facilitating are helping members stay on the topic, summarizing what has been said or decided, and letting other members know their feelings are accepted. Because of their skills, social workers can help the group state problems so that they can be worked on. Workers can partialize problems, which is done by breaking a problem into parts, prioritizing which part should be worked on, and/or deciding the order for working on the various parts. They can identify strengths and resources.

Some behaviors to avoid are criticizing others or their values, forcing ideas on the group, making decisions that belong to the group, and talking too much. The social worker studies the group and its functioning and decides what will most help the group at any point in time.

A third task, *coordination*, calls for monitoring to assess whether all members are carrying out their assigned tasks and whether, in carrying out the tasks, the work of each group member is done in a way that complements that of other members. Coordination ensures that the work of various members does not conflict but rather complements the work of other group members. Social workers are especially able to perform this role because of their broad view of personal and social functioning. They can view the various parts of a plan, ascertain how the parts fit together, and when misfit exists, identify means of modifying misfitting plans.

Much of this coordination is done by building relationships. The social worker attempts to understand the position of every other group member and to gain an appreciation of the needs of each member in relation to the group's task. Through relationships with group members, the social worker can mediate differences and provide observations about group functioning. In this way, the social worker assists the group in its work and helps the group coordinate its work.

Social workers can contribute a great deal to groups of which they are members. Knowledge of group process; understanding of issues that can inhibit group functioning; and skill in carrying out the tasks of consultation, facilitation, and coordination provide the social worker with a firm base for making this contribution.

Task groups usually end when the task has been completed, when the group gives up its efforts to effect a change, or when its authority to operate ends, as might be the case for a time-limited task group. Generally, a celebration of some sort is in order when the task is completed. If the group fails to complete its task, some sort of debriefing may be necessary, and a report may be generated, outlining its accomplishments and analyzing the reasons that the effort failed. This may help group members resolve some of their disappointment and can help future groups avoid some of the same difficulties. Such a report may also be needed for accountability to various authorities with an interest in the outcome.

Unlike small groups in which relationships are important, task groups are focused on the task itself, and relationships are secondary to the group's purpose. When individual members drop out, the decision regarding follow-up is generally made based on how critical the person or their organization is to the task at hand and whether they are likely to support or oppose the group's efforts. Follow-up can be done by any member.

## Using Task Groups to Develop Services

Volunteers are a resource that has historically been very important in the delivery of social services. Before the development of the social work profession, most social services were delivered by volunteers. In fact, the early social workers were volunteers. With cutbacks in governmental support for social services at all levels, it has become increasingly urgent that volunteer efforts be enhanced to fill service gaps. Issues of competence, confidentiality, and dependability have been raised when considering volunteers as a resource. Professionals believe that they are best suited to deliver services. Also, the type of volunteer has changed. Women are now a large segment of the workforce and so are not available for volunteer roles or during agency work hours. Because their numbers are increasing, retired persons are now seen as an important source of volunteer efforts.

Effective use of volunteers calls for the development of a volunteer program. Someone must be responsible for helping identify the roles and tasks suitable for volunteers to carry out. Job descriptions and agency policy must be written. To carry out these tasks, a volunteer manager must develop an understanding of clients and the services required and of the factors that motivate people to volunteer. The volunteer manager should be able to work with staff persons to identify services volunteers can provide. The worker also needs skill in motivating people. A volunteer program should have a means of recruiting and screening volunteers, matching the volunteer with a job, and orienting and training volunteers.

The volunteer coordinator should not be the only person involved in planning the development of a volunteer program. Prior to appointing the coordinator, a group should determine the need and focus of the program and set goals and objectives for it. The group should represent agency staff, concerned community members, influentials, possible volunteers, and clients to be served. This group can then serve as a board of directors or advisory group when the coordinator is chosen; the group should have input into, and responsibility for, choosing the coordinator.

When an understanding is developed of what a functional volunteer program entails and of the planning process used in developing such a program, the resource of volunteers can be added to those resources already available to clients. Clients thus can be better served.[11]

Self-help groups are another resource social workers can help develop. These are discussed as groups in Chapter 7. These voluntary small groups are an important component of mutual aid. In the modern world, it is not always possible on one's own to find a supportive group. Social workers can help those with similar life situations and challenges find one another and provide mutual aid to one another.

Because people facing a new situation or difficulty often feel helpless, it is advisable to include individuals who have had some opportunity to work on the same issue or adjust to a similar situation. They often are glad to help others, for doing this further facilitates their return to more stable functioning. The widow-to-widow program is a good example. Newly widowed persons can be visited by others who have been widowed for a year or more; the visitor can encourage participation. In the group, the newly widowed person finds others who can help with the many concerns and decisions they face. Much needed information is shared.

Brian and Gail Auslander have suggested that a *consultation model* is appropriate when working with self-help groups. They identify three roles for the consultant: (1) discussion of client-related needs and possible interventions, (2) discussion of the self-help group's policies and procedures in the hope of obtaining desired change, and (3) a link between resources that the group or individuals in the group may need.[12] The latter role would include providing information about and consulting on the procedures for accessing needed resources. Information about how similar groups function can also be provided.

Self-help groups are not the answer for all clients. Some groups foster inappropriate dependence or encourage simplistic solutions to complex situations. Some develop a strong antiprofessional bias. Some of these negative characteristics can be avoided if, in the process of development, an ongoing consultative role for the social worker can be planned. Social workers can support self-help groups by helping groups find a meeting place, encouraging them to find needed financial resources, providing them with information and training, referring appropriate persons to them, helping the group develop credibility with the community and with professionals, and providing social and emotional support.

### Client Task Groups

Another type of task group in organizations are groups that include clients. Most of the time these groups are advisory groups that give feedback to administrators from a client's perspective. These groups can assist in improving existing service delivery as well as giving feedback about new programs. Typically, the group is composed of former clients who have received services from the organization. The group will usually meet with the director of the program to discuss issues related to service delivery. Care must be taken to maintain confidentiality when discussing services to clients. Most of the time these groups are chaired by a member of the group as opposed to having the agency staff serve as chair. The social worker may need to assist the chair in developing skills in chairing a meeting. Most advisory boards or groups are more informal than formal. However, minutes should be taken and approved, an agenda prepared and approved, and votes taken and recorded when the group takes a position on a particular matter.

A special form of client group are resident councils. These are task groups for residents of various facilities such as retirement communities, nursing homes, assisted living facilities, adolescent residential care, inpatient units, and the like. Resident councils typically provide advice and feedback to administration about conditions in the facility. They may also communicate complaints from residents and suggest ways of resolving these. The councils may engage in problem-solving and advocacy activities. They may also provide information and communications to residents through newsletters and meetings. Some resident councils may plan and implement improvements in the facility such as gardens, landscaping, pictures, and the like. They may also plan and implement outings and excursions, activities, and special events.

Resident councils are usually elected by the residents. This gives members the authority to represent and speak for the residents of the facility. The role of social worker is to provide a link between residents and administration and to serve as a coordinator or resource person as needed or to assist members in carrying out these tasks. Frequently, the worker may be put in the role of advocate or may advise the council on various forms of advocacy when change is needed, especially if those changes run into resistance.

## Group Development with Task Groups in Organizations

Stages of group development with task groups in organizations are similar to what we have described for other groups. There is typically an orientation stage, followed by an authority stage, which is then followed by a negotiation stage. These stages make up what would be considered the stages of group formation. The functional stage follows these stages and the final stage is disintegration. Although the stages are similar, there are significant differences in the group and in the use of the change process at each stage.

The first three stages of group formation is likely to be different for task groups within organizations than it would be for other groups, including task groups in the community. There are several major reasons for these differences. First, most if not all of the members will probably know one another, since they work for the same organization. It is possible in larger organizations that some members will not know one another very well, but it is likely that most will. Second, organizations typically have a structure that includes a hierarchy or chain of authority. Differences in level of authority will have an effect on the task groups having members from different levels of the organization. A third factor concerns the politics of the organization. Relationships outside of the group will tend to influence members' behavior within the group. Even if the level of authority is the same, how members relate to one another outside of the group is likely to have an effect on their relationships within the group. For example, if two members are rivals and compete with each other for promotion and status in the organization, there is a high probability that this will have an effect on their actions within the group.

The first three stages of group formation are likely to be somewhat brief and should be focused on getting organized and beginning the task rather than on building relationships, as is the case for other groups we discuss in Part Two. The purpose of task groups is not to form relationships that will help members to achieve their goals. Rather, it is to accomplish the task. Members do not need to have an intimate relationship with one another. They do not even have to like one another, although it helps if they do. Theoretically, members can accomplish the task without liking or caring about one another. In reality, not liking one another can lead members to act in a way that does not contribute to the success of the group. However, within organizations there can be severe penalties for doing so.

Maintenance task groups such as staff meetings, case conferences, and the like have a built-in structure to them and they typically follow the chain of authority with the highest ranking member serving as chair. The board is chaired by the president or chair. In his or her absence, the vice president or vice chair presides. Committees typically have a chair who is either appointed by the president or chair or by vote of the board, depending on how the bylaws are structured. Boards have to follow parliamentary procedure when conducting official business such as passing budgets, approving spending, setting policy, and the like. Committees tend to be less formal. Maintenance task groups within the organization also tend to be less formal. However, taking minutes may be necessary in order to report on or keep a record of their functions and decisions.

Other task groups may be formed within the organization to accomplish various purposes such as developing new programs, recommending changes in programs, developing new policies and procedures, and the like. Typically, when a new task group is formed or when a new member joins an existing group, members introduce themselves by name, the position they hold, and the program in which they work. The chair of the group may be appointed, usually by the CEO, or he might be elected by the group. Generally, the highest-ranking member is appointed or elected chair. The chair is responsible for preparing an agenda and presiding over meetings. The introductions are part of the orientation stage. The election or appointment of a chair and the setting of an agenda represent the authority stage. A new group will need to review their charge, which outlines who is authorized to serve in the task group, the purpose or goal of the group, time frames for accomplishing its task, and the authority that the group has with respect to accessing various parts of the organization or its resources. The charge will typically come from the CEO or the board. This also represents the authority stage. The negotiation stage is usually characterized by the group getting organized and deciding on how it will conduct its business. Meeting times and dates need to be set and decisions made about subgroups and assignments. It is better if members volunteer for various responsibilities, but sometimes they may need to be drafted or appointed.

The social worker uses assessment, planning, and action skills during the first three stages of group formation. If she is the chair, the worker needs to facilitate members getting acquainted with one another and organizing the task group. She solicits items for the agenda and prepares it before the meeting. After the meeting is called to order, she asks for approval of the minutes and the agenda. The agenda represents the plan for the meeting. As a group member, the social worker participates in discussions and decision making. She volunteers for responsibilities that are commensurate with her knowledge, skills, and experience. She makes suggestions and helps to negotiate agreements. Planning for a new group, planning for group sessions, and planning during the group are forms of planning that are discussed in Chapter 4.

Actions during the first three stages are centered on facilitating group formation and organization. The actions identified in Chapter 4 are especially relevant for this phase of the group. These include actions to facilitate group formation, group development, and discussion leadership, actions to resolve conflict, enhance group interaction, and structure group activities. As with other elements of the change process, these are used differently for task groups as opposed to other groups that we studied in Part Two. In task groups in organizations, the worker participates in developing good relationships and models this in his actions within the group and when he is acting on behalf of the group. He asks questions, makes suggestions, facilitates discussions, negotiates, and mediates as the group engages in discussions and experiences disagreements. He helps group members to sort out roles, rules, and norms as the group moves toward group formation. He accepts leadership roles and supports others as they become leaders. All of this is done with an eye toward helping the group to reach a point at which it can function as a group and accomplish its tasks.

During the action phase of task group formation, the group may be engaging in actions that set the stage for working on the tasks that will accomplish the group's purpose. This might include conducting a needs assessment as described earlier and in the next chapter. The group might be a product of a needs assessment and charged with planning and implementing a program to meet the needs that were identified and documented in the needs survey. The group may need to gather feedback about the tasks that it was formed to accomplish. Changes in policies and procedures should include feedback from staff before changes are recommended. To the extent that members of the task group represent various interest groups within the organization, they need to gather information from those whom they represent.

As with other groups, evaluation takes place throughout the group. During formative stages, the worker evaluates the group as it moves through the first three stages and becomes a group. She observes and evaluates group and member functioning. She considers the quality of the relationships within the group and seeks to alleviate negative interactions and replace these with more functional positive ones that will move the group toward success.

As with any group, a task group may revisit or recycle back through these early stages even though it has progressed to the functional stage. In fact, each meeting might have some elements that represent any or all of these first three stages. Typically, reviewing minutes and obtaining approval of an agenda represent these stages. The chair gathers information about a potential agenda before the meeting. He reviews unfinished business from previous meetings and puts these under old business. He adds new business based on member input and events that occur between meetings. When the group is called to order, minutes from the previous meeting are reviewed and approved. This is done not only for accuracy but it also serves to remind the group of what was done at the last meeting. It is a form of orientation. The agenda orients the group to the work that needs to be done at this meeting. Approval of the agenda represents the authority and negotiation stages as the group reaches an agreement about the business to be conducted at the meeting.

As with any group, task groups may experience disintegration at any point in time. However, because organizational task groups are set up by organizations to accomplish their mission and goals, they are less likely to disintegrate prematurely. Disintegration during the early stages might occur because it is determined that the wrong mix of members was selected or members are not able to reach the point at which they can work together. There is usually a great deal of pressure to get along and accomplish the task, but negative relationships may persist. If these are overt, they tend to be quite destructive in terms of having the group develop cohesion. Often, these negative relationships are exhibited more covertly and can result in resistance and even sabotage.

Planning also occurs at meetings as the group or subgroups meet to share information and develop plans for each phase of the work. During the functional stage of group development, planning involves activities that are related to accomplishing the group's purpose. Planning during the first three stages was focused on forming and organizing the group and laying the foundation for working on the tasks that the group will need to undertake to be successful. Planning during the functional stage is aimed at actually accomplishing those tasks. Members report on their activities between meetings and plans are made for activities that will take place between now and the next meeting.

Actions take place at meetings as the group analyzes information and makes decisions. Actions also occur outside of the group between meetings as members carry out tasks, gather information, and implement plans. If she is the chair of the group or a subgroup, the worker is responsible for coordinating the efforts of the group and reporting back to the larger group. Members may also have responsibility for coordination, but are primarily responsible for accomplishing tasks that contribute to the success of the group. Many of the social worker's actions in carrying out tasks will involve similar actions that we have identified. She uses assessment, planning, action, and evaluation skills. She builds relationships with key members of the organization and seeks their input and support. She contributes to enabling and empowering the group in carrying out its tasks. She intervenes when there is a crisis and seeks to resolve it so the group can get back on track in conducting its business. The worker uses her knowledge about resources. She supports the group and its members by being positive and encouraging and facilitating discussion. She mediates disagreements within the group and with other individuals or entities outside of the group. The work of task groups typically involves the environment of the worker and often that of clients of the agency. When the group is involved in planning and implementing new or modified programs or services, it is planning and implementing environmental change. The social worker should engage in proactive advocacy to ensure that changes benefit clients and staff, especially staff at lower levels of the organization who might be vulnerable to detrimental changes without having a voice in those changes. The worker uses her skills in coordination to coordinate the efforts of the group and subgroups and to assist with the implementation of planned changes.

Evaluation during the functional stage is focused on evaluating progress toward accomplishing the purpose of the task group. This should include consideration of the effectiveness and efficiency of any planned changes as well as their effect on staff and clients.

While disintegration can occur during the functional stage, it is highly unlikely since the group will have reached the point at which they are accomplishing the task. Disintegration might occur because the group runs out of time and exceeds its authorized time limit. Typically, an extension is secured, especially if the group is close to achieving its purpose. Disintegration does occur at the end of each meeting and the group needs to review what it has accomplished and what needs to be done between meetings.

An assessment of the group's work, complete with accomplishments and failures, is conducted as the group nears an end to its work. A plan is developed for writing reports and wrapping up the group's work. Actions are taken that complete whatever needs to be finished and data are collected and analyzed. The final report represents an evaluation of the effectiveness of the group's efforts in accomplishing its task.

As the group reaches the point at which it has achieved its purpose, disintegration and termination need to be planned. As we indicated, the group needs to develop a final report. If it has not accomplished its task, then some debriefing needs to occur and a report written and submitted identifying what was accomplished and what was not and reasons for each. Successful endings need to have a report on what was accomplished and what might still need to be done.

## Summary

Changing organizations from within may be the strategy of choice when agency functioning is the cause of the block to client need fulfillment. To use this strategy, the worker first assesses the social system of the agency. Emphasis is placed on decision making and resistance to change. This strategy is important because of the ethical responsibility of social workers to work for humane delivery of social services. Self-help groups and volunteer programs are two means for enhancing the resources available to clients.

The generalist social worker provides services to individuals, families, small groups, organizations, and communities. The focus is on transactions among systems, that is, on social functioning. This approach to social work calls for a wide variety of strategies, including those that do not focus on the client. These strategies involve action with other systems on behalf of clients, and focus on situations in the client's environment that affect social functioning. Ethically, a social worker must not only work with the client but also with systems that impinge on the client.

CASE **11.1**

**Working with Task Groups
in a Retirement Facility**

As the social worker at Sunnyside Assisted Living Facility, Sue meets with the resident council each month. The facility is part of a larger complex that includes a retirement facility as well as a facility to serve residents who require nursing home care. Each program has its own resident council. There is also a coordinating resident council made up of the officers from each of the facility councils. During a meeting, a member brought up the idea of having a newsletter. While the organization already has a quarterly newsletter, the majority of residents felt that there is a need for more frequent news and they wanted to have more focus on the residents and on items of interest to them. There was a discussion about what they could do with a newsletter and whether to include the other facilities and even families. Several members volunteered to organize an effort and the chairperson agreed to bring the matter up at the next coordinating resident council meeting. Sue pointed out the need to discuss the proposal with administration and the need to identify funding. She volunteered to discuss it with her supervisor and with the social workers from the other units and with her family support group.

Sue discussed the idea with her supervisor and her colleagues at the next social work staff meeting and they were all supportive. Sue had found some unused funding in the activities budget that could be used for clubs for residents. She suggested that the residents could form a newsletter club. The other social workers agreed to take this idea back to their resident councils. There was some discussion regarding whether to make this a newsletter for the whole organization or to let each unit have their own. It was decided that this should be left up to the residents. If enough people were interested then each unit could have their own, but if there was not enough interest, then an organization-wide option might be best. Their supervisor agreed to bring the proposal up at the next administrative staff meeting. At the next family support group meeting, Sue also raised the possibility of a

newsletter by and for residents and their families. The families were very supportive of the idea. One member worked at a print shop and offered to approach her boss about sponsoring the project and letting her help.

At the next staff meeting, Sue's supervisor indicated that administration was not opposed if they could find funding for it. Sue reported that the coordinating resident council had met and decided to form a newsletter club and apply for funding. They also considered the possibility of selling some space for advertising. Several residents had already come forward to gather and write stories and articles. The coordinating council decided to appoint an editor and have that person serve on the council as a nonvoting member since the position was not one that would be elected by the residents. A decision had been made to try an organization-wide newsletter first. Then, if there was sufficient interest, other options would be considered. Sue also reported that the family member who worked in the print shop had been told by the owner that they would copy the newsletter at cost and he would do the first one for free.

As Sue worked within the organization to assist her residents with this project, she used her skills as a social worker and as a group member. Sue facilitated the discussion and planning within the resident council while still allowing the residents to be in charge of their meeting. Her primary role was that of resource for the group. She advocated for them with her supervisor, who in turn secured support for the project at the administrative staff meeting. Sue led the discussion with her colleagues and secured their support. In turn, they were able to get support from their resident councils. When the chairperson of Sue's resident council proposed the project to the coordinating resident council, Sue provided information regarding potential funding and reported that her family support group was enthusiastic about the project.

## QUESTIONS

1. Identify a need in your community. Discuss how you would go about developing a task group within an organization that would be designed to address that need.

2. How would you see the task group progressing through stages of development as it met the need you identified in Question 1?

3. Describe a role you would play as a social worker in a task group within an organization organized to meet the need you identified in Question 1. What organization did you select and why? Who would you want to have as members of your task group? Why would you select these people?

4. What are the ethical considerations of working in an agency that is not meeting the needs of clients (needs for which it has responsibility)? How much risk would you be willing to take in bringing about needed change in an agency? At what point do you think it would be appropriate for you to use a change-from-within strategy?

5. What is meant by *proactive advocacy* and when should a social worker engage in this form of advocacy? Describe a situation in which you would consider using proactive advocacy within an organization.

## SUGGESTED READINGS

Johnson, Louise C., and Yanca, Stephen J., *Social Work Practice: A Generalist Approach*, 9th ed. Boston: Allyn & Bacon, 2007 (Chapters 7, 14, and 15).

Brueggemann, William G. *The Practice of Macro Social Work*, 3rd ed. Belmont, CA: Thomson-Brooks/Cole, 2006 (Chapters 9–12).

Erlich, John, Rothman, Jack, and Teresa, Joseph G. *Taking Action in Organizations and Communities,* 2nd ed. Dubuque, IA: Eddie Bowers Publishing, 1999.

Fatout, Marian, and Rose, Steven R. *Task Groups in the Social Services*. Newbury Park, CA: Sage Publications, 1995.

Kettner, Peter M. *Achieving Excellence in the Management of Human Service Organizations*. Boston: Allyn & Bacon, 2002.

Long, Dennis D., Tice, Carolyn J., and Morrison, John D. *Macro Social Work Practice: A Strengths Perspective*. Belmont, CA: Thomson-Brooks/Cole, 2006.

Netting, Ellen F., Kettner, Peter M., and McMurtry, Steven L. *Social Work Macro Practice,* 4th ed. Boston: Allyn & Bacon, 2008.

Netting, Ellen F., and O'Connor, Mary K. *Organization Practice: A Social Worker's Guide to Understanding Human Services*. Boston: Allyn & Bacon, 2003.

Rae, P. Ann, and Nicholas-Wolosuk, Wanda. *Changing Agency Policy: An Incremental Approach*. Boston: Allyn & Bacon, 2003.

Weinbach, Robert. *The Social Worker as Manager,* 5th ed. Boston: Allyn & Bacon, 2008.

# CHAPTER

# 12 Generalist Practice with Communities

1. Understanding the need to work with communities in generalist social work practice.
2. Understanding communities as social systems.
3. Understanding needs assessment in generalist practice with communities.
4. Knowledge of various approaches to generalist practice with communities.
5. Understanding the change process in working with communities.

This chapter deals with the change process in generalist social work practice with communities. As with direct practice with organizations, it is rare for the BSW or inexperienced MSW social worker to be called on to work directly with large communities as client systems in bringing about change. In rural areas, social workers may work more directly with communities. This is mostly related to developing services. Social workers often work with various groups in the community as they serve their clients. It is also important that the worker understands the community in which she is practicing and the community as an ecosystem for her clients. The worker may become involved with the change process as a participant in community task groups. When the social worker engages in these activities, she acts on behalf of clients to ensure that changes that are made at the community level benefit clients who are in need of services and resources. The worker brings her knowledge and skill in working with groups and in assessment, planning, direct and indirect practice actions, and evaluation to working with communities.

The first part of the chapter discusses the community as a social system and this is followed by a presentation of approaches to generalist practice with communities. Finally, the chapter examines the use of the change process in working with communities including assessing the community, conducting a needs assessment, planning with communities, practice actions with communities, policy change, and evaluation with communities.

## The Community as a Social System

The **community** is the environment of the worker, the client system, and the agency. Different units of that community will have different impacts and influences on each. The interactions of worker and client system are influenced by the transactions of the community.

Service delivery is a part of the community system. Understanding these impacts and influences is an important aspect of generalist social work knowledge. To gain this understanding, it is first necessary for the worker to see the community as a social system. This knowledge is important not only because the environment influences the worker–client system interaction but also because the community may be the client or it may be the target for intervention. In either of these cases, the worker usually works with individuals and small groups to bring about change in the community structure and functioning. For the generalist social worker, effort is usually focused on changing or developing a community resource that will in turn enhance the functioning of individuals and families. Whether the community or some element of it is the client or is the target of change, it is important to understand the community as a social system so that its strengths and resources can be included in promoting growth and change. Particular attention needs to be paid to these elements as the worker seeks to understand the community.

At a minimum, such knowledge calls for awareness of the boundaries of the community, its component parts (individuals, families, associations, neighborhoods, organizations, institutions, etc.), and its environment. The worker also needs to be aware of the way the community functions and of its historical development.

The identification of a community's boundaries poses a substantial problem in a society of large cities and multiple institutional catchment areas. Is an agency's community a geographic place, the catchment area from which the clients come? Is a group of persons who support and sanction the agency its community? Is it the immediate geographic neighborhood in which it is located? Should the entire metropolitan area be considered a community? Or are community and neighborhood the same? Each of these questions may be answered affirmatively under certain circumstances.

There can also be a time element in the concept of community. The *community system* functions in relation to issues and to provide services (e.g., education). The *community units* may interact only when dealing with those issues and in providing services. Community units are groups (both formal and informal), organizations, institutions, and other social systems that function within the boundaries of the community. Thus, the community system also may have a time element and exist only under certain circumstances.

The community may be seen as a geographic place. *Community* is a term also used to describe "nonplace" associations such as the professional community or the religious community. When considering the kinship group, the extended family, or certain cultural groups, community is a related concept. The community system can have a wide variety of forms that can influence the transactions among individuals, families, and small groups.

Sociology furnishes us with several ways of considering a community. Ferdinand Tönnies saw a change in the relationships among people with the industrialization of society. He described this change as one from **Gemeinschaft** (rural "we-ness") to **Gesellschaft** (individuals related through structures in the community).[1] These differences among communities still exist. Rural or small communities function rather informally; urban or large communities tend to function more through formal structures. In searching for understanding of a community, a worker will find it useful to determine the kinds of relationships that exist in the community. Usually, there are different kinds of relationships, depending on the community functions involved.

Understanding the use of land adds another dimension to the study of a community. One method of using this concept is to draw maps of a community showing retail stores; wholesale businesses; industry (light and heavy); schools, churches, and other institutions; various types of residential dwellings; and the locations of various ethnic and socioeconomic groups.

Floyd Hunter's studies of community power are also useful.[2] The location of the community power structure is particularly important when trying to develop new services or to change existing services. This power structure may be formal or informal, elected or assigned. The impact of the power is varied depending on how the power holder and others perceive the power. It is exercised through initiating activity, legitimizing activity, giving approval to ideas and plans, implementing decisions, or blocking discussion of issues and of decisions. Usually, the impact of a particular power holder depends on the issue at hand. Some in power tend to have greater influence over economic issues than over social welfare issues. In larger communities, where power is more dispersed, there is a greater chance that power is related to specific segments of community life. In smaller communities, power tends to reside with one small group of people. Identification of not only the individuals in the power structure but also how they exercise that power and over what issues they have significant influence is another important ingredient of any community assessment.

Eugene Litwak's work on the significance of the neighborhood points out the neighborhood's importance for client systems in meeting need. He identified several types of neighborhoods and their effectiveness in meeting need. The *mobile neighborhood* manages to retain its cohesion despite a rapid turnover of residents. The *traditional neighborhood* is one in which residents are long term and that maintains stability. The *mass neighborhood* is one in which there is no mechanism of integration.[3] Understanding the kind of neighborhood a client lives in helps a worker understand a client and the resources that may be available for that client.

Roland Warren's work, which considers the community as a social system, is especially useful. He identified the locally relevant functions of a community as (1) production-distribution-consumption, (2) socialization, (3) social control, (4) social participation, and (5) mutual support. Each community has community units that carry out these functions. The business community has a major responsibility for production, distribution, and consumption. The schools are involved in socialization. Government is concerned with social control. Various clubs and organizations fulfill social participation needs. Social welfare organizations are involved in mutual support. Warren also noted that many community units have ties with structures and systems outside the community. These links are known as *vertical patterns;* relationships within the community are known as *horizontal patterns*. An example of this conceptualization as it relates to a church (a community unit) would be that the horizontal link would be a local council of churches or ministerial group; the vertical link would be to a denominational body. Warren saw the exploration of these patterns as a primary means for studying a community.[4]

There are differences among communities, just as there are among any category of social system. It is almost impossible to develop a scheme for classifying communities because of the many variables involved. Dennis Poplin identified three areas that seem important when considering differences among communities: size, the nature of a community's hinterland, and social-cultural features.[5]

Differences in size usually have been discussed on a rural-urban continuum. The U.S. Census Bureau uses a population of 2,500 as the division point between rural and urban. This leaves many different types of communities in the urban category. Another division point frequently used is 50,000, the population necessary for a Standard Metropolitan Statistical Area. In looking at nonmetropolitan community service delivery systems, Louise Johnson identified four types of communities: the small city, the small town, the rural community, and the reservation community.[6]

In subsequent work, Johnson identified two additional types of small communities: the bedroom community and the institutional community. The bedroom community is found near a larger community that furnishes jobs and often a variety of services for residents of the bedroom community. The institutional community contains a large institution, such as a state mental hospital, an educational institution, or a government site (state capital), which is the major employer in that community. She found that community characteristics are heavily influenced by the distance between communities that contain services (e.g., medical, social, and retail). Small communities that are at considerable distance from services in another community have a richer service system than do communities of the same size that are near communities from which they can obtain services.[7]

Metropolitan areas contain communities that differ: there are the central city, the suburban community, and the satellite city. In addition, some communities are inhabited by the upper class. Some may have a reputation for being inhabited by bohemian, intellectual, or artistic persons, such as Greenwich Village in New York City; others are middle-class communities. There also are the ghettos and the barrio communities that have typically been a particular concern of social workers. Ethnic communities have particular characteristics that come in part from the culture of the groups occupying them. A social worker should possess an understanding of the characteristics of the particular kind of community with which she is working.

A community, then, can be considered as a social system that has a population, shared institutions and values, and significant social interactions between the individuals and the institutions. The institutions perform major social functions. A community usually but not always occupies space or a geographic area and has many forms. In modern society several communities may overlap. Communities differ in the amount of autonomy they have and the extent to which persons living in the community identify with their community. When considering the community as a social system, understanding from many sources can be used to provide a theoretical base or to point to characteristics that should be considered in specific communities. In other words, different communities, because of differing characteristics, often call for different choices as to what is important to include in a community study.

In trying to attain understanding about a community and its impact on people, agencies, and institutions, a social worker faces two major problems. First is the identification of the system itself, which varies depending on the situation. Often a political unit is the defined system; this is a fairly easy way to define boundaries, but it is artificial and does not really consider parts of the community system that may lie outside the political boundaries. When looking at the neighborhood system, it is difficult to define boundaries.

Understanding a community calls for identifying the boundaries of the unit to be considered. Too large an area makes the study unwieldy; too small an area makes it too limited.

In nonmetropolitan areas, the choice may be a small city or town. In metropolitan areas, the choice may better be a neighborhood or some other manageable unit. Creativity is necessary in deciding how to define the community.

Social workers function in many different kinds of communities: large metropolitan areas, neighborhood settings, small cities, rural communities, large institutions, Native American reservations, and so on. Each kind of community has different characteristics. The study of any community as a social system provides understandings that can lead to greater degrees of client-congruent culture, to better use of available resources, to identification of when the community should be the focus of change, and to better identification of which work strategy is best suited to a particular situation.

Of special concern to social workers are diversity factors that exist in the community. The racial and ethnic makeup of the community are important to know. With regard to race and ethnicity, the worker should have knowledge about the degree to which various groups are integrated or segregated. He should note the attitudes of various groups toward each other. Is there respect or valuing of differences? Are there coalitions that have been formed? Are there adversarial relationships? How tolerant or intolerant are these groups toward one another? What groups hold power? Who has little or no power, and how does this reflect the general population? Similar questions should also be asked with respect to gender, age, and sexual orientation.

Some information about diversity can be obtained from census data or community surveys. However, much of this information is obtained more informally, through observation and discussion with key informants who know the history and have personal knowledge about various populations. For instance, knowledge about the gay or lesbian community may be available only from someone who is a member of the gay or lesbian community or from someone who works with this community.

The diversity competent social worker tunes in on the attitudes and stereotypes toward diverse groups and the affect that these have on members of each population. She is also aware of the values that each group holds and is alert to value conflicts and their affect on relationships. The worker identifies ways of helping that each group uses and seeks to improve her skills so that she can serve members of each group in a manner with which they are comfortable.

The second problem social workers face in understanding a community is the fact that the information that can be collected about any community is vast. It is never possible to obtain complete information. Some decisions must be made as to when there is sufficient information for understanding. Care needs to be taken to ensure that the information is representative of all units in a community. Some information can be found in a library in local history books, census reports, directories, and the like. Other helpful written material can be obtained from chambers of commerce, local government units, and volunteer organizations. Some information is not as easy to obtain; it may be known within the community but not shared with outsiders. This includes information about relationships among people and institutions and the community's decision-making and power structure. Information about norms and values may be obtainable only after observing and being a part of the community for some period of time.

In order to understand community interaction, gathering information from many individuals and small groups is essential. The generalist social worker uses both formal and informal interviews and observes and participates in small groups. The worker carefully observes a wide range of community interactions in order to develop understanding about the community and its impact on the functioning of individuals, groups, and families.

Because of the amount of material, in terms of both volume and variety, it is helpful if an organized plan is developed for gathering such material. Social workers can begin to gather some material before entering a new community. They also need to add to this material as long as they work in the community. As with all social systems, the community system continues to change. In Table 12.1, one means of organizing a community study considers major subsystems related to Warren's locally relevant functions. The table provides a means to identify possible impacts, influences, and resources in the community system and looks for both horizontal and vertical relationships.[8] Table 12.1 provides a social worker with a guide for developing a working understanding of a community. The community study represents the assessment document for community practice.

Once a social worker has the necessary information, it becomes possible to identify and understand current concerns in the community, the community decision-making process, and the manner in which that community usually solves its problems. Issues relative to community autonomy become clearer, as do differing service areas for different community agencies and institutions. For instance, the school district, the political boundaries, and the shopping service area are often different. Also, at this point it is possible to identify strengths and limitations of the community system. Because of the size and diversity of the units (subsystems) within the community system, different parts of the system will show different strengths and different limitations. One way of focusing the consideration of strengths and limitations is to consider the overall quality of life as perceived by community residents.

A community study should include at least some consideration of the strengths and limitations of the community system, the manner in which that community solves its problems, and the capacity and motivation for change. Communities that seem most able to fulfill their functions and meet people's needs have the following characteristics:

1. At least some primary relationships exist.
2. They are comparatively autonomous (not overly impacted by outside influences).
3. They have the capacity to face problems and engage in efforts to solve those problems.
4. There is a broad distribution of power.
5. Citizens have a commitment to the community.
6. Citizen participation is possible and encouraged.
7. There are more homogeneous than heterogeneous relationships.
8. They have developed ways of dealing with conflict.
9. There is tolerance for and valuing of diversity.

It is difficult for a community to meet citizen need when (1) the problems lie beyond the capacity of the community to solve, (2) the organizations and institutions of the community lack sufficient autonomy, and (3) the citizens lack identification with the community. These community characteristics should be considered when identifying strengths and limitations of any community system.

**TABLE 12.1    Schema for the Study of a Geographic Community**

**I.** Setting, history, demography
  **A.** Physical setting
    **1.** Location, ecology, size
    **2.** Relationship to other geographic entities
      **a.** Ecological, political, economic, social
      **b.** Transportation, mass media from outside the community
  **B.** Historical development
    **1.** Settlement, significant events, change over time, cultural factors
  **C.** Demography
    **1.** Population
      **a.** Age and sex distribution
      **b.** Cultural, ethnic, racial groups
      **c.** Socioeconomic distribution
    **2.** Physical structure
      **a.** Who lives where?
      **b.** Location of businesses, industry, institutions
    **3.** Other
      **a.** Mobility
      **b.** Housing conditions
  **D.** Cultural setting
    **1.** Community norms, values, and expectations
    **2.** Community traditions and events

**II.** Economic system
  **A.** Employment
    **1.** Industry: nature, who is employed, number of employees, influence from outside community, relationship to community and employees
    **2.** Distribution-consumption: retail and wholesale business, kind, location, ownership, employees, trade territory
    **3.** Institutions that employ large numbers of persons: nature, number of employees, types of employees, relationship to community, influence from outside community
  **B.** Other economic factors
    **1.** Stability of economy
    **2.** Leading business persons
    **3.** Organizations of business or organizations that influence the economic system

**III.** Political system
  **A.** Government units (structure and functioning)
    **1.** Span of control
    **2.** Personnel, elected and appointed
    **3.** Financial information
    **4.** Way of functioning—meetings, etc.
  **B.** Law enforcement, including court system
  **C.** Party politics: dominant party and history of recent elections
  **D.** Influence on social service system
  **E.** Services provided

**IV.** Educational system

  **A.** Structure and administration (all levels)

  **B.** Financing, buildings

  **C.** Students

    **1.** Numbers at each level or other divisions

    **2.** Attendance and dropout rates

  **D.** Instructional factors

    **1.** Teacher–student ratio

    **2.** Subjects available, curriculum philosophy

    **3.** Provisions for special-needs students

  **E.** Extracurricular activity

  **F.** Community relations

**V.** Social–Cultural system

  **A.** Recreational–cultural activities, events

    **1.** Parks, public recreation programs

    **2.** Cultural resources: libraries, museums, theaters, concerts

    **3.** Commercial recreation

  **B.** Religious institutions and activities

    **1.** Churches: kind, location, membership, activities, leadership

    **2.** Attitudes: values, concern for social welfare issues, concern for own members

    **3.** Influence on community

  **C.** Associations and organizations

    **1.** Kind, membership, purpose, and goals

    **2.** Activities, ways of functioning, leadership

    **3.** Intergroup organizations and linkage within and outside the community

    **4.** Resources available

  **D.** Mass media in community

    **1.** Radio, TV, newspapers

  **E.** Ethnic, racial, and other diverse groups

    **1.** Way of life, customs, child-rearing patterns, etc.

    **2.** Relationship to larger community

    **3.** Structure and functioning of group

  **F.** Community persons

    **1.** Power persons; how power is manifested

    **2.** Leadership and respected persons

**VI.** Human service system

  **A.** Health care services and institutions

    **1.** Doctors, dentists, and other professionals

    **2.** Hospitals, clinics, nursing homes

    **3.** Public health services

    **4.** Responsiveness of health care system to needs of people

  **B.** Formal social welfare system

    **1.** Agencies in community: function, persons eligible for service, how supported and how sanctioned, staff, location

(*continued*)

**TABLE 12.1 (Continued)**

---

   **2.** Agencies from outside that serve community: location, services available, conditions of service, control of agency
   **3.** Conflicts among, overlaps, complementary factors of social welfare agencies
**C.** Informal helping system
   **1.** Individuals and organizations
   **2.** How help is given, to whom
   **3.** Relationship to formal system
**D.** Planning bodies
   **1.** Fundraising, regulatory, consultative

**VII.** General considerations
   **A.** Current concerns of community. Who is concerned? Why? What has been done about the concern?
   **B.** Customary ways of solving community problems. Who needs to be involved?
   **C.** Community decision-making process
   **D.** How autonomous is the community? Do various service areas coincide or are they different? How strong is the psychological identification with the community?
   **E.** Strengths of community in terms of "quality of life"
   **F.** Challenges to community in terms of "quality of life"

---

The community can be a nebulous entity that is often understood only intuitively. It can also be a defined system understood through organized study. In fact, through organized study a social worker is most apt to grasp the impacts and influences the community has on the social work endeavor. Skill in understanding a community includes:

1. A framework to organize information
2. The ability to locate information and resources
3. The ability to identify the information needed in specific situations
4. The ability to analyze the information obtained and to identify linkages and relationships among information and among subsystems in the community system
5. The ability to interact with individuals and small groups for purposes of developing relationships and gathering information about a community
6. The ability for careful observation of community functioning

It is also through organized study that the social worker gains knowledge about the resources a community provides for all members of that community. Knowledge of impacts, influences, and resources leads to effective practice with individuals, families, and small groups. It also leads to a practice that considers interventions into the system of the community and/or its subsystems when these larger systems impact on individuals, families, and small groups. Negative impacts, then, may become legitimate targets for change.[9]

The community is a social system. Like any social system, it has a structure, a way of functioning, and a history. It has energy and organization. The functioning of the helping system cannot be fully understood apart from the environment in which it functions, the community.

# Approaches to Generalist Practice with Communities

Community organization is a field of study unto itself and is beyond the scope of this book. However, community organizing will be discussed here briefly, so that the reader has some awareness of its role in generalist social work practice and how it can be used to bring about change in a community. Rothman and Tropman presented three models of community organization practice that can be used to address social issues and promote change, as follows:

**1.** *Locality development*—This model is used when the desired change is to facilitate community cooperation and interaction, and foster self-help. It is primarily a process model in that it focuses on efforts to involve large numbers of concerned citizens in an area rather than on a specific change per se.

**2.** *Social planning*—This model is used when the goal is planned change regarding a specific issue. It utilizes "experts" rather than grassroots planners and is commonly used in governmental, educational, and private institutional settings. There may be very little, if any, community involvement in the process.

**3.** *Social action*—This model utilizes a coalition of a disadvantaged segment of the population to take action regarding a social problem that affects them directly. This is discussed in more detail in a following section.[10]

Rothman and Tropman's models are classic examples of professional community organizing strategies. They provide an excellent base for understanding community practice as a professional social worker working as a community organizer. However, many generalist social workers need to understand community practice from a generalist perspective and as a worker who needs to work with the community as a part of her work with other client systems. It is also important for her to understand how to work with various task groups in the community. From this perspective it is important to consider the involvement of the worker, the involvement of members of the community, the involvement of community organizations, and the involvement of governmental agencies and bodies. Each of these may vary considerably. In addition, the unit of attention for the change effort may be the community or a segment of the community, organizations in the community, or governmental systems. In an ecosystems approach to change, the unit of attention could also be the interaction among any of these systems. The role of the worker and the use of the change process in these various configurations is explored below. First let us look at the various types of change efforts.

The community or neighborhood or segment of the community may be the initiator of the change effort or the unit of attention. When change is initiated by the community or any group of community members, we generally refer to it as a *grassroots movement*. In working with a grassroots movement, the worker may be a participant as either a representative of his organization or as a private citizen. In either case, the worker may provide valuable knowledge and skills in organizing, campaigning, advertising, media relations, and similar activities that may be vital to the success of the change effort. When the worker initiates the change effort, either alone or with a group, we consider this to be an *activist movement*. As with a grassroots movement, similar activities typically take place, but an effort to involve the community or affected segments of it is generally the first priority in using this approach. In a grassroots movement, the community is already involved and the worker joins the effort and lends his expertise. In either of these instances, community organizations may or may not be involved as supporters of the change effort. Some community organizations may be the unit of attention. Most often, these two approaches do not involve governmental systems as partners in the change process, at least not initially. However governmental systems are frequently the unit of attention either primarily or secondarily. In the first instance the change effort is aimed directly at a governmental unit. In the second instance, influencing the governmental unit may be necessary in order for the effort to be successful.

One or more community organizations may initiate a change effort that is directed at the community or a segment of it or at governmental systems or at other organizations. We will refer to this as an *organizational task force*. It might also be called an *organizational* or *agency collaborative* or *cooperative*. Governmental systems may also set up a task force that we refer to as a *governmental task force*. When members of the community are included in an organizational task force, we refer to it as a *community partnership*. When members of the community are included in a governmental task force, we call it a *community task force*. Community task forces may also include representatives of community organizations. Most often task forces are developed to address social or economic issues in either the community at large or a segment or area of it. Task forces might be set up to reduce crime or drug activities or to reverse urban decay or promote economic revival. The worker is usually a representative of her organization and her knowledge and skills are used in a more formal way by the task force to facilitate the change effort.

# Using the Change Process with Communities

As the social worker works with client systems she comes into contact with the community. She also works with communities to bring about change. In doing so she uses her knowledge and skills in the change process to serve her clients and her community. The worker uses assessment, planning, direct and indirect practice actions, and evaluation as she works with communities.

## Assessment with Communities

Assessment with communities can take many different forms. One form is the assessment of the community itself which was covered earlier and is outlined in Table 12.1. The worker might limit this assessment to a particular section of the community such as a neighborhood. She might consider an ethnic community or a segment of the community such as the human services system. The form of the assessment is dictated by the purpose or the need. In large metropolitan areas it may be too cumbersome and unnecessary to gather all the information outlined in Table 12.1. Typically, a study of a neighborhood may be more appropriate. Conversely, in rural areas, the worker might consider an entire county or even several counties as the community. When working with Native Americans, the reservation may be the community that needs to be studied. Community assessments may be used by any of the situations we described under various change efforts (task forces, partnerships, and movements). Typically, assessments of the community with grassroots or activist movements are informal and limited to certain elements of the schema in Table 12.1 that are necessary for the change effort. Assessments with task forces and partnerships are more formal.

Quite often, the most valuable use of assessment in the community is a needs assessment. Assessment of a community and its resources, assessment of a group of people, or assessment of a client in a situation may result in the realization that needed resources are not available. Social workers have a responsibility to work toward the development of needed resources. One of the first steps is carrying out a needs assessment. A needs assessment represents a very practical application of the assessment process to working with communities. Funding sources usually require some data relative to the nature and extent of need be gathered before they will support new projects or programs. Some governmental funding agencies and accreditation bodies require a needs assessment as part of their ongoing review of programs. A needs assessment may be undertaken by an agency, a group of agencies, or a community group.

Sometimes a needs assessment may have been done before any of the task forces or community partnerships are formed. Typically, this would have been initiated by an organization, a group of organizations, or a governmental system. The task force or partnership may represent the next step after the needs assessment is completed. Other times, a needs assessment may be undertaken by the task force or partnership to lay the groundwork for planning. Usually, this is a more formal assessment, especially if it will be used to secure funding for the effort. Social workers may have conducted the original needs assessment or may be involved in conducting one with a task force as representatives of community organizations or governmental systems. This may include designing and implementing the study.

The needs assessment can be carried out in several ways. First, general opinions about the service or the need for service can be obtained from various segments of the community, such as service providers, consumers, and community influentials. A major problem with this type of information gathering is that it represents opinions, not hard facts. However, this mechanism can provide information that may not be obtainable through other means. It can be a preliminary step in designing an assessment instrument that captures a complete picture of the problem and can be used to involve the community in the assessment.

A second mechanism for needs assessment is to survey current users of service. Often professionals forget that the "I need" perspective is just as important as the "they need" perspective. Involving users in needs assessments may provide important information about the design of services. However, it is not always possible for users to articulate their needs, so the mechanism may not provide a complete picture of the need. For example, people who are older may have some difficulty admitting to need. They may feel that the admission of limitations would force them into a nursing home or to come to grips with the aging process in ways they prefer to avoid.

Another mechanism of determining need is through the use of statistical data. For example, if a community has a high percentage (compared to similar communities) of people who are older or people below the poverty level, it is likely that there are needs not being met. The worker must be careful in using statistical data, as the use of this mechanism may lead to assumptions that later prove unfounded.

Usually, in designing a needs assessment it is desirable to use several means for collecting data. Need can be identified in terms of gaps in services, redundancy of services, availability of services to various groups of people, accessibility of services to those who are in need, and usability of service (e.g., is it provided within a framework that can be used by various diversity groups?).

Before designing a needs assessment instrument, it is important to be thoroughly familiar with the community, the need area, and the population to be targeted. The schema for the study of a community (Table 12.1) should be used for this purpose. Involving community influentials or community organizations can also be very helpful in planning the assessment. These people can help interpret the need for the assessment, give it community sanction, and provide input for its construction; this will make the assessment acceptable to the community and result in a greater chance of an accurate response. Other social systems significant to the study also need to be identified, as well as all possible data sources. The latter category includes demographic statistical profiles, key informants (those in direct contact with those experiencing problems), consumers of service, individuals experiencing difficulty or having potential for doing so, and the general public. A preliminary statement of the concern or need should be developed at this stage and assumptions about the nature of the concern or need and potential resources stated.

When the needed background information has been gathered, the worker is ready to begin the design of the needs assessment. Decisions must be made about the type of data needed, the individuals who can best provide the information, and the most appropriate means for gathering that information. Information can be gathered in person, by phone interviews, through mailed questionnaires, or through existing data such as agency or census records. Generally, it is wise to develop an instrument that will allow the collection of the same information from each respondent. Information sought may include demographic data, such as race, gender, age, marital status, educational level, and length of residence in the community; perceived problems; where information about services is obtained; factors that hinder the seeking of help; and services needed. The development of the needs assessment design requires creativity to individualize it for the situation.

As the needs assessment design is being developed, two other areas need attention. The first is the development of a publicity campaign. Public knowledge of the assessment and its purpose is necessary if people are to provide accurate information. A publicity campaign can include news releases, television and radio spots, posters, and announcements at meetings and community activities. It can make use of the community members who have been involved in the development of the needs assessment. These individuals can give sanction and lend credibility to the effort. When considering a needs assessment, it is important to consider timing of the survey. The worker must be aware of other activities going on in the community and plan the assessment for an appropriate time.

Another consideration relates to the confidentiality of information obtained, or the human rights concern. All publicity should indicate how the information will be used and assure confidentiality. Interviewers must be trained not only in confidentiality issues but also in how to conduct the interview. Often, it is helpful to first test an instrument with a small sample of people representative of those who will be contacted during the assessment. This test case can alert the designer to questions that are problematic and apt to be misinterpreted or not answered. This helps ensure that the outcome of the assessment will be accurate. The evaluation and interpretation of information are part of the assessment design and relate to the particular information. Once this stage has taken place, it is important to share the findings with those who have participated in the assessment. Needs assessment, when properly carried out, is an involved process but an important part of meeting the needs of individuals and families.

## Planning with Communities

As with assessment, planning can take several forms in working with a community. Different forms of community organization practice may require different types of planning. Planning may be formal or informal. Planning needs to take place for everything from planning meetings to planning campaigns to planning programs that address the results of needs surveys.

Governmental systems and task forces in urban areas will typically have individuals or even whole departments devoted to urban planning. In addition, there are private engineering firms that may be contracted to plan developments and renovations. In suburban and rural areas, local governments typically have planning bodies that are appointed to develop and oversee zoning ordinances. These often use private firms to assist with these endeavors. Other governmental systems develop plans and budgets either to continue to provide various services or to develop new ones. Whenever tax dollars are involved, there are processes for plans and budgets to be reviewed by governmental bodies, usually elected officials who must conduct their business at public meetings. This provides individuals and community groups with opportunities to influence the process and the results. Public meetings are a frequent target for grassroots and activist movements. Many public meetings are also covered by the media, so this also provides an opportunity to get their message out to the larger community. The social worker can assist with organizing these efforts and may act as a spokesperson or assist with developing a message and may even prepare and deliver news releases.

Organizational task forces or collaboratives or cooperatives need planning processes that will allow the member organizations to develop and maintain mutually beneficial service delivery systems. Good planning is more likely to result in good cooperation and good services. Planning may need to take place at many levels across several organizations. Meetings need to be planned and organized and plans developed, implemented, and monitored. The organizations may undertake a needs survey and plans are then made to address those needs. The social worker may participate in planning activities as a representative of her agency. She might be involved within her agency with planning for her program that will contribute to the overall plan for services with other agencies.

Planning within organizations can be top down, bottom up, or some blending of these. Top down refers to planning that occurs at higher levels of the agency without much involvement from below. Bottom up is the opposite of this. Organizations that do top down planning need accurate data and a realistic view of what is possible along with an understanding of the impact that plans have on service delivery. Otherwise, plans may interfere with effectiveness and efficiency. At the very least, top down planning should include feedback from supervisors and direct services staff before being finalized and implemented. Bottom up planning can be effective but may not always be efficient. Planning takes time; if direct services staff have to devote too much time to planning, it takes away from service delivery. In addition, staff at lower levels of the organization may not have sufficient understanding of the larger picture either within the organization or in the community. Many organizations find that a blend of these works well. Typically, planning groups are formed.

Some may be permanent and others temporary, formed to deal with a specific project. Planning groups need representation from affected departments or programs and may include staff at several levels of the organization. One of the advantages of this approach to planning is that management is more likely to have the support of staff when staff have had input into the plan. A disadvantage is that some staff may act more on self-interest and may not consider the interests of the larger organization. Planning in organizations is discussed in Chapters 10, and 11. Planning in community task groups is discussed in Chapter 13.

Planning with grassroots and activist movements tends to be much less formal than with organization and government groups. Activist movements will typically plan activities that are designed to recruit affected members of the community. Activities may range from door to door and word of mouth to various forms of media coverage. Once groups are formed by either of these movements, planning usually involves a campaign that is designed to bring about desired changes. The unit of attention for the campaign usually includes winning support from the larger community and influencing members of various power structures who have decision-making powers that are necessary for the success of the change effort. A successful campaign generally results in further planning by governmental systems or organizations to plan and implement the changes. Planning with groups for grassroots and activist movements are discussed in the next chapter.

Program planning can take place within an existing agency structure or from a community base. If the program is to function within an existing agency structure, the support and involvement of the agency administration and staff are crucial. If the program is to develop from a community base, community members will carry primary responsibility for its functioning. These people need to be involved in the planning as early as possible. Usually, it is important to discuss the proposed plan with several community influentials as a first step. This discussion will provide the social worker with information needed for developing the plan. It also involves these important persons in obtaining support for the project. Often, it is advisable for a community person to initiate and conduct a meeting to discuss the project. The social worker may need to identify and motivate a suitable leader. The worker then prepares the leadership person for the meeting by making the arrangements for a meeting place, attending to the meeting details, and evaluating with the leadership person after the meeting. Program planning in groups will be addressed in the next chapter.

## Practice Actions with Communities

As we discuss in Chapter 3, social work practice actions are divided into direct and indirect actions. Direct actions take place directly with clients. Indirect actions take place on behalf of clients. Because BSWs and inexperienced MSWs do not typically work with communities as clients, most of their practice actions with communities are indirect or on behalf of clients. However, when workers are working with grassroots and activist movements, some of their actions could be classified as direct. At the same time, most of the actions with communities take place with groups. We concentrate on working with community groups in Chapter 13 and so most of the practice actions, especially with groups, is covered there.

The worker facilitates relationship building and good relationships as he works with the community. At times he may do this with individual members of a group, an organization, or a governmental system, but mostly this is done in groups. He models, facilitates, and promotes good communication, problem solving and decision making, and conflict resolution.

In working with the community, both written and oral communication skills are a necessity. As the worker works with the community in the various groups identified earlier, good written skills are needed to write letters, press releases, petitions, reports, agendas, and the like. Good oral communication skills are needed to facilitate meetings and communicate with supporters, opponents, potential supporters, the media, decision makers, influentials, and the like. Problem-solving skills are needed to resolve issues within groups and with opponents and decision makers. Decision-making skills are used within groups and in influencing decision makers. Conflict resolution can also be used within groups and with opponents and decision makers.

While teaching the use of the change process is not a central focus of practice with communities, the use of the change process is vital to the success of any change effort. Assessment, planning, action, and evaluation are used within groups, in dealing with opposition to the change effort, and in influencing the community at large and those in positions of power who are either responsible for making decisions related to the change effort or who are in a position to influence those who are.

Knowing and using resources are used in a similar way as the use of the change process. Teaching knowledge and use is secondary to the worker actually knowing and using resources. This is typically one of the most valuable contributions that social workers make to community change efforts. Knowing and using resources in the community are major areas of expertise for social workers. Community members and others in various organizations and governmental systems usually have either a general knowledge about some of the resources available or they may have more in-depth knowledge about a narrow focus related to receiving or delivering services in their area of need or their area of service delivery. Generalist social workers are expected to have a much broader knowledge of resources because they have skills in working with a broad range of client systems including individuals, families, groups, organizations, and communities. Often, generalist social workers are called on to be a resource person when working with community change efforts.

Empowering and enabling client systems are both a goal and a means of achieving goals in community work. It is especially important to influence community change when working with populations who are marginalized or disadvantaged or who have a history of experiencing prejudice, discrimination, and oppression. Often, the challenges to meeting needs for these populations lie in removing barriers to opportunity and empowering them so that they can bring about the environmental and systems changes necessary to open doors to opportunities. Empowering and enabling as a group are usually the preferred mechanisms for community change. Because these groups are marginalized, grassroots and activist movements are more likely to be used. However, when the social worker works in any capacity as a member of a task force, partnership, or other community group, she has an obligation to speak on behalf of and represent those who do not have a voice or whose voice is not likely to be heard. She advocates for these segments of the community and advocates for their inclusion in the decision-making process in a meaningful way. We call this **proactive advocacy**. Generally, in describing advocacy activities, the social worker acts in response to a barrier to meeting need by acting on behalf of the client system. This is what we call *reactive advocacy*. Proactive advocacy involves promoting the interests of a disadvantaged or disenfranchised group before barriers are erected. By anticipating their needs and advocating for inclusion, the social worker can empower and enable these groups before they experience further exclusion or marginalization. This is a vital role for social workers in all areas of practice, but in particular practice with organizations and communities. It represents much of what is referred to as social justice.

Actions taken in crisis situations in working with the community are more likely to be associated with crises that arise within a group or as groups undertake various change efforts. That is not to say that the worker will not encounter individuals who are experiencing personal crises. In any area of practice this can and will occur. Whenever it does, the worker uses his skills in crisis intervention at least to stabilize the situation. He ensures that the person receives assistance from organizations in the community that provide services to deal with the crisis. In rural areas, this may not be readily available and the worker may be the only professional help available, in which case he should provide whatever services he is able and competent to provide while preserving confidentiality.

Actions taken to provide support for clients are similar to those described under crisis intervention. The worker may provide support temporarily while referring individuals to resources in the community. In rural areas, this may not be readily available and it may be necessary for the worker to provide support while mobilizing members of the individual's natural support system such as family, friends, church, and the like. Providing services that include support or promoting this as an aspect of the community change effort is another way that social workers include support in community work. In addition, members of groups may experience support by being group members even if support is not the primary focus or purpose of the group. They may also form support systems for other matters as a result of their group experiences.

While structured activities are not typically used in working with communities, group members are expected to engage in activities that are part of the change effort within the group and subgroups and between meetings. Activities within the group or subgroups are covered in Chapter 13. Activities between meetings may take place with individuals and smaller or informal groups undertaking them. Without activity between meetings nothing of any substance will take place. Meetings are typically used to plan and monitor change activities. These may include activities related to campaigning, mobilizing the community, influencing decision makers and influentials, and the like. Members may need to prepare mailings, postings, signs, and other materials. They may conduct surveys and petition drives. They may attend and speak at rallies and board or governmental meetings. Developing and maintaining momentum and support are critical to any change effort in the community and activity is the best way to do this.

The indirect practice actions identified in Chapter 3 are central to the work that is done in community work. Mediation is used within groups, with opponents, and with power structures in the community, various organizations, and governmental systems. Because social workers have skills in mediating, they are valuable resources whenever conflict arises. The worker maintains a neutral position and uses her skills to help formulate compromises without undermining the change effort. She negotiates and proposes potential remedies that will bring opposing individuals or groups together.

The use of influence is another central skill in community work. While the worker may use his influence within a group, the primary mechanism for bringing about change in communities is most often influence. This is particularly true for grassroots and activist movements. Members of these groups are typically outside of the power structure. Mobilizing community groups to influence the political process or to change public or organizational policies is the main means of bringing about change for these movements. The worker will often need to use influence or may need to recruit influentials when working within or with organizations or governmental systems.

Community work is all about actions designed to change the environment. The community is the environment for all other client systems. Thus, community work may be undertaken as a practice area in and of itself or it may be part of working on behalf of other client systems. In either case, community change means environmental change at some level. It is vital that the worker not only keep this in mind at all times, but she also needs to remind other members of the change effort. Beneficial changes for some groups may not be beneficial for others. The social worker pays special attention to the impact of change on disadvantaged and underrepresented populations. She engages in proactive and reactive advocacy for those who are less powerful to ensure that community change benefits them too. She seeks to ensure that those who are most affected by environmental change will have a voice in the process and that their voice is heard.

Coordination is another strength of the generalist social worker. He uses this in service to the groups with whom he works. Coordination of services in community work is not the same as with individuals or families. Case management is the approach most associated with those client systems. Instead, the worker uses his coordination skills to facilitate effective and efficient implementation of plans for change. He uses these skills during meetings and assists in coordinating activities between meetings.

## Policy Change

Much of the service delivery system is heavily influenced by actions that take place in the political arena. Because public policy is so important in working with communities, we discuss it here in a separate section. Public social policy is an outcome of legislative action. Policy determines which programs will be supported and to what extent by governmental funds. Some social workers have always attempted to influence that political process, with varying degrees of success. The political process is heavily influenced by the climate of the times, so in times of a more liberal political climate, social workers tend to have more influence; in times of conservatism, less influence.

Recently, the political climate in the United States has increasingly tended toward conservatism. Nonetheless, it is critical that social workers continue to advocate, especially since there are fewer avenues available for populations at risk to voice their concerns. All social workers, not just those in indirect service positions, should become politically active. Direct service workers are in the best positions to fully understand the impact of social and political change on their clients.

As with all social work strategies, influencing the political process takes understanding and skill. A thorough understanding of local, state, and national political processes is a must, as is a thorough understanding of the issues involved. It is important to view political decision makers as individuals and know how they respond to others. Reliable data about how the issue of concern affects people are very important. These data should include not only how the problem affects the client group but also how it affects other segments of the population. The cost of proposals under consideration is important knowledge to have.

Also, an assessment should be made of possible sources and nature of resistance to any proposed change.

Gathering the information needed to develop this understanding of the political process takes time and skill. Social workers should learn how to use governmental publications and documents as well as statistical material. These materials are available through state and federal representatives, libraries, and various Internet sources. Participating in political activities and establishing working relationships with key political figures can be a means of gathering other needed information.

After the social worker has gained information and understanding about the political process and the particular issue involved, a decision should be made about the appropriate tactics to use in influencing that process. This decision will depend in part on where that issue is in the political process. If it is still in the discussion stage, then suggestions for possible legislation might be the option to pursue. Some of the means social workers use to influence the political process include:

1. Researching issues and providing facts to decision makers
2. Testifying at hearings (using facts whenever possible)
3. Lobbying or being present while the legislative process is taking place and influencing legislative votes when possible
4. Forming coalitions with service providers to present information to legislators regarding the local impact of current policies
5. Sharing disguised anecdotal information regarding the impact policies have on clients with state and national groups concerned with the issues
6. Working for the election of candidates who are sympathetic to social issues and to the needs of people
7. Letter-writing/e-mail campaigns to inform decision makers

Influencing the political process is a complex endeavor. Although most social workers are not in a position to be heavily involved, they can and should use the tactics available to them to influence the political process. Workers have an obligation to develop an understanding of the process and of the issues so they can participate in political advocacy in a responsible manner.[11]

Social action organizing has been a part of the social work response to human need from its earliest days. Jane Addams organized for social action when she advocated improved social conditions. The approach was widely used during the period of social unrest in the 1960s. Since that time, a theory base has developed that supports the use of this approach to organizing oppressed peoples. The focus is on changing the societal power base and basic institutional change. A theory proposed by Saul Alinsky and by Richard Cloward and R. Elman is sometimes referred to as a grassroots approach.[12] It begins with people who see themselves as victims, not with professionals who decide what is needed.

The principal thrust of this approach is the organizing of groups of people so that they can exert pressure on power structures, institutions, and political bodies. Adherents believe that equity in society will come about only when existing power structures recognize the power of oppressed peoples—in other words, when the societal power base is broadened to include new groups of people. Tactics used include: (1) crystallization of issues and action against a target; (2) confrontation, conflict, or contest; (3) negotiation when appropriate; and (4) manipulation of mass organizations and political processes.

The social worker's first task is to organize people and get them involved in the action. In many ways, this is a self-help approach in that it relates directly to client empowerment and may be an outgrowth of a mutual aid group. The worker then enables the individuals to carry out the action.

Social workers need to develop advocacy skills if they are to help social institutions become more responsive to the needs of all people. How the individual social worker uses these skills depends on three variables:

**1.** *The position of the worker in the social welfare system*—Some agencies place constraints on workers' involvement in cause advocacy. Also, workers who work cooperatively with decision makers will probably not want to use conflict tactics.

**2.** *The client's desires regarding action*—If clients do not wish to take the risks involved in an advocacy action, these desires should be respected.

**3.** *The risks involved in the action*—If advocacy actions have the potential for bringing about backlash or negative influences on the client or on the social service system, advocacy should be used cautiously and only when the client or service system fully understands the possible negative ramifications.

The worker serves as an expert, an enabler, a negotiator, or whatever is needed by the people who direct the change activity.[13] Chapter 13 examines working with various groups in the community.

## Evaluation with Communities

As with other client systems, evaluation is both formal and informal in community work. In fact, formal and informal evaluations are similar to formal and informal assessments identified earlier. Typically, most evaluation with grassroots and activist movements is informal. With other forms of community change efforts, there tends to be a mixture of formal and informal evaluation. Formal evaluation may be required by current or potential funding sources. Typically, if the instrument and design are submitted with grants or funding requests then there is an opportunity for the funding source to accept these ahead of time rather than finding out too late that the method or the mechanism is not sufficient. Governmental and policy-making bodies may need formal evaluations to change policies or approve the expenditure of tax dollars. Evaluations may be designed to evaluate the results of a change effort or to provide a basis on which to approve one.

Informal evaluation takes place throughout any change effort with any client system. Both effectiveness and efficiency should be monitored from assessment to completion. Data and information that are collected need to be evaluated for validity and reliability. Plans need to be efficient and effective, along with the actions that implement them. Goals, objectives, and tasks need to be measurable and monitored.

# Summary

Generalist social work practice with macrosystems includes working with and changing communities on behalf of client systems. Often, this involves developing and making needed resources available to clients. The assessment process typically begins with a needs assessment.

Approaches to community organization include working with groups made up of organizations, governmental systems, and members of the community. The worker uses her skills in generalist practice as a member of these groups and in service to them. She advocates for members of the community who are disadvantaged and ensures that their interests are represented.

The worker uses her knowledge and skills in the change process to work with community groups in change efforts. This includes assessment, planning, direct and indirect practice actions and evaluation.

Program planning and development involve the use of the planning process to develop new resources. Program planning may take place within an agency or be used by a community group.

Policy change is an important aspect of working with communities. The worker develops her knowledge of policy change and uses her skills to influence policy especially on behalf of groups that are not represented in the community power structure.

---

C A S E   **12.1**

## Using a Community Task Group to Conduct a Needs Survey

Sally Jones is an adult services worker in a social services agency in an area where about eighteen percent of the population is over sixty-five years old. The agency is concerned about the unmet needs of these people who are older and has developed a program that involves workers and communities working together to discover unmet needs and develop resources to meet those needs.

Sally has been working for about a year with this community, which has a population of about 5,000. She has already carried out a very thorough community study (see Table 12.1). She knows that it is important to find out if this community recognizes the needs and accepts responsibility for its senior citizens. She has found that there is an active senior citizens' center and several very active women's church groups that are interested in community projects. Because Sally does not live in this community, she needs sanction for the project from the community.

As a first step, Sally makes appointments with the president of the senior citizens' center and the presidents of three church women's groups. She learns these presidents are concerned, and they acknowledge that they have never thought of a formal or systematic means of trying to identify needs. Sally then introduces the idea of a formal needs assessment. She has some guidelines from the state office on carrying out an assessment. She also has some information on what similar communities have done as a result of their needs assessment, and she shares these findings in each of the interviews. She states her belief that the community could benefit from such a process and asks if the organization that each individual represents would be willing to help. Sally could have worked with just one organization, but she knows it will be important to have a broadly based community organization if plans for community projects are to be developed based on the needs assessment. She

CASE **12.1** Continued

believes that establishing this broad base early in the process, through involving several groups in the needs assessment, will increase the chances of services being developed.

The group leaders express interest, as long as it does not involve too much time. Guidelines indicate that one hundred calls to senior citizens and one hundred calls to the general public will provide the information needed. She hopes for a total of twenty volunteers, five from each organization, so that each would only have to make ten phone calls in a two-week period. She also tells the president of the senior citizens' center that she will need some help in identifying those over age sixty in the phone book for the random sampling of that group. The president says they have a meeting in two weeks and asks Sally to come and talk to them about the project.

The first church group president wants to discuss the project with the members and get back to Sally. She does this in a month's time and says they are ready to help. The second church group president says she will have to talk to the pastor and see if he approves of the project, and she will then get back to Sally. She never does and is very evasive when Sally calls her back. Sally does not pursue this group, as she has found another group of ten women in the community who are eager to be included in the project. The third church group president says that her group is too busy on their own projects to help right now, but she does want to be informed about the results.

The design for this assessment has been developed in the state office. Phone calls are made to a random sample of the general community and to those over age sixty in the community; an instrument has been developed for use with each group. The community sample is asked opinions about need in the community around five areas: loneliness and isolation, ability to care for a home, nutrition, transportation, and activities of daily living. Those over age sixty are asked about their needs in these areas. Respondents are also asked their age, whether they have family living within a thirty-mile radius, and how they would rate their health.

Once the surveys are completed, they are sent to the state office for computer tabulation.

Sally goes over this procedure with the group of volunteers and asks if they would add any other questions unique to people living in this community. She explains that this assessment is their attempt to understand their own town and that it needs to reflect what they want to know. She says that any data they collect that are not appropriate for state office analysis will be gone over by her and any of the volunteers that want to help.

When it becomes apparent that community groups will be able to obtain the needed volunteers and when a date for the survey has been set, Sally begins a public relations campaign. This campaign is designed to inform the community of the upcoming survey and its purpose. The use of the information is carefully discussed, including the confidentiality of individual answers and how the findings will be shared with the community through news releases to the local weekly newspaper and public meetings. The campaign also uses announcements at meetings of various organizations.

When all the community respondents have been identified, when the senior citizens have completed their identification of those over age sixty in the community, and when Sally has chosen the random sample to be called, a meeting is held with the volunteers. At this meeting Sally passes out the instrument to be used in collecting data during the phone call. She suggests that the telephone volunteers jot down any remarks or questions that respondents make about needs or present services. She tells the group that after the forms have been sent to the state office for tabulation, they will get together to discuss the experience and the remarks and questions of the respondents. She notes that this information may reveal additional needs in the community and of older persons as well as providing responses to the survey questions. She carefully goes over all details and stresses confidentiality of the information obtained. She discusses how to handle various situations that may be encountered and has the group engage in role-play of the phone call.

(continued)

CASE **12.1** Continued

Each volunteer is then given ten names to call, with five alternates if they cannot complete the first ten calls. Sally stresses the need to get all the calls completed in a two-week period. She tells the volunteers to be sure to get in touch with her if they have any problems and that she will check with them at the end of a week and collect their forms at the end of two weeks. As a result of Sally's thorough knowledge of the community and her careful planning with community leaders and volunteers, all but five of the calls are completed in the two-week period. Two volunteers agree to complete the remaining calls that one volunteer, with unexpected family stress, could not finish. A month after sending the data to the state office for analysis, Sally receives the results. Sally is aware that the true meaning of the data will only be determined within the context of this specific community. She knows that the volunteers and club officers are the real experts on this community. Thus, she calls a meeting of the involved individuals so that they may begin the work of data analysis to determine the unmet needs of people who are older in the community and move toward deciding what to do about those needs.

## QUESTIONS

1. Identify a need in your community. Discuss how you would go about conducting a needs assessment.

2. How would you go about planning and developing a program to meet the need you identified in Question 1?

3. Describe a role you would play as a social worker in a task group organized to meet the need you identified in Question 1. Who would you want to have as members of your task group? Why would you select these people?

4. How much risk would you be willing to take in bringing about needed change in a community? At what point do you think it would be appropriate for you to use a grassroots or activist movement as a strategy?

5. How might you use proactive advocacy to prevent an injustice? How might you use reactive advocacy?

## SUGGESTED READINGS

Johnson, Louise C., and Yanca, Stephen J. *Social Work Practice: A Generalist Approach*, 9th ed. Boston: Allyn & Bacon, 2007 (Chapters 7, 14, and 15).

Brueggemann, William G. *The Practice of Macro Social Work*, 3rd ed. Belmont, CA: Thomson-Brooks/Cole, 2006.

Edwards, Richard L., Ed. *Encyclopedia of Social Work*, 19th ed. Washington, DC: NASW Press, 1995 ("Citizen Participation"; "Community"; "Community Needs Assessment"; "Community Organization"; and "Community Practice Models").

Haynes, Karen S., and Mickelson, James S. *Affecting Change: Social Workers in the Political Arena*, 5th ed. Boston: Allyn & Bacon, 2003.

Homan, Mark S. *Promoting Community Change—Making It Happen in the Real World*, 3rd ed. Belmont, CA: Thomson-Brooks/Cole, 2004.

Long, Dennis D., Tice, Carolyn J., and Morrison, John D. *Macro Social Work Practice: A Strengths Perspective*. Belmont, CA: Thomson-Brooks/Cole, 2006.

Netting, Ellen F., Kettner, Peter M., and McMurtry, Steven L. *Social Work Macro Practice,* 4th ed. Boston: Allyn & Bacon, 2008.

Rothman, Jack, Erlich, John L., and Tropman, John E. *Strategies of Community Organization—Macro Practice*, 6th ed. Belmont, CA: Thomson-Brooks/Cole, 2001.

Rubin, Herbert J., and Rubin, Irene S. *Community Organizing and Development,* 4th ed. Boston: Allyn & Bacon, 2008.

Tropman, John E., Rothman, Jack, and Erlich, John L. *Tactics and Techniques of Community Intervention*, 4th ed. Belmont, CA: Thomson-Brooks/Cole, 2006.

# 13 Task Groups in Communities

1. Understanding the need to work with communities in generalist practice.
2. Understanding various forms of group work with the community.
3. Understanding group work and various methods of community organization practice.
4. Knowledge of facilitating task groups in the community.

Generalist social workers work with individuals, families, groups, organizations, and communities. This final chapter examines how generalist social workers facilitate task groups in the community as leaders and as participants. As we have mentioned, it is rare that BSWs or inexperienced MSWs will find themselves employed as community organizers or will have the community as their client system. However, social workers may have opportunities to participate in community change efforts either as representatives of their agencies or as private citizens. When they do, they invariably will be working in groups.

## Community Change

Community change requires a great deal of effort, much more effort than one or two people can muster. Community change typically involves segments of the community as participants in the change process or as units of attention or both. Thus, the worker needs to develop skills in working with community task groups. Chapter 12 identifies several approaches to community change using different types of task groups. These include organizational task forces, community partnerships, governmental task forces, community task forces, activist movements, and grassroots movements. In this chapter we examine how the worker participates or facilitates each of these types of task groups as she works for community change.

As community task groups are formed and undertake their work, several types of change may be needed. Among these may be changes in public policy, program planning and resource development, and cause advocacy. In the process of making these changes, the worker may need to network with other workers and involve influential people from the community. It is important that the social worker understand these areas of community change as she works with various groups in the community.

## Changing Public Policy

Most community change efforts will involve changing public policy some time during the process. Thus, it is important for the worker to understand how public policy is formulated and enacted and how it is changed. Here, we give a brief overview that will set the stage for understanding how various task groups can become involved in influencing public policy.

In essence, the legislative branch of federal, state, and local government is responsible for developing public policy in conjunction with the executive branch. The executive branch then implements or "executes" the policies. The judicial branch ensures that policies are legal and constitutional. Because our form of government uses a system of checks and balances, no single branch of government has sole responsibility for public policy. Thus, influencing public policy can be complicated, but it can also be influenced strategically if the worker understands how both the formal and informal power structures operate. While members of the executive branch are responsible for implementing policy, they can be heavily influenced by legislators. In turn, legislators can be influenced by constituents in areas that they represent. In addition, legislators are influenced by one another because it takes the cooperation of a majority of any legislative body to pass any form of legislation. They need support from others to pass laws that will benefit their constituents. As a result, legislators rely on support from one another to pass bills that will affect the communities in the areas that they represent.

Most of the work of state and federal legislative bodies takes place in committees and subcommittees. In addition, most of the details of public policy is formulated by the staff of the legislator. Thus, working closely with the staff can influence policy before it is introduced as a bill. Once a bill is introduced, it needs to be considered by one or more committees before it reaches the legislative body as a whole. Typically, the chair of the committee or subcommittee is responsible for scheduling hearings on the matter. The chair is a very powerful position because he may or may not schedule items for consideration. Issues can be brought to the committee by a vote of the membership, but members are reluctant to do this if it is likely to cost them too much goodwill because they want other measures that they favor to move through the process. Once hearings are scheduled, the process can be influenced in several ways. The worker or a group can testify on behalf of or against a proposed bill. They may organize letter-writing or telephone or e-mail campaigns to influence members of the committee. They can influence members of the committee to speak out and to use their influence to represent the group's position.

If a bill receives a favorable vote in a subcommittee or committee, it moves to the next level. Subcommittee issues move to the committee level, where the process is repeated and committee work moves to the chair of the legislative body. At each level a similar process occurs, as the chair decides if and when to schedule a vote. Once again, chairs have considerable power because they can decide not to schedule a vote. However, chairs of legislative bodies are elected by a majority of the membership, so they must take this into consideration in their actions as chair. When a piece of legislation is scheduled for a vote, there is considerable activity behind the scenes if it is controversial or has limited support. Members will try to influence one another to vote for or against it. They will "wheel and deal" with each other regarding this and other pieces of legislation in order to garner enough support for their position. If a bill is passed, it is then sent to the other chamber, where it must go through the same process. This occurs on both the federal and state levels, except in Nebraska, which has only one legislative body.

Once legislation is passed in both houses of the legislature, it goes to the president or governor for his or her signature. If the president or governor signs it, the measure becomes law. If he or she vetoes it, it can go back to the legislature, where a two-thirds majority is needed to override the veto.

Local legislative bodies generally operate somewhat differently than state and federal governments. At the local level, there is usually only one legislative body and there may not be an executive that is separate from that body. So, a mayor may be a member of the city council or he or she may be elected separately and serve as the chief executive officer (CEO) of the city. Counties may have a similar structure. Townships usually have the supervisor or CEO as a member of the township board.

Larger local governments may conduct their business in committees. Smaller ones typically act as a committee of the whole at their meetings. It is important for the social worker to know what level of government has the power to act on a particular piece of legislation and how that level of government is structured and acts. The worker can get this information directly from governmental entities or it may be available online by visiting a website. Most states have copies of their code of laws available online. State law affects both the structure and functioning of state government and local government. A similar process of influencing individuals and governmental bodies can be used to bring about changes in public policy on the local level. In addition, organized groups at the local level can be used more directly by having members attend public meetings of local government. They can engage in petition drives to place measures on the ballot and conduct political campaigns for or against ballot proposals. Writing letters and influencing public opinion through the media are also tactics that can be used. These are discussed further in this chapter.

## Networking and Coordination

**Networking** is a form of coordination.[1] Networking is the development and maintenance of communication and of ways of working together among individuals of diverse interests and orientations. This technique can facilitate macro level coordination. It can be used for movements and task forces. Networking also holds promise as a means for formal system helpers and natural helpers to work together. The technique of networking calls for developing some means of face-to-face communication among people who have the potential for developing a relationship based on a common interest.

One technique used to develop a service network is a "fair." People delivering services in a particular area (such as services for women) are invited to set up displays and provide an informed person to be present to discuss informally the services provided. The fair is usually seen as an opportunity for the community to find out about the services. In informal, open discussion at the fair, professional and other helpers discover commonalities of interest and concern. From this discussion, decisions begin to be made about working together. A sensitive facilitator can then encourage further planning for activity that will strengthen the network.

Another networking technique is a monthly meeting of community agencies that can be expanded to include a wide range of community resources. Agendas for these meetings can consist of various agencies presenting their programs and services. Time should be provided for informal discussion and discussion of current community needs. The long-term goal is for relationships to develop among the participants and for a network to emerge.

Because of the differing patterns of functioning and communicating, formal systems must not expect informal systems to accept their approach. Service networking calls for the establishment of innovative patterns that allow both formal and informal systems to function together. Informality must not be stifled but rather respected and encouraged when using this form of coordination.

When coordinating with natural helpers, it is important not to place professional expectations on them. Professionals tend to consider these individuals in a paraprofessional capacity and take a supervisory stance in the relationship. This is not appropriate, for two reasons. First, it may destroy any chance of developing the relationship because the natural helper feels demeaned in such a relationship. Second, it may destroy the natural helper's distinctive way of helping and thus his contribution to the situation.[2] Professionals who use a consultative stance are more likely to develop coordinative relationships with natural helpers.

Blocks to effective coordination in service **networks** include lack of respect for, or confidence in, the other helpers involved; lack of adequate sharing of information among helpers; differing perspectives or values about what is to be done regarding clients; lack of capacity to share and work together; lack of time to develop cooperative relationships; and lack of agency sanction and support for coordination. A productive, satisfying coordination is possible when mutual understanding, shared goals, a feeling that it is advantageous to work cooperatively, a capacity to work together, and the sanction needed to develop cooperative relationships are present.

Three social work skills are useful for social workers in facilitating coordination: (1) skill in sensing commonalities and differences and in communicating them appropriately to those involved in the situation; (2) skill in facilitating communication among the participants; and (3) skill in exciting and motivating helping persons to see the advantages of coordinating services. Underlying these skills is the capacity to develop opportunities creatively for open and relaxed communication.

Much has been said about the need for, and the advantages of, coordination in interorganizational and interprofessional relationships. Less has been identified with respect to skills and techniques in developing and maintaining those relationships. Applying understandings about the nature of other relationships and the means for encouraging and maintaining them can enhance this knowledge base. Coordination is needed for providing complex services in complex situations and for ensuring that activities take place for community task groups. Coordination depends on functional relationships among people.

## Cause Advocacy

Social workers using a systemic approach to assessment should be sensitive to situations in which the block to need fulfillment lies in the functioning of societal institutions. Often these blocks affect not just one person or family but groups of individuals. In these situations, a strategy that focuses on change in societal institutions needs to be considered. A cause advocacy strategy is one option.

**Cause advocacy** has been a concern of social work since its earliest days. Early-twentieth-century social workers in settlement houses were concerned with social conditions as they affected the people with whom they worked. During the unsettled 1960s, cause advocacy was a major focus of some social workers. The cause-function debates of the profession relate to social work's concern with changing social institutions.

The literature on advocacy recognizes both *case advocacy* (advocacy in service of a client) and cause advocacy (advocacy in service of a class of persons who are victims of a social problem). George Brager has identified an advocate as the professional who identifies with the victims of social problems and who pursues modification in social conditions.[3] According to Robert Teare and Harold McPheeters, the advocate role is helping clients obtain services in situations in which they may be rejected or helping expand services to persons in particular need.[4]

There are several means to use in advocating for a class of persons. Robert MacRae identified the following:

1. Preparation of carefully worded statements of policy on lively social welfare issues
2. Careful analysis of pending legislation
3. Individual consultation with key legislators on the implications of pending measures
4. Persuasion of influential organizations outside the welfare field to oppose or support pending legislation
5. Creation of an ad hoc citizens' committee composed of representative citizens of influence and prestige
6. Continuous interpretation of social needs[5]

J. Donald Cameron and Esther Talavera discussed an advocacy program in which the emphasis was on participation in "important community planning and development groups, and other community organizations." The goal of this activity was "to keep the community needs of Spanish-speaking people visible and to effect the flow of resources to meet these needs."[6] Almost all the literature on social work with diverse racial groups calls for advocacy as an important component of any service provided to these groups.

Robert Sunley suggested the following as useful in a family advocacy program: (1) studies and surveys, (2) expert testimony, (3) case conferences with other agencies, (4) interagency committees, (5) educational methods, (6) position taking, (7) administrative redress, (8) demonstration projects, (9) direct contact with officials and legislators, (10) coalition groups, (11) client groups, (12) petitions, (13) persistent demands, and (14) demonstrations and protests.[7]

There are two major approaches to cause advocacy. The first is influencing the political process; the second is organizing the people affected, or social action. Before discussing each of these major approaches, we need to consider some issues pertinent to the use of advocacy. First is the position of an agency employee, particularly an employee of a public agency, in advocacy activity. Constraints in public employment policy make it difficult if not impossible for public employees to engage in cause advocacy. This fact places an additional responsibility on social workers not so constrained to be cause advocates. However, public employees can find some legal means to advocate. These include taking annual leaves to testify at legislative hearings, providing factual data on the effects of policy on individuals, and giving clients information about organizations that can help them fight for their rights.

Advocacy activity may cause a backlash. Policies and procedures meant to assist one group of clients may cause additional difficulties for another group of clients. Money used to fund a needed program for one group of clients may be taken from an equally valuable program for another group. All workers who engage in advocacy need to carefully assess the possibility of backlash or the effect of the desired change on other parts of the service delivery system. They then must make interventive decisions in light of ethical considerations.

Another issue is related to the ethics of engaging in cause advocacy for persons who have not asked for or do not want such action. Some clients are afraid of recriminations and feel they have more to lose than gain from advocacy activity on their behalf. Others do not trust professionals.

Before engaging in cause advocacy, a social worker should carefully assess and thoroughly understand the situation. The worker should be certain that other means for alleviating the difficulty are not available. The risks involved should be thoroughly explored and seem worth taking for the anticipated outcomes. The expected outcomes should be realistically determined. Resources needed to complete the project should be available. Facts to be used should be verified, appropriate, and to the point. Research techniques should be used when possible, since they strengthen the case for change. With all the facts at hand, the social worker can then decide whether to work to influence the political system or to organize the people affected by the problem.

## Involvement of Influentials

One means of gaining support is through the involvement of **influentials**—people within a community or an organization who have power and/or authority. Individuals may have power because they have a reputation that assigns power to them. They may have power because they are in a position to make crucial decisions, such as which projects get funded, who reports to top administrators, or how regulations are written. Other individuals have power because their role or function involves control over ideas, information, fiscal resources, and so on.

Influentials have the ability to use power to affect the actions of others. These people can persuade others to act in specific ways, gain support for their point of view or way of functioning, and effect compliance with desired ways of functioning. They often have control of needed resources (money, manpower, etc.), can reward or punish others, and can effectively block action they do not favor. They may be influential in all aspects of an organization or community or only in certain segments of the system's functioning. Influentials relate to one another in patterns; this is called the *power structure*.

Social workers can work with influentials in several ways:

1. Approval for projects or programs must be obtained from influentials in order to facilitate development of the projects or programs.
2. An attempt must be made to have an influential initiate the action in order to gain the support of others.
3. Influentials must be informed about what is being planned and why to prevent them blocking a project.

The first step in working with influentials is to identify these persons. This can be done by asking those who know the system well ("system knowledgeables") which people have the reputation of being influential or who of these must be included in decision making. Influentials are not always the same as those who hold authority positions; often, they are less visible and function behind the scenes in the informal system. An understanding of the community and its power structure is essential when working with influentials.

When social workers work with influentials, they need to be clear about the desired change and why it is needed. They can then present facts in a convincing, logical manner. It is often useful to show the influential how the desired change is in her self-interest. This first step for involving influentials allows them to see that the social worker can be an ally in carrying out community projects. Social workers should remain open and flexible when working with influentials. It is important to incorporate appropriate input from influentials into the plan.

The art of opportunity seizing is another important skill useful for working with influentials. This involves a keen sense of timing and a sense of when influentials are ready to become involved and make use of the social worker's help and expertise. Involvement in community activities can provide social workers with opportunities to get to know influentials and for influentials to get to know workers.

Persuasion skills are important when working with influentials and often can be useful in helping an influential understand the desirability of working for change. Social workers need to learn how to work with and utilize the support of influentials to effect change in organizations and communities.

## Program Planning and Resource Development

Program planning can take place within an existing agency structure or from a community base. If the program is to function within an existing agency structure, the support and involvement of the agency administration and staff are crucial. If the program is to develop from a community base, community members will carry primary responsibility for its functioning. These people need to be involved in the planning as early as possible. Usually, it is important to discuss the proposed plan with several community influentials as a first step. This discussion will provide the social worker with information needed for developing the plan. It also involves these important persons in obtaining support for the project. Often, it is advisable for a community person to initiate and conduct a meeting to discuss the project. The social worker may need to identify and motivate a suitable leader. The worker then prepares the leadership person for the meeting by making the arrangements for a meeting place, attending to the meeting details, and evaluating with the leadership person after the meeting.

If the decision is made to develop a program, some kind of structure should be set up to do the necessary work. This can be a provisional board or a planning committee and should allow for appropriate involvement of community persons in the process. This group may find it useful to conduct a needs assessment. The group should also be involved in the development of the program structure and policies. Other tasks are to obtain support for the proposed program, which may involve grant writing and other fund-raising activities, and recruitment and hiring of personnel. The social worker can fill the role of enabler by helping the community group reach the goals it has adopted. Also, the worker can fill the role of technical expert by providing information about how to accomplish certain tasks.[8]

Sometimes an established community group becomes aware of a need and wishes to do something about it. In this situation, a social worker can help the group document the need, obtain support (money, people, etc.), and develop the program or resource. For example, a community group was concerned with services for the elderly. The social worker helped the group carry out a needs assessment that indicated that housing for older single women was a prime need in this community. The group was able to interest a local realtor in focusing on this need and worked with the realtor to develop an understanding of the housing needs of older women and plans for making more suitable housing available for them.

At other times, groups of people interested in a particular problem emerge. Social workers can also work with these groups to develop community resources. For example, a women's group was concerned about battered women. The social worker's function was to provide understanding about battered women and their needs. This group talked to women who had worked on the problem in other communities. The group set up a training program and developed a telephone response service, a safe house, and a self-help group.

As these examples show, grassroots groups can be useful when developing community resources for clients. When working with such groups, social workers should not take over the planning; they should respect the group's way of functioning and facilitate the work. Workers must gain and maintain the trust of the group. They should enable individuals to carry out the necessary tasks, suggest ways of proceeding and resources to be tapped, and mediate the group's difficulties with professionals and other community groups. This latter task is sometimes necessary because established services or other professionals may be threatened by a grassroots group or concerned about its ability to provide quality service. In a time of shrinking federal and state resources, maximizing local resources is necessary if human needs are to be met. Program planning and resource development with grassroots groups thus become important tasks for social workers.

The social worker who attempts to mobilize the community or a group of concerned individuals to address a particular issue may want to form a task group. Task groups are groups organized to reach a specific goal. They tend to have clear lines of responsibility and specific tasks. Because task groups often include influentials, potential consumers, and service providers (people with various agendas and varying social statuses), it is important to address both interpersonal and task issues throughout the work of the group. Each member must feel he has something valuable to contribute, and this contribution needs to be perceived by other members. It is important to have members who can offer various skills, resources, or services to achieve the goal. For example, if the goal is to establish a hospice service for persons with terminal illness, it would be important to have a member who can raise funds, an influential who can work effectively with the community to allay fears or concerns, and someone who can network with the population and their families. In task groups, the work is generally divided into subgroups, which then work toward various objectives to reach the goal. This implies that there must be shared leadership, with each leader and subgroup given a specific charge and sufficient autonomy to attain the desired objective. Typically, subgroups meet frequently, with the group as a whole coming together less often to share progress, ensure coordination of efforts, and reevaluate the overall plan.[9]

The planning process may take up a considerable amount of the group's time. Just as in small groups, it is important to establish a common goal that is inclusive and relates to the purpose of the group. Initially, the common goal may be stated in very broad terms. However, care should be taken to avoid stating the goal in terms of solutions. Task groups are usually made up of factions or representatives of organizations who may have a considerable

**335**

investment in the outcome. For example, a community task force on juvenile gangs is likely to be made up of representatives from law enforcement, juvenile court, schools, substance abuse agencies, and youth organizations. Each of these brings its own perspective on the problem and is invested in solutions related to that perspective. Usually, the solution is viewed as a need for more resources for that particular organization or a need for a different response from one of the other organizations. Thus, law enforcement is likely to see the problem as related to not having enough police officers or of the courts not being tougher on juveniles. The juvenile court may see the problem in terms of needing more court workers or more money for placement options. The schools may see the goal as the need for a new program in the schools or for the court to be stricter with school truants. The substance abuse agencies and youth organizations are likely to see a need for more programs to treat substance abuse or to keep young people off the street. Generating a common goal that involves a community response is the key to holding these groups together. For example, the group could be encouraged to adopt a community goal of reducing gang membership by half. To accomplish this goal, each organization would have to do its part and make a collaborative effort.

Social workers can sometimes use program planning to mobilize different and creative kinds of resources that are relatively inexpensive financially. Two resources that fall into this category are volunteers and self-help groups.

Program development uses the planning process developed in Chapter 10. As the plan is developed, special attention must be given to means of generating support for the plan. Support must come not only from the agencies involved (both workers and administration) but also from the community. Most programs needing community resources cannot be developed without community support.

Usually, in developing a new program it is advisable to begin small or to serve at first only a portion of the population that might benefit from the program. It is also advisable to begin with that portion of the population with which the chances of success are the greatest. If done in this way, it is easier to find and correct the deficiencies in the plan. Another point to remember is that it is easier to obtain support for small programs that relate to popular causes.

Jack Rothman, John Erlich, and Joseph Teresa discussed promoting an innovation in an agency. This idea can be used in planning new community programs. They pointed out that the literature on the "diffusion of innovations" supports the advisability of beginning small and of demonstrating the new program before planning for widespread use. Three guidelines are helpful when planning programs to develop or mobilize new resources:

1. Develop and rely on good relationships.
2. Clarify goals and plans for developing the program.
3. Be realistic about the resources that may be available to the program.[10]

## Group Development with Community Task Groups

Stages of group development with community task groups are similar to what we have described for task groups in organizations and in other groups. There is typically an orientation stage followed by an authority stage and a negotiation stage. These first three stages would be considered the stages of group formation. The functional stage follows, and the final stage is disintegration. While the stages are similar to other groups, there are significant differences in the various types of community task groups and in the use of the change process at each stage.

## Community Task Forces and Partnerships

The first three stages of group formation is likely to be different for community task groups than it would be for other groups including task groups in organizations. A lot depends on the type of community task group. An organizational task force, collaborative, or cooperative is typically made up of several community organizations who initiate a change effort that is directed at the community or a segment of it or at governmental systems or at other organizations. Representatives of these organizations meet in task groups to work on the change effort. This typically begins with meetings among the chief executive officers (CEO) of the organizations. It may begin at lower levels, but this is usually informal until CEOs get involved. As the change effort proceeds, members of the organizations at other levels typically meet to develop and implement plans for the effort. Generally, most of the CEOs will know one another, but there is still a need for some formal or informal introductions. Usually, the organization that originates the idea will host the meeting and take responsibility for introducing the issue or issues that bring the group together. This constitutes the orientation stage. There may be several sessions in which members discuss the formation of a task force, a collaborative, a cooperative, or a community partnership.

As the group's discussion moves from presenting various views of the issues to discussing a response to the issues, the authority and negotiation stages have begun. Most of the time, CEOs will need to take the results of these discussions back to their boards of directors for permission to proceed with participating in setting up any form of cooperative venture. This represents the authority stage, in which there is an official sanction to proceed. There may be considerable discussion within each board on whether the organization should be involved and at what level. This might erupt into disagreements about whether and how to proceed. There may be political considerations, such as competition among agencies for funding, clients, services, publicity, and the like.

Similar situations often arise in the formation of a governmental task force made up of governmental systems and possibly community organizations. In the case of a governmental task force, a legislative body of some sort will need to officially sanction its formation. This might be the state legislature, the county board, the city council, or a township board. Preliminary work is typically done by members of the executive branch, such as a member of the governor's cabinet, the county executive, the mayor's office, or the township supervisor.

Community partnerships are organizational task forces that include members of the community, and community task forces are governmental task forces that include the community. These groups function somewhat differently because they include representatives of the community who are not elected to public office. The primary issue initially for these types of groups is representation. If community members are appointed or recruited, there may be questions raised about whom they represent. It behooves those who are appointing or recruiting to take this into consideration. Conversely, there may be people who are considered community leaders who have broad support from the community at large because of their position or reputation. It is essential that community members have ties to segments of the community that are affected by the issues and will also be affected by the response. Community members need to be made to feel welcome and have their role respected by professionals who are on the task force or partnership.

Most of the time, BSW workers or MSWs at lower levels will not become involved until task groups made up of lower-level staff are formed. Program directors, supervisors, and line staff from various organizations may work together on a regular basis or may have worked together in the past. Therefore, some members may already know one another, although introductions are still in order at the beginning of the first session. This represents the orientation stage. Some sort of preliminary organization and agenda should be developed. There may have been a charge given by other task groups made up of those in higher positions in the organizations or governmental systems involved. If so, this should be reviewed along with deciding on the type of organizational structure for the group and ongoing tasks such as chairing the meetings and taking minutes. Once the group has begun to accomplish these tasks, the authority and negotiation stages are under way. When a permanent structure is established, these stages are complete. They may be revisited in the future if issues arise around authority, power, and control.

The first three stages of group formation may be somewhat brief if members know one another and have worked together. These stages should be focused on getting organized and beginning the task. Building relationships comes out of working together, but this is not the primary purpose of the group. The purpose of task groups is not to form relationships and help one another with individual goals, but to accomplish the task. Members do not need to have close relationships. As we mentioned with other task groups, members do not have to like one another, although it helps if they do. They can accomplish the task without liking or caring about one another, but this can lead members to act in a way that does not contribute to the success of the group.

The worker uses assessment, planning, and action skills during the first three stages of group formation with various task forces or partnerships. If the worker serves as chair, she facilitates members getting acquainted with one another and organizing the task group. She solicits items for the agenda and prepares it before the meeting. After calling the meeting to order, the chair asks for approval of the minutes and the agenda which represents the plan for the meeting. As a member of a community task group, the social worker participates in discussions and decision making. She volunteers for responsibilities that are commensurate with her knowledge, skills, and experience. She makes suggestions and helps to negotiate agreements. Planning for a new group, planning for group sessions, and planning during the group are forms of planning that are used. These are discussed in Chapter 4.

Actions during the first three stages are focused on facilitating group formation and organization, which are identified in Chapter 4. These are especially relevant for this phase of the group and are similar to actions with organizational task groups we describe in Chapter 11. They include actions to facilitate group formation, group development, and discussion leadership; and actions to resolve conflict, enhance group interaction, and structure group activities. As with other task groups, the worker participates in developing good relationships and models this in his actions within the group and when he is acting on behalf of the group. He asks questions, makes suggestions, negotiates, and mediates as the group engages in discussions and experiences disagreements. He helps group members to sort out roles, rules, and norms as the group moves through the stages of group formation. He accepts leadership roles and supports others as they become leaders. All of this is aimed at helping the group to develop so it can function as a group and accomplish its tasks.

During the action phase of task group formation, the group may be engaging in actions that lay the foundation for working on the tasks that will achieve the group's purpose. This might include conducting a needs assessment or the group might be a product of a needs assessment. The group might be charged with planning and implementing a program to meet the needs that were identified and documented in the needs survey. The group may gather information about the tasks that it was formed to accomplish. To the extent that members of the task group represent various interest groups in the community, they need to gather information from those whom they represent.

As with other groups, evaluation takes place throughout the life of the group. During group formation, the worker evaluates group dynamics and actions as it moves through the first three stages and becomes a group. She observes and evaluates the functioning of the group as a whole as well as individual members. She evaluates the quality of the relationships within the group. The worker identifies negative interactions and facilitates the development of more functional, positive relationships that will move the group toward success.

As with any group, community task groups may revisit these early stages even when it has progressed to the functional stage. Each meeting will have some elements that represent any or all of the first three stages. Reviewing minutes represents orientation and obtaining approval of an agenda represents authority and negotiation stages. The chair gathers information for a preliminary agenda before the meeting. He reviews minutes, identifies unfinished business from previous meetings, and puts these on the agenda under old business. He identifies and solicits new business from members and from events that occur between meetings. When the meeting is called to order, minutes from the previous meeting are reviewed and approved. This is done for the sake of accuracy and to remind the group of what was done at the last meeting. The agenda is an agreement about work that needs to be done at this meeting.

As with any group, community task groups may experience disintegration at any point in time. Premature disintegration of community task groups is generally the result of either excessive conflict about some aspect of the endeavor or because members lose interest in the project. Sometimes it may be because the initial barriers to change may be seen as too formidable or members are not be able to reach the point where they can work together.

The group or subgroups meet regularly to share information and develop plans for each phase of the work. During the functional stage, planning is focused on activities that are related to achieving the group's purpose. Planning during the first three stages is centered on forming and organizing the group and laying the foundation for working on the tasks needed for success. Planning during the functional stage is aimed at accomplishing those tasks. Members report on the activities that take place between meetings. Plans are made for future activities.

The group engages in actions during meetings to analyze information and make decisions. Actions occur between meetings as members carry out tasks, gather information, and implement plans. The chair is responsible for coordinating the efforts of the group and either reporting back to the larger group or calling on various members to report on their activities. Members may have responsibility for coordinating the efforts of subgroups. Members engage in tasks that contribute to the success of the group. Many of the social worker's actions in carrying out tasks will involve similar actions that we have identified. The worker uses assessment, planning, action, and evaluation. She builds relationships with key members of the community and seeks their input and support. She facilitates enabling and empowering the group in carrying out various tasks. The worker engages in crisis intervention when there is a crisis and assists the group in resolving it so the group can proceed with achieving its goals. The worker contributes to the group by using her knowledge about resources. She provides support by being positive and encouraging. She mediates disagreements within the group and with other individuals or systems outside of the group. Working with community task groups affects the environment of the worker, the worker's organization, and their clients. Planning and implementing new or modified programs or services means planning and implementing environmental change. The social worker needs to use proactive advocacy to ensure that changes benefit clients and community members, especially those who might be vulnerable to detrimental changes or who do not have a voice in the changes that are planned. The worker uses coordination skills to facilitate the efforts of the group and subgroups and to assist with the implementation of planned changes.

During the functional stage, evaluation is focused on the progress toward achieving the purpose of the task group. This should include evaluating the effectiveness and efficiency of any planned changes as well as their affect on clients and community members.

While disintegration can occur during the functional stage, it is less likely because the group will be moving toward achieving the task. Disintegration might occur because the group runs out of time and exceeds its authorized time limit. However, an extension is likely to be granted especially if the group is close to achieving its purpose. Disintegration occurs at the end of each meeting as the group reviews what it has accomplished and what needs to be done before the next meeting.

As the group reaches the point at which it has achieved its purpose, disintegration and termination should be planned. The group typically develops and submits a final report to the organizations and governmental systems participating in the effort. If it has not accomplished its task or some tasks are incomplete, then some debriefing needs to occur. A report should be written and submitted identifying what was accomplished and what was not and reasons for each. Groups that are successful should report on what was accomplished and what might still need to be done.

The group assesses and evaluates the work that it has done and the accomplishments and failures as it nears the end of its work. It develops a plan for writing reports and wrapping up its work. Actions are taken to complete whatever needs to be finished and data are collected and analyzed. The final report is an evaluation of the effectiveness of the group's efforts in accomplishing its task.

## Community Movements

We use the term *movements* to refer to task groups that are associated with change that arises from community members as opposed to change that involves community organizations or governmental systems. This is because movements are substantially different from these other change activities. Typically, movements occur because community organizations or governmental systems have not been responsive to some segment of the community. Thus, the change effort is frequently aimed at changing that response. There are exceptions to this. Community members may come together to change some aspect of the community or to respond to social issues within the community. An example of this is a neighborhood with a high crime rate that decides to initiate a community response to reduce crime. Usually, such an effort will eventually include governmental systems and organizations. When it does, if leadership for the change effort shifts to governmental systems or community organizations, we classify it as a community task force or community partnership. If leadership remains in the hands of community members, we classify it as a movement.

As we indicated, movements that are initiated by community members are grassroots movements and those that are initiated by professionals, including social workers, are activist movements. Activist movements typically require a campaign aimed at involving and mobilizing community members. Once the community is involved, leadership may remain in the hands of the professionals, in which case we continue to call it an activist movement. If there is a transition to leadership by community members, we call it a grass-roots movement.

A campaign to involve and mobilize the community by an activist movement is typically aimed initially at a neighborhood or a segment of the community. Later, this may be expanded to a campaign to gain support from the larger community in some cases. The initial campaign is usually determined by the resources that are available and the nature of the segment of the community at which it is aimed. The activist or her group of activists need to assess the resources that are available and the unit of attention for the initial campaign. They need to plan the campaign and take actions to implement the plan.

At the first few meetings, members of the activist group need to work through the first three stages of group development and become a group. Group members may or may not know one another, so introductions are in order. Typically, members will identify themselves and give reasons they are there. They might be asked to contribute what they see as issues faced in the community, the neighborhood, or the segment of the community. This represents the orientation stage. There may be some agreement regarding these issues, but there may also be some differences. The social worker facilitates a discussion of these differences and helps the group to identify preliminary goals that are inclusive or encourages the group to seek further information so they can resolve their differences. The group also needs to develop some organization. This tends to be mainly informal, but the group might decide to have certain leadership positions or a steering or executive committee. Sometimes the group may need to agree on the issues it will address before it will be ready to decide on its leadership structure. These activities represent the authority and negotiation stages. The group may be able to accomplish these stages in the first session or it may take several to do so. Once these stages have been achieved, group formation has taken place and the group is ready to undertake actions during the functional stage.

For activist movements, it will be necessary to revisit these stages as the group gains members for the community. Grassroots movements will have similar experiences as they struggle through the stages of group formation. If the group makes a transition from an activist movement to a grassroots movement or some combination of these, the group will revisit these stages as it moves through reforming itself. Community members will also have their own view of the community and the issues and may have different agendas. The worker facilitates these transitions and helps to mediate differences, negotiate compromises, and resolve conflicts. The strongest motivation for this can be serving the needs of their community and achieving changes that will benefit the community.

Time and money are two very important resources for any campaign and are factors in both planning and action phases of the change process. Movements with larger numbers of people may have more of both, but at the very least they have more time. This means that there are more people available to do the work that needs to get done. In general, campaigns that make personal contact with members of the community are more likely to be successful than those that rely on some form of publicity. If there are sufficient numbers of members to go door-to-door or to attend community meetings, then this might be a good plan. Conversely, if the activist group is small or considerably smaller than the segment of the community it is trying to reach, then a publicity campaign may be a better format. Sometimes both of these methods are possible. In any case, some sort of written material will be needed. Fliers should be prepared that deliver a message appealing to potential members. It is best to try to make a connection between the issues and people's own circumstances. The message should also identify actions that people can take. It may ask people to attend a meeting or a rally or to attend a governmental meeting such as a city council or county board meeting. It may ask for financial assistance or volunteer activities. It may ask people to sign a petition or to vote for or against an issue or a candidate. When money is spent on a political campaign or ballot measure, the group needs to be careful to abide by campaign finance laws. These may be obtained from the city or county clerk or may be downloaded from state government websites (type in the state's abbreviation in www.state.gov). Other written materials may include posting fliers announcing meetings or rallies; issuing news releases to newspapers, radio stations, and television outlets; advertising in newspapers and other media including cable television; arranging public service announcements with the media; and the like.

Campaigns need to take into consideration different methods of communication in diverse segments of the community. There may be local newspapers or newsletters for various groups, including those that are written in languages other than English for various ethnic groups. Church bulletins or meetings may be a good place to advertise meetings. Posting fliers at grocery stores, community centers, and locations with heavy pedestrian traffic should be considered. Some communities rely heavily on word of mouth, so key members of the neighborhood system need to be contacted for support.

Regardless of whether the movement is activist or grassroots, there is usually a small group that takes responsibility for leadership. It may be quite informal and called a *steering* or *executive committee* or *leadership council* or similar title. We prefer steering committee, which implies a more democratic and spontaneous group. The size of this group is usually between five and twenty members. In larger groups, subgroups are generally formed that take responsibility for various aspects of the campaign. Confidentiality can be important when the group is planning various measures and size plays a role in maintaining confidentiality. A general rule is that the larger the group, the less likely it is that confidentiality will be maintained.

Space is a consideration whenever a community task group plans for a meeting. Unlike organizations or governmental systems that are more likely to have meeting rooms, movements need to arrange for meeting space. Sometimes meeting rooms may be available at churches, neighborhood centers, schools, halls, government buildings, restaurants, and other facilities. Space may actually be the main factor in determining the size of the group or the type of public meeting that is held. Rallies are usually held outdoors, but weather can be a factor in turnout. Anytime the group plans any type of public support, it is vital that the group is able to deliver numbers that are sufficient to exhibit support. Otherwise, those in power will discount the group's efforts. If the group asks for people to come to a rally or attend a public meeting, an effort must be made to generate a moderate to high turnout.

Money may be needed for materials, copying, mailings, meeting rooms, publicity, and the like. Mass mailings are expensive and also take time and energy. Address lists of registered voters can usually be obtained from the city or county clerk for a nominal fee. Most have these on Excel or another program that can be manipulated to create various types of address labels. Any type of contact can be used to generate funds, but usually funding comes from a small number of people. This might include the activists, members of the steering committee, and a few members of the community. Large fund-raising drives take considerable time, effort, and money and may actually drain energy and resources from the change effort itself. Soliciting funds at rallies and meetings can generate some financial support. Often, the segments of the community that are being asked to participate have been marginalized and may lack power and wealth. Thus, they may not be able to help much with the financial aspects. However, there may be other segments of the community who have resources and are interested in supporting efforts to bring about change.

Rural communities face additional challenges including fewer resources, large distances to travel, and transportation issues. There may be few if any places for groups to meet. Distance and sparse population require either travel on the part of group members to reach the larger community or travel by members of the community or both.

Once the community is mobilized, some type of steering committee is formed that assesses, plans, acts, and evaluates the efforts of the larger group. Social workers have these skills and others that are especially valuable for leadership task groups. Most community members will generally not have these skills. In activist movements, the worker may serve as a leader or will typically be on the steering committee or may serve on subgroups or subcommittees. In grassroots movements, the worker will usually serve as an adviser or resource person for the leadership and the group.

Assessment and planning take up a considerable amount of time and energy for task groups involved in movements. Changing the direction of the community, neighborhood, community organizations, or governmental systems requires a great deal of planning, which in turn requires good assessment. Assessment tends to be more informal than formal in that written assessments are not as likely to be produced. Planning is also more informal, but should exist in some type of written form so that everyone knows the goals, objectives, and tasks and their roles in carrying them out. As the group begins to implement plans for change, the functional stage of the group takes place. The social worker participates and engages in assessment, planning, actions, and evaluation throughout the stages of group development.

The actions of the social worker in contributing to task groups for movements include those identified in Chapters 3 and 4, and in Part Three. Facilitating good relationships is vital to any group. Members may not know one another well or may have had negative relationships before they joined the group. Members may have different agendas. They may compete for power and control. Any of these situations can present challenges for the group in accomplishing tasks and achieving its goals. The worker encourages positive relationship skills including good communication, effective problem solving and decision making, and conflict resolution that is constructive rather than destructive. It is easy to see how critical these skills are in task groups. The worker assists members in learning and using these skills. She models them and intervenes when members fail to exhibit them. She makes suggestions, mediates, and negotiates. She reminds the group about the need to maintain a focus on achieving the greater goals of the group.

The social worker has knowledge about resources that are valuable for the group. He helps the group to access those resources. He enables and empowers members by helping them to develop leadership skills and to achieve their goals. There is nothing more empowering for a population in the community that has been marginalized than to discover its power through collective action. The worker facilitates that collective action. He supports individuals and groups as they become more empowered and engaged in actions to change their community or change the response to their community by those in power. He helps coordinate and takes part in activities that bring about change.

With almost any movement, crises will occur. These can be personal crises experienced by individual members, difficulties with key relationships within the group, meeting timelines and deadlines, and addressing barriers or unanticipated challenges to carrying out important activities. The worker uses her crisis intervention skills to assist members and the group to overcome these challenges and devote their attention and energy to a successful outcome. The worker also uses her skills in mediating to assist in resolving issues within the group and with individuals and systems outside of the group.

The social worker takes action to recruit influential members of the community to the change effort. She influences individuals and systems in the environment directly or indirectly. Direct influence involves working directly with key individuals and systems to access power and resources for the movement. Indirect influence is getting influential members of the community to do this on behalf of the movement. She uses her skills as an advocate to speak for the group and the change effort. This may include speaking at public meetings and meetings of governmental units or organizations, talking with individuals and groups who are in power, conducting news conferences or interviews with the media, and the like.

In terms of group facilitation skills, the social worker uses these skills throughout the stages of group development. He encourages group discussion within the group that is productive and respectful. He helps the group to focus on the tasks and the overall goal. He encourages discussion from every side of an issue and then helps the group to resolve their differences. He seeks to enhance group interaction by encouraging the group to listen to one another and to solicit opinions and ideas from those who are more quiet. He helps the group through the first three stages of group formation and helps them to achieve their goals during the functional stage of development.

Disintegration for movements can occur at any time. These groups may not be able to get through the stages of group formation because of conflicts or an inability to develop a common goal or purpose. They may lose critical leadership or may not be able to reach enough members of the community to form a critical mass for change. The group may be able to mobilize the community but the change effort may still fail if the power structure is able to weather the pressure for change or the group fails to generate enough support from the community at large. Opposition groups may be formed that are successful at resisting the change effort.

Evaluation occurs throughout the group and the change effort. This tends to be quite informal since most movements do not have a formal structure and do not receive grants or funds from governmental units or foundations. The group evaluates information that it receives to determine its reliability and validity. The group evaluates the progress toward goals as it proceeds through the functional stage. If the change is successful, the group evaluates the extent of its success.

As the group reaches the end of its life as a movement, it may disintegrate or it may become a more permanent organization or it may be absorbed into an existing group or organization. In any case, the group needs to end its work and members need to terminate with one another or with those who are leaving the group. Successful change efforts usually call for some type of celebration. Unsuccessful change efforts generally call for debriefing and some expression of appreciation for the efforts and the experience.

## Summary

Generalist social work practice with macro systems involves changing communities on behalf of client systems or working with client systems to change communities. The social worker may be called upon to act as a member of a community task group. She uses her skills to facilitate successful achievement of the group's goals and purposes. Often, this involves using her knowledge of the change process and using her skills in facilitating groups.

Often, community change means changing public policy. The social worker needs to be knowledgeable about public policy and how it is formulated. She needs to know where the key figures are and how to influence them.

Program planning and development involve the use of the planning process to develop new resources. Program planning may take place within an agency or be used by a community group. Self-help groups and volunteer programs are two means for enhancing the resources available to clients.

Cause advocacy is concerned with changing societal institutions. Two main approaches are used: influencing the political process and organizing the victims.

The generalist social worker provides services to individuals, families, small groups, organizations, and communities. The focus is on transactions among systems, that is, on social functioning. This approach to social work calls for a wide variety of strategies, including those that do not focus on the client. These strategies involve action with other systems on behalf of clients and focus on situations in the client's environment that affect social functioning. Ethically, a social worker must not only work with the client but also with systems that impinge on the client.

## CASE **13.1**

# A Community Task Group

A group of people began to discuss the need for a hospice program for people with terminal illnesses in their community of 40,000 people after several dying patients and their families expressed a need for supportive help. A social worker became involved with this group as a technical expert in group process. The group was able to involve several community influentials in the planning process, including a lawyer, a physician, the superintendent of schools, a representative of the county health department, and two pastors. The group, which also included nurses, family members of people with AIDS, and a representative of the local cancer society, involved about fifteen people.

The worker's first task was to develop a working atmosphere in which each member understood and valued the potential contributions of the others. At the same time, the first business of the group included developing a legal structure and applying for nonprofit status. The group worked with the local hospital and obtained office space in the hospital. During this phase, the social worker used her understanding of group process and the technical aspects of forming an organization to function as a contributing member of the group. She also obtained materials from another organization forming a hospice, which provided some guidance in the group's deliberations. A lawyer took major responsibility for the legal aspects of the group's formation.

The next step was to form subgroups charged with various tasks that needed to be accomplished. This included developing several working papers, such as job descriptions and forms covering the various aspects of service (e.g., request for service, nursing and psychosocial assessments, doctors' orders, care plan). It also included planning for work with the community at large to educate the residents regarding the need for

the service as well as addressing concerns that might exist. Subgroups also worked on fundraising and volunteer structure and recruitment. A service flow chart was developed. The social worker assisted the subgroups to adapt materials that had been developed by other hospices to the local situation.

The social worker was active in working with the cancer society and the family members of persons with AIDS in planning and coordinating a very successful training program, which resulted in an attendance of over fifty persons at each session and a recruitment of thirty individuals as volunteers for the program. The success of the training program was due in part to an excellent public relations campaign. The social worker did not need to be involved, as other members of the board were skilled in this area. Several members were very successful in fund-raising. Funds were obtained from several community groups, from individuals as memorials, from the county commissioners, and from the local United Way. One difficult task was obtaining liability insurance.

After nine months, the program was operational, though still needing refinement of its procedures and policies. Patients were referred and service was provided to patients and their families through the bereavement stage. The social worker served as coordinator of social services and worked with others who provided the service to the patients and their families. The board, composed of several members of the original task group, was functional and planned monthly training sessions for the volunteers. An active public relations program continued to be carried out to heighten community awareness of the service and to recruit additional volunteers. Plans were under way to develop closer ties with the health care network of the community.

CASE **13.2**

## An Activist Task Group

About a year after David, a family services social worker, had organized community-wide efforts to develop a homeless shelter, the housing issue in his community became the focus of attention. Many homeless people were employed or had income from various social welfare programs but were unable to find affordable housing. During the year since the shelter had opened, David and his original task group had gathered information regarding the lack of low-income housing in the community. Many existing low-income housing units had been lost to other purposes or had been torn down for commercial or other housing developments.

The issue came to a head when the city council was asked for a zoning change that would allow a parking ramp to be built on property now containing an apartment that housed many low-income people. David organized and met with a small group, including a member of the city council who showed concern about the homeless, a former state legislator, the director of the county social services agency, a low-income resident housed in the apartment, and several other concerned citizens from the original task group.

This group needed to move quickly because a zoning change proposal was to come before the city council in about two weeks. The group assessed the information David had gathered about affordable housing for low-income people in the city. They asked the newspaper to run a feature article, which aroused some citizen concern. With the help of the city council member, they contacted city council members and city staff who had been involved in planning the zoning proposal and discussed the impact of the loss of housing on low-income people. They planned and carried out public testimony at public hearings regarding the zoning change. They were present with the apartment residents at the council meeting at which the matter was considered.

The outcome was that the city council tabled the zoning change and appointed a committee made up of council members and concerned citizens to study the situation further. David and his committee planned to continue to monitor the work of this committee, to collect and provide them with needed information, and to testify as needed.

## QUESTIONS

1. Identify a need in your community. How would you go about organizing an organizational task force to address that need? A community partnership? A community task force?

2. How would you go about organizing an activist movement to meet the need you identified in Question 1? A grassroots movement?

3. Describe actions you would take as a social worker in any of the task groups in Question 1

or 2 that you would organize to meet the need you identified in Question 1.

4. How much risk do you think there would be in working with activist or grassroots movements to bring about needed change in a community? How much risk would you be willing to take?

5. When engaging in cause advocacy, should the response be to injustice or to client wishes? How can these two perspectives be reconciled?

# SUGGESTED READINGS

Johnson, Louise C., and Yanca, Stephen J. *Social Work Practice: A Generalist Approach*, 9th ed. Boston: Allyn & Bacon, 2007 (Chapters 7, 14, and 15).

Alinsky, Saul D. *Rules for Radicals: A Pragmatic Primer for Realistic Radicals*. New York: Random House, 1971.

Bobo, Kimberly A. *Organizing for Social Change: A Manual for Activists in the '90s*. Santa Ana, CA: Seven Locks Press, 1996.

Brueggemann, William G. *The Practice of Macro Social Work*, 3rd ed. Belmont, CA: Thomson-Brooks/Cole, 2006.

Edwards, Richard L., Ed. *Encyclopedia of Social Work,* 19th ed. Washington, DC: NASW Press, 1995 ("Citizen Participation"; "Community"; "Community Needs Assessment"; "Community Organization"; and "Community Practice Models").

Erlich, John, Rothman, Jack, and Teresa, Joseph G. *Taking Action in Organizations and Communities,* 2nd ed. Dubuque, IA: Eddie Bowers Publishing, 1999.

Ewalt, Patricia L. *Social Policy: Reform, Research, and Practice*. Washington, DC: NASW Press, 1997.

Ewalt, Patricia L., Freeman, Edith M., and Poole, Dennis L. *Community Building: Renewal, Well-Being, and Shared Responsibility*. Washington, DC: NASW Press, 1998.

Fatout, Marian, and Rose, Steven R. *Task Groups in the Social Services*. Newbury Park, CA: Sage Publications, 1995.

Haynes, Karen S., and Mickelson, James S. *Affecting Change: Social Workers in the Political Arena,* 5th ed. Boston: Allyn & Bacon, 2003.

Homan, Mark S. *Promoting Community Change—Making It Happen in the Real World*, 3rd ed. Belmont, CA: Thomson-Brooks/Cole, 2004.

Long, Dennis D., Tice, Carolyn J., and Morrison, John D. *Macro Social Work Practice: A Strengths Perspective*. Belmont, CA: Thomson-Brooks/Cole, 2006.

Netting, Ellen F., Kettner, Peter M., and McMurtry, Steven L. *Social Work Macro Practice,* 4th ed. Boston: Allyn & Bacon, 2008.

Rothman, Jack, Erlich, John L., and Tropman, John E. *Strategies of Community Organization—Macro Practice*, 6th ed. Belmont, CA: Thomson-Brooks/Cole, 2001.

Rubin, Herbert J., and Rubin, Irene S. *Community Organizing and Development,* 4th ed. Boston: Allyn & Bacon, 2008.

Tropman, John E., Rothman, Jack, and Erlich, John L. *Tactics and Techniques of Community Intervention*, 4th ed. Belmont, CA: Thomson-Brooks/Cole, 2006.

# APPENDIX

# Chapter Notes

## Chapter 1

1. For a good discussion of settlement work, see Donald Brieland, "The Hull-House Tradition and the Contemporary Social Worker: Was Jane Addams Really a Social Worker?" *Social Work*, 35, 2 (March 1990): p. 134. For a recent biography of Jane Addams, see Louise W. Knight, *Citizen: Jane Addams and the Struggle for Democracy* (Chicago: University of Chicago Press, 2005).

2. For further discussion of this history see Gisela Knopka, *Social Group Work: Helping Process*, 2nd ed. (Englewood Cliffs, NJ: Prentice-Hall, 1972), chap. 1; Gertrude Wilson, "From Practice to Theory: A Personalized History," in Robert W. Roberts and Helen Northern, Eds., *Theories of Social Work with Groups* (New York: Columbia Press, (1976); and Albert S. Alissi, *Perspectives on Social Group Practice* (New York: Free Press, 1980), chap. 1.

3. Knopka, *Social Group*, p. 9.

4. Allissi, *Perspectives*, p. 17.

5. For a good discussion of this, see Janice Andrews, "Group Works Place in Social Work: A Historical Analysis," *Journal of Sociology and Social Welfare*, 28, 4 (2001): 45–65.

6. Wilson, *From Practice to Theory*, p. 5.

7. See Gisela Knopka, "The Generic and the Specific in Group Work Practice in Social Work Settings," *Social Work*, 1, 1 (1956): 73–80.

8. For a review of many of these approaches, see Alissi, op. cit. chap. 24.

9. Catherine P. Papell and Beulah Rothman, "Social Group Work Model: Possession and Heritage," *Journal of Education for Social Work*, 2 (Fall 1966): 66–77.

10. This material is found in Roberts and Northern *Theories of Social Work*.

11. See *NASW Code of Ethics*, at www. socialworkers.org/pubs/code/default.asp.

12. Ibid.

13. David E. Pollio, "The Evidence-Based Group Worker," *Social Work with Groups*, 25, 4 (2002): 57–70.

14. Mark J. McGowan, *A Guide to Evidence-Based Group Work* (New York: Oxford University Press, 2008).

15. See Papell and Rothman, *Social Group Work*, pp. 66–77.

16. Ibid.

17. Ibid.

18. Ibid.

# Chapter 2

1. Mary E. Richmond, *Social Diagnosis* (New York: Russell Sage Foundation, 1917; reprint, Free Press, 1971).

2. Ibid., p. 357.

3. Helen Harris Perlman, *Social Casework: A Problem-Solving Process* (Chicago: University of Chicago Press, 1957).

4. Ibid., p. 4.

5. Ibid., p. 171.

6. Ibid.

7. Florence Hollis, *Casework: A Psychosocial Therapy* (New York: Random House, 1964); and Ruth Elizabeth Smalley, *Theory for Social Work Practice* (New York: Columbia University Press, 1967).

8. Hollis, *Casework,* 2nd ed. (1971).

9. Carol H. Meyer, *Social Work Practice: A Response to the Urban Crisis* (New York: Free Press, 1970).

10. Harriett M. Bartlett, *The Common Base of Social Work Practice* (New York: National Association of Social Workers, 1970).

11. Max Siporin, *Introduction to Social Work Practice* (New York: Macmillan, 1975); Beulah Roberts Compton and Burt Galaway, *Social Work Processes* (Homewood, IL: Dorsey Press, 1975); Howard Goldstein, *Social Work Practice: A Unitary Approach* (Columbia: University of South Carolina Press, 1973); and Allen Pincus and Anne Minahan, *Social Work Practice: Model and Method* (Itasca, IL: F. E. Peacock, 1973).

12. Pincus and Minahan, *Social Work Practice,* p. 103.

13. Ibid., p. 247.

14. See Catherine P. Papell and Beulah Rothman, "Social Group Work Models: Possession and Heritage," *Journal of Education for Social Work* 2 (Fall 1966): 66–77; and Jack Rothman, "Three Models of Community Organization Practice," in *National Conference on Social Welfare Social Work Practice* (New York: Columbia University Press, 1968), pp. 16–47.

15. Robert W. Roberts and Robert H. Nee, Eds., *Theories of Social Casework* (Chicago: University of Chicago Press, 1970).

16. For a fuller development of the model, see Louise C. Johnson and Stephen J. Yanca, *Social Work Practice: A Generalist Approach*, 9th ed. (Boston: Pearson Education, 2007).

17. Harriett M. Bartlett, *The Common Base of Social Work Practice* (New York National Association of Social Workers, 1970).

18. For another formulation of the knowledge base, see Betty L. Baer and Ronald Federico, *Education of the Baccalaureate Social Worker: Report of the Undergraduate Curriculum Project* (Cambridge, MA: Ballinger, 1978), pp. 75–78.

19. Betty L. Baer and Ronald Federico, *Education of The Baccalaurate Social Worker: Report of the Undergraduate Curriculum Project* (Cambridge, MA: Ballinger, 1978), pp. 75–78.

20. See *Educational Policy and Accreditation Standards* (Washington, DC: Council on Social Work Education, 2001), pp. 9–12.

21. Dennis Saleebey, Ed., *The Strengths Perspective in Social Work Practice,* 2nd ed. (New York: Longman, 1997), pp. 12, 15.

22. See *Educational Policy and Accreditation Standards* (Washington, DC: Council on Social Work Education, 2001), p. 5.

23. See *NASW Standards for Cultural Competence*, (Washington, DC: NASW, 2001)

24. Martha Ozawa, "Demographic Changes and Their Implications," in *Social Work in the 21st Century,* Michael Reisch and Eileen Gambrill, Eds. (Thousand Oaks, CA: Pine Forge Press, 1997).

25. W. Nichols, "Portfolio," unpublished analytical paper (University of Vermont, Burlington), as cited by Marty Dewees in "Building Cultural Competence for Working with Diverse Families: Strategies from the Privileged Side," *Journal of Ethnic and Cultural Diversity in Social Work* 9, 3 (2001): 41.

26. Yuhwa Eva Lu, Doman Lum, and Sheying Chen, "Cultural Competency and Achieving Styles in Clinical Social Work: A Conceptual and Empirical Exploration," *Journal of Ethnic and Cultural Diversity in Social Work* 9, 3/4 (2001): 7.

27. Doman Lum, *Culturally Competent Practice: A Framework for Understanding Diverse Groups and Justice Issues* (Pacific Grove, CA: Brooks/Cole, 1999), chap. 6.

# Chapter 3

1. Robert J. Teare and Harold L. McPheeters, *Manpower Utilization in Social Welfare*, (Atlanta, GA: Southern Regional Education Board, 1970), p. 34.

2. Ibid.

3. Lorraine M. Gutierrez, "Working with Women of Color: An Empowerment Perspective," *Social Work* 35 (March 1990): 149–153.

4. Barbara Bryant Solomon, *Black Empowerment: Social Work in Oppressed Communities* (New York: Columbia University Press, 1976); and "Social Work Values and Skills to Empower Women," in *Women, Power, and Change,* Ann Weick and Susan T. Vandiver, Eds. (Washington, DC: National Association of Social Workers, 1980), pp. 206–214.

5. Ruth J. Parsons, "Empowerment: Purpose and Practice Principle in Social Work," *Social Work with Groups* 14, 2 (1991): 7–21. Also contains an excellent case example.

6. Silvia Staub-Bernasconi, "Social Action, Empowerment and Social Work—an Integrative Theoretical Framework for Social Work and Social Work with Groups," *Social Work with Groups* 14, 2 (1991): 35–51.

7. Karla Krogsrud Miley, Michael O'Melia, and Brenda L. DuBois, *Generalist Social Work Practice: An Empowering Approach* (Boston: Allyn & Bacon, 1995), p. 31.

8. Good discussions of techniques are found in Gutierrez, "Working with Women," and in Solomon, "Social Work Values."

9. The approach that follows is a simplified version of cognitive and behavioral approaches. See *cognitive therapy* and *behavioral therapy* in the Glossary. Also see Albert Ellis, *Better, Deeper, and More Enduring Brief Therapy: The Rational Emotive Behavioral Therapy Approach* (New York: Brunner/Mazel, 1996); Judith Beck, *Cognitive Therapy: Basics and Beyond* (New York: Guilford, 1995); Jim Lantz, "Cognitive Theory and Social Work Treatment," in *Social Work Treatment,* 4th ed., Francis J. Turner, Ed. (New York: Free

Press, 1996); Mark Mattaini, *Clinical Practice with Individuals* (Washington, DC: NASW Press, 1997); and Bruce Thyer and John Wodarski, *Handbook of Empirical Social Work Practice* (New York: Wiley, 1998).

10. See Louise C. Johnson and Stephen J. Yanca, *Social Work Practice: A Generalist Approach*, 9th ed. (Boston: Allyn & Bacon, 2007), chap. 16.

11. Florence Hollis, *Casework: A Psychosocial Therapy* (New York: Random House, 1972), pp. 89–95.

12. Judith C. Nelson, "Support: A Necessary Condition for Change," *Social Work* 25 (September 1980): 388–392.

13. Patricia Ferris and Catherine A. Marshall, "A Model Project for Families of the Chronically Mentally Ill," *Social Work* 32 (March–April 1987): 110–114.

14. James Kelley and Pamela Sykes, "Helping the Helpers: A Support Group for Family Members of Persons with AIDS," *Social Work* 34 (May 1989): 239–242.

15. Carolyn Knight, "Use of Support Groups with Adult Female Survivors of Child Sexual Abuse," *Social Work* 35 (May 1990): 202–206.

16. Robert Vinter, "Program Activities: An Analysis of Their Effects on Participant Behavior," in *Readings in Group Work Practice,* Robert Vinter, Ed. (Ann Arbor, MI: Campus Publishers, 1967).

17. See Ruth R. Middleman, "The Use of Program: Review and Update," *Social Work with Groups* 3 (Fall 1980): 5–23. The Suggested Readings in this text contain many important sources for this material as well.

18. William Schwartz, "The Worker in the Group," in *Social Welfare Forum 1961,* Robert Clifton Weaver, Ed. (New York: Columbia University Press, 1961), p. 154.

19. William Schwartz, "On the Use of Groups in Social Work Practice," in *The Practice of Group Work,* William Schwartz and Serapio R. Zalba, Eds. (New York: Columbia University Press, 1971), p. 5.

20. See Schwartz and Zalba, *The Practice of Group Work*; and Lawrence Shulman, *A Casebook of Social Work with Groups: The Mediating Model* (New York: Council on Social Work Education, 1968), and *The Skills of Helping Individuals and Groups,* 2nd ed. (Itasca, IL: F. E. Peacock, 1984).

21. See Shulman, *The Skills of Helping Individuals and Groups,* pp. 9–10.

22. See Shulman, *A Casebook of Social Work with Groups.*

23. Irving Spergel, *Community Problem Solving* (Chicago: University of Chicago Press, 1969), p. 106.

24. William Schwartz, "The Social Worker in the Group," in *The Social Welfare Forum Proceedings* (New York: Columbia University Press, 1961), p. 157.

25. See Charles S. Levy, "Values and Planned Change," *Social Casework* 53 (October 1972): 488–493, for another discussion of these factors.

26. For additional discussion, see Anthony N. Maluccio, "Promoting Competence Through Life Experience," in *Social Work Practice: People and Environments,* Carel B. Germain, Ed. (New York: Columbia University Press, 1979), pp. 282–302.

27. Irene A. Gutheil, "Considering the Physical Environment: An Essential Component of Good Practice," *Social Work* 37 (September 1992): 391–396.

28. See Carel B. Germain, "'Space': An Ecological Variable in Social Work Practice," *Social Casework* 59 (November 1978): 515–529.

29. For further consideration of this topic, see Brett A. Seabury, "Arrangement of Physical Space in Social Work Settings," *Social Work* 16 (October 1971): 43–49; and Thomas Walz, Georgina Willenberg, and Lane deMoll, "Environmental Design," *Social Work* 19 (January 1974): 38–46.

30. See Richard E. Boettcher and Roger Vander Schie, "Milieu Therapy with Chronic Mental Patients," *Social Work* 20 (March 1975): 130–139.

31. Carel B. Germain, "Time: An Ecological Variable in Social Work Practice," *Social Casework* 57 (July 1976): 419–426.

32. Karen Orloff Kaplan, "Recent Trends in Case Management," in *Encyclopedia of Social Work,* 18th ed. (supplement), Leon Ginsberg, Ed. (Silver Spring, MD: NASW Press, 1990), pp. 60–77.

33. Ibid., p. 62.

34. Jack Rothman, "A Model of Case Management: Toward Empirically Based Practice," *Social Work* 36 (November 1991): 520–528.

35. Stephen T. Moore, "A Social Work Practice Model of Case Management: The Case Management Grid," *Social Work* 35 (September 1990): 444–448.

# Chapter 4

1. Another excellent source on group process is Margaret E. Hartford, *Groups in Social Work* (New York: Columbia University Press, 1972).

2. This discussion of the small group as a social system is a synthesis of knowledge about small groups primarily based on three schools of thought: (1) Field theory or group dynamics. The work of Kurt Lewin is the original source; Darwin Cartwright and Alvin Zander, *Group Dynamics: Research and Theory* (Evanston, IL: Row Peterson, 1960), is another source. (2) Interactional process analysis. Paul A. Hare, Edgar F. Borgotta, and Robert E. Bales, *Small Groups: Studies in Social Interaction* (New York: Alfred A. Knopf, 1965), is a source for this school of thought. (3) Homans's systems theory. George Homans, *The Human Group* (New York: Harcourt, Brace and World, 1960), is the third primary source.

3. Henry W. Maier, "Models of Intervention in Work with Groups: Which One Is Yours?" *Social Work with Groups* 4 (Fall/Winter 1981): 21–34.

4. For a full description of this technique, see Mary L. Northway, *A Primer of Sociometry,* 2nd ed. (Toronto: University of Toronto Press, 1967).

5. Kenneth D. Benne and Paul Sheats, "Functional Roles of Group Members," *Journal of Social Issues* 4 (1948): 41–49.

6. John K. Brilhart, *Effective Group Discussion* (Dubuque, IA: Wm. C. Brown, 1974), p. 5.

7. Based on a formulation developed by Henriette Etta Soloshin, "Development of an Instrument for the Analysis of Social Group Work Method in Therapeutic Settings" (Ph.D. diss., University of Minnesota, Minneapolis, March 1954). Also see William Schwartz, "The Social Worker in the Group," in *Social Welfare Forum 1961* (New York: Columbia University Press, 1961), pp. 146–171.

# Chapter 5

1. Helen Harris Perlman, *Relationship: The Heart of Helping People* (Chicago: University of Chicago Press, 1979), p. 2.

2. Ibid., p. 24.

3. Ibid., p. 62.

4. See Lawrence M. Brammer, *The Helping Relationship: Process and Skills,* 3rd ed. (Englewood Cliffs, NJ: Prentice-Hall, 1984); and Beulah Roberts Compton and Burt Galaway, *Social Work Processes,* rev. ed. (Homewood, IL: Dorsey Press, 1979), chap. 6.

5. Compton and Galaway, *Social Work Processes,* p. 224.

6. See Anthony N. Maluccio, *Learning from Clients: Interpersonal Helping as Viewed by Clients and Social Workers* (New York: Free Press, 1979).

7. See Felix P. Biestek, *The Casework Relationship* (Chicago: Loyola University Press, 1957), for a full description of the seven principles.

8. Ann Templeton Brownlee, *Community, Culture and Care* (St. Louis: C. V. Mosby, 1978), chap. 3.

9. Joel Fischer, Diane D. Dulaney, Rosemary T. Frazio, Mary T. Hadakand, and Ethyl Zivotosky, "Are Social Workers Sexists?" *Social Work* 21 (November 1976): 428–433.

10. Joanne Mermelstein and Paul Sundet, "Education for Social Work in the Rural Context," in *Educating for Social Work in Rural Areas: A Report on Rural Child Welfare and Family Service Project of the School of Social Work,* Lynn R. Hulen, project coordinator (Fresno: California State University, June 1978).

11. Yvonne L. Fraley, "A Role Model for Practice," *Social Service Review* 43 (June 1969): 145–154.

12. Adapted from Brett A. Seabury, "Communication Problems in Social Work Practice," *Social Work* 25, 1 (January 1980): 40–44.

13. Floyd W. Matson and Ashley Montagu, *The Human Dialogue: Perspectives on Communication* (New York: Free Press, 1967), p. 6.

14. See Lawrence Shulman, *The Skills of Helping: Individuals and Groups,* 2nd ed. (Itasca, IL: F. E. Peacock, 1984), chaps. 2 and 4.

15. See Doman Lum, *Culturally Competent Practice: A Framework for Understanding Diverse Groups and Justice Issues* (Pacific Grove, CA: Brooks/Cole, 1999).

16. Ibid., p. 155.

17. Ibid.

18. James V. Leigh, *Communicating for Cultural Competence* (Boston: Allyn & Bacon, 1998), p. 19.

19. Ibid., chap. 8.

20. Ibid., chap. 5.

21. Ibid., p. 19.

22. Lum, *Culturally Competent Practice,* pp. 152–154.

23. This triad is based on the work of C. B. Truax and R. R. Carkhuff, *Toward Effective Counseling and Psychotherapy* (Chicago: Aldine, 1967). For an excellent discussion of this material, see Eveline D. Schulman, *Intervention in the Human Services,* 2nd ed. (St. Louis: C. V. Mosby, 1978), chap. 8, "Traux Triad."

## Chapter 6

1. See Rosemary Smead Morganette, *Skills for Living: Group Counseling Activities for Young Adolescents,* Vol. I (Champaign, IL: Research Press, 1990) and Vol. II by Rosemary Smead (2000).

2. For an excellent discussion of the art of group work and for balancing individual and group needs and goals see: Helen Harris Perlman, *Relationship*: *The Heart of Helping People.* (Chicago: University of Chicago Press, 1979), chap. 7. Also see Allen E. Ivey, Paul B. Pederson, and Mary Bradford Ivey, *Intentional Group Counseling: A Microskills Approach.* (Belmont, CA: Thomson/Wadsworth, 2001), pp. 108–115 for a discussion of theme-oriented groups which use an "I-we-it" focus for group discussion. Our description is different than this in that we see the need to balance "I-we" as part of the group process similar to how Perlman describes the need to balance individual needs and goals when working with groups and families.

3. Allen E. Ivey, *Intentional Interviewing and Counseling: Facilitating Client Development in a Multicultural Society,* 3rd ed. (Belmont, CA: Thomson: Brooks/Cole, 1994), p. 192.

## Chapter 7

1. Florence Hollis, *Casework: A Psychosocial Therapy* (New York: Random House, 1972), pp. 89–95.

2. Judith C. Nelson, "Support: A Necessary Condition for Change," *Social Work* 25 (September 1980): 388–392.

3. See *The Big Book Online*, Alcoholics Anonymous Worldwide Services www .alcoholics-anonymous.org, and click on *The Big Book*, chap. 5, pp. 59–60.

4. Florence Hollis, *Casework: A Psychosocial Therapy* (New York: Random House, 1972), pp. 89–95.

5. Judith C. Nelson, "Support: A Necessary Condition for Change," *Social Work* 25 (September 1980): 388–392.

## Chapter 8

1. See Abraham Maslow, *Motivation and Personality* (New York: Harper and Row, 1954).

2. Table 8.1 is based on updated material developed by Louise Johnson in the late 1960s. Published in Harleigh Trecker, *Social Group Work: Principles and Practices* (New York: Association Press, 1972), pp. 247–249.

## Chapter 10

1. Barbara Oberhofer Dane and Barbara L. Simon, "Resident Guests: Social Workers in Host Settings," *Social Work* 35 (January 1990): 63–68.

2. Ralph Morgan, "Role Performance in a Bureaucracy," in *Social Work Practice 1962* (New York: Columbia University Press, 1962), pp. 115–125.

3. See Robert Pruger, "The Good Bureaucrat," *Social Work* 18 (July 1973): 26–32, and "Bureaucratic Functioning as a Social Work Skill," in *Educating for Baccalaureat Social Work: Report of the Undergraduate Social Work Curriculum Development Project,* Betty L. Baer and Ronald Federico, Eds. (Cambridge, MA: Ballinger, 1978), pp. 149–168.

4. Christina Maslach, "Job Burnout: How People Cope," *Public Welfare* 36 (Spring 1978): 56–58.

5. Martha Bramhall and Susan Ezell, "How Burned Out Are You?" *Public Welfare* 39 (Winter 1981): 23–27.

6. These ideas are further developed in Martha Bramhall and Susan Ezell, "Working Your Way Out of Burnout," *Public Welfare* 39 (Spring 1981): 32–39.

# Chapter 11

1. Herman Resnick and Rino J. Patti, Eds., *Change from Within: Humanizing Social Welfare Organizations* (Philadelphia, PA: Temple University Press, 1980), pp. 5–6.

2. This strategy is based on the work of Resnick and Patti, *Change from Within*, and the discussion that follows is heavily influenced by their work. For an earlier version, see Rino J. Patti and Herman Resnick, "Changing the Agency from Within," *Social Work* 17 (July 1972): 48–57.

3. See Rino J. Patti, "Organizational Resistance and Change: The View from Below," *Social Service Review* 48 (September 1974): 367–383.

4. Resnick and Patti, *Change from Within*, pp. 9–11.

5. Patti and Resnick, "Changing the Agency from Within."

6. Jack Rothman, John L. Erlich, and Joseph G. Teresa, *Promoting Innovation and Change in Organization and Community: A Planning Manual* (New York: John Wiley, 1976), chap. 2.

7. See James D. Jorgensen and Brian W. Klepinger, "The Social Worker as Staff Trainer," *Public Welfare* 37 (Winter 1979): 41–49.

8. Edward J. Pawlak, "Organization Tinkering," *Social Work* 21 (September 1976): 376–380.

9. Resnick and Patti, *Change from Within*, p. 12.

10. John J. Horwitz, *Team Practice and the Specialist* (Springfield, IL: Charles C. Thomas, 1970), p. 10.

11. Marlene Wilson, *The Effective Management of Volunteer Programs* (Boulder, CO: Volunteer Management Association, 1976), is a good resource on developing volunteer programs.

12. Brian A. Auslander and Gail K. Auslander, "Self-Help Groups and the Family Service Agency," *Social Casework* 69 (February 1988): 74–80.

# Chapter 12

1. Ferdinand Tönnies, *Fundamental Concepts of Sociology* (Gemeinschaft und Gesellschaft), trans. Charles P. Loomis (New York: American Books, 1940).

2. Floyd Hunter, *Community Power Structure* (Chapel Hill: University of North Carolina Press, 1953).

3. Eugene Litwak and Ivan Szelenyi, "Primary Group Structures and Their Function: Kin, Neighbors, and Friends," *American Sociological Review* 34 (August 1969): 465–481; Phillip Fellin and Eugene Litwak, "The Neighborhood in Urban American Society," *Social Work* 13 (July 1968): 72–80; and Eugene Litwak, *Helping the Elderly* (New York: Guilford Press, 1985), chap. 8.

4. Roland L. Warren, *The Community in America* (Chicago: Rand-McNally, 1963).

5. Dennis E. Poplin, *Communities,* 2nd ed. (New York: Macmillan, 1979), chap. 2, "Community Types."

6. Louise C. Johnson, "Human Service Delivery Patterns in Non-Metropolitan Communities," in *Rural Human Services: A Book of Readings,* H. Wayne Johnson, Ed. (Itasca, IL: F. E. Peacock, 1980), pp. 55–64.

7. Louise C. Johnson, "Services to the Aged: Non-Metropolitan Service Delivery" (unpublished paper delivered at NASW Symposium, Chicago, IL, November 1985).

8. Roland L. Warren, *The Community in America* (Chicago: Rand-McNally, 1963).

9. Padi Gulati and Geoffrey Guest, "The Community-Centered Model: A Garden Variety Approach or a Radical Transformation of Community Practice?" *Social Work* 35 (January 1990): 63–68.

10. Jack Rothman, with John E. Tropman, "Models of Community Organization and Macro Pratice Perspectives: Their Mixing and Phasing," in *Strategies of Community Organization*, 4th. ed., Fred Cox, John L. Erlich, Jack Rothman, and John E. Tropman, Eds. (Itasca, IL: F. E. Peacock, 1987), pp. 3–26.

11. It is expected that understandings to carry out these activities will come from political science courses and a course in social welfare policy.

12. Saul D. Alinsky, *Reveille for Radicals* (Chicago: University of Chicago Press, 1946); and Richard Cloward and R. Elman, "Advocacy in the Ghetto," in *Strategies of Community Organization: A Book of Readings*, Fred M. Cox, John L. Erlich, Jack Rothman, and John E. Tropman, Eds. (Itasca, IL: F. E. Peacock, 1970), pp. 209–215.

13. Cox, Erlich, Rothman, and Tropman, *Strategies of Community Organization*, 4th ed. (1987), pt. III, sec. IV, "Social Action," is an excellent source for this.

# Chapter 13

1. For further discussion, see Seymour B. Sarason, Charles Carroll, Kenneth Maton, Saul Cohen, and Elizabeth Lorentz, *Human Services and Resource Networks* (San Francisco: Jossey-Bass, 1977); and Louise C. Johnson, "Networking: A Means of Maximizing Resources in Non-Metropolitan Settings," *Human Services in the Rural Environment* 8, 2: 27–31.

2. See Alice H. Collins and Diane Pancoast, *Natural Helping Networks: A Strategy for Prevention* (Washington, DC: National Association for Social Workers, 1976).

3. George A. Brager, "Advocacy and Political Behavior," *Social Work* 13 (April 1968): 15.

4. Robert J. Teare and Harold L. McPheeters, *Manpower Utilization in Social Welfare* (Atlanta, GA: Southern Regional Education Board, 1970), p. 30.

5. Robert H. MacRae, "Social Work and Social Action," *Social Service Review* 60 (March 1966): 1–7.

6. J. Donald Cameron and Esther Talavera, "Advocacy Program for Spanish-Speaking People," *Social Casework* 57 (July 1976): 427–431.

7. Robert Sunley, "Family Advocacy: From Case to Cause," *Social Casework* 51 (June 1970): 347–357.

8. For more information about each of the tasks identified, see Bradford W. Sheafor, Charles R. Horejsi, and Gloria A. Horejsi, *Techniques and Guidelines for Social Work Practice*, 4th ed. (Boston: Allyn & Bacon, 1997), pt. IV, sec. B.

9. Ronald W. Toseland and Robert F. Rivas, "Working with Task Groups: The Middle Phase," in *Strategies of Community Organization*, 4th. ed., Fred Cox, John L. Erlich, Jack Rothman, and John E. Tropman, Eds. (Itasca, IL: F. E. Peacock, 1987), pp. 114–142.

10. Jack Rothman, John L. Erlich, and Joseph G. Teresa, *Promoting Innovation and Change in Organizations and Communities: A Planning Manual* (New York: John Wiley, 1976), chap. 2.

# GLOSSARY

**action**  The process of carrying out a plan developed through the assessment and action phases of the social work process.

**action system**  System of people and resources involved in carrying out tasks related to goals and strategy of the helping endeavor.

**activity**  Doing something or performing tasks as opposed to talking about what to do or talking about feelings or ideas.

**advocate**  A role that consists of fighting for services for clients whom the service system would otherwise reject.

**agency**  The organization that employs the worker and manages resources used to help the client.

**assessment**  Ongoing process of the social work endeavor that develops an understanding of person in situation to use as the basis for action.

**bond**  The cohesive quality of a relationship in a group or family.

**boundary**  Point at which the interaction around a function no longer has the intensity that interaction of system members or units has. For example, when considering who is a member of a family system, the boundary is the point that divides those who are continually interacting around family concerns and issues and those who have little or no input into family functioning.

**broker**  A social work role in which the worker provides the client with information about available resources and helps link the client with the resource.

**burnout**  Feelings of stress that lead helping professionals to lose positive feelings, empathy, and respect for their clients.

**case advocacy**  Advocacy for a single client or client system.

**case management**  A method for coordinating services in which a worker assesses with a client which services are needed and obtains and monitors the delivery of the services.

**cause advocacy**  Advocacy that serves groups with similar difficulties.

**change-oriented groups**  Groups intended to facilitate change such as problem-solving, decision-making, and counseling groups.

**change process**  The blending of an ecosystems and a strengths approach with problem solving to form a process for helping various client systems through assessment, planning, action, and evaluation and termination.

**collaboration**  The working together of several service providers with a common client toward a common goal.

**community**  Immediate environment of worker, client, and agency that is manifest as a social system.

**concern**  A feeling that something is not right. Interest in, regard for, and care about the well-being of self and other persons.

**conflict**  A struggle for something that is scarce or thought to be scarce.

**congruity**  A situation in which the interactions or transactions within an ecosystem are balanced, resulting in mutual benefit for the person and the environment.

**coordination**  The working together of two or more service providers in activity focused on a particular client or focused on persons in a particular category (e.g., the aged). Coordinative mechanisms include allocation of services, networking, linking, case management, collaboration, and a team approach.

**cope**  A person's efforts to deal with some new and often problematic situation or encounter or to deal in some new way with an old problem.

**counseling groups**  Groups made up of members who are capable of making decisions and carrying them out.

**crisis**  A state of disequilibrium or a loss of steady state due to stress and precipitating event in the life of a person who usually has a satisfactory level of functioning.

**culturally competent practice**  The ability to provide services to clients from a particular cultural group in a manner that is consistent with the norms and customs of that culture.

**diagnosis**  A term borrowed from the medical field. It relates to developing a statement as to the nature of the client's need and the situation related to that need. A more contemporary term is *assessment*.

**diagnostic approach**  A historic model of social work practice that places a primary emphasis on diagnosis.

The contemporary model is usually referred to as the *psychosocial approach*.

**direct practice**   Action with individuals, families, and small groups focused on change in either the transactions within the family or small group or in the manner in which individuals, families, and small groups function in relation to individuals and social systems in their environment.

**diversity competence**   The ability to provide services to clients with a particular diversity factor in a manner that is acceptable within that diversity group.

**ecological perspective**   A way of thinking about practice that involves a focus on the client's surrounding environment.

**ecosystem**   A system of systems including the person(s) and all of the interacting systems in the environment along with the transactions among the person(s) and systems.

**ecosystems perspective**   An approach that examines the exchange of matter, energy, or information over time among all the systems in a person in environment approach.

**ecosystems strengths approach**   A blend of the ecological and strengths perspectives with the problem-solving approach to form a process for facilitating growth and change.

**empowerment**   A process for increasing personal, interpersonal, or political power so that individuals can take action to improve their life situation.

**enabling**   Making it possible for an individual or system to carry out some activity they might not be able to engage in without support or help.

**engagement**   The establishment of a helping relationship between the worker and the client system.

**environmental manipulation**   A strategy to bring about change in a client's environment in order to enhance the client's social functioning.

**extinction**   The technique of ignoring undesirable behavior as a way of eliminating it.

**feeling**   An intuitive sense of a situation or solution to a problem. Facts have not been sought, it is more of an emotional process than a cognitive one.

**felt need**   A need identified by a client.

**focal system**   The primary system upon which the social work process focuses in the change activity.

**functional approach**   A historic model of social work practice that places emphasis on the role and tasks of the social worker in the helping situation rather than on a client's deviance or illness.

**Gemeinshaft**   A characteristic of communities that demonstrates a sense of "we-ness" and informal functioning.

**generalist practice**   Practice in which the client system and worker together assess the need in all of its complexity and develop a plan for responding to that need. A strategy is chosen from a repertoire of responses appropriate for work with individuals, families, groups, agencies, and communities. The unit of attention is chosen by considering the system needing to be changed. The plan is carried out and evaluated.

**Gesellschaft**   A characteristic of communities in which individuals tend to relate through institutions and other formal structures.

**goal**   The overall, long-range expected outcome of an endeavor.

**group**   A system of clients or a multiclient system.

**group-building (group maintenance) roles**   Roles that focus on the maintenance of the group as a system.

**group-task roles**   Roles related to the accomplishment of the function or task of the group.

**growth and development groups**   Groups formed to promote healthy social, physical, emotional, or spiritual growth of their members.

**human development perspective**   A way of viewing human need that sees people as developing over the life cycle.

**human diversity approach**   A way of viewing persons in situations that considers culture, race, gender, and disabling conditions as they affect human functioning. It views human behavior as highly relative to the social situation in which persons function.

**incongruity**   A situation in which the interactions or transactions within an ecosystem are out of balance, resulting in unmet needs for the person and/or the environment.

**indirect practice**   Action taken with persons other than clients in order to help clients.

**individual roles**   Roles that satisfy individual need but detract from the work of the group.

**inductive learning**   Learning that involves moving from making observations of phenomena to searching for patterns that may lead to theory development. It means adopting an open-minded inquisitive approach, laying aside preconceived notions, and listening to the experiences of the client.

**influence**   General acts of producing an effect on another person, group, or organization through exercises of a personal or organizational capacity.

**influentials** Persons in a community or an organization who have power or authority.

**interactional process** The process by which a worker and a client work together on a concern/need in an environment.

**interactional skill** The capacity of social workers to relate to both clients and significant others, both individuals and social systems, in such a manner as to be helpful and to support the work at hand.

**interface** A point of contact between two systems at which transactions occur.

**intervention** Specific action by a worker in relation to human systems or processes in order to induce change. The action is guided by knowledge and professional values as well as by the skillfulness of the worker.

**interventive repertoire** The package of actions, methods, techniques, and skills a particular social worker has developed for use in response to needs of individuals and social systems.

**knowledge** Picture of the world and the place of humans in it. Ideas and beliefs about reality based on confirmable or probable evidence.

**leadership** Roles that facilitate effective group functioning.

**mediation strategy** A strategy in which a worker helps a client and a system in the immediate environment to reach out to each other and find a common concern or interest and to do the work necessary to bring about a desired change.

**medical model** Used in medical field and often appropriated by social workers. Characterized by a process of study, diagnosis, and treatment.

**mutual goals** Goals that require two or more family or group members to participate or act in certain ways regardless of the actions of others.

**natural helpers** People who possess helping skills and exercise them in the context of mutual relationships, as opposed to professionals trained in certain helping skills who are not part of a client's immediate community.

**natural helping systems** A client's friends, family, and coworkers. Those in an individual's informal environment to whom one turns in time of need.

**naturalistic inquiry** An inductive learning process that begins with the position that one does not know what one does not know, which leaves one open to hearing the client's story without preconceived notions.

**need** That which is necessary for either a person or a social system to function within reasonable expectations, given the situation that exists.

**network** A loose association of systems. Not a social system but an entity that operates through mutual resource sharing.

**networking** Development and maintenance of communication and ways of working together among people of diverse interests and orientations. One means of coordination.

**norming** The process by which implicit norms or expected ways of behaving are made explicit.

**objectives** Intermediate goals that must be reached in order to attain the ultimate goal.

**plan of action** The way or method for carrying out planned change in the social work endeavor. It is structured and specifies goals and objectives, units of attention, and strategy.

**prevention groups** Any group whose primary purpose is to prevent the development of unhealthy functioning in the biological, psychological, or social aspects of the lives of an "at risk" population by promoting healthy functioning through group experiences or the acquisition or enhancement of skills and abilities.

**proactive advocacy** Advocating for clients before barriers are encountered by avoiding policies that are not in the best interests of clients.

**problem** (in social work) A social functioning situation in which need fulfillment of any of the persons or systems involved is blocked and in which the persons involved cannot by themselves remove the block to need fulfillment.

**problem-oriented record** A four-point record containing a database of pertinent information, a problem list, plans and goals, and follow-up notes (including outcomes).

**problem-solving process** A tool used by social workers to solve problems in a rational manner. It proceeds through identifiable steps of interaction with clients. These steps include identification of the problem, statement of preliminary assumptions about the problem, selection and collection of information, analysis of information, development of a plan, implementation of the plan, and evaluation.

**process** A recurrent patterning of a sequence of change over time in a particular direction.

**process recording** Narrative report of all that happened during a client contact, including worker's thinking and feeling about what happened.

**professional relationship** A relationship with an agreed-upon purpose, a limited time frame, and in which the professional devotes self to the interest of the client.

**psychosocial approach** See *diagnostic approach*.

**reciprocal goals** Goals that require different actions on the part of two or more family or group members.

**referral** The process by which a client is made aware of another service resource and helped to make contact with that resource to receive a needed service.

**reframing** Stating a concern or a problem in a new way, from a different point of view.

**relationship** Cohesive quality of the action system. Product of interaction between two persons.

**scientific philanthropy** Systematic, careful investigation of evidence surrounding the need for service before acting on the need.

**self-help groups** Voluntary groups in which members with common problems help each other.

**skill** A complex organization of behavior directed toward a particular goal or activity.

**small group** Three or more persons who have something in common and who use face-to-face interaction to share that commonality and work to fulfill needs, their own or those of others.

**social history** A form of assessment of individuals or families. It includes information (historical and current) needed for understanding and working with clients.

**social system** A system composed of interrelated and interdependent parts (persons and subsystems).

**social work process** A problem-solving process carried out with clients to solve problems in social functioning that clients cannot solve without help. It is conceptualized as study, assessment, planning, action, and termination.

**sociogram** A pictorial assessment technique used with small groups to show the relationships between group members.

**strengths approach** An approach to social work practice that emphasizes the strengths and capabilities of the client system and the resources within the client's natural environment.

**summary record** A form of recording that contains basic information and summaries describing significant information and actions taken by the worker and a statement of what was accomplished.

**support** The use of techniques that help clients feel better, stronger, and more comfortable in some immediate way.

**support groups** Groups that provide help with coping with challenging situations that members are experiencing.

**task group** A group formed to accomplish a task or achieve a goal.

**tasks** Steps necessary to achieve a goal.

**team** A group of persons, often representative of various professions, who work together toward common goals and plans of action to meet the needs of clients.

**termination** The last phase of the social work process when the emphasis is on disengagement, stabilization of change, and evaluation.

**thinking** Use of a cognitive process to sort out information or to engage in a problem-solving process.

**transaction** The exchange of matter, energy, and/or information among persons or systems within an ecosystem.

**treatment** Term used for action segment of the social work process. Very often used in clinical social work.

**unit of attention** The system or systems on which the change activity is focused; also called *focal system*.

**values** What is held to be desirable and preferred. Guides for behavior.

# INDEX